DAVID LEWIS-WILLIAMS

The Mind in the Cave

CONSCIOUSNESS AND THE ORIGINS OF ART

with 94 illustrations, 27 in color

 **Thames & Hudson**

© 2002 Thames & Hudson Ltd, London

All Rights Reserved. No part of this publication may be reproduced or transmitted
in any form or by any means, electronic or mechanical, including photocopy,
recording or any other information storage and retrieval system, without
prior permission in writing from the publisher.

First published in hardcover in the United States of America in 2002 by
Thames & Hudson Inc., 500 Fifth Avenue, New York, New York 10110

thamesandhudsonusa.com

Library of Congress Catalog Card Number 2002102597
ISBN 0-500-05117-8

Printed and bound in Slovenia by Mladinska Knjiga Tiskarna

Contents

Preface

Mankind always sets itself only such problems as it can solve; since, looking at the matter more closely, it will always be found that the task itself arises only when the material conditions for its solution already exist or are at least in the process of formation.

KARL MARX, *A CONTRIBUTION TO THE CRITIQUE OF POLITICAL ECONOMY* (1859)

The publication of this book marks the end of a century of research on Upper Palaeolithic art – and the beginning of another. It was in 1902 that Emile Cartailhac, an influential French archaeologist who had vehemently contested the authenticity of the finds that had been made in the French and Spanish caves, recanted and published his now-famous article *Mea culpa d'un sceptique*. The widespread, though not complete, scepticism that had denied the prehistoric people of the Upper Palaeolithic period the ability to produce art at once fell away. At a stroke, the study of Upper Palaeolithic art became respectable, and a new academic industry was born.

Now, just over a century later, we ask how much we have learned since Cartailhac changed his mind. Certainly, our knowledge of the facts of Upper Palaeolithic art has increased enormously. We know of far more sites, both underground and in the open air; we have detailed inventories of the images in most of the major sites; many caves have been surveyed, and we have maps showing the precise location of each and every image; we know the dates of many of the images; we have huge collections of beautifully made portable art; caves and rock shelters have been meticulously excavated; we even know the ingredients of some of the paints that the ancient images-makers used. Yet, despite all this information, we seem no closer to knowing why the people of that period penetrated the deep limestone caves of France and Spain to make images in total darkness – in addition to those in daylight areas and on pieces of portable stone, bone, ivory and antler. We do not know what the images meant to those who made and those who viewed them. At least, there is no unanimity on these key points, and the greatest riddle of archaeology – how we became human and in the process began to make art – continues to tantalize.

Many researchers, especially those in France and Spain, believe that still more 'facts' are required before we can 'theorize'. But how will we know when we have 'enough' data to begin work on explanation? Will our data reach a critical mass, implode and automatically reconfigure as an explanation? Hardly. Or is it not so much a matter of quantity of data as some crucial piece of information, some exceptionally perceptive observation still to be made in the caves, that will cause all the other accumulated data to fall into place and provide us with a persuasive explanation? We may as well search for the Holy Grail.

Although Karl Marx may be overly optimistic in the epigraph to this Preface, I believe that a century of research has indeed provided us with 'enough' data, the 'material conditions', to hazard a persuasive, general explanation for a great deal of – not all – Upper Palaeolithic art, and, moreover, to explain some hitherto inexplicable features of the imagery and its often bizarre contexts. What is now needed is not yet more data (though more data are always welcome), but rather a radical re-thinking of what we already know.

This is not to say that each and every question can now be answered; *we do not have to explain everything in order to explain something*. Rather, we can form a broad idea of why Upper Palaeolithic people made images and, especially, what drove them into the dark caves to make hidden images. We can go further: moving beyond such generalizations, we can understand some precise specifics about caves and images. Yet, I repeat, there is still much to find out. This book does not attempt to answer each and every question that may be asked. The explanation that I propose is not a ringing down of the curtain on Upper Palaeolithic art research. On the contrary, it will, as I make plain in chapter after chapter, open up new and more searching questions.

What is missing today is not a massive collection of data or some crucial but lost piece of a jig-saw puzzle. We need a *method* that will make sense of the data that we already have. Methodology, the study of method, is the crucial issue. Methods should not be confused with techniques, such as radiocarbon dating, computer analysis, or the making of accurate copies of images. Method is the mode of argument that a researcher uses to reach explanatory statements. Today all researchers agree on the need for accurate techniques of dating and so forth, but they do not agree on what form of argument is likely to reach a convincing conclusion. As a result, communication between researchers who are trying to explain the phenomenon of Upper Palaeolithic cave art is at a low ebb. Misunderstandings abound, pile up and topple over into vilification. Small wonder, then, that many researchers today are resolute agnostics. They distance themselves from the explainers and concentrate on data collection.

A lack of methodology in Upper Palaeolithic art research has led to confusion of priorities. We need to have a clear idea of which questions need to be answered before others can be essayed; we need to know which questions, fascinating though they may be, can be safely left alone without impeding the progress of our explanation. This is what I try to do in this book: I circumnavigate many a reef on which debate has foundered and move on to the crucial questions that we can answer.

I begin by outlining the way in which the nineteenth-century discovery of Upper Palaeolithic art, together with the massive impact of Charles Darwin's work on evolution, radically changed the way in which we think about ourselves and our place in nature and history (Chapter 1). Indeed, it is hard to overestimate the effect of these changes in Western thought. Yet, as I repeatedly point out in later chapters, pre-Darwinian ways of thinking and belief in the existence of a non-material realm, though greatly reduced, have not disappeared. At a gross level, there are still Creationists who argue for a single, miraculous moment when all of life and earth as we know it came into being by divine edict. The explanation for this uncomfortable dichotomy in modern thought lies, I argue, deep in the human brain.

To prepare for a discussion of the working of the brain, I describe the discovery of Upper Palaeolithic art (Chapter 2) and some of the highly charged debates of the time. These controversies have cast long shadows. I then examine a series of successive explanations that writers have advanced to account for this art (Chapter 3). Each was, in a sense, of its own time, for we cannot easily escape from the social and philosophical context in which we live. No doubt that contextuality is also true of the explanation that I advance. But I contest the forms of relativism, popular in some quarters today, that deny the very possibility of getting nearer and nearer to a past that really happened in the way that it did.

Human beings did evolve in one way and not in others; they did begin to make art for certain reasons and not for others. To sort valid hypotheses from futile ones, I consider the role of intelligence and consciousness in prehistory (Chapter 4). I argue that most researchers have consistently ignored the full complexity of human consciousness and have concentrated on only one slice of it and made that slice the defining characteristic of what it is to be an anatomically and cognitively fully modern human being. Here I examine interaction of mental activity and social context: how, I ask, do notions about human experience that are shared by a community impinge on the mental activity of individuals and how does socially controlled access to certain mental states become a foundation for social discrimination?

To consolidate the conclusions to which the first four chapters come, I offer two case studies of the ways in which mental imagery can be translated into rock art. The two instances are the San of southern Africa and the early people of the far west of North America (Chapters 5 and 6). It is important to notice that my method is not to argue by analogy from these case studies to the art of Upper Palaeolithic western Europe, for that would be to stumble into the same trap as a number of early researchers. Southern Africa and North America merely provide enlightening instances of what can happen when mental imagery is turned into visual imagery on rocks and in caves.

Chapter 7 moves on to explore the possibility that the people of the Upper Palaeolithic harnessed what we call altered states of consciousness to fashion their society and that they used imagery as a means of establishing and defining social relationships. It considers two types of consciousness: primary consciousness, and higher-order consciousness. I argue that the development of higher-order consciousness made image-making possible – though not inevitable. It was at this time that image-making (art), religion and social distinctions appeared in western Europe: at that particular time and in that place (this book does not cover the whole world), image-making, religion and social discriminations were a 'package deal'.

Chapter 8 uses the insights developed in earlier chapters to address some highly enigmatic features of Upper Palaeolithic cave art. I show that the puzzles of this art are not, as they may at first appear, disparate enigmas. Rather, they interlock and respond to a unified, though multi-component, explanation. To demonstrate the effectiveness of this explanation I consider the broad sweep of Upper Palaeolithic cave art. But such generalization cannot provide a final answer.

I therefore turn in Chapter 9 to two contrasting caves and consider their topographies and how people responded to the highly varied chambers, passages and small *diverticules*. Here we see that the embellished caves were not mere reflections of Upper Palaeolithic society and thought. On the contrary, they were deeply implicated in the fashioning of the life of that period.

Finally, Chapter 10 examines the other side of the coin: society does not develop and evolve without conflict, without individuals who contest the *status quo*. Here, we are dealing with the origin of human society, its tensions and discriminations. The Upper Palaeolithic was not Eden before the Fall. The forbidden fruit was tasted as soon as our ancestors ceased being pre-human and became fully human.

To my way of thinking, there is no greater archaeological enigma than the subterranean art of Upper Palaeolithic western Europe. Anyone who has crouched and crawled underground along a narrow, absolutely dark passage for more than a kilometre, slid along mud banks and waded through dark lakes and hidden rivers to be confronted, at the end of such a hazardous journey, by a painting of an extinct woolly mammoth or a powerful, hunched bison will never be quite the same again. Muddied and exhausted, the explorer will be gazing at the limitless *terra incognita* of the human mind.

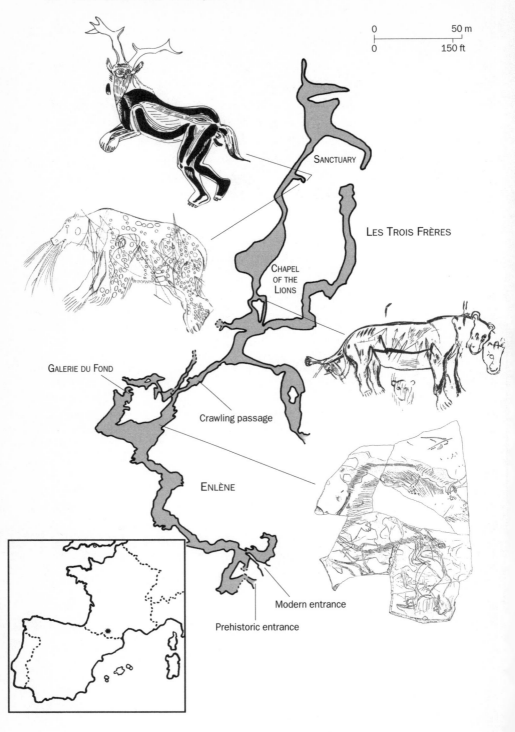

0   50 m

0   150 ft

SANCTUARY

LES TROIS FRÈRES

CHAPEL
OF THE
LIONS

GALERIE DU FOND

Crawling passage

ENLÈNE

Modern entrance

Prehistoric entrance

Three Caves:
Three Time-Bytes

Time-Byte I

TIME Between 13,000 and 14,000 years ago
PLACE The Volp Caves (Enlène and Les Trois Frères), Ariège, France

A man enters the narrow opening of a limestone cave. Clutching a flickering tallow lamp and a small, precious object, he moves slowly into the dark depths. Soon he is aware of thick smoke and the overpowering odour of burning animal bone. He hears strange sounds echoing from the darkness. He knows that, in that smoke, people are scratching images of animals on small pieces of stone, and cutting across them with multiple lines.

The darkness, apart from his wavering tallow lamp, is absolute. He skirts a seemingly bottomless pit from which rise the sounds of rushing water. Then, kneeling, he turns to his right and crawls along a low tunnel. Suddenly, he emerges into a high-vaulted chamber. His lamp light does not reach to its dark extremities; he stands in a pale island of light, suspended in darkness.

Groping his way farther into the depths, he finds a small side chamber. There he is confronted by a lion. It seems to float out of the wall into which it is carved. Carefully, he thrusts his valuable object – a cave bear tooth – into a niche in the wall. Part of his mission is complete. But there is more to be done.

He descends still farther into the depths of the central passage of the cave. At the foot of a slippery, muddy slope, he finds a wall densely covered with images of animals and scratched lines. After trying to decipher the tangled images, he raises his lamp above his head and looks up: there, on a ledge high above him, looms a figure, part human, part animal, with spreading antlers.

1 Two of the Volp Caves: Enlène and Les Trois Frères. During the Upper Palaeolithic, access to Les Trois Frères was probably through Enlène.

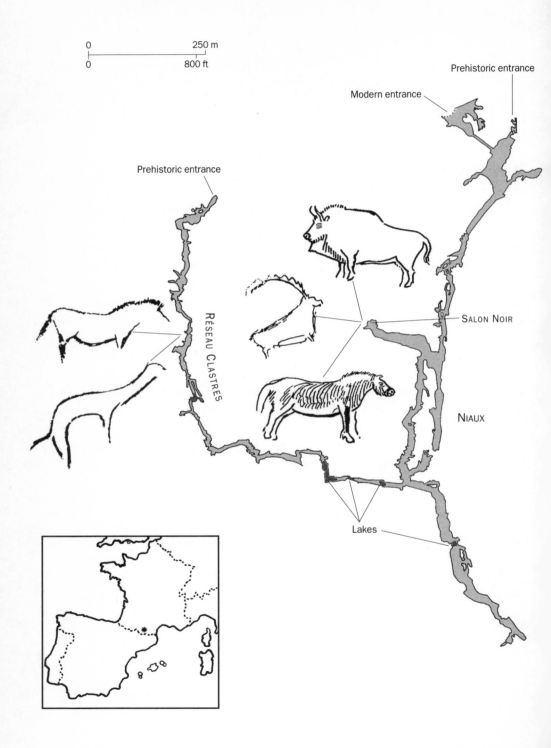

0 ———————————— 250 m

0 ———————————— 800 ft

Prehistoric entrance

Modern entrance

Prehistoric entrance

RÉSEAU CLASTRES

SALON NOIR

NIAUX

Lakes

Time-Byte II
TIME AD 1660
PLACE Niaux Cave, Ariège, France

Ruben de la Vialle and some companions enter a deep cave near the small town of Tarascon. The cavern is a local tourist attraction – a natural wonder. De la Vialle penetrates a high-vaulted, 450-metre-long passage, turns into a side gallery and climbs 200 metres up to the chamber that is now known as the Salon Noir.

Here the passage ends, and he commemorates his visit by inscribing his name and the date on the wall of the chamber. His florid inscription, which can still be seen, is less than a metre from large, well-preserved and extraordinarily striking depictions of bison and ibex painted in black. Every convolution of this section of the cave wall reveals another set of images: bison, some of which seem to be impaled by spears, heavy-jowled horses, ibexes with large curving horns, and a stag with impressive antlers.

Yet neither he nor anyone else at that time seems to pay much attention to the images.

2 Niaux Cave, with its extension, the Réseau Clastres. In prehistoric times access to the Réseau Clastres was at what is now its farthest point. Today the passage leading from Niaux to the Réseau Clastres is blocked by deep underground lakes.

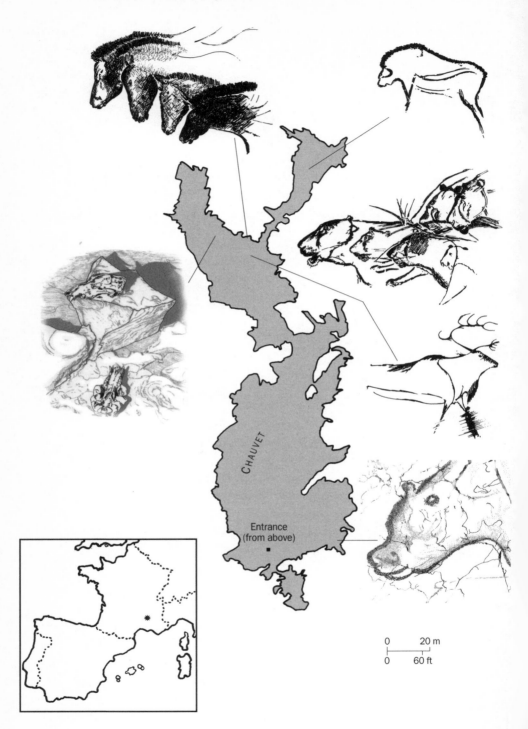

CHAUVET

Entrance
(from above)

0	20 m
0	60 ft

Time-Byte III
TIME AD 1994
PLACE Chauvet Cave, Ardèche, France

Three friends are in search of Upper Palaeolithic art. On 18 December, Jean-Marie Chauvet, Eliette Brunel Deschamps and Christian Hillaire detect a draught coming from behind a pile of rubble in an unexplored, and not very promising, cave. Having removed enough of the stones, Eliette squeezes through a very narrow tunnel and, after about 10 metres, comes out on a ledge overlooking a large, echoing chamber; the floor is at least 10 metres below her. Together they return to their car to fetch a ladder.

Back in the cave, they unroll the ladder, descend to the floor and begin to explore what they soon realize is a major discovery. As they edge forward, their lamps catch images of animals, handprints and series of dots; depictions of a mammoth and a rhinoceros especially impress them. Taking care to step in the footprints of the leader so as not to damage possible evidence on the floor, they move deeper and deeper into the richly embellished chambers.

In a large chamber they find a panel of horses' heads, exquisitely painted. Then, ahead of them, they spot a low square rock: resting on it is the skull of a cave bear, its canine teeth hooked over the edge. In another, still deeper, chamber they find a series of startling lion heads.

Later, they recall the experience:

Alone in that vastness, lit by the feeble beam of our lamps, we were seized by a strange feeling. Everything was so beautiful, so fresh, almost too much so. Time was abolished, as if the tens of thousands of years that separated us from the producers of these paintings no longer existed. It seemed as if they had just created these masterpieces. Suddenly we felt like intruders. Deeply impressed, we were weighed down by the feeling that we were not alone; the artists' souls and spirits surrounded us. We thought we could feel their presence; we were disturbing them.[1]

3 The Chauvet Cave. The prehistoric entrance is now blocked and access is through a small tunnel at a higher level.

CHAPTER I

Discovering Human Antiquity

The questions raised by Time-Byte I are the principal subject of this book. Why did the person of 13,000 and more years ago undertake such a hazardous journey? What emotions did he experience? Was the person a man, as we so easily assume, or was it a woman? How old was the person? Why did he or she believe it was important to place the bear tooth in the wall of the cave? It was not the only object placed in the cave walls: there are also pieces of bone, stone tools and core-stones.[2] What did he or she believe about the images on the walls? What did the subterranean journey 'do' for him or her?

These questions are not just about ancient history. They take us to the heart of what it is to be human today. It is not simply that we are more intelligent than other creatures, that we are masters of complex technology, or even that we have complex language. These are glittering jewels in the crown of humanity with which we are comfortable. On the contrary, the essence of being human is an uncomfortable duality of 'rational' technology and 'irrational' belief. We are still a species in transition. The unknown person of Time-Byte I had the rational, 'scientific' knowledge and skill to make a tallow lamp and also a set of beliefs that were the imperative for his or her apparently irrational underground journey. That duality in human behaviour did not disappear at the end of the Stone Age. Even in the twentieth century, people were 'rational' enough to travel to the moon and back and yet still 'irrational' enough to believe in supernatural entities and forces that transcend, and in effect make nonsense of, all the laws of physics on which their moon journey depended. Does the human *brain* construct spaceships and the human *mind* fashion unseen forces and spirits? What is the difference between brain and mind? What is intelligence and what is human consciousness? How did early people reach a stage of evolution that allowed them to make and understand pictures? These are just some of the issues with which we shall have to grapple when we try to answer the questions posed by Time-Byte I.

What the seventeenth-century people of Time-Byte II thought the images in Niaux were or who they thought made them we do not know. Perhaps Ruben de la Vialle and others who had been there before him believed that the pictures had been made by recent visitors like himself, and so he added a contribution of his own – his name and the date. At that time, Western thought had no concept of prehistory; the received view was that the world had been created by God. According to Archbishop James Ussher (1581–1656), this miraculous event occurred in 4004 BC. Later, Bishop John Lightfoot refined Ussher's calculations and announced that creation took place at nine o'clock on the morning of 23 October 4004 BC. Not everyone, even at that time, may have accepted the happy fortuity of creation coinciding so neatly with the beginning of the Cambridge University academic year, but virtually everyone believed that human history started miraculously at a moment that was not so very long ago. De la Vialle had no conceptual framework into which to fit the significance of what he was seeing, so, in effect, he did not 'see' it at all.

What happened during the years between Time-Byte II and Time-Byte III? Why did Jean-Marie Chauvet and his friends see what de la Vialle missed? The answer is both simple and momentous. The Western world had learned that it had a deep past, its concept of humanity had undergone profound changes, and its yearning to know the truth about its origins had risen to a level of unprecedented intensity: finding evidence for 'Human Origins', be it stone artefacts, fossils or genes, had become an absorbing passion. The chasm created by the passing of, not merely Archbishop Ussher's 6,000 or so, but 30,000 years, suddenly closed. As Chauvet himself wrote, 'Time was abolished.' Despite the enormous time gap, he and his friends felt as if they could sense the 'souls and spirits' of the artists surrounding them; the hidden images invoked not only 'scientific wonder' but also awe and 'spiritual' proclivities. They used words like 'artists' and 'masterpieces'. They were identifying with people whom they took to be their remote ancestors. Shared consciousness, they believed, was a bridge to those ancestors. They were right, though perhaps not in a way that they would have recognized.

A revolution in Western thought

The story of the sea-change in Western thought that took place between Time-Bytes II and III began in the first half of the nineteenth century. At that time, the influence of writers such as Sir Charles Lyell (1797–1875) was beginning to be felt. Lyell, Professor of Geology at King's College, London, published his immensely important *Principles of Geology* in 1830. He argued that layered sedimentary rocks and the fossils they contain point to an antiquity of the earth until then unsuspected. At first, conservative fundamentalist Christians, and not a few geologists, accommodated the fossils by suggesting that they came from a barbaric antediluvian period. For them, the fossils simply confirmed the historical accuracy of the Biblical account of the catastrophic flood that Noah and his family survived. The Church championed this idea because it fitted well with the Biblical record. Given the short span of time allowed for human history, catastrophes had to be invoked, and so-called Diluvialists debated not just Noah's flood but also the number of pre-Noachian floods.

Lyell, however, firmly rejected catastrophism of this kind and argued instead for the operation of gradual processes – the same erosional, depositional, volcanic, faulting and folding processes that are evident today sculpted the earth from the beginning. This idea was enshrined in the lengthy title of his great work: *Principles of Geology, Being an Attempt to Explain the Former Changes of the Earth's Surface by Reference to Causes Now in Action.* Lyell later allowed that the intensity of change may have varied, but the notion of uniformitarianism was born: at least in geological terms, the past was no different from the present, and the fossil record showed that a lot happened *before* 4004 BC. Immediately, the battle lines were drawn.

Yet, despite conservative resistance, the old way of seeing human history was beginning to crumble. The notion of slow evolutionary change was in the air. Sensationally, an anonymous evolutionary tract appeared in 1844; it was entitled *Vestiges of the Natural History of Creation.* Much later, the author turned out to be Robert Chambers, who had worked for Sir Walter Scott and who eventually, with his brother William, founded the Edinburgh publishing house W. & R. Chambers. *Vestiges* outlined the history of the world from a gaseous cloud, through the fossil record and up to the transmutation of apes into human beings. Chambers, privately a sceptic, nevertheless insisted on the presence of God and believed in phrenology and spiritualism. Still, many readers considered the book to be dangerously atheistic. What Chambers's scheme really lacked was a mechanism that would account for the transformations that he described. That key was supplied by a far more rigorous thinker.

Charles Robert Darwin (1809–82), who as a young man had circumnavigated the globe and studied a broad range of botanical and zoological topics, was the catalyst (Fig. 4). Darwin set out on that voyage holding the view that the world had indeed been created by God and that species were separate creations. He began to sharpen his more scientific ideas in debates with the captain of the *Beagle*, Robert Fitzroy, a fanatical proselytizer, but at that time Darwin had enough in common with him to publish a jointly authored article in the *South African Christian Recorder* in 1836.[3] The article was a plea for more missionaries to be sent to the Pacific. Darwin's easy relationship with Fitzroy was, however, doomed.

Before long Darwin realized that what was missing from biological thought was a persuasive account of the *mechanism* of change: *how* could one species evolve into another? As early as 1844, he prepared an article that encapsulated the main tenet of his answer to this question – natural selection. But he did not publish his work; he showed it only to a friend, the celebrated botanist Joseph Hooker. After 1844 Darwin continued to collect data to support his theory. As part of this work he produced a highly detailed and definitive study of barnacles. It contains no mention of his ideas on evolution.

Darwin's theory of evolution did not come to him fully formed as he stood on the shores of the Galapagos Islands. Rather, his conversion proceeded gradually and in close co-operation with numerous celebrated specialists in taxonomy and systematics. But it was he, not they, who perceived the wood and not just a scatter of trees. At the beginning of his work, he was as prejudiced against evolutionary ideas as they, but something in his make-up, some hard-to-define 'genius in science', allowed him to see connections that escaped the meticulous inspection of others.[4]

Then came a decisive moment. On 18 June 1858, Darwin received an essay from Alfred Russel Wallace (1823–1913), a naturalist who was then 12,000 miles away in the Moluccas Islands.

Wallace's essay was entitled *On the Tendencies of Varieties to Depart Indefinitely from the Original Type*. Darwin's previous correspondence with Wallace had not prepared him for the content of the article. For Darwin, it was 'a bolt from the blue'. He realized that Wallace's ideas about how species changed and evolved into other species were very similar, even identical, to those on which he had been brooding for so long. Wallace, he feared, was about to seize

4 Charles Darwin, catalyst of modern thought. It was his penetrating insights into the mechanism of evolution that made a modern, rational assessment of prehistory possible.

the initiative, but, being a man of great magnanimity, he did not wish to deprive him of his due. At once, Darwin consulted Lyell, who, ever active and influential in such matters, facilitated the reading of papers on natural selection by both Darwin and Wallace at the Linnean Society in London. The occasion was scheduled for 1 July of the same year.

In the event, the papers were read not by the authors but by the secretary of the Society: Darwin, as became his habit, remained at home, and Wallace was in the Moluccas. Surprisingly, few of those present seem to have found the occasion especially noteworthy. Perhaps the secretary's delivery was soporific. The President recorded in his annual report that the papers did not deal with one of those 'striking discoveries which at once revolutionize, so to speak, the department of science on which they bear'.[5] This stunningly banal evaluation of the explosive material contained in the two papers says something about the unpredictable nature of the receptivity of 'scientific' minds. A more decisive blow needed to be struck.

It came in 1859 with the publication of Darwin's hastily completed, but as always meticulous and erudite, book *On the Origin of Species by Means of Natural Selection* (Fig. 5). Despite its more than 400 pages, Darwin regarded it as an 'abstract'.[6] He subtitled it *The Preservation of Favoured Races in the Struggle for Life*, and the popular phrase 'survival of the fittest' became part of Western thought – together with a series of attendant racist notions of which Darwin would certainly not have approved. The actual phrase, 'survival of the fittest', was first used by the English philosopher Herbert Spencer in 1865, and Darwin acknowledged it in the 1869 edition of *On the Origin of Species*. Darwin himself neatly summed up his central idea thus: '…the theory of descent with modification through natural selection'.[7] The first printing of 1,250 copies of *On the Origin of Species* was sold out on the first day, an achievement that few, if any, subsequent scientific writers have been able to equal. By 1872, six editions and 24,000 copies had been published; by 1876, the book had been translated into every European language. Here was the conceptual framework that de la Vialle lacked, a framework that opened up an entirely new perspective on humanity. Suddenly, Westerners who had access to Darwin's ideas could 'see' things that they had never noticed before.

The most famous public clash came in 1860 at an Oxford meeting of the British Association. Darwin was again not present. Expectation was running high because it was common knowledge that the Church, as embodied in Bishop Samuel Wilberforce, was, as the Bishop himself said, about to 'smash Darwin'. The event exceeded even the noisy students' hopes. In one of science's

5 *The book that changed the world: the title page of the first edition of* On the Origin of Species. *It became the foundation of modern thought and philosophy.*

ON

THE ORIGIN OF SPECIES

BY MEANS OF NATURAL SELECTION,

OR THE

PRESERVATION OF FAVOURED RACES IN THE STRUGGLE FOR LIFE.

By CHARLES DARWIN, M.A.,

FELLOW OF THE ROYAL, GEOLOGICAL, LINNÆAN, ETC., SOCIETIES; AUTHOR OF 'JOURNAL OF RESEARCHES DURING H. M. S. BEAGLE'S VOYAGE ROUND THE WORLD.'

LONDON:
JOHN MURRAY, ALBEMARLE STREET.
1859.

The right of Translation is reserved.

most infamous foolishnesses, Wilberforce asked Thomas Henry Huxley if it was through his grandmother or his grandfather that he was descended from an ape.

Huxley (1825–1895), trained as a surgeon, was at that time Professor of Natural History at the Royal School of Mines; he was a popular lecturer who was able to make abstruse matters plain to ordinary people. He coined the word 'agnostic' to describe his own position on religious issues and was happy to call himself 'Darwin's watchdog'. When the absurdly facetious question was put to him he was heard to murmur, 'The Lord hath delivered him into mine hands.' When he rose to reply to the Bishop, Huxley said that he would rather be descended from an ape than from a bishop who prostituted the gifts of culture and eloquence in the service of falsehood. At once there was an uproar. The students loved it, but Fitzroy, the *Beagle*'s former captain who happened to be present, was heard to yell above the hubbub that he had warned the young Darwin about his dangerous thoughts. The rest of his words were drowned by the tumult. Less than five years later, overwhelmed by religious despair, Fitzroy took his own life.

The following year, also in Oxford, Benjamin Disraeli coined an enduring phrase.[8] First, he asked, 'What is the question now placed before society with a glib assurance the most astounding? The question is this – Is man an ape or an angel?' His response to his own question turned out to be memorable: 'My Lord, I am on the side of the angels.'

In his epoch-making book, Darwin skated around the implications of his theory for human evolution, though he did say briefly that the theory of evolution by natural selection would throw light on 'the origin of man and his history', and that psychology will show 'the necessary acquirement of each mental power and capacity by gradation'.[9] His circumspection was prudent because, at that time, there was virtually no fossil evidence for human evolution. Nevertheless, this was a topic to which he turned in his 1871 book, *The Descent of Man, and Selection in Relation to Sex*. He did not shy away from the profound implications of his work. But others had seen those implications too. In 1863, Huxley, Darwin's great advocate, published *Man's Place in Nature*, and this book was followed in 1864 by Wallace's article in the *Anthropological Review*, similarly arguing for human evolution by natural selection.

By the end of the 1870s, it was clear to many people that human history, every bit as much as geology and animal species, was not exempt from the concepts of uniformitarianism and evolution. Indeed, as long ago as 1836, Danish archaeologists had divided human antiquity into the now well-known Stone, Bronze and Iron Ages. Those stages of human development found a home in Darwinian theory. Then, after the sensation created by *On the Origin of Species*, Sir John Lubbock (later, and appropriately, Lord Avebury) published his immensely popular book *Prehistoric Times* (1865). In it he subdivided the Stone Age into two parts and coined the terms Palaeolithic and Neolithic. The Palaeolithic period was one of flaked stone artefacts and hunting and gathering as a way of life. The Neolithic, by contrast, saw the introduction of polished stone axes and the beginnings of farming. Much later, Gordon Childe (1892–1957), an influential Australian archaeologist who adopted a Marxist perspective, described the change from the Palaeolithic to the Neolithic as the 'Neolithic Revolution', and thus started a line of archaeological thought about the nature of the process of becoming human.[10] In accordance with Marxist social theory, he argued that society was 'driven' by its material foundations, and, through evolutionary processes, 'contradictions' developed. These contradictions were resolved by comparatively sudden periods of change – revolutions. So it was that Childe also proposed an 'Urban Revolution'.[11] We return to the supposed revolutionary nature of change in later chapters. It has become a central – and contested – topic in disputes about the evolution of human consciousness and art. How swift does evolution have to be before we can call it revolution?

As we know, the dust raised by all the debates that Darwin's work sparked has not yet entirely settled. Most people still accept both the laws of physics and the existence of supernatural forces that operate beyond those laws. Others continue to challenge the very notion of evolution. The human duality of material and 'spiritual' has proved more stubborn than some nineteenth-century scientists expected. There are thus two questions that we can ask. First, what is it that leads some people to accept a revolutionary[12] idea like evolution? Secondly, why do many people persist in believing in an invisible dimension populated by spirit beings? Both questions will concern us at various points in this book as we consider explanations for such difficult notions as consciousness and art.

As a provisional answer to the first question, we may say, not for the last time, that 'proof' is an inappropriate concept in discussions of this kind. The philosopher John Stuart Mill realized this and pointed out, 'Mr Darwin has never pretended his theory was proved'.[13] He did not say that he rejected Darwin's ideas, only that 'proof' is an elusive concept in such contexts. Rather than seek 'proof', we should speak about – and assess – the diversity and weight of evidence for a proposition. Darwin himself provided a key part of the answer. In the *Origin* he wrote, 'Now this hypothesis…explains several large and independent classes of facts'.[14] He repeated this important idea in a subsequent book, *Variations of Animals and Plants under Domestication*: 'I believe in the truth of the theory, because it collects under one point of view, and gives a rational explanation of many independent classes of facts'.[15] He was pointing to the elegance and parsimony of the theory of evolution. It covers not only all species of plants but also all species of creatures. As we proceed in our quest for an explanation of the earliest art and why the human mind works as it does, we shall, like Darwin, examine disparate bodies of data. If we can find a hypothesis that explains and co-ordinates those bodies of data, we shall be drawn to it.

Darwin had a further and equally important thing to say about hypotheses. In an 1860 letter to Lyell, he wrote, '…without the making of theories I am convinced there would be no observation'.[16] De la Vialle did not see the painted images in Niaux because he had no 'theory' to bring them into focus. Many subsequent philosophers of science agreed with Darwin. Scientists do not collect data randomly and utterly comprehensively. The data they collect are only those that they consider *relevant* to some hypothesis or theory. Otherwise they, like de la Vialle, would not even recognize that some, not all, of their observations (things they notice during the course of their work) can be used as data in a sustained argument. Certainly, scientists do not collect 'irrelevant' data.

This is currently one of the problems besetting research on the topics discussed in this book. On the one hand, many researchers are afraid of theories. They say that it is 'too soon' to formulate hypotheses about the making of Upper Palaeolithic art. First, they argue, they must collect 'all' the data in an indiscriminate way. But we know, and philosophers of science have pointed out time and again, that explanations (or hypotheses) do not emerge inexorably and naturally out of data. Human insight is what discerns explanations. Those students of Upper Palaeolithic art who say that they are methodically collecting theory-free data should realize that they cannot make observations and discern relevant data without some theory in mind. At the outset of our enquiry, we need to be aware that theory directs observation, at least to a substantial extent. But there is another side to the coin. In day-to-day research, theory and data must interact; they must illuminate one another. When we notice, perhaps even stumble upon, observations that do not accord with received theory, and then make the leap to a new hypothesis, we are fortunate indeed. We may even be on the threshold of a 'revolution'.

With these important ideas about discovery, theory and evidence in mind we can move on from the antiquity and evolution of humankind to another discovery that many found hard to swallow, even though they had a conceptual framework into which they should have been able to fit it. Acceptance of Stone Age *art*, even in the adventurous intellectual climate of the late nineteenth century, was another matter altogether. The very idea of Palaeolithic art was deeply disturbing. Was not art one of the great achievements of high civilizations?

Controversial art

The first pieces of Upper Palaeolithic art came to light as long ago as the 1830s in the Chaffaud Cave (Vienne) in France, but their antiquity was not recognized; Western thought was then still of the order evinced by de la Vialle in 1660.[17] The Darwinian Rubicon had not yet been crossed. The pieces were small, decorated objects that ancient people could have carried around with them. Today we know that portable art (*art mobilier*), as these objects are known, comprised a wide variety of items: beads, pendants, carved spear-throwers, statuettes, flat pieces of stone (known as 'plaquettes') inscribed with images and multitudes of scratched lines, elaborately embellished batons made from long bones, and so forth.[18] Many of these pieces bear engraved or carved images of animals, fish, birds and, less commonly, what appear to be human figures, as well as complex arrangements of parallel lines, chevrons and notches (Fig. 6). These *objets d'art*, as people tend to think of them, were made from bone, stone, mammoth ivory, amber and antler. The particular pieces found in the 1830s were made from bone and antler and were decorated with engravings of ibex, a horse's head and hinds.

Some 30 years later, at the beginning of the 1860s and thus immediately after the publication of *On the Origin of Species*, the French archaeologist

6 *Portable Upper Palaeolithic art. (Right) A spear-thrower carved in the shape of a gracefully leaping horse; Magdalenian. From Bruniquel, Tarn-et-Garonne. (Centre left) A spear-thrower carved in the form of an ibex looking back over its shoulder; Magdalenian. From Mas d'Azil, Ariège. (Approximately 30 cm). (Centre right) A mammoth ivory carving of a bison apparently licking its flank; Magdalenian. From La Madeleine, Dordogne. (Below) A carved bone baton; images are shown 'unrolled'; Magdalenian. From Lortet, Hautes-Pyrénées.*

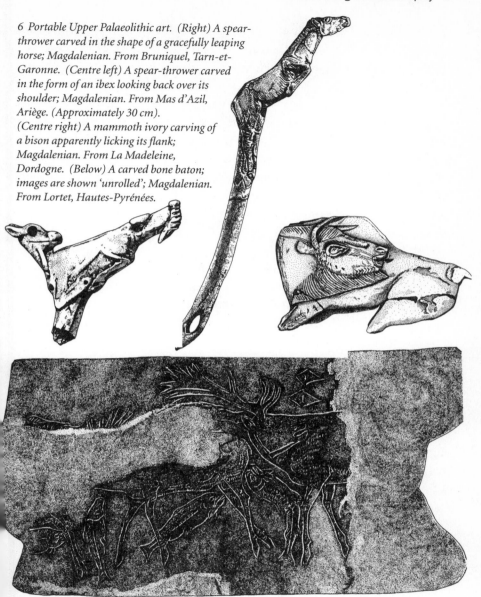

Édouard Lartet was excavating in the cave Massat in the Ariège Département of France. He found more engraved portable art. Amongst the items was a beautiful pierced bone baton engraved with a bear's head and some other motifs. By this time, the advances in geology had established the existence of an Ice Age populated by now-extinct animals – including huge cave bears

(*Ursus spelaeus*),[19] mammoths with long woolly coats to protect themselves against the cold, and sabre-toothed tigers. The association of the engraved pieces with fossils of extinct species indisputably confirmed the great age of the 'art'. When, in 1861, Lartet published his finds, he included a drawing of a piece that had been discovered nearly a decade earlier but that had not been recognized for what it was. At once there was a wave of reassessment of earlier finds and debate about the antiquity of human beings and, especially, their supposed primeval savage mental state. Surely, many felt, their consciousness was not the same as ours. As one, probably apocryphal, Victorian lady remarked, 'Let us hope it is not true, but if it is, let us pray that it will not become generally known.'[20] Her prayer went unanswered, and further discoveries continued to be made.

The dispute over portable art was, however, as nothing to that which preceded the acceptance of parietal art – images painted or engraved on the walls and ceilings of caves. Today, we know that parietal art is not confined to deep caves; that was true of only the first discoveries. Some was made in the open air on vertical rock surfaces, some is in open rock shelters, and some is in the entrances to caves but not beyond the reach of daylight. Time-Byte I took us back to the time when people were penetrating for more than a kilometre underground to make deep, seemingly hidden, images. That most of the parietal art known today is of this kind may be a result of the effects of natural weathering on art in exposed places – though we cannot be certain about this point.

Parietal images were made by diverse techniques, some of which were combined in a single image. Some painted images, such as those in the Hall of the Bulls in Lascaux, are as much as 2 m (6 ft 7 in) long and executed in a number of brilliant colours (Pl. 1); others are only a few centimetres in length and made by a few deft strokes in one colour only (Pl. 12). Others were engraved or scratched into the surface, without the use of paint (Fig. 44). Some parietal art is not merely engraved, but deeply carved into the walls to create bas-reliefs. Often, too, images were made by fingers trailing through the soft mud on the walls of caves (Pl. 16). Images of this kind were even made on the floors of caves; such is the case in Niaux, though de la Vialle did not notice them. Perhaps he and others of the time trampled most of them into oblivion. One of the most intriguing techniques was to use a natural rock fold, a crack or step to provide the outline of an animal's body. Then a few strokes of paint supplied the missing parts. In some cases such images are visible only when one's light is in a particular position. The presence of a human being with a lamp or torch is necessary to bring them into view (Pls 17 and 18).

The motifs of parietal art include animals, such as bison, horses, aurochs, woolly mammoths, deer and felines. An interesting study of bison images showed that they depict aspects of that species' behaviour.[21] There are also occasional anthropomorphic figures that may or may not represent human beings. Some of these are therianthropes (part-human, part-animal figures). Researchers have argued that they depict masked and costumed people performing rituals, but close inspection shows that they are essentially a blend of human and animal features. Some, for instance, have a human body and an animal head and have been thought to depict masked 'sorcerers'. Then there is an image type that is exceptional in the ways that it is made – handprints. Some of these are positive: paint was applied to the palm and fingers and then the hand was pressed against the rock. Others are negative: a hand was placed against the rock wall and then paint was blown from the mouth (or through a hollow bone) over it so that, when the hand was removed, its outline remained in the midst of the surrounding paint. Finally, there is a multiplicity of 'signs', geometric forms such as grids, dots, and chevrons. These subterranean signs include some of those found on portable art, but others are unique to parietal art.

Parietal art does not depict such a wide range of species as that associated with portable art. Why, we may ask, is there this distinction? Some researchers think of portable art as having been 'secular' and parietal art, especially that deep inside caves, as having been 'sacred'. There may be some merit in this distinction, but a dichotomy between secular and sacred is largely a Western construct; it is not a distinction that Upper Palaeolithic people are likely to have recognized. Rather than unthinkingly take over a Western notion like this we should try to be more explicit about what we mean; simply to invoke the secular:sacred dichotomy is not to provide an explanation of the data in all their complexity. Certainly, we should not ignore the substantial similarities between the imagery of portable and parietal art. As soon as researchers start to draw on a neat Western analogy to explain Upper Palaeolithic art, we should become uneasy.

Discovery and debate

The story of the first discovery of parietal art is well known.[22] Impressed by pieces of portable art that he had seen at the 1878 Paris Universal Exhibition and by his discussions there with the great French prehistorian Édouard Piette, Don Marcelino Sanz de Sautuola began to explore a cave on his property on the northern Spanish coast. In 1879, as the story goes, he was looking for stone

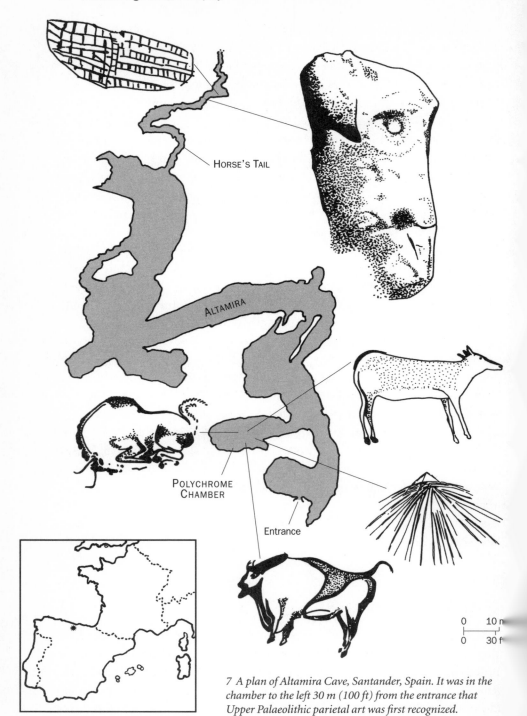

Horse's Tail

Altamira

Polychrome
Chamber

Entrance

0   10 m
0   30 ft

*7 A plan of Altamira Cave, Santander, Spain. It was in the
chamber to the left 30 m (100 ft) from the entrance that
Upper Palaeolithic parietal art was first recognized.*

artefacts and pieces of portable art in his excavation in the Altamira cavern when his young daughter, Maria, discovered the now-famous images of bison, some of which were painted on bosses projecting down from the ceiling of the cave (Fig. 7; Pl. 2).[23] He had kept his eyes fixed on the floor; she looked up. Years later, Picasso was to say, 'None of us could paint like that.'[24]

De Sautuola was dumbstruck. But similarities between the portable art that he knew from the Paris exhibition and his own Altamira paintings convinced him that he, or rather his daughter, had discovered a hitherto unknown kind of ancient art. At first there was a flurry of interest in the find. Even the King of Spain came to have a look at the paintings. Unwittingly following de la Vialle's example, the King allowed a servant to trace in candle-smoke the inscription 'Alfonso XII'.[25]

In 1880, de Sautuola published a soberly entitled booklet: *Breves apuntes sobre algunos objetos prehistóricos de la provincia de Santander* (*Brief Notes on Some Prehistoric Objects from the Province of Santander*). In it he described the stone tools, bone ornaments, pigments and food remains that he had found in his excavation in the entrance to Altamira. In dealing with the paintings, he identified the extinct bison and stressed their artistic merits. He also linked the pieces of portable art that he had seen in France to the paintings in Altamira and declared the Spanish paintings to be of Palaeolithic age.[26] All in all, the booklet was a model of sensible thought, way ahead of its time.

Years later, Maria de Sautuola told Herbert Kühn, Professor of Pre- and Protohistory at the University of Mainz, that the discovery of the painted ceiling was 'the greatest adventure of my life…and, also, my bitterest disappointment'.[27] There was no smooth road ahead. By 1880 interest in the Altamira paintings had dried up. In that year, Juan Vilanova y Piera, Professor of Palaeontology in Madrid, arranged a visit to Altamira for delegates to the Congress of Prehistoric Archaeology in Lisbon, but no one wished to go.[28] De Sautuola was not to enjoy success of the kind that Darwin garnered with *On the Origin of Species*. On the contrary, the implacable and virulent scepticism that he encountered is today considered one of the great scandals of the study of Upper Palaeolithic art. The elaborately executed art on the ceiling in the Altamira cave did not fit current notions of Palaeolithic 'savagery'; it was too 'advanced' for the period. Members of the archaeological establishment were therefore quick to denounce Altamira as a fraud. In 1882, Édouard Harlé, a French scholar, confirmed this opinion after a visit to Altamira. He argued that the images had been made between de Sautuola's two visits to the cave, that is, between 1875 and 1879. The implication was obvious: either de Sautuola had been duped or he was himself a forger. At this point, the rejection of the authenticity of Altamira recalls the incomprehension that Darwin's and Wallace's papers encountered at the 1858 meeting of the Linnean Society. Thirty years on, the minds of 'scientists' were no better able to 'see' something new.

De Sautuola died in 1888, embittered and discredited. Right from their first discovery, or rather from recognition of their antiquity, images of the kind seen in Time-Byte I had the power to excite and amaze, but also to inflame. Western thought was poised on the brink of a revolution as profound as the shift in belief from a geocentric to a heliocentric solar system, but the sceptics demanded more evidence.

Although Piette himself accepted the authenticity of Altamira, another prominent French prehistorian, Émile Cartailhac, seized the limelight with his strident denunciations of de Sautuola and any others who dared to confront him. Personal status and religious sentiments rather than detached, rational thought poisoned debate. Then, finally, in 1902, when he could no longer withstand the growing weight of evidence, Cartailhac astutely turned events to his own advantage and published a paper entitled, in part, *Mea culpa d'un sceptique*. He admitted 'an error, committed for twenty years, an injustice that must be acknowledged and made reparation for publicly…. For my part I must bow to reality, and render justice to M. de Sautuola.'[29]

Perhaps the most influential evidence that led to Cartailhac's change of mind came from a comparatively small cave in the Dordogne Département of France. In 1895, at La Mouthe, a farmer had cleared some debris from a small rock shelter that he wished to use for his agricultural activities. He exposed the existence of a tunnel behind the infill. Soon after, four boys entered the underground passage and discovered an image of a bison. Then Émile Rivière, a French prehistorian, began excavations in the cave. In 1899, he turned up a stone that had been hollowed out to serve as a lamp and that was engraved on the underside with the head of an ibex (Fig. 8). It seemed as if art was being used to enhance, or beautify, technology. On a more practical level, finds such as this told researchers how the person of Time-Byte I managed to grope his or her way through the labyrinth of subterranean passages and chambers: people of that time used not only large, flaming torches but also delicate tallow lamps. Most importantly, the manner in which the entrance to the underground passage had been blocked by accumulated ancient debris made it clear that the images on the walls of the cave must be of Palaeolithic age. This situation may not have constituted 'proof', but the weight of evidence was telling. Still, true to

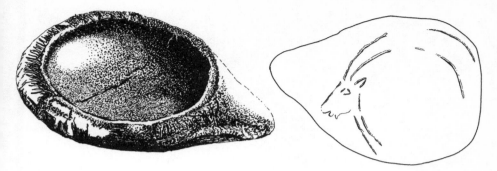

8 *A stone lamp found in the Dordogne cave La Mouthe. An ibex head with exaggerated curving horns is carved on the underside. The image suggests that the object was in some way 'special'. The lamp was primed with tallow and burned by means of a wick.*

form, some archaeologists claimed that Rivière had been deceived. Then, in 1901, Louis Capitan and the Abbé Henri Breuil published the images they had copied in Les Combarelles Cave, also in the Dordogne, claiming that they were from the Upper Palaeolithic. Cartailhac and others could hold out no longer: the evidence for sophisticated Palaeolithic art was now overwhelming. After recognizing Breuil's skill in copying images in Marsoulas, Cartailhac invited him to accompany him on a visit to Altamira. 'What we saw plunged us in deep amazement.'[30] The 'savage mind' of Stone Age people was by no means as primitive as had been supposed.

Soon the Abbé Henri Breuil (1877–1961), whose name will crop up in subsequent chapters, became recognized as a leading researcher (Figs 9, 10). He was known as the 'Pope of Prehistory', a sobriquet that suited his demeanour. His central role in the exciting discovery in 1912 of an art form in some ways between portable and parietal art is therefore not surprising. The three sons of Count Henri Bégouën had been

9 *The Abbé Henri Breuil, the 'Pope of Prehistory'. His influence was supreme until his death in 1961.*

10 A fanciful sketch by the Abbé Henri Breuil shows a copy of a rock painting of a bison 'coming alive' and facing two wolves.

exploring a system of caves on their father's property in the Ariège Département, near the foothills of the Pyrenees. The caves, two of which feature in Time-Byte I, are associated with the Volp River, which flows deep underground for part of its course. Max, Jacques and Louis used a home-made boat, 'a contraption of boxes and empty petrol tins',[31] to enter a cave from which the Volp flows. This part of the cave system is known as Tuc d'Audoubert and, today at any rate, does not seem to be connected by any passages to the adjacent caves of Time-Byte I. The three boys beached the boat and left it after they had penetrated into the darkness for some distance. Soon they found passages with Upper Palaeolithic engravings; a seventeenth-century inscription told them that they were not the first people of modern times to enter these passages. The event of Time-Byte II had been played out here too. But it was time to return home. They could hardly wait to get back to the cave.

Later, on 12 October 1912, Max Bégouën, acting on a hunch that more wonders awaited them, decided that a wall of translucent stalagmitic material that was preventing them from entering a deeper passage would have to be removed (Fig. 11). They set about the task with axes.[32] When the gap had been opened, he found a narrow opening, a 'cat's hole', as the French call it, through which one can still squeeze only with difficulty. It led upwards to a new passage at a higher level. A few hours later, Max and Louis, now on the higher level, made their way down a long tunnel scattered with the skeletons of ancient cave bears. They noticed that the canine teeth had been removed from the skulls, perhaps to make pendants. Towards the end, the ceiling sloped down and there, where one has to crouch down, they found two magnificent bison moulded in clay, one male, the other female. Each is a little over 60 cm (24 in) long, and both lean up against a large rock. The hole from which the makers of the bison had scraped the clay could be seen a short distance away.

At once their father, who was a friend of both Émile Cartailhac and Henri Breuil, despatched the now-famous telegram to Breuil: 'The Magdalenians modelled in clay!' 'Magdalenians' is the term used to denote people who lived during the later part of the Upper Palaeolithic period; the name derives from a Dordogne cave known as La Madeleine. At once Breuil replied, 'I'm on my way!' His telegram is preserved in the Bégouën family museum. Four days later Breuil and Cartailhac made their way along the underground river, disembarked in the darkness, and climbed into the long upper passage to see, at the

11 A 1912 photograph of the discoverers at the entrance to Tuc d'Audoubert. From left to right: Jaques Bégouën, Comte Bégouën, Max Bégouën, Abbé Breuil, Louis Bégouën and Emile Cartailhac.

far end, the new find. A hitherto unknown type of art had been discovered. Today, there is no more moving sight than to see the Tuc d'Audoubert clay bison, lit, as they were in Palaeolithic times, by a solitary lamp at the end of the shadowy passage. The variety, fecundity and mystery of Upper Palaeolithic art seem inexhaustible.

The significance of Altamira

In the decades following the authentication of Upper Palaeolithic art, new finds were made in quick succession, and the diversity of the art became increasingly apparent. Discoveries of unnoticed images, and even whole chambers, were also made in caves such as Altamira. Niaux, too, the cave that de la Vialle and many subsequent visitors had explored, yielded up hitherto unnoticed images. Today, looking back to those heady days of discovery, we can see that Altamira, the cave where it all started, encapsulates many features of Upper Palaeolithic cave art, features that will assume increasing importance as we proceed. We need to examine them briefly now so that we can have a mental framework into which we can fit the questions that will arise.

One of the most noticeable characteristics of Upper Palaeolithic caves is their diversity of form. Some have a single entrance; others have multiple entrances. Some entrances are huge stone arches that allow light to penetrate for some distance; others are small openings through which only one person at a time can squeeze and which permit very little natural light to enter. Some are long, totally dark, narrow passages; some have large chambers, others do not. Altamira itself is, overall, a long, sinuous passage, wider in some parts than in others.[33] The side chamber in which Maria de Sautuola made her sensational discovery is on the left, about 30 m (100 ft) from the entrance; some light may have filtered through to it in Palaeolithic times. The middle portion of the cave is a winding corridor with a few side extensions; there are images in the narrower parts. Then the cave suddenly narrows markedly at the beginning of the final section, a passage about 55 m (180 ft) long; it is known as the Horse's Tail (Fig. 7).

At the time of its discovery, the richly decorated ceiling was much lower than it is today; de Sautuola and subsequent archaeologists excavated the floor extensively. There are 25 polychrome images and several black paintings. Some of the images appear to be 'unfinished'. The well-known polychrome bison are on bosses of rock 'hanging' from the ceiling, rather like the decorated bosses of Gothic vaulting (Pl. 2). The making of these bison images was not a simple, quick process. It seems that their outlines were first engraved; then painting began. Finally, some details, such as eyes, nostrils and horns, were engraved. The curled-up postures of some of the bison, at least partly governed by the shape of bosses, have been interpreted in various ways – sleeping, giving birth and dying. It has also been argued that the combination of males and females suggests the rutting season. Whatever the case, it is of interest that the painters tried to fit the animals onto the bosses and, at the same time, to fill the spaces available; if they had made the images slightly smaller, they could have depicted the animals in the more usual standing position. There was clearly some sort of *interaction* between the depictions and the rock formations. The painters transformed the shapes of the rock. Perhaps the unknown person of Time-Byte I was involved in a related process of interaction with the rock wall when he or she placed the bear tooth in the niche. I return to this intriguing thought in a subsequent chapter.

Along with the remarkable bison on the Altamira ceiling there are depictions of horses, hind (Pl. 3) and signs of the dot, grid and claviform (vertical lines with an off-centre bulge on one side) kind. The cave also contains handprints and meandering patterns traced by fingers in the soft clay. Some of these tracings embrace images, such as the head of a bull. These and other examples led to the idea that representational imagery grew out of random markings, another notion to which I return.

The deepest part of the Altamira Cave, the Horse's Tail, has many images, principally but not exclusively engravings. It is particularly interesting for the so-called 'masks' (Pls 4, 5). Protuberances from the walls have been marked with paint so that they appear to be faces looking out at the visitor; one at least appears to be the face of an animal. They are not found in other parts of the cave. Here is another instance of interaction between image-maker and cave wall. The wall itself was given significance; it was not simply a neutral support for an image.

Having passed through the passages and chambers of Altamira and reached the end of the Horse's Tail, we encounter one of the most profound problems of Upper Palaeolithic art research. Did the people who used the caves recognize specific areas where, perhaps, they performed rituals appropriate to each area?

If we are to try to distinguish sections of caves that may have meant somewhat different things to Upper Palaeolithic people, our results will depend upon the criteria we choose as significant. Do we note the distribution of animal species, or of techniques of depiction (e.g., engraving or painting), or the sizes of images, or total numbers of images regardless of subjects, or what? The possible criteria seem infinite; change the criterion and we change our division of the cave into hypothetically significant areas. How much store should we set by the configuration of the cave itself? In what ways do the images interact with the caves? Is there any evidence, apart from parietal images, that will provide us with clues to the kinds of activities that people performed in the caves? These will be recurring questions as we proceed.

Remarking on the diverse Altamira images, Breuil, who recorded them as early as 1902, remarked, 'We search in vain for any composed scene, but most of the figures are placed near together in more or less large groups...'.[34] He was raising an issue that many researchers were to confront from various points of view: To what extent can the images of Upper Palaeolithic art be said to be 'placed' in meaningful combinations? Do the caves contain 'ensembles' of images? Why are some images superimposed on top of others? Breuil did not find any repeated patterns and concluded that, by and large, the images should be seen as scatters of disparate items. But was he right?

Periods and dates

Breuil, Cartailhac, Piette, Rivière, Capitan, indeed all those early researchers, used words like 'Palaeolithic' without having any idea – beyond intelligent guesses – of what they meant in terms of years. How long ago was the Palaeolithic? How long did it last? Strata in caves could be assigned relative dates – the lower down the stratum, the older it must be. But absolute dating given in numbers of years seemed impossible. This problem was solved, at least partially, in the 1950s. An American physicist, Willard F. Libby, who had worked on the Manhattan Project that led to the detonation of the first atomic bomb in New Mexico in 1945, discovered the radiocarbon (^{14}C) dating technique. Archaeology was transformed, and Libby was awarded the 1960 Nobel Prize for Physics. Perhaps this is an instance in which we can legitimately speak of a 'revolution'. Very briefly, the radiocarbon technique is based on the fact that all living matter, whether plant or animal, contains a radio isotope of carbon known as ^{14}C. It is absorbed from the atmosphere and taken in with food. The rate at which this carbon breaks down is constant. By measuring both the broken down and the remaining ^{14}C, researchers can calculate the time at which the organism died, that is, when it ceased to absorb ^{14}C. Libby had discovered a natural clock. But the technique has practical limits: it ceases to be effective between 40,000 and 50,000 years before the present, and this limitation has placed a question mark over the date of the beginning of the Upper Palaeolithic.

Still, radiocarbon dating strongly suggests that the Upper Palaeolithic period, that part of the Palaeolithic in which people began to make art, lasted from about 45,000 to 10,000 years ago (Fig. 12). Since the 1950s, other dating techniques have tended to confirm these dates. At once I must add that the dates apply to western Europe; we shall see the significance of this restriction later. The Upper Palaeolithic in western Europe was the period of fully anatomically human people no different from ourselves, the period of *Homo sapiens*. They had the same bodies and – more importantly – brains as we do. The art we have been discussing all comes from this period.

The period that preceded the Upper Palaeolithic in western Europe is known as the Middle Palaeolithic. It was characterized by *Homo neanderthalensis* – famed 'Neanderthal Man'. The Neanderthals did not make art, had a simpler stone tool kit, and were more opportunistic in their hunting than *Homo sapiens*. Techniques other than radiocarbon show that the Middle Palaeolithic Period lasted from perhaps as much as 220,000 years ago to about 45,000 years ago. All these dates are approximate.

The period that preceded the Middle Palaeolithic is known as the Lower Palaeolithic and lasted from nearly three million to about 130,000 years ago, depending on where in the world one means (and the scientist making the

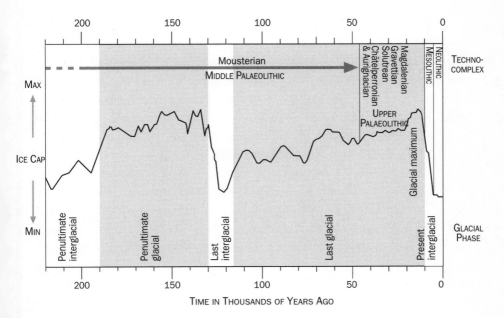

12 *The glaciations, archaeological periods, dates and techno-complexes of the Middle and Upper Palaeolithic.*

estimate). The Lower Palaeolithic was characterized by the presence of a number of hominids, including *Homo erectus* and *Homo habilis*, whose fossils have been found in Africa. *Homo habilis* made the first stone tools.

For the moment we need not go further back in time or introduce more accurate, regional dates and subdivisions of the three major periods. All I want to do at this juncture is point to what has become known as the Middle to Upper Palaeolithic Transition. In western Europe this Transition lies between 45,000 and 35,000 years ago. During this period, the Neanderthals gave way to *Homo sapiens*, the two forms having lived side by side, at least in some areas, for some thousands of years. Clearly, this transition was a crucial period in the human story: it has long been believed, not, as we shall see, altogether correctly, that this is when and where 'art' began. Following in Childe's footsteps, researchers have labelled the Middle to Upper Palaeolithic Transition the 'Upper Palaeolithic Revolution' or, even more dramatically, the 'Creative Explosion'. Suddenly, so it seems to many researchers, art appeared and human life became recognizable.

If a couple of trained anthropologists who had worked with small-scale communities in various parts of the world were to be transported back in time to the Middle Palaeolithic and given the opportunity to live with, study and learn the language of the Neanderthals, I believe they would be at a loss, marooned in an incomprehensible world. But were the same anthropologists allowed to move forward just a few thousand years to the early Upper Palaeolithic, they would immediately set about learning the language, studying kinship systems and other human relationships, the economy, and even the religion of their hosts. In short, they would be 'at home' every bit as much as they would be 'at home' among any human community anywhere in the world today.

What happened during the Middle to Upper Palaeolithic Transition that made all the difference? The following chapters try to answer that question and, at the same time, show that what appears to be a 'revolution' was something much more complex. We need to ask wider questions than those that are usually posed. Essentially, we need to know how human consciousness evolved – not just intelligence. In what ways is consciousness linked to the making of art? Or, to put the question another way, is art-making simply a part of being human, as language appears to be, and therefore hardly in need of explanation (though the how, where and when of language acquisition are debated)? The ways in which writers have tried to answer these questions and explain Upper Palaeolithic art lead through labyrinths of Western thought, social circumstances and philosophy.

CHAPTER 2
Seeking Answers

The end of the controversy over the antiquity and authenticity of Upper Palaeolithic art simply started another one that has endured to this day. Why did Upper Palaeolithic people make these images? The philosophical and religious turmoil that still rages around Darwin's theory of evolution suggests that large, emotive issues are involved in all aspects of human origins.

Perhaps the most insidious of these issues, one that covertly skews our thinking, is our use of the word itself – 'art'.[1] It is one of those terms (others crop up in subsequent chapters) that everyone believes he or she understands – until asked to define them. All too readily people assume that 'art', as they understand the term, is a universal phenomenon, and they tend to ascribe not only the word itself but also all its connotations to non-Western contexts. As a result, we have come to think of 'the artist' as a special kind of person who, because of some universal, almost mystical, principle of inspiration, is found in all societies. But notions of 'art' and 'artists' are formulations that are made at specific points in history and in specific cultures. For instance, 'art', as we think of it in present-day London, New York or Paris, did not exist in the Middle Ages, when people did not distinguish between 'artisan' and 'artist'. The notion of inspired individuals who, by their almost spiritual status, are set apart from ordinary mortals is a concept that gained acceptance in the more recent West during the Romantic Movement (c. 1770–1848), a period when writers and philosophers asserted the ascendancy of individual experience and a sense of the transcendental.

Some writers on Upper Palaeolithic art, such as the Berkeley archaeologist Margaret Conkey,[2] rightly highlight the dangers of importing Western connotations by the unthinking use of 'art'. Certainly, the word has misled many researchers to understand Upper Palaeolithic imagery in terms of Western art. But, that said, I believe that we can become over-sensitive to this problem. 'Art' is a handy monosyllable, and, provided we are aware of the dangers of its Western connotations, we can use it with caution.

The various ways in which researchers have explained Upper Palaeolithic art constitute a long historical trajectory that moved from simplicity to more complex hypotheses and then on to the collapse of the whole interpretative enterprise, and thus to present-day agnosticism. Today many researchers believe that it is impossible to know what Upper Palaeolithic art was all about. I start with an apparently simple catch-phrase that brings into the foreground the problematic word.

Art for art's sake

At first, notions of early 'savage man' tended to discredit any suggestion that Upper Palaeolithic images had a symbolic purpose. Art was simply decorative, and it would be foolish to see abstruse symbolic meanings in the images of savages. As early as 1864, Édouard Lartet and Henry Christy, a wealthy English banker who financed much of Lartet's work, tried to get around the problem of such sophisticated portable art coming from people who were, by all accounts, startlingly primitive. They argued that the environmental conditions of the Upper Palaeolithic spawned an abundance of animals that made hunting easy and so, despite their primitiveness, people had plenty of leisure time during which they could decorate themselves, their tools and their otherwise drab living spaces. Art, then, was born of leisure: the images were made for simple enjoyment, fun and decoration once people had achieved a measure of control over their environment. Importantly, Upper Palaeolithic art had no symbolic content and was, in accordance with Romantic ideals, essentially an individual rather than a social activity. This rejection of symbolic interpretation of Upper Palaeolithic art and emphasis on individual 'inspiration' arose from the belief that such primitive people could not possibly have had a religion.

The idea of a link between leisure and the development of aesthetic practices was taken up by Édouard Piette in his study of mobile art. He deployed bouquets of romantic phrases, such as 'exclusively artistic', 'seeking perfection in art' and 'eternally concerned with the cult of beauty'.[3] Illustrations of the time show, principally, bearded Upper Palaeolithic men absorbed in solemn contemplation in the making of art, while women kneel nearby, assistants or acolytes rather than role-players.[4] This idea of art as something exalted and something that could be achieved only after the natural environment had been tamed, is still kept alive by textbooks that argue that art is the fruit of an 'aesthetic sensibility', an innate desire to produce beautiful things, that can be indulged only in leisure time. This is the explanation for Upper Palaeolithic art that became known, not altogether correctly, as *art pour l'art*, art for the sake of art.

The art-for-the-sake-of-art explanation did not enjoy prolonged acceptance after it was first mooted. In 1987, long after it had been abandoned, John Halverson, an American art historian, tried to revive it, albeit in a much more sophisticated form, but he met with little success.[5] From the beginning, there were two principal reasons why early twentieth-century researchers began to doubt *art pour l'art* as a general explanation for Upper Palaeolithic images. First was the discovery of more and more subterranean art. It was understandable that people would decorate their weapons, wear pendants, and make statuettes; after all, these were activities with which researchers themselves were familiar. But why would they make works of art in inaccessible, dark, underground places? The seemingly obvious fact that art is made to be looked at is contradicted by deep Upper Palaeolithic cave art.

Secondly, Sir Baldwin Spencer and F. J. Gillen's 1899 ethnographic report from Australia told of people who lived under very harsh conditions but who nevertheless made a vast amount of complex art in rock shelters. Cartailhac himself also pointed to the 'Bushmen' of southern Africa as a people who made art in circumstances that he believed (incorrectly) left little time for leisure. Then, too, in the 1890s, Sir James Frazer's compendious collection of 'primitive' folklore from around the world, entitled *The Golden Bough* (a phrase he derived from one of Turner's paintings), began its influential career; it did nearly as well as *On the Origin of Species*. Frazer (1854–1941), a man of astounding scholarship and erudition, showed conclusively that 'primitive' people *did* have religion, though it has to be said that his monumental study is a mishmash of little understood exotica.[6] All this evidence, first from deep cave art and then from Spencer and Gillen, and Frazer, seemed to point to the, for some people, unpalatable conclusion that Upper Palaeolithic people did, after all, have a religion of some kind. Art in such societies was therefore not necessarily *art pour l'art*.

Today we recognize other problems with the *art pour l'art* explanation. First, from the point of view of logic, it may be expressed thus:

1 How do we know that human beings have an innate aesthetic sense or drive?

2 We infer it from the existence of what we believe to be the beautiful creations of the earliest art and from *objets d'art* around the world.

3 We then use this inferred sensibility to explain the existence of art.

The argument is thus clearly circular: a state of mind is inferred from the art, and then used to explain it without any other supporting evidence.[7] Some researchers may question this conclusion by pointing to the symmetry of very ancient – as much as one million years old – stone hand-axes and by suggesting that an aesthetic sense originated in an in-built predilection for symmetry. The idea is engaging but not convincing. If a desire for symmetry is indeed in-built, there is no reason to suppose that the symmetry of the hand-axes had anything to do with 'aesthetics'; the symmetry more probably resulted from (not necessarily linguistically) learned motor skills than a desire for beauty. In any event, there is next to no evidence in Upper Palaeolithic art for an interest in symmetry.[8]

Moreover, art historians have developed much more penetrating explanations for the making of art. At the root of many of these explanations is the realization that the making of art is a social, not a purely personal, activity. Art serves social purposes, though it is manipulated by individual people in social contexts to achieve certain ends. Art cannot be understood outside its social context.

Another point follows directly from this one. It is not possible for someone to depict an animal without in some way giving resonance to part of its symbolic associations, and those associations are socially created and maintained. For instance, in Western thought the lion has associations of regality and strength, the lamb of innocence and gentleness. The lion does not stand for deceit, nor the lamb for treachery, no matter what an individual person may believe. If an Upper Palaeolithic artist were to depict an animal because it had exclusively personal and arcane associations for him or her, those associations would be lost on most viewers who would, inevitably, see the picture in terms of other, socially sanctioned, associations. True, as we shall see, individuals manipulate images and their meanings for their own ends, but they do so within limits established by society; otherwise their new 'take' on a symbol would be totally obscure to viewers.

Essentially, it is the context of an image that focuses its meaning. For instance, a depiction of a lamb on the wall of a nursery will resonate differently from a lamb in an ecclesiastical stained-glass window. Yet perhaps not entirely so, for the symbolic associations of animals are all interrelated; they constitute a richly affective spectrum rather than a conglomeration of separate meanings. William Blake wondered at the 'fearful symetry' of the tiger that burned brightly in the forests of the night, while T. S. Eliot startlingly took up another segment of the tiger's semantic spectrum: 'In the juvescence of the year Came Christ the tiger'.

In all societies, many animals have rich associations of this kind, and it seems highly improbable that Upper Palaeolithic people would, repeatedly and in remote contexts, have depicted horses and bison if those creatures did not have some non-trivial, shared meaning for them. Indeed, the narrow range of painted and engraved subjects suggests social norms rather than personal predilections. Upper Palaeolithic artists were, essentially though not entirely, bound by rules of custom.

These thoughts on a supposed innate aesthetic sense in *Homo sapiens*, a species-specific drive that led to the broad set of objects and behaviours that we term 'art', has been summed up in a striking way. At the beginning of his immensely popular *The Story of Art*, Ernst Gombrich wrote, 'There is really no such thing as Art. There are only artists.' That is the view that I take in this book. I seek a practical, down-to-earth goal: I enquire about the origin of image-makers ('artists', if you will), not the genesis of some impossible-to-define philosophical concept. I argue that the first image-makers were acting rationally in the specific social circumstances that I describe in later chapters; they were not driven by 'aesthetics'. That amorphous, changing concept that we, in our particular place in history, call 'art' came *after* the first image-makers.

The next attempt to understand the meaning of Upper Palaeolithic art was far more enduring than *art pour l'art*. It has indeed entered popular thought about 'cavemen' and has given rise to innumerable cartoons. It is also the explanation that is most commonly encountered not only in popular accounts of Upper Palaeolithic art but also in textbooks.

Totemism and sympathetic magic

At the beginning of the twentieth century, and in the years immediately following, anthropology and sociology were coming into their own as respectable fields of study, and popular interest in 'primitive' people around the world was growing as a result of European imperial expansion. Writers such as Franz Boas, Henry Schoolcraft and Lewis Henry Morgan in America, Sir Henry Maine, Sir Edward Tylor and Sir James Frazer in England, Sir Baldwin Spencer and F. J. Gillen in Australia, Arnold van Gennep, Marcel Mauss and Émile Durkheim in France, to mention but a few, were prominent in this tidal wave of interest. In 1865, Tylor (1832–1917) had sensed an affinity between magic and prehistoric art.[9] But the writer who most effectively turned the insights of anthropology and ethnography to an understanding of Upper Palaeolithic art was Salomon Reinach.

In 1903, the year after Cartailhac's *mea culpa*, Salomon Reinach

(1858–1932), who was at that time curator of the Musée des Antiquités at Saint-Germain-en-Laye, published an article entitled *L'art et magie: à propos de peintures et des gravures de l'Age du Renne* in the journal *L'Anthropologie*. He proceeded from the fundamental assumption that the only way in which we can gain some understanding of Upper Palaeolithic art is by examining the lifeways of existing 'primitive' peoples. Here, right at the beginning of Upper Palaeolithic art research, Reinach created a problem that still dogs the footsteps of all workers: is it possible to understand Upper Palaeolithic art without recourse to analogy?[10] By using analogies, do we not simply create a past in the image of the present?

Reinach tried to handle the problem by insisting that researchers should strictly limit their analogical sources to hunters and gatherers – those people who, in his view, are closest to the way in which Upper Palaeolithic people lived. He was a good deal more cautious than some of his successors. Nevertheless, it is today recognized that twenty-first-century hunters and gatherers are not living fossils of the Upper Palaeolithic but people with a long history. Still, it has to be admitted that there are commonalities among hunter-gatherer communities that probably bear some resemblance to the ways in which Upper Palaeolithic people lived. Being sure of exactly what those commonalities are and which features are culture-specific is the problem.

One of the ideas to emerge from a reading of the Australian ethnography was totemism. Today, researchers recognize that the word has been ill-defined,[11] but at the beginning of the twentieth century it had a fairly straightforward meaning. The word itself derives from a North American Indian Ojibwa word that denotes an animal, or sometimes a plant, that is the emblem of a clan. One could speak of 'Eagle-people' or 'Bear-people'. Similar beliefs and social entities are found in Australia. Armed with this information, some researchers suggested that the images in the caves were totems. But the explanation did not acquire many supporters.[12] If the depicted animals were totems, so the counter-argument ran, one would expect to find clusters of images of single species, each cave being a kind of 'totem-pole'. But, came the response, if a few totemic groups constituted a single residential group then a comparatively small number of species would be found together – which we do find. The argument seemed to go round and round.

Reinach, however, was taken with other information that Spencer and Gillen published in 1899 about the Australian Aboriginal Arunta people. According to those two writers, the Arunta painted pictures of certain creatures in the belief that their actions would cause the depicted species to breed and multiply. It seemed to Reinach that the animals depicted in the European caves were the very ones that Upper Palaeolithic people would wish to multiply. It was like playing a game of 'snap': two similar cards turned up, one in Australia, the other in western Europe. The match was convincing, and so Reinach inferred similar motives for the production of art in both contexts.

Later, the Abbé Henri Breuil and others extended this hypothesis to hunting magic. The images, they argued, were intended to give hunters power over their prey. This idea, of course, fitted in well with what people in Europe knew about witchcraft, wax dolls and pins. With, perhaps, witchcraft in mind, Breuil claimed that many images had spears or projectiles sticking into them. Perhaps, he thought, the act of painting these weapons effected the death of a real animal. Breuil may well have been especially influenced by Niaux, the cave that de la Vialle and many others visited in 1660, and even before the seventeenth century. Here there are indeed a number of paintings of animals with what could easily be taken to depict weapons stuck into them. But, overall, only 15 per cent of Upper Palaeolithic bison images seem to be wounded or dying.[13] Most appear to be alive and well.

At first, the explanation seemed to explain why so many of the images were hidden in dark chambers: magic would be performed out of sight. Then, too, the explanation seemed appropriate to the species depicted in the caves. When images of felines and other dangerous animals were found, ones that it seemed unlikely people would consciously hunt or wish to increase, Breuil explained their presence by saying that the artists hoped to acquire the strength and hunting skill of the predators. The elasticity of the explanation did not end there. Quadrangular signs, such as those in Lascaux (Fig. 58), were said to depict traps into which animals would fall. Other signs were taken to be hunters' hides or the dwellings of spirits.

Today, there is little point in arguing all the pros and cons of either *art pour l'art* or sympathetic magic. To be sure, the image-makers may well have taken pride in their handiwork, and hunting, a hugely important Upper Palaeolithic activity, may well have had *something* to do with image-making. But so many of the arguments for these two explanations can easily be turned on their heads. For some writers, the complex, entangled superimpositions of many engraved panels of images obliterated any possibility of aesthetic appreciation. But that is a purely Western supposition: the confusion of lines and difficulty of decipherment may, for all we know, have been considered aesthetically pleasing. Then, too, some writers argued that leisure time was necessary for the making of art, and that art would not have been made during seasons of privation and incessant searching for food. Others responded that it could equally be argued that rites of sympathetic magic would be performed precisely during those difficult times in order to ensure an adequate food supply. Similarly, depictions of weapons may be taken as an indication of hunting magic; but, then, where no weapons are shown, it may have been the simple act of making the pictures that was considered efficacious. Either way, the explanation emerges unscathed. All the debate that went on through the twentieth century certainly exposed the weakness of these explanations, but, ultimately, as in many research contexts, explanations are discarded only when better ones are devised.

Making judgments

How does one recognize a 'better' explanation? If we are to understand the rollercoaster history of Upper Palaeolithic art research in the twentieth century, we need some insight into how science advances – or fails to advance. Broadly speaking, there are two schools of thought on this matter; they are not necessarily exclusive, though they are sometimes presented as if they are. On the one hand, there are researchers totally committed to the objectivity of science; they believe that there are established rules and procedures of verification that lead to sure knowledge. At the other extreme, there are those who see all knowledge claims as relative and the product of social forces and cultural perceptions.

First, it needs to be repeatedly emphasized that no explanation of Upper Palaeolithic art can ever be 'proved'. As we saw in Chapter 1, Darwin did not claim to have proved his explanation of the mechanism of evolution. Proof is a concept that should be restricted to closed systems, such as mathematics. At the end of an algebraic problem, a student can write 'Q.E.D.' – that which had to be demonstrated. But in archaeology, nothing of interest will ever be proved in that way. Philosophers of science have devoted much attention to this problem. We cannot now enter into a detailed account of scientific methodology, fascinating though that field is, but before we proceed to the far more complex explanations that succeeded art for art's sake and sympathetic magic it will be useful to pause and consider how we shall be able to judge them. I therefore note a few of the common criteria by which scientists judge and compare hypotheses.

Fundamentally, an explanation for some phenomenon or other must accord with received, well-supported general work and with overall theory.

One cannot, for instance, explain an aberration in a planet's orbit by invoking laser beams directed at it from beings living in the vicinity of Alpha Centauri, while all other orbits are adequately explained by gravitational fields within the solar system.

Secondly, a hypothesis must be internally consistent. In other words, all parts of a hypothesis must depend on the same premises and must not contradict one another.

The third criterion is one on which, as we have seen, Darwin insisted. A hypothesis that covers diverse fields of evidence is more persuasive than one that pertains to only one, narrow type of evidence. For example, if the theory of gravity applied only to inanimate objects, such as tennis balls, and not to living creatures, such as people, its explanatory value would be so limited that scientists would reject it.

Fourthly, a hypothesis must be of such a nature that verifiable, empirical facts can be deduced from it: a hypothesis must relate explicitly to observable features of data. Art for art's sake fails this test because there are no verifiable features of images that it explains and that cannot be explained by other hypotheses. Aesthetic judgment is so vague that any image can be declared to be the result of an innate aesthetic impulse, even if, by today's Western standards, its draughtsmanship is not very 'good'.

Fifthly, useful hypotheses have heuristic potential, that is, they lead on to further questions and research. Art for art's sake fails on this criterion too because, once stated, it closes off further research. It (apparently) says all that there is to say.

These five points are but a brief summary of some of the ways in which scientists judge hypotheses. But it should not be thought that these criteria are a simple check-list that scientists can tick off and then reach agreement. Many of the criteria are themselves problematic when it comes to practical application.

A more serious reservation, one that we must accept if we are to understand the historical trajectory of Upper Palaeolithic art research, concerns the social embeddedness of scientific work.[14] Social constructivists point out that science is a lot less objective than many of its practitioners would have us believe. Thomas Kuhn,[15] physicist turned historian of science, argued that scientific knowledge does not accumulate incrementally as scientists methodically tick off a list of agreed criteria. Rather, science advances by the comparatively sudden abandonment of one theoretical and methodological structure – or paradigm – and its replacement by another. Kuhn entitled his influential book *The Structure of Scientific Revolutions*. Such revolutions, he went on to argue, can be explained only if we see them in terms of the sociolog-ical characteristics of scientific communities. Even as the art of antiquity was produced in a specific social context, so too the production of knowledge about that art is today also socially embedded.[16] Kuhn's work has not gone unchallenged: the revolutions that he cites may be special cases. Moreover, the notion of 'social construction' has been applied too enthusiastically to a great many 'constructs' that are not entirely socially constructed – including the dif-ferent kinds of environments in which people live.[17] Still, it is fair to say that today researchers realize that social factors do influence the acceptance or rejection of new ideas.[18]

We need to have these preliminary points, both 'objective' and sociological, in mind as we move on to a much more thought-out explanation than *art pour l'art* or sympathetic magic, one that gripped the imagination of rock art researchers during the second half of the twentieth century and that contains elements that still permeate researchers' thinking about Upper Palaeolithic art. We need to know why it was so exciting at the time and why it has been so comprehensively abandoned.

Structure and meaning

'Structuralism' was one of the great informing notions of the second half of the twentieth century. It was a philosophical movement that had roots deep in Western thought. It has also been a diverse movement that has opened up enquiries into the relationship between the human mind and the material world. To guide us through the maze of structural approaches it is useful to distinguish between, on the one hand, 'structural analysis', a general method of analysis that examines the ways in which a 'structure', framework or mental template, of which people may not be aware, orders the ways in which they think and act,[19] and, on the other, 'Structuralism' (with an upper-case S) which refers to a specific kind of structure comprising binary oppositions and medi-ations of those oppositions.[20] Both kinds of structural theory can be discerned in an important eighteenth-century book.

Giambattista Vico (1668–1744) was an Italian jurist and classical scholar. In 1734 he published *Principii di una scienza nuova* (*Principles of a New Science*). Impressed by the work of such natural scientists as Newton and Galileo, Vico proposed a science of human society, what today we would call 'social science', as opposed to the 'natural science' of physicists, zoologists, astronomers, chemists, and so forth.

Writing in a period of European expansion and intense interest in the 'primitive' people and 'savages' whom the explorers were encountering, Vico began by challenging the current notion that such people had a different kind of mind from 'civilized' people. Rather, he said, the myths and explanations that they gave for natural phenomena were not simply nonsense based on ignorance; they were 'poetic' or 'metaphoric' and not intended to be taken literally. Way ahead of his time, Vico was ignored and the notion of a 'primitive mentality' endured through to the beginning of the twentieth century – and beyond.

Vico was astonishingly modern, even post-modern, in another way. He argued that the human mind gives shape to the material world, and it is this shape, or coherence, that allows people to understand and relate to the world in effective ways. The world is shaped by, and in the shape of, the human mind, despite the fact that people see the world as 'natural' or 'given'. In performing this task of shaping the world, humanity created itself. This being so, there must be a universal 'language of the mind', common to all communities. Structuring, making something coherent out of the chaos of the natural world, is the essence of being human. In succeeding chapters I argue that Vico was correct, though in a way that he may not have fully appreciated. The problem with his work is that 'mind' is taken as an intellectualizing organ that mediates between a material world and an inner, mental world. But, as we shall see, there is more to the mind than just intelligence: there is also consciousness.

The notion of structure was greatly developed by Ferdinand de Saussure (1857–1913), a Swiss linguist, and it is from linguistics that twentieth-century structuralism sprang. Saussure must surely be the only modern Western influential figure who did not write a book. The key text, *Course in General Linguistics* (1915), was compiled by (no doubt unusually attentive) students from notes taken during his lectures. For our present purposes, we need consider only a few of the important distinctions that he drew, ones that eventually influenced the study of Upper Palaeolithic art.

The first is between *langue* (language or grammar) and *parole* (speech or utterances). *Langue* is thus the structure and *parole* the individual items produced in terms of that structure. Saussure illustrated this distinction by pointing to chess: the rules and conventions of the game constitute the *langue* of chess, while embodiments of those rules in actual games are examples of *parole*. The similarity with Vico's earlier ideas about 'the language of the mind' is obvious.

Saussure also distinguished between diachronic studies and synchronic studies. The diachronic approach, as in philology, studies the development of language through time; synchronic studies examine a language at a given time, that is, its structure, its *langue*. Structure is therefore synchronic.

Related to these notions is one that became all important in Upper Palaeolithic art research. Meaning consists not so much in things themselves as in the relationship between things. For example, 'life' can have no meaning without 'death', 'light' without 'darkness', and so forth.

There is, of course, much more to Saussure's linguistics, but these few points enable us to turn now to a researcher whose most penetrating ideas have been consistently overlooked or undervalued, not because they are demonstrably wrong but because the social and political circumstances of Upper Palaeolithic art research in the second half of the twentieth century militated against their propagation.

Society, structure and Karl Marx

Today, Max Raphael,[21] a German Marxist art historian, is seldom remembered, and then only as the source of some of André Leroi-Gourhan's and Annette Laming-Emperaire's structuralist ideas. Before we consider the massive contribution that these two researchers made to the study of Upper Palaeolithic art, we need to resurrect Raphael, not to see him simply as a source from which others selectively borrowed.[22] It is unfortunate that writers who review the history of Upper Palaeolithic art research remark only, if at all, on his inchoate structuralist explanation, that is, his indebtedness to the earlier writers to whom I have referred, and ignore his heavy emphasis on the social context and character of the art. It is impossible to understand Raphael's structuralist contributions without an appreciation of his use of social theory. The nature of society was, after all, the foundation and *fons et origo* of his thought.[23]

As a young student, Raphael moved to Paris where he visited the studios of Rodin, Picasso and Matisse.[24] After brief incarceration in French detention camps, he moved in 1941 to New York, where he died in 1952, his work on Upper Palaeolithic art incomplete.[25] Raphael wrote his book *Prehistoric Cave Paintings* in the aftermath of the Spanish Civil War and during World War II, when the threat of fascism was tangible. He claimed that art historians and archaeologists of his day were reluctant to allow that Upper Palaeolithic people practised an art that was fundamentally, though not in all respects, similar to that of the mid-twentieth century. They chose to belittle the achievements of Upper Palaeolithic people 'in order to maintain the misleading doctrine of progress from nothing to something',[26] and, by implication, thereby to parade the achievements of capitalism. By the beginning of the twenty-first century the tide had turned. Now, many art historians and archaeologists share Raphael's position (even though they may never have heard of him) and are at pains to emphasize the modernity of Upper Palaeolithic people, both behaviourally and conceptually, and even to push modern behaviour further back in time as they rehabilitate the Neanderthals of the Middle Palaeolithic.

Following in Saussure's footsteps and distinguishing between diachronic and synchronic studies, Raphael began by arguing that the 'transverse section of historical existence…unfolds the qualities contained in the longitudinal section'.[27] These qualities consist in 'the economic reproductive process and the struggle of economy, society and politics against religion, morality, art and science'; both of these elements were in the hands of the ruling classes.[28] All the fundamental social categories, forces and tensions that Marxist theory identifies were thus present at the lowest stage of fully human social evolution; Raphael explicitly challenged the then-current view that hunting bands, both historic and prehistoric, were egalitarian.[29] Upper Palaeolithic peoples were, in Raphael's telling phrase, 'history-making peoples *par excellence*'.[30]

Marxist social theory, a putative key to history-making, is a complex tradition, not a monolithic canon.[31] Still, one may say, all too briefly, that purist Marxist theory argues that a social formation (a 'society') comprises an infrastructure and a superstructure. The economic base of a social formation, the infrastructure, includes the social relations of production that produce the material necessities of life. In doing so, it determines the superstructure, that is, ideology, belief, religion and juridical controls. The content, or 'message', of art is thus part of the superstructure, though its production may derive from the social relations of production, which are part of the infrastructure. The social relations of production govern who shall perform what work and how the product of labour shall be distributed. It is the task of a rigid Marxist art historian to uncover the ways in which the infrastructure determines the superstructure. This determination may be detailed or conceived in broader terms, depending on the individual writer's view. At this infrastructural level, class struggle principally operates and may be masked by the ideology of the superstructure, an ideology fashioned by the ruling class to conceal, or 'mystify', the social relations of production.

Upper Palaeolithic art, says Raphael, tells us nothing about the people's instruments of production, their hunting techniques, or their habitations –

that is, about the material component of the infrastructure. What it does tell us about is social struggle, and it does so by means of a *structured* code. As in totemism, social groups were represented in the art by animals. Animals depicted in combat represent antagonistic 'clans' (a term he does not adequately define). Often, in such instances, the animals are depicted 'crossed', that is, partially superimposed with heads facing in opposite directions. These compositions depict conflict. Conversely, animals pictured one inside the other depict alliance in social struggle and may stand for 'domination, mediation or a promise of support'.[32]

Then, more perceptively, he noted that researchers have interpreted the apparent disorder of Upper Palaeolithic parietal art as an absence of unity.[33] Their error arises from their failure to allow that there are different kinds of order. If researchers seek only the kinds of order with which Westerners are today familiar, they will miss, or reject as disorder, all other orders. Time and again in the history of Upper Palaeolithic art research, workers have fallen into this trap and failed to discern an order different from the one which they were seeking.

Let us now focus on the kind of order, or structure, that Raphael discerned in Upper Palaeolithic art. Essentially, he challenged Breuil's position that the images should be seen as isolated instances and emphasized instead that they should be studied as compositions, a notion that had been tentatively suggested for a few panels some decades earlier. Because the structures of these compositions recur in panel after panel and cave after cave, we can, Raphael believed, infer the compositional devices (*langue*) that underlay their construction. Further, he argued that researchers should interpret the elements in relation to the whole composition. In this he was echoing Saussure's structural insistence on relationships: as 'death' is meaningless without 'life', so bison are (to a large degree) meaningless without horses. The notion of planned compositions was thus born: these compositions were instances of *parole* derived from a *langue* that could, in turn, be inferred from them.

Raphael went on to note that different species tended to predominate numerically in specific caves. For instance, at La Pasiega in Spain stags and does predominate. In Lascaux, it is horses and aurochs (wild cattle). Most significantly in the light of Leroi-Gourhan's subsequent work, Raphael declared that, in Les Combarelles, in the French Dordogne, 'horses are repeatedly represented as hostile to the bison and bulls'.[34] Then at nearby Font de Gaume, 'the bison fight against the horses they have found there before them'.[35] Later in his book, he somewhat imprecisely developed the opposition between these two species: 'In Palaeolithic art horses and bison represent man and society.'[36] But this was not all. He more specifically anticipated a key feature of Leroi-Gourhan's work when he wrote that the magical battle of clans on the ceiling at Altamira was a vehicle for further meanings. The delicate hind confronting the large bison could, he claimed, be read as '...a conflict between feminine tenderness and masculine bulk' (Pls 2 and 3). The opposition (female:male) thus acquired a 'universal human significance'.

Raphael carried this binary opposition over to an interpretation of signs. He distinguished one set of signs as representing male sex: 'arrow points, phallus, act of killing or death'. The other he saw as 'feminine sex, woman, life-giving, life'.[37] Faced with what Raphael calls 'tragic dualism', the Upper Palaeolithic artists 'confronted the task of harmonizing the opposition'.[38] The 'message' of Upper Palaeolithic art was produced, reproduced and transmuted by means of oppositions and mediations. This is a fully Structuralist position, though it predates Lévi-Strauss.

Raphael's work has been comprehensively ignored. As we shall now see, Leroi-Gourhan and Laming-Emperaire tacitly rather than explicitly developed his structuralist (and Structuralist) insights but completely passed over his social analyses. They were more interested in cracking the 'code' (*langue*) of Upper Palaeolithic art than in the functioning of the society that produced it. Similarly, writers on Leroi-Gourhan may mention Raphael fleetingly and merely as a source of Leroi-Gourhan's and Laming-Emperaire's ideas. Certainly, any murmur of Marx is suppressed.

Structuralism and mythograms

Our consideration of how Raphael's social theory controlled his interpretation of Upper Palaeolithic art brings us to two researchers who, at least in my view, made the greatest twentieth-century contribution to the study of Upper Palaeolithic art.[39] They are Annette Laming-Emperaire and André Leroi-Gourhan (Fig. 13). Sadly, some recently published works, ones that in fact depend heavily on their ideas, hardly mention them; they are suffering the same fate as Raphael. Our historical rollercoaster ride continues.

Laming-Emperaire (1917–78), or Laming as she then was before her marriage, published a short book about Lascaux in 1959. The site had been sensationally discovered on 8 September 1940. Three schoolboys found the cave by chance when 17-year-old Marcel Ravidat's dog, Robot, tumbled down a sink hole that had been known to local people since before World War I.

13 André Leroi-Gourhan, philosopher, ethnographer, archaeologist and innovator. He re-examined Upper Palaeolithic cave art and devised a new, all-embracing explanation.

Farmers had tried to block the hole to prevent cattle falling down it. The boys retrieved Robot and decided to return later with better equipment, including rope.

On 13 September, Ravidat and three other friends, including two boys who had been evacuated from wartime Paris, returned. They widened the hole, and Ravidat was the first to slide down the steep slope beneath it. When they all gathered at the foot of the slope, they found themselves in a large sub-terranean chamber. They had a lamp, but could see little in the vast space. They advanced into what is now known as the Axial Gallery (Pls 21–23), where they first spotted images of animals. In great excitement they explored the rest of the cave and found more and more wonders (Pls 1, 20, 26–28).

Realizing the importance of the find, they resolved to tell their schoolmaster, Léon Laval. Because of his age, he was at first unable to get down the difficult incline, so he asked one of his former pupils to copy some of the images. Thus convinced of the importance of the discovery, he arranged for the Abbé Breuil to be contacted. Breuil had fled from German occupied Paris and was sheltering in Brive. He soon authenticated the discovery. It was a stunning find, unequalled until, in 1994, Chauvet and his two friends found the cave that features in our Time-Byte III and that now bears his name. No wonder that Lascaux provided material for a brand-new approach to and explanation for Upper Palaeolithic cave art.

In a general discussion of Upper Palaeolithic art that precedes her analysis of Lascaux, Laming-Emperaire seems to follow Raphael in a number of important ways. She

   – questions the value of ethnographic parallels,
   – argues that the difficulty of access to many subterranean images pointed to 'sacred' intentions,
   – rejects any simple form of totemism,

– proposes that 'the mentality of Palaeolithic man was far more complex than is generally supposed',[40] and

– argues that images should be studied as planned compositions, not as scatters of individual pictures painted 'one at a time according to the needs of the hunt'.[41]

Her work thus shifted emphasis from magical concerns to symbolic meanings. More specifically she argued that horses and bovids are deliberately and repeatedly paired. She remarked that this sort of association raises 'a problem which has hitherto never been considered at all'.[42] She also wrote that deliberate associations of images 'which have hitherto been interpreted as juxtapositions or superpositions should in fact be regarded as deliberately planned compositions'.[43]

All these points seem to derive from Raphael, yet she does not mention him in the Lascaux book. Did she consider it imprudent to mention Marxist Raphael in the days of the Cold War? Yet, when she came to prepare her Ph.D. thesis,[44] she acknowledged Raphael as the originator of the ideas that she later developed and said that Raphael let her have 'typed notes' as early as 1951.[45] Then, in an inexplicable *volte-face*, she concluded that Raphael's hypothesis that some panels 'represent the struggle of the sexes or of totemic clans...[is] unfortunately useless. It is difficult to accept Raphael's conclusions.'[46]

In *La Signification de l'Art Rupestre Paléolithique*,[47] her major work, Laming-Emperaire suggested that the horse may be associated with 'femaleness' and the bison with 'maleness'. Later, she revised her views and, although she continued to allow that horse and bison were in some way fundamental to Upper Palaeolithic cave art, she rejected the notion that they 'stood for' sexual duality.[48] Instead, she developed Raphael's suggestion that 'clans' and social organization, along with creation myths, were at the root of the art.

Laming-Emperaire died tragically in a motor accident in 1978 but the methodology and techniques that she proposed became the procedures that she, Leroi-Gourhan and numerous other researchers would follow. In her early Lascaux book, she advocated 'compiling inventories and collating all the archaeological evidence in order to extract the utmost information from both sources'.[49] She argued that researchers should prepare 'distribution maps according to the following criteria: position of the works in a cave, associated archaeological remains, signs of use, and content or form of a representation'.[50]

Laming-Emperaire's methodological suggestions were exactly what André Leroi-Gourhan (1911–86) adopted to prepare for his complex hypothesis. He was an anthropologist and ethnographer who taught at the Collège de France in Paris. Earlier in his career, he was an assistant director at the Musée de l'Homme along with Claude Lévi-Strauss (b. 1908), the enormously influential French savant and father of the Structuralist movement in anthropology and archaeology. To understand Leroi-Gourhan's contribution to the study of Upper Palaeolithic art we must first consider Lévi-Strauss's work.

The son of a musician and himself an accomplished musician, Lévi-Strauss studied law and philosophy; he acknowledges also the influences on his thought exercised by geology, Freudian psychology and Marx.[51] Before World War II, Lévi-Strauss taught at the University of São Paulo and did ethnographic work in Brazil amongst the Caduveo and Bororo Indians. After leaving the university he led a year-long expedition to the South American Nambikwara and Tupi-Kawahib communities. But theoretical work interested him more than fieldwork, which he found slow and time-consuming.[52] During the war he taught in the New School for Social Research in New York.[53] There he met and was influenced by numerous European linguists, including Roman Jakobson.[54] He was thus in New York at the same time as Raphael, but there does not seem to be any evidence that they met, though they may well have. After the war, he was appointed French Cultural Attaché in the United States of America. He returned to France in 1948.

Lévi-Strauss is a Marxist and thus has that in common with Raphael, though in exactly what sense he is Marxist is hard to say;[55] indeed, much of what Lévi-Strauss says is hard to pin down. The Cambridge anthropologist Edmund Leach[56] perceptively remarks that Lévi-Strauss seems to admire Verlaine's dictum 'pas de couleur, rien que la nuance' ('no colour, nothing but nuance'). Lévi-Strauss's Structuralism played itself out in a number of arenas but most famously in his mythological studies. Of these, 'The Story of Asdiwal',[57] a Northwest Coast of America Tsimshian myth, is the most persuasive, and the four volumes of *Mythologiques* (*The Logics of Myth*), an analysis of over 800 myths (plus more than 1,000 variations of them) from South America through to the Northwest Coast of North America, the most spectacular. Lévi-Strauss's work is founded on the notion that binary oppositions and mediations of those oppositions constitute a unifying thread, a hidden logic, that runs through all human thought. Binary oppositions comprise two 'opposite' terms, for example, up:down, life:death and male:female. 'Structure' is concerned with logical categories like these and the kinds of relations between them. According to Lévi-Strauss, every society's language, kinship system and mythology are variations on this binary theme.[58]

Inevitably, in every such system of classification and relations there are anomalies: real history sometimes contradicts present conditions; and there are always people and animals that do not fit neatly into the system of categories. For Lévi-Strauss,[59] 'the purpose of myth is to provide a logical model capable of overcoming a contradiction (an impossible achievement if, as it happens, the contradiction is real)'. Because myth is ultimately fated to fail, large numbers of variants are generated, each slightly different from the others. As Lévi-Strauss himself says, 'Thus, myth grows spiral-wise until the intellectual impulse which has produced it is exhausted.'[60]

Leroi-Gourhan had little to say about the way in which his and Lévi-Strauss's paths crossed – they sometimes took coffee in the same common-room – but there can be no doubt that he owed his philosophical and methodological position to Lévi-Strauss. Leroi-Gourhan's references to his colleague at the Collège de France may be sparse, but it would be obtuse to suggest that he tried to claim originality for what were so clearly Lévi-Strauss's developments of Structuralism: Leroi-Gourhan accepted his debt to Lévi-Strauss as patent.

Leroi-Gourhan says that he and his team of associates began work on his monumental *The Art of Prehistoric Man in Western Europe* [61] in 1957. He published a shorter book, *Les Religions de la Préhistoire*, in 1964. From the beginning, he says, he did not find the disorderly scatter of images that he expected to find; rather, he was impressed by 'the unity each of the sets of figures embodies'.[62] Early on, he and Laming-Emperaire realized that they were both 'very much on the same track'. Leroi-Gourhan says that the grouping of images had been 'entirely overlooked' until Laming-Emperaire noticed it,[63] though we know that this was not true: Raphael had certainly noticed groupings. At this point, they decided to pursue their researches separately. When they later compared their finished work, they found that if they had both gone 'off track', they had 'done so with the same sense of direction, which fact deserves at least a certain interest'.[64]

As I outline Leroi-Gourhan's work, it will be apparent that it *seems* to answer the five criteria that I mentioned for judging hypotheses. Certainly, it is in accordance with what was then a well-established philosophical position (Structuralism); it is internally consistent; it covers (to a certain extent) different bodies of data; it appears to connect with 'real' data; it seems to open up new avenues of research. Shortly, I shall show that some of these accords are illusory.

Leroi-Gourhan began by rejecting as too vague and imprecise all the old generalizations that had appeared in book after book for 50 years. For

instance, the rather naive division of animals into food and dangerous creatures was, in his view, superficial and tendentious. Paralleling Raphael and
Laming-Emperaire, he also rejected the use of ethnographic analogies;
researchers should, he said, derive their explanations from the data of the art.
Yet, like Raphael and Laming-Emperaire, he found that this admirable-sound-
ing precept is impossible. He also decided to begin his study with parietal
rather than portable art; the parietal images, he noted, remained where people
had placed them, a key consideration if one is to study spatial structure.
Importantly, he followed Raphael and Laming-Emperaire in acknowledging
that the art was not a scatter of individual images, as Breuil had argued, but
rather a carefully composed series of groupings that had to be understood in
their relationships with one another.

A number of Leroi-Gourhan's principles have their roots in Vico's ideas.
The first is that Upper Palaeolithic people had the same brain/mind as we and
all people living today have: theirs was no 'primitive mentality'. This was a
point that Lévi-Strauss convincingly demonstrated in such works as *The
Savage Mind*.[65] Another principle is that Upper Palaeolithic people imposed
the 'shape' of their minds on their material world. A third principle is that close
study of the products of the Upper Palaeolithic mind will reveal something of
its functioning. This last point, it has to be admitted, has more than a whiff of
circularity about it: if we decide, as a result of received notions from linguistics
and Structuralism, that the mind works in a particular way and then analyse
the data of the art in that very way, the outcome of our work will be to a certain
extent predetermined.

More precisely, Leroi-Gourhan accepted Lévi-Strauss's proposition that the
mind works like a computer in binary oppositions and that meaning lies in the
relationships between the elements of those oppositions. If, at this point, one
recalls binary oppositions such as light:darkness, male:female, divine:human
and so on, all seems well. But what binary oppositions are specifically discernible in Upper Palaeolithic cave art?

Setting out from these principles, Leroi-Gourhan analysed the numerical
data of the images and their locations in 66 caves. He prepared detailed maps
of the caves along the lines that Laming-Emperaire advocated and analysed
the numbers of images and their locations by means of punch-cards. But, in all
cases like this, the categories fed into the system and the possible relationships
between images all derive from the mind of the researcher. In a sense, it was
Leroi-Gourhan who was asking himself questions of his own devising.

Let us now consider the pivotal elements of Leroi-Gourhan's rather complex hypothesis; he himself frankly refers to 'a labyrinth of hypotheses'.[66] To complicate matters further, he changed his mind about aspects of his work in response to criticism and, especially, as a result of discrepancies between his explanation and the 'real' data of the art. We need not explore all the changes that he allowed, though the 'dialectic' between his thought and the criticisms directed at his work is fascinating;[67] we are more concerned with the foundations and principles of his work.

To begin with, he believed that he could divide the depictions of animals into four groups:[68]

A Smaller herbivores: horse, ibex, stag, reindeer, hind.

B Large herbivores: bison, aurochs.

C Peripheral species: mammoth, deer, ibex.

D Dangerous animals: feline, bear, rhinoceros.

Then he went a stage further. He designated the Group A animals as 'male' and the Group B animals as 'female'. Here he is not referring to sex of the individual images. Rather, he is saying that Group A species represent 'maleness' and Group B species 'femaleness', as metaphysical properties (Fig. 14). Group C comprised species that seemed to be painted peripherally to those of A and B. Group D was a separate group of animals that people would have feared.

Next he tackled the signs. Again seemingly influenced by more than just the germ of an idea in Raphael's work he distinguished two categories: a and b.

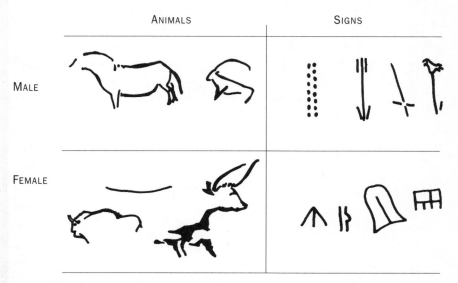

14 A tabulated summary of Leroi-Gourhan's male : female binary opposition as manifested in images and signs. In the caves, these were 'opposed' or 'paired'.

Group a comprised what he called 'narrow' signs: hooked or 'spear-thrower' signs; barbed signs; single and double strokes; and rows of dots. Group b comprised 'wide' signs: triangles; ovals; quadrangular signs; and claviforms. Both groups seem to be derived, he argued, from schematic representations of, respectively, male and female genitalia. This binary grouping (a:b) was linked to the A and B animal groups; 'narrow' signs were considered male, and 'wide' signs female. The sets of groups, both animals and signs, could thus 'stand for' one another (Fig. 14). In short, Upper Palaeolithic art could be summed up by the principal binary opposition A + a (male) : B + b (female).

This was Leroi-Gourhan's response to the suggestion that the images and the signs have nothing whatever to do with each other. On the contrary, he saw them as complementary signifying systems, perhaps like text and diagrams in a book – both say the same thing, though in different ways. In a subsequent chapter, I argue that *some* of the signs are actually of the same order and system as the images of animals; they are not different, though parallel, systems: some of the signs and the animals derive from the same source.

Leroi-Gourhan, then, saw A and B as constituting a binary opposition, with C animals as peripheral additions. He was thus able to construct a summary 'mythogram': A + B – C (the dash does not mean a minus sign). He argued that this mythogram was a mental template – the *langue* – of Upper Palaeolithic art for the entire period. Leroi-Gourhan thus took the Saussurian notion of *langue* and turned it into a Lévi-Straussian binary opposition.

We now come to the way in which Leroi-Gourhan related these sets of images to the caves (Fig. 15). First, he divided the caves into a number of areas: entrances, central areas, and deep areas (he also allowed for *diverticules*, small

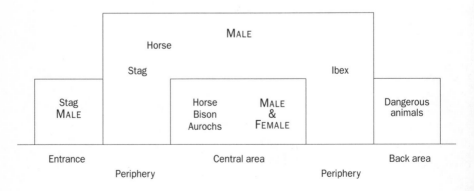

15 A simplified version of Leroi-Gourhan's conception of an idealized Upper Palaeolithic cave. Entrance and deep areas flanked an all-important central area of 'paired' images and signs.

side chambers). Male animals and signs were, he claimed, distributed throughout the caves, while female animals and signs clustered in the central areas. In those central areas, the horse:bison/aurochs pairing was central; Group C animals were peripheral. The deep, end chambers were said to be associated with dangerous animals. The cave itself was thus an integral part of the 'message'. He saw it as largely female. In his own words:

Palaeolithic people represented in the caves the two great categories of living creatures, the corresponding male and female symbols, and the symbols of death on which the hunters fed. In the central area of the cave, the system is expressed by groups of male symbols placed around the main female figures, whereas in the other parts of the sanctuary we find exclusively male representations, the complements, it seems, to the underground cavity itself.[69]

In sum, Leroi-Gourhan[70] believed that the art was 'the expression of ideas concerning the natural and supernatural organization of the living world'. Prudently, he added that, in that ancient thought system, 'the two might have been one'. Here, we seem to have a clear version of Lévi-Strauss's Structuralism: Leroi-Gourhan's mythogram is apparently exhibiting and trying to overcome a fundamental contradiction, or parallel contradictions, as, says Lévi-Strauss, does myth. Can we echo Lévi-Strauss[71] and say that Upper Palaeolithic art grew 'spiral-wise until the intellectual impulse which…produced it [was] exhausted'? Is panel after panel, ranging in time from the beginning to the end of the Upper Palaeolithic, dealing with male:female, culture:nature, and other parallel oppositions and contradictions?

In a couple of absorbing conversations that I had with Leroi-Gourhan in 1972 in Valcamonica, Italy, I found that he was at that time convinced of the validity of the mythogram and the patterned distribution of motifs in the caves. It was the predictive potential of his work that he found persuasive: he felt that, in a cave he had never before entered, he could foretell the presence of, say, a horse to complement an image of a bison that he had just been shown – to the astonishment of his guide. But he registered an important reservation: he believed that the horse:bison :: male:female opposition was only one characterization of the mythogram. For him, the mythogram was a *vehicle* that could carry a wide range of meanings. Though he did not say so, he was perhaps influenced by Lévi-Strauss's tireless reiteration of the great culture:nature and male:female binary oppositions, and he would have been better advised to choose some more neutral characterization of the mythogram than male:female.

When one compares Leroi-Gourhan's work with the old art-for-art's-sake and sympathetic magic explanations, one cannot but be astounded by his combination of industry and ingenuity. Why, then, did researchers come to abandon his explanation? In reciting his failings, some critics adopt an unbecoming triumphalism; they are more interested in his errors than his insights. Some illogically present him as paradigmatic of the failure that must necessarily await all who attempt to understand Upper Palaeolithic art.

Essentially, the principal reason for Leroi-Gourhan's fall from academic grace has to do with the criterion that demands articulation with hard data. Although he himself stressed the empirical component of his work and believed that more empirical work in the caves would expand the explanatory potential of his insights, the opposite turned out to be the case.

For one thing, the diversity of the topography of the caves makes it impossible to compare them with one another in terms of entrance/central/deep/*diverticule* areas (Figs 1, 2, 3, 7, 54, 56). Sometimes this problem led Leroi-Gourhan to identify a 'central' or a 'deep' area by means of the species depicted, not the topography – a circular argument. Sometimes his identification of a mark on a cave wall as a particular species seems to be a result of his preconception of that area of the cave. Then, too, his statistics have been criticized on various grounds.[72] As the years went by and more and more caves were discovered, such empirical problems multiplied until researchers concluded that the whole Structuralist edifice was built on friable empirical foundations. The mythogram was too good, too neat, to be true. Leroi-Gourhan's idea did not have the adaptability that Breuil's sympathetic magic enjoyed. Ironically, Leroi-Gourhan's was a 'good' hypothesis in that it had the capacity to be invalidated by empirical work; in Karl Popper's term, it was refutable. Whatever other qualities the mythogram hypothesis may have, it foundered on empirical grounds.

Towards the end of the twentieth century the feature of the mythogram hypothesis that most troubled researchers was Leroi-Gourhan's insistence that the formula for the embellishment of the caves persisted through the entire Upper Palaeolithic. His explanation was derided as 'monolithic'. Such a long period, his critics reasoned, must have embraced far-reaching changes; there must have been more diversity through time and across space than he allows. This is, in fact, an equivocal objection. The passage of time does not *cause* change; it merely allows for it. Beyond researchers' hunch that there must have been considerable change, there is no good reason why change *must* have taken place. Then, too, we need to be explicit about what sort of change we mean. If we say that the mythogram may have remained essentially the same, but its content, or meanings, may have changed, we have made a point with which Leroi-Gourhan agreed. Certainly, horse and bison are enduring Upper Palaeolithic motifs, but did they always carry exactly the same meanings? So we need to be more specific when we complain that so many changeless millennia seem an unlikely proposition. Both change and stasis must be demonstrated, not assumed.

Still, we must note exactly what was falsified. It was the grouping/pairing of species and their distribution through the caves that was shown to be incompatible with the more varied data – not the *notion* of structure. Raphael, Laming-Emperaire and Leroi-Gourhan may all have been wrong in the specifics of their hypotheses but correct in their beliefs that the caves are indeed patterned. The crux of the matter is to identify the criteria that inform, and will therefore reveal, the (or, rather, 'a') pattern. This is a point to which subsequent chapters return.

Strangely, although Leroi-Gourhan produced the most thorough-going use of Structuralism in archaeology, his influence was limited, even in his heyday and in his native France. This limitation may explain why it has now become easy to ignore him and yet still benefit from his work. It is also true that Leroi-Gourhan produced his Structuralist work at a time when archaeology, greatly influenced by the so-called New Archaeologists who strove for a strictly 'scientific' discipline, was turning its back on attempts to get at the meanings of ancient symbols and belief systems.[73] Scepticism about such matters became the order of the day.

A return to society...and more

Leroi-Gourhan's work, in all its complexity and with all its problems, is the vertex of this chapter. It flourished (though it was contested from the beginning) for a couple of decades, but its abandonment was swift and decisive; the historical rollercoaster went into a steep plunge. Unfortunately, the entire structuralist position was discarded along with many of its valid principles. The baby went out with the bathwater before it could grow to maturity. As a result, the study of Upper Palaeolithic art is in danger of losing some of its greatest practitioners. Today, there seems to be what Lévi-Strauss[74] calls 'a desperate eagerness which drives us to forget our own history' – or at any rate to forget its positive elements as we concentrate on the failures and errors of our predecessors. Today few researchers want to be seen as structuralists. In 1997

Lévi-Strauss himself put the general point forcefully:

It is quite popular in the United Kingdom to criticize and reject old masters. This happens periodically in the history of any scientific discipline. But science should progress by incorporating past evidence into the new and not rejecting it.[75]

In the structuralist wake came an anti-theoretical age of agnostic empiricism.[76] Researchers did not abandon structuralism for another theoretical perspective that would make better sense of the data: on the contrary, they abandoned theory altogether. Or, at least, so they believed.

But it has not been entirely a Dark Age of obscurantism. Some researchers, such as Georges Sauvet,[77] Denis Vialou[78] and Federico Bernaldo de Quirós,[79] have usefully pursued structuralist explanations. For Sauvet, a pattern is discernible in formal analysis of signs; for Vialou, it is in the distribution of species in specific panels. Bernaldo de Quirós sees Altamira as a planned structure comprising three principal sections, or nuclei, linked by passages: 'Indeed, the decoration of the cave seems to conform to a pattern that invariably takes advantage of the natural relief, as do the masks in the Horse's Tail, the doe's head in the Pit, and the figures of bison on the Great Panel'.[80] He believes that the sections of the cave were designed as a location for initiation rites.[81] Structure is thus implicated in the reproduction of social order through initiation rites.[82] Whether Sauvet, Vialou and Bernaldo de Quirós are correct in the specific patterns that they believe they have uncovered, the important point is that they continue to argue that there must be some pattern.

Other researchers have followed up social approaches to the problem. In her last statement, Laming-Emperaire[83] returned to Raphael's sociological position. She remained convinced of the salience of horse and bison, but she reverted to the idea that the different species depicted in the caves represented social groups and that some of the panels told the myths of the origins of these groups. The art was essentially a social phenomenon. Mythogram and myth were thus coming together in her thought.

The mythogram alone did not, indeed did not attempt to, explain the greatest of all enigmas: why Upper Palaeolithic people made images in deep, dark caves. The number and types of data that it covered were strictly limited. The reason for this curious subterranean Upper Palaeolithic practice must have been social; there must have been enduring social pressures that kept driving people underground throughout the Upper Palaeolithic, and, if we restrict our enquiry to the 'meaning of the message' and ignore its social context, we shall unnecessarily hobble ourselves.

Shifting emphasis from the content of the message to its form and the reasons for it, some researchers have linked the startling topographical contexts of many images to 'information transmission' and have drawn on recent developments in 'information theory'. Initiates and others, they argue, were psychologically prepared by the circumstances of the caves for the reception of crucial information about social customs and so forth.[84] Others have linked this supposed 'information' to relations between geographically scattered but interdependent communities that constituted alliance networks.[85] The 'appearance of parietal art in Late Pleistocene Europe resulted from the closing of social networks under conditions of increasing population density'.[86] Antonio Gilman[87] developed a Marxist approach to this sort of alliance theory and argued that tensions within alliance networks led to the Middle to Upper Palaeolithic Transition and eventually art as a response to a need for symbols of identity. How classless societies could develop internal contradictions that would lead to major social change has long been a problem for Marxist theorists.[88] Unfortunately, Gilman has not followed up this work.

These information theory explanations in some ways state the obvious (pictures meant something) and, at the same time, accept the disputable proposition that pictures carry enormous loads of information, more than words. But as the art historian Ernst Gombrich[89] has pointed out, pictures have the power to move, but they in fact convey very little information: because people read pictures in different ways images always remain semantically equivocal. The best that can be said for pictures is that they trigger memories of information that has been absorbed in different ways, that is, by experience and verbally. So whilst the Upper Palaeolithic images may have sometimes functioned as mnemonics, their capacity to store or convey information was limited. They were not like the hard drives of modern computers.

One final explanation for the appearance of art requires comment because it is alluringly attached to evolutionary theory. Ellen Dissanayake of Edinburgh University argues that art is a characteristic of our species and defines it as a way of 'making special', a process that includes all the 'arts'.[90] According to her, it is this 'making special' that is adaptive, not just image-making or one of the other 'arts'. To my mind, this definition and explanation are too broad: we need to distinguish types of art and explore the specific problems that each poses. Then we need to explain art in social terms – how it functioned in society, not simply how it promoted survival.

These considerations bring us back to a central theme of this book – methodology. If we have learned anything from a century of research on the meanings and purposes of Upper Palaeolithic art it is that we have no agreed method for tackling the problems that they pose, and that we have to address different kinds of questions, such as the meanings of images and their strange placement in caves. To begin to confront such diverse issues we need to intertwine a number of strands of evidence;[91] one 'pure' method, be it inductive, deductive or analogical, will not suffice, a point that I develop in Chapter 4.[92] Proof, it is true, will remain elusive, but complementary types of evidence that unite to address the complex problems posed by Upper Palaeolithic art can, I believe, produce persuasive hypotheses. Alive to the influence of our own social context and the ways in which the 'scientific' community is moulded by social pressures, we need to develop a more complex method than those hitherto used to address specific, isolated aspects of Upper Palaeolithic art.

Throughout this chapter I have adopted what is essentially a modernist, or realist, approach. It would, I believe, be a serious error to suppose that, because science is a social activity, all explanations are simply products of their own times and therefore cannot be said to approximate more or less closely to a situation that was part of a past that did indeed happen as it did. I believe that it is possible to produce knowledge of a real world 'out there'. We need not embark on an endless programme of deconstruction. We do not live in a world composed entirely of representations. Clearly, I cannot enter now into a full consideration of these contentious ideas. All I can do is state my position: I believe that some representations (such as hypotheses about the past) correspond more nearly to reality than others, and we can discern which they are. If this were not so, there would be no telephone, radio or interplanetary travel.

Allowing the effects of social contexts and at the same time emphasizing a real historical past and the possibility of constructing hypotheses that approximate to it, we can proceed to address the enigma of what happened to the human mind in the caves of Upper Palaeolithic western Europe. This is the epistemological principle on which the following chapters are posited. To identify a key evidential strand that is currently ignored, we need to go back to Vico and other early writers and recall that the human mind tends to impose itself, or rather aspects of its structure, on the stream of undifferentiated sense impressions that come to us in daily life. We must therefore look more closely at the brain, the mind, intelligence and the shifting, mercurial consciousness of human beings. But first we must see what happened in western Europe at about 45,000 to 35,000 years ago and understand that those events were but a slice of a much wider shift in human behaviour. The brain and changing social relations were shaping the mind.[93]

CHAPTER 3

A Creative Illusion

Two years before Darwin received Wallace's stunning essay and realized that he would have to hurry up with the publication of his own ideas on the mechanism of evolution, an accidental discovery ignited controversy in Germany. Workmen who had been digging out a cave known locally as Feldhofer Grotto showed some of their finds to Johann Fuhlrott, a local schoolmaster and amateur naturalist.[1]

The cave was high up in a limestone cliff overlooking the Neander Valley, through which the Düssel River flows on its way to its confluence with the Rhine at Düsseldorf. Contrary to a widespread belief, the stream below the cave is not called the Neander. The name derives from Joachim Neander, a seventeenth-century theologian and teacher, who was relieved of his post at a Düsseldorf school because he refused to take Holy Communion. As he pondered his theological dilemma, he took frequent walks up the valley, and it became known locally as Neander's Valley – Neanderthal.

Then, in 1857, the valley itself presented a dilemma with theological implications. The workmen showed Fuhlrott some limb bones, part of a pelvis and, most strikingly, a cranium (the top part of a skull). They assumed that the bones came from one of the extinct cave bears, the remains of which they frequently found. Fuhlrott disagreed: it was certainly not part of a bear skull. He particularly noticed the extraordinarily pronounced supraorbital ridge, the bone that, in a double curve, runs horizontally across the face over the eye sockets. Above this bony ridge, the forehead was thick and sloped sharply back (Fig. 16). It was therefore also unlike a modern human skull. The limb bones, too,

16 *The Neanderthal cranium found in 1857. This is how the sensational discovery was illustrated in T. H. Huxley's book* Man's Place in Nature *(1863).*

were especially robust. All the bones were encrusted with mineral accretions that, Fuhlrott knew, took a very long time to form.

After examining the bones, Fuhlrott set off for the cave, but he found no further specimens. He did, however, learn that the bones had come from beneath a thick layer of sediment. Unquestionably, they were decidedly ancient. But were they human, perhaps the remains of some diseased or mentally retarded person? Or were they of some other, non-human species that he could not identify? With no Darwinian concept of human evolution to guide him, Fuhlrott was baffled.

He therefore contacted Professor Hermann Schaaffhausen, a noted anatomist in the University of Bonn. Together, they presented descriptions and discussions of the finds at Bonn scientific gatherings on 4 February 1857 and, in more detail, in June of the same year. Schaaffhausen was a remarkable man, and the events in which he participated bore some resemblance to those taking place at the same time in England. Like many intellectuals of the period, he was leaning towards some form of evolutionary theory and had published his doubts concerning the supposed immutability of species.[2] But he and Fuhlrott lacked Darwin's and Wallace's notion of natural selection, and they had to fall back on vague generalizations in their explanation of the bones from the Neander Valley. They suggested that they came from a 'barbarous and savage race' that co-existed with the extinct animals, the bones of which were well known.[3] In tune with the burgeoning prescience of the time, Schaaffhausen wrote: 'Many a barbarous race may…have disappeared, together with the animals of the ancient world, while the races whose organization is improved have continued the genus'.[4] This is getting very close to a concept of human evolution and, moreover, natural selection. One has the feeling that an intellectual dam was about to burst; all that was needed to crack the wall was Darwin's *Origin of Species*.

Needless to say, given all the other bitter controversies of the time, there were many who fiercely challenged Schaaffhausen's interpretation of the finds. August Meyer, a pathologist in the University of Bonn, argued as late as 1864 – five years after the publication of *Origin of Species* – that the bones came from a Cossack soldier whose regiment had pursued Napoleon in 1814. Mortally wounded, the unfortunate man crept into the Neanderthal cave to die. The eminent anatomist Rudolf Virchow supported Meyer's rejection of the find, and exercised his influential authority to prevent recognition of the discovery. Inevitably, one recalls what happened after the discovery of Altamira (Chapter 1).

On the other side of the Channel, the scientific climate was more receptive, thanks to the energetic work of Darwin, Lyell and Huxley. In 1863, Huxley himself recognized the importance of the Neanderthal finds in his *Evidence as to Man's Place in Nature*. In the same year, William King, a former student of Charles Lyell and himself Professor of Geology at Queen's College in Galway, Ireland, coined the famous term *Homo neanderthalensis* – Neanderthal Man. The two-part Latin name indicates that King believed that the bones from the Neander Valley represented a species distinct from modern people, that is, from *Homo sapiens*.

Transition to modernity

King, Huxley and many others seriously pondered whether Neanderthal Man was a 'missing link' between ape-like ancestors and modern people. In doing so, they were the first to tackle the problems of what is now known as the Middle to Upper Palaeolithic Transition, the time in western Europe when the Neanderthals gave way to fully modern people.[5] Hereafter, I refer to this time simply as the 'Transition'.

Before we examine some of the characteristics of this crucial time in human history, we need to be more precise about places and dates than we have hitherto been. At first, our discussion will centre on western Europe, especially southwestern France and northern Spain where the Transition is well documented and studied. In this region, the Transition took place between 45,000 and 35,000 years ago; the periods and dates of the west European Transition and the principal subdivisions of the Upper Palaeolithic itself are set out in Figure 17. At the end of this chapter, I consider evidence from Africa that predates the west European data; the syntheses of the African evidence that researchers are now making provide a better understanding of the Transition as it took place in western Europe. The picture of change in human society that emerges from this recent research throws new light on that aspect of the Transition that has been called the 'Upper Palaeolithic Revolution' and the 'Creative Explosion' – that time when recognizably modern skeletons, behaviour and art seem to have appeared in western Europe as a 'package deal'.

As well as questioning the inevitability implied by the 'package deal' theory – that the whole indivisible package was simply part of the evolutionary process – we need to examine the kind of role that art played in the Transition, especially in western Europe. But first we must briefly return to the question of appropriate methodology.

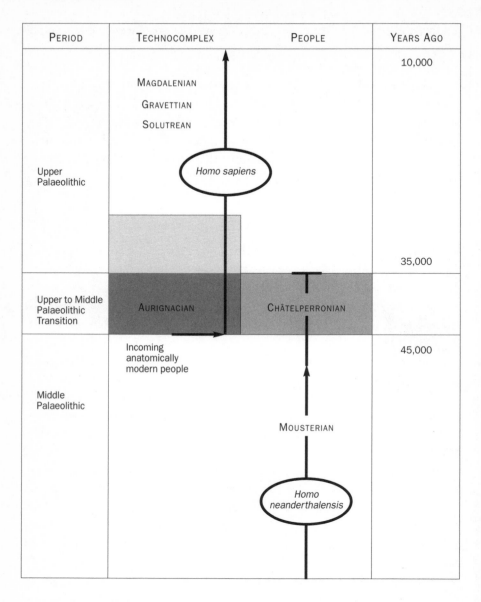

PERIOD	TECHNOCOMPLEX	PEOPLE	YEARS AGO

MAGDALENIAN

GRAVETTIAN

SOLUTREAN

Upper Palaeolithic

Homo sapiens

10,000

35,000

Upper to Middle Palaeolithic Transition   AURIGNACIAN   CHÂTELPERRONIAN

Incoming anatomically modern people

45,000

Middle Palaeolithic

MOUSTERIAN

Homo neanderthalensis

17 A diagrammatic representation of the Middle to Upper Palaeolithic Transition. Homo sapiens *lived side by side with* Homo neanderthalensis *before the archaic species died out.*

Most accounts of the Transition start with the climate and ecology of western Europe and then move on to human technology and thereafter to social organization, and end with a brief section on art, as if the making of images was to be expected and was, in any event, of no great consequence. The effect of this apparently logical approach is methodologically comparable with the one that Laming-Emperaire and Leroi-Gourhan adopted when they mapped the caves and plotted the locations of images on their maps: it carries with it the danger of predetermining a particular kind of answer (that was in all probability in mind from the beginning). Laming-Emperaire's and Leroi-Gourhan's structuralist and mythogramatic hypotheses were inevitably founded on the locations of species in the caves because that was the way in which they collected and handled their data (Chapter 2). They believed that their explanations derived from, rather than determined, their methods, but belief in such linear ordering of method and explanation is somewhat naive. Similarly, the descriptive chain favoured by many writers on the Transition tends to lead to the conclusion that 'art' (image-making, body decoration, music, dance) was a unified, symbolic or aesthetic component of a package that came at the end of a causal chain of *environmental* factors. The type of method that researchers employ thus determines the nature (if not the details) of the type of explanation that they eventually come up with.

In contrast to an explanation that sees art as an inevitable part of a symbolic package, I argue that art – let alone an 'aesthetic sense' – should not be seen as the simple *result* of something else, be it ecological stress occasioned by expanding ice sheets or social stress consequent upon the onset of glaciation. Rather, art-making, *if* and *when* it appears, is an active member of a dynamic nexus of interdigitating factors. Art was not simply a foregone conclusion, the final link in a causal chain. It was not the inevitable outcome of an evolving 'aesthetic sense', as some writers suggest. On the contrary, I argue that an aesthetic sense (if there is such a thing) was something that developed *after* the first appearance of art in the sense of image-making; it was a consequence, not a cause, of art-making, a consequence, moreover, that real people living in specific times, places and social circumstances constructed, not one that they inherited in the make-up of their brains.[6]

Contrasts

Bearing in mind these caveats about the relationship between method and explanation and, at the same time, questioning the supposed inevitability of art, we can now examine the changes that are observable in the west European archaeological record between 45,000 and 35,000 years ago – over and above the appearance of portable and parietal art, which is our principal interest.

What caused these changes in the material evidence left by human communities is the question that we must answer.

The first point to notice is that the Transition cannot be explained by climatic change alone: human change was not the direct result of marked environmental change. The crucial period did see a colder climate peaking at about 35,000 years ago, but Neanderthals had survived previous climatic instability. During the Transition, vast ice sheets extended across the northern parts of Ireland and England, the whole of Scandinavia and parts of northern Germany. Separate ice caps covered the Pyrenees and the Alps. South of the polar ice sheet was a broad band of tundra and steppe – barren, windswept, treeless areas of frozen subsoil. The Ice Age reached its peak at about 18,000 to 20,000 years ago, long after the Transition. There were minor fluctuations during the period, as, for example, between 50,000 and 30,000 years ago. Throughout the time of glaciation, there would have been marked contrasts between summer and winter temperatures, but, overall, the temperature was as much as 10° C below today's levels. During the winters, heavy snow falls would have made human movement difficult, but during the summers an absence of dense forests had the opposite effect: people could travel freely. Moreover, with so much water locked up in the ice sheets, the sea-level fell and parts of the North Sea were dry, thus affording access to England and Ireland. This land-bridge remained until the end of the Ice Age, that is until about 8,000 years ago.

The open tundra and steppe was inhabited by herds of bison, wild horse, aurochs and reindeer, as well as mammoth and woolly rhinoceros, creatures whose thick coats were strikingly adapted to the cold.[7] These species were migratory, and the herds followed regular routes from summer to winter pastures and back again. For communities that could take advantage of these reasonably predictable, mobile herds, it was a time of plenty, and researchers estimate that, at least during the Upper Palaeolithic itself, population densities may have equalled those of the first agricultural communities.

Such was the setting for (not the cause of) the west European Transition: a stable climate, severe but with compensations. Before 45,000 years ago the anatomically archaic Neanderthals had this landscape to themselves. By 35,000 years ago they had vanished from France, and their place had been taken by anatomically modern *Homo sapiens*; the last Neanderthal outposts, isolated enclaves, hung on in the Iberian Peninsula until about 27,000 years ago. From Gibraltar, the last Neanderthals looked out across to Africa, their ancestral homeland, but a place by that time occupied by *Homo sapiens*. The earliest members of the incoming *Homo sapiens* communities are often called Cro-Magnons, after a site near the Dordogne town of Les Eyzies. This change from Neanderthals to Cro-Magnons is clearly discerned in the kinds of tool kits that the two groups made and used. We need consider the contrasts – and the overlaps – in tool types only briefly; it is the behaviour and identities of the communities that made the tools that are our chief interest.

Archaeologists have long defined periods of the Stone Ages by reference to types of stone tools and the ways in which they were made. The stone tool industry practised by the Middle Palaeolithic Neanderthals is called the Mousterian technocomplex; the earliest industry practised by Upper Palaeolithic *Homo sapiens* communities is called the Aurignacian technocomplex (Fig. 17).

During the Middle Palaeolithic, the Neanderthals used what is called the Levallois technique for flaking flint and other stone types (Fig. 18). This technique required preparation of core stones so that standardized *flakes* could be struck from them. The flakes were wide, fairly thick and heavy and were used for cutting, scraping and so forth; they were probably mostly hand-held. During the Upper Palaeolithic *Homo sapiens* communities manufactured much thinner and longer *blades* from distinctively conical cores of flint. Once detached from the core, these blades were often carefully shaped by further and finer flaking; they were probably hafted rather than hand-held. But the distinction is not absolutely clear-cut. Some Middle Palaeolithic people had begun to make more refined stone artefacts that can be called blades. What is important is that there was a proliferation of blade-making after the Transition.

Along with the new blade techniques of manufacture came a wider range of tool types. These include a diversity of spear-points, as well as a novel kind of scraper called an 'end-scraper' that was probably used for preparing skins and other such tasks. People also made burins (blades notched at one or both ends so that they could be used as chisels) for working bone, wood and antler. These new tool types suggest the adoption of new hunting techniques and more carefully made clothing. But many writers point out that some of the tool types, such as the finely made and highly standardized Solutrean points (Fig. 18), go well beyond functional necessity. During the Middle Palaeolithic, tool forms were much more uniform, and their function seems to have been paramount. It is as though, in the Upper Palaeolithic, the *shape* of the tool, not simply its function, began to matter. This development seems to imply that the forms of the tools symbolized social groups, within or between settlements.[8]

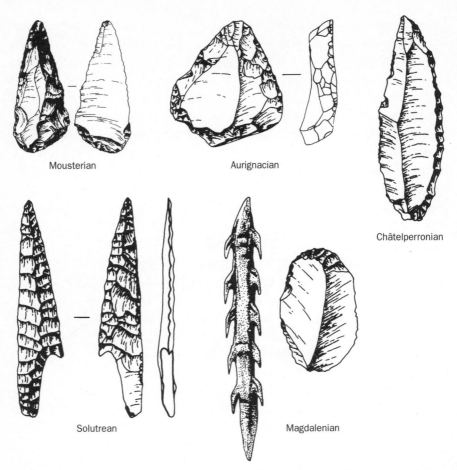

Mousterian

Aurignacian

Châtelperronian

Solutrean

Magdalenian

18 Stone tool kits. The more recent artefacts are more finely made and include items made from bone, mammoth ivory and antler.

(Some researchers link this development to the acquisition of fully modern language, but that is a matter we can leave for the moment.) So it seems that Upper Palaeolithic people had a clearer, more precise mental picture of what they wanted their tools to look like, and that picture was linked to the social groups to which they belonged. But that is not all. Upper Palaeolithic tool shapes varied frequently both geographically and through time: the shapes of one's stone artefacts (rather like a car today) signalled one's social group. It is hard to escape the implication that society was diversifying and was much more dynamic than during the Middle Palaeolithic. If so, it is important to notice that human creativity and symbolism was linked to social diversity and change, not to stable, history-less societies. Change stimulates; homeostasis anaesthetizes.

A new creativity is also seen in the exploitation of raw materials – bone, antler, ivory and wood. Whilst Neanderthals sometimes used these materials, they did not exploit their 'malleability': the new raw materials can be carved and bent into an endless variety of shapes. Quite suddenly, at the Transition, excavators of archaeological sites begin to find bone, ivory and antler awls, 'batons', beads, pendants, bracelets, 'pins' and exquisitely carved statuettes.[9] As the American archaeologist Randall White puts it: 'Aurignacian body orna-mentation explodes onto the scene in southwest France during the early Aurignacian…It appears to have been complex conceptually, symbolically, technically and logistically right from the very beginning.'[10] In other words, there was a kind of cognitive quantum leap.

The techniques employed to make these objects were far from simple. For instance, stone burins were used to gouge out long splinters of bone or mammoth ivory that could then be fashioned into needles and so forth. Some of these objects are remarkably fine. For example, people collected fox, wolf and bear teeth and then carefully bored through the roots of the teeth to make pendants and necklaces. White argues that French sites such as Abri

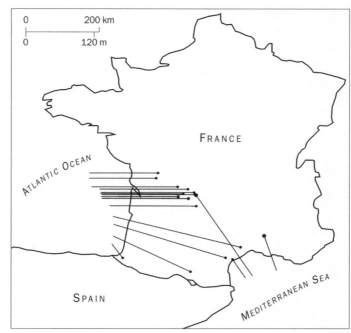

19 Upper Palaeolithic trade in seashells. The lines representing movements of seashells extend beyond the modern coastline because sea levels were lower at that time.

Blanchard, Abri Castanet and La Souquette seem to have been 'factories' where skilled artisans made beads and pendants according to complex sequences of techniques; the manufacture of items of personal adornment became an industry in itself.[11] Remarkably, some beads seem to have been shaped to resemble species of seashells that were traded over considerable distances across southwestern Europe. Shells from the Mediterranean coast have turned up in sites in the Périgord area of France (Fig. 19).[12] It would be rash to suppose that these exotic items point to long-distance movements of people. The selectivity, or 'special-ness', of the items suggests rather that they had exchange value and that it was the items not so much the people that moved. The value of the items was therefore social; they were not merely 'trinkets' or souvenirs picked up by aimless wanderers.[13] As White[14] points out, the ethnographic literature strongly suggests that the process of extended exchange had profound social implications.[15] Some form of trade in items of decoration – and also in fine flint artefacts – was operating in the Upper Palaeolithic.

Trade, of course, implies social complexity and communication. Social integration beyond a nuclear family comprising parents and children is also evident in the organization of hunting, especially of migrating herds of bison, horse and reindeer. The steep-sided valleys of the Vézère and the Dordogne, for instance, channelled herds of animals migrating from the Massif Central down to the plains that lie to the west. Valleys such as these have high densities of Upper Palaeolithic sites. To take advantage of animal migrations, people had to be able to predict the times and places best suited to hunting and then to organize parties to be present at the right times and to perform different but complementary functions. Upper Palaeolithic people were also able to predict the early spring salmon runs when these fish swim upstream to spawn. Being at the right place at the right time meant a great harvest of fish that they could dry and store. Upper Palaeolithic people thus tended to concentrate on a single species, especially at certain times of the year; these included reindeer, wild horse and salmon. Some writers, such as the influential American archaeologist, Lewis Binford, have argued that the Neanderthals were, by contrast, merely scavengers and that they lived off the remains of kills made by carnivores and hence off a wide variety of animals over which they had no control.[16] Others have challenged this rather extreme view and have argued that there are signs of planned hunting in the Middle Palaeolithic (some Neanderthal sites do show a focus on selected species). Either way, there can be no doubt that, at the beginning of the Transition, hunting became a much more effective and highly organized social activity.

Overall, in southwestern France, there are four to five times as many Upper Palaeolithic sites as there are ones dating back to the Middle Palaeolithic; the contrast is striking. We also need to note the presence of large Upper Palaeolithic settlements, far more extensive than any Mousterian sites. These settlements were probably aggregation sites.[17] Communities split up into small bands during some seasons of the year and then united at recognized aggregation sites at others. Places of this kind were probably associated with rituals, such as rites of passage to adulthood and marriage.

Then, too, archaeologists have found evidence that points to increased social complexity within individual Upper Palaeolithic sites. Although post-depositional disturbance and superimposed series of Neanderthal occupations have blurred the evidence, excavations have shown that in some Middle Palaeolithic sites certain activities were performed close to a hearth; others were conducted closer to the periphery. Does this pattern indicate the early beginnings of a type of social complexity that we could call modern rather than archaic? Some archaeologists believe, probably correctly, that this kind of distribution was simply a matter of convenience and not a result of social distinctions. In support of their position they cite the distribution of activities in some chimpanzee nests[18] and much earlier Lower Palaeolithic hominid sites. By contrast, living structures and spatial differentiation are common in early Upper Palaeolithic sites. There are, for instance, stone arcs and postholes in the Arcy-sur-Cure site that probably supported discrete shelters.[19] Perhaps the most impressive evidence comes from Pincevent, an open-air Magdalenian site some 60 km (37 miles) southeast of Paris. Here, researchers, initially under the direction of André Leroi-Gourhan, uncovered a large settlement area with numbers of hearths and evidence for shelters. Analysis of stone tools and bones indicated relationships between these nodes. Such complex settlement patterns suggest that Upper Palaeolithic people had more precise ideas about the spatial distribution of activities and people within sites than did their Middle Palaeolithic predecessors and that they distinguished between social categories of people.

There is thus evidence, right from the beginning, for an Upper Palaeolithic mental template (or structure) that controlled (but which people probably also contested) the way in which sections of society interacted with and left their mark on available living space. Society superimposed its social and technological divisions on space: different categories of people were visibly distinct within the area of a camp. People's movements between designated areas made powerful, *visible* social statements about belonging to or differences between groups. Space thus became a malleable template that people constructed to express, to reproduce through time, and also to challenge social order and divisions. This is a point that we must bear in mind when, in later chapters, we consider the diverse ways in which Upper Palaeolithic people adapted the topography of deep caves for arcane purposes.

Social differentiation is also implied by elaborate Upper Palaeolithic burials, such as the astonishingly rich ones at Sungir in Russia.[20] At this extensive living site, approximately 150 km (95 miles) east of Moscow, archaeologists have excavated five burials (though two are partial); they are probably as much as 32,000 years old.[21] Randall White, one of the few Western archaeologists to have studied the material first-hand, believes that Sungir can be seen as a northeastern extension of the Aurignacian. Two of the burials are of adolescents laid in shallow graves dug into the permafrost; the corpses were placed on their backs with their hands folded across their pelves. One of these bodies, said to be that of a boy, was covered with strands of beads, 4,903 in all; he also had a beaded cap with some fox teeth attached. Around his waist was the remains of a decorated belt with more than 250 canine teeth of the polar fox; a simple calculation shows the minimum number of foxes (63) – animals that must be individually trapped or hunted – required to supply so many teeth. In addition, the boy was buried with a carved ivory pendant in the form of an animal, an ivory statuette of a mammoth, an ivory lance made from a straightened mammoth tusk, a carved ivory disc with a central perforation, and other items. The lance was probably too heavy to have served a practical purpose. The adjacent burial, said to be that of a girl, was accompanied by no fewer than 5,274 beads and other objects. If White[22] is correct in estimating that it took more than 45 minutes to fashion a single bead, the beads in this female burial took more than 3,500 hours to make.

This brief description gives but a glimpse of the richness of the Sungir burials. Nevertheless, it is clear that, at Sungir, selected people were buried with grave goods that suggest social ranking or leadership of one kind or another, but that was not necessarily linked to age. People used meaningful items, such as fox teeth, to construct their identities in life and to construct a special, perhaps enhanced, identity for specific dead. The high status that these young people enjoyed may have been inherited, but it may also have been acquired in a manner similar to the selection of a Dalai Lama. Moreover, the sheer quantity of the grave goods suggests that the items were contributed by an extensive social network, not by a single family. This was no simple, isolated, egalitarian hunting band.

That said, we must allow the possibility that in cases such as the extraordinarily rich Sungir burials people may have 'robbed' earlier graves in order to provide goods for later ones, as apparently sometimes happened in ancient Egypt. The rich Upper Palaeolithic burials may therefore point not so much to individual status but to cumulative status, perhaps through a descent lineage of one kind or another. Either way, we cannot doubt that these burials suggest the functioning of complex societies.

Neanderthal burial practices are much more controversial than those implied by sites such as Sungir.[23] The Neanderthal archaeological evidence itself is often questionable, the excavations having been undertaken a long time ago. Still, it seems unlikely that *all* the supposed Neanderthal burials could have been accidental, as has been suggested. One reason for accepting a limited number is that the skeletons have remained articulated. Their completeness indicates that they were deliberately placed in the ground and thus protected from human, animal and physical factors that would otherwise have scattered the bones. This judgment is, however, not the final word in the controversy. Robert Gargett, in a detailed re-examination of the evidence, has concluded that there are 'natural depositional circumstances in which articulated skeletons might be expected to occur' and that these conditions are in evidence in all cases of claimed Neanderthal burials.[24] If this is so, it is not clear why no other articulated animal skeletons of creatures that could be expected to die in a rock shelter have been found. It seems that we must leave a question mark over some but not all the Neanderthal 'graves'.

On the other hand, the evidence for Neanderthal grave goods, or 'offerings', is unquestionably weak, a point on which there is major agreement. When, or if, they did bury their dead, they did so without the complex accompanying rituals that Upper Palaeolithic people often (though perhaps not always) practised. In sum, it seems likely that *some* comparatively late Neanderthals *may have* buried their dead, though there is little evidence in any of these burials to suggest ritual or religious beliefs; burial alone might have been done for hygienic reasons if people did not wish to abandon a rock shelter in which someone had died. This is, in the context of our enquiry, a highly significant point.

It is important to recall that all the diverse and sophisticated Upper Palaeolithic activities that we have noted did not proliferate gradually or severally in western Europe. They *all* seem to appear right at the beginning of the Upper Palaeolithic, though some may have intensified in later periods. At one time some researchers believed that art, both portable and parietal, was somewhat different from other components of the Upper Palaeolithic package in that it started hesitantly, evolved gradually through the Upper Palaeolithic and reached its apogee during the Magdalenian. Breuil[25] argued that this trajectory was characterized by two stylistic cycles, each starting with 'simple' art and evolving into more complex images. Leroi-Gourhan,[26] on the other hand, postulated a single stylistic cycle moving from simple to complex.[27] The 1994 discovery of the Chauvet Cave put paid to that misapprehension.[28] The sophisticated, 'advanced' images in that cave have been dated to just over 33,000 years before the present, that is, within the Aurignacian, the earliest Upper Palaeolithic period. This early date should not really have come as a surprise to archaeologists because the finely carved statuettes found decades earlier at Vogelherd and Hohlenstein-Stadel in southern Germany had been dated to the Aurignacian.[29] These carvings include representations of horses, mammoths, felines, and a remarkable therianthropic statuette that has a human body and a feline head (Figs 45, 46). One of them in particular, an exquisite image of a horse, is polished as if it had been carried around in a pouch or, perhaps, fingered in a ritual; it also has a clean-cut chevron that was incised on the shoulder after the horse had been polished.[30]

There can now be little doubt that – in western Europe – the Transition saw a range of marked innovations, nearly all of which imply mental and social changes of great significance. Upper Palaeolithic people were behaving very differently from their Middle Palaeolithic predecessors, and these changes can be dated back to the beginning of the Aurignacian. We can understand why many researchers speak of a 'Creative Explosion'. So far, their case looks strong.

Causes

Researchers have advanced two explanations for the changes that we have now examined. These contrasting explanations hold very different implications for our enquiry into the origins of art and, more especially, into the proliferation of subterranean cave art during the west European Upper Palaeolithic.

On the one hand, some researchers argue that local Neanderthal populations gradually *evolved* into anatomically modern people.[31] Others argue that there was a fairly swift *replacement* of Neanderthals by anatomically modern *Homo sapiens* who migrated across Europe, both north and south of the Alps, and ended up in southwestern France and the Iberian Peninsula. This has been a highly controversial issue, but I believe it is fair to say that, today, most researchers favour the population replacement explanation. We need not rehearse all the data and positions involved in this debate. Instead, I briefly note five important points that persuasively favour the replacement hypothesis. We shall then be able to move on to the intriguing implications of Neanderthals living for perhaps as much as 10,000 years in proximity to incoming *Homo sapiens* communities.

1 A clearly Neanderthal skeleton at the site Saint-Césaire has been dated to 35,000 years before the present, in other words, to the very end of the Transition. Other Neanderthal remains, at Arcy-sur-Cure, have been dated to 34,000 years before the present.[32] Finds in the Iberian Peninsula suggest a pocket of surviving Neanderthals as late as perhaps 27,000 years ago. If Neanderthal populations lasted this long, there would simply not have been enough time for them to evolve into anatomically modern people.

2 Fully modern skeletons have been found at the sites of Qafzeh and Skhul in Israel and have been dated to as early as 90,000 to 60,000 years before the present. As we shall see, Israel is on the route that fully modern people would have taken on their way to western Europe. Without doubt, anatomically modern populations existed some 50,000 to 60,000 years before they begin to register in the west European archaeological record. In other words, they did not evolve out of west European Neanderthals.

3 New DNA evidence suggests that the anatomically archaic Neanderthals did not contribute significantly to the genes of modern populations and, moreover, that the two types did not interbreed.[33]

4 The Aurignacian technocomplex, the one that characterizes the first fully modern populations, extends with remarkable uniformity from Israel all the way to the Iberian Peninsula. Such a wide spread is better explained by fairly rapid migration than by local, evolutionary developments from geographically scattered and somewhat different Mousterian industries.

5 Lastly, and convincingly, dates for Aurignacian settlements from eastern Europe through to western Europe become more recent as we move towards the west – which is what we would expect if *Homo sapiens* communities moved in this direction. The Cambridge archaeologist Paul Mellars has usefully collated the dating evidence to show this temporal sweep across Europe (Fig. 20).

Clearly, the replacement hypothesis answers the criteria for successful hypotheses (Chapter 2) better than local evolution. Yet, despite all these and numerous other points, the debate is not dead. All the evidence, but especially

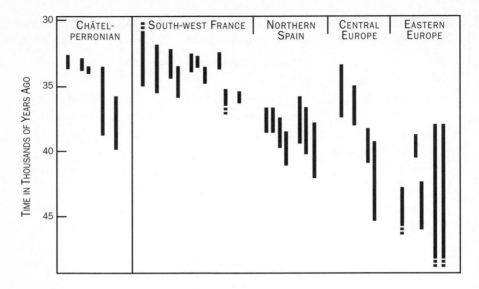

20 Dates showing movement of Homo sapiens *communities across Europe from east to west; the oldest dates are in the east. The bars represent the ranges of dates from specific sites.*

that from the rich Arcy-sur-Cure site, was aired and discussed in a 1998 Special Issue of *Current Anthropology*. Francesco d'Errico and four colleagues argued for independent development of the Arcy-sur-Cure Mousterian into the Châtelperronian, an early Upper Palaeolithic technocomplex that I describe below.[34] Nine specialists contributed to the debate. Whilst most expressed sympathy with a research programme that re-evaluates this important site, the broad consensus was that the distinctive features of the Châtelperronian developed as a result of contact with in-coming Aurignacian communities.

Responding to the *Current Anthropology* debate, Mellars has effectively summed up the position. Referring to recent dates, he points out that they leave

entirely open the possibility that the appearance of a range of distinctively 'modern' behavioural features among the late Neanderthal populations of western Europe – including the presence of simple bone and ivory tools and perforated pendants at Arcy-sur-Cure – was the product of some form of contact and interaction between the two populations, regardless of whether we refer to this as 'acculturation', or by some other term. The alternative is that after a period of around 200,000 years of typically Middle Palaeolithic technology and behaviour, the local Neanderthal populations in western Europe independently, coincidentally, and almost miraculously 'invented' these distinctive features of Upper Palaeolithic technology at almost exactly the same time as anatomically and behaviourally modern populations are known to have expanded across Europe.

The notion of population replacement brings us to what are perhaps the most fascinating questions of all. If anatomically modern people moved fairly swiftly into western Europe, they must have encountered and even lived along-side Neanderthal communities. How did these two groups regard one another? Did they interact? If so, was their interaction violent or peaceful? Did they learn from one another? Could they communicate by means of language? In what, if any, ways did their minds/brains and type of consciousness differ? Could interaction between archaic west European Neanderthal and anatomi-cally modern communities in some way have triggered the efflorescence of art that we find in that region? We have no historical record whatsoever of two species of *Homo* living side by side to guide our thinking: for the last 35,000 years only one species of human beings has occupied the world.

To answer some of these questions, we concentrate on the early Upper Palaeolithic technocomplex known as the Châtelperronian (Fig. 17).

New neighbours

The archaeological record in western Europe shows that the beginning of the Upper Palaeolithic was characterized by two distinct groups of people who made different kinds of artefacts. The *Homo sapiens* people, who moved from the east into western Europe, brought with them the Aurignacian tool kit, the art and new ideas that we have already noticed. Then, for the first 5,000 years and more of the Upper Palaeolithic, the Châtelperronian, a technocomplex associated with Neanderthals, flourished in the Dordogne, southwestern France and parts of the Pyrenees.[35] During that period, there was undoubtedly contact between the Aurignacians and the Châtelperronians. At some sites, such as Roc de Combe and Piage in the Dordogne, Aurignacian strata are interstratified with Châtelperronian strata:[36] it is therefore clear that the two cultures not only co-existed but that they also occupied the same rock shelters alternately. By 35,000 years before the present, the Châtelperronians had dis-appeared and the Aurignacians had the landscape to themselves.

We should not envisage this process of replacement as an inexorable wave sweeping across Europe. Rather, we should think of a series of 'steps' or 'jerks'.[37] Discrete, advance colonies of *Homo sapiens* appeared, expanded and coalesced as the people struck out from one ecological locality to another. At the same time, the Neanderthal population was contracting according to its own dynamic. Co-existence was therefore probably not a universal feature of the replacement process. But that there were areas, especially central France and the Pyrenees, where Neanderthals and *Homo sapiens* lived side by side for some thousands of years is a scenario about which there is no doubt.

What happened during the period of overlap? We need to distinguish between the evidence of stone tools and that of human physical types.

Strong continuities between Mousterian and Châtelperronian stone tools and the ways in which they were made are evident (we need not go into the details).[38] For instance, it has long been thought that the Châtelperronian curved, blunt backed flint knives derived from the naturally backed knives characteristic of the Mousterian.[39] It thus seems that the Châtelperronian stone industry developed out of the Mousterian. It is also clear that the Châtelperronian was associated with Neanderthals.[40] By contrast, no Aurignacian sites are associated with Neanderthals. There is in fact a clear, decisive break between the earlier Mousterian and the intrusive Aurignacian in both artefacts and hominid types. The Châtelperronian can therefore be seen as a terminal expression of the Mousterian, both industries being made by Neanderthals, while the in-coming Aurignacian technocomplex was independent of the local Mousterian and was made by *Homo sapiens* (Fig. 17).

In eastern Europe and the Italian peninsula there are two technocomplexes comparable to the Châtelperronian. They are, respectively, the Szeletian and the Uluzzian. Both seem to have developed out of earlier Mousterian industries, and both extend into the Aurignacian period. They appear to be local responses to the juxtaposition of Mousterian and Aurignacian communities.[41] We shall, however, concentrate on the Châtelperronian of western Europe because it is there that the great flowering of art took place.

There are some highly significant parallels between the Châtelperronian and the Aurignacian that complicate any simple explanation that proposes *exclusive* origins for the Châtelperronian in the Mousterian. There is, in the Châtelperronian, a strong component of blade technology that seems to have come from the makers' Aurignacian neighbours, not out of their Mousterian ancestry. There are also end-scrapers and burins, as well as items made from bone and antler that show a technology that seems to have originated in the Aurignacian industry rather than in the earlier Mousterian. Perhaps most interesting are items of personal adornment, especially grooved and perforated animal teeth, and abundant pieces of red ochre that may have been used for body decoration.[42]

All these borrowed features developed at a late stage of the Châtelperronian, long after the first appearance of the Aurignacian in western Europe. Were they spontaneous developments among the Châtelperronian Neanderthals, or were they the result of selective imitation of, and exchange with, Aurignacian communities, that is to say, a consequence of acculturation?[43] As we have seen, most researchers now believe that the best explanation for the combination of inherited and the borrowed features evident in the Châtelperronian is that there was a process of acculturation that resulted from contact between the two species of *Homo* – *Homo sapiens* and *Homo neanderthalensis*. The precise nature of that contact is more debatable. We need to consider it now. Thereafter we shall examine the significance of those Upper Palaeolithic features that the Neanderthals did *not* adopt. As we shall see, they are more instructive than those they did adopt.

Interaction

The first scenario for contact between the Aurignacians and Neanderthals that springs to many people's minds is violent conflict, an early form of genocide. They imagine Aurignacian hoards rampaging through the land, viciously destroying all the slow-witted Neanderthals they found. The actuality was probably rather different. There were probably many ways in which the two groups interacted at different times and places.[44]

To be sure, it seems unlikely that there was no conflict at all, but it was probably intermittent rather than sustained genocide. When there was conflict, it seems likely that it was the *Homo sapiens* men who killed the Neanderthal men and ravished their women. But the *Homo sapiens* communities were intelligent enough to realize that the offspring of such unions would be infertile and probably mentally inferior to themselves.[45] How would the *Homo sapiens* communities have regarded such offspring? At this point imaginative reconstruction of what bi-species society was like reaches its limits. We need to turn to the archaeological record for more substantial clues than imagination alone can provide.

Writers such as Clive Gamble[46] have pointed out that, certainly at first, the in-coming Aurignacians may have sought different kinds of landscape to exploit from those favoured by the Neanderthals. It seems that, at first, the Aurignacians moved around a Neanderthal pocket that hung on in the Dordogne. If the Neanderthal and *Homo sapiens* hunting strategies were different – the Neanderthal's being more general than that of *Homo sapiens* who, as we have seen, tended to focus on single species – competition for resources and particular kinds of landscape may have at first been rare.

Different hunting strategies in turn suggest different social structures.

Gamble[47] has subtly developed this implication. He explores the effects of different kinds of social networks for the two groups. In brief, he argues that, in Châtelperronian society, contact was face-to-face: people met other people and exchanged artefacts and information. By the production of symbolic artefacts that signified different social groups and kinds of relationships, Aurignacian people were able to maintain wider networks that could exist even between people who had never set eyes on one another. If the Aurignacians were able 'to go beyond the confines of face-to-face society and achieve wider system integration performed across a social landscape',[48] they would have been able to construct a geographically wider power base. As a result of their more complex networks, 'individuals were both constrained and enabled in the scale and effects of their actions over others'.[49]

Because they were able to forge symbolically sustained networks and fields of power, the Aurignacian population built up. Eventually, competition for resources became more intense and perhaps violent. If we recall that at the time of the Transition there was a comparatively cold period and that Neanderthals had survived such problems before, we can isolate a major difference between those earlier cold periods and the Transition: at the Transition there was another human species on the landscape and therefore greater competition for resources. Even small disadvantages, such as higher infant mortality, can tip the balance. If *Homo sapiens* communities were able to store food through the winter and the Neanderthals were not able to do so, *Homo sapiens* child survival rates would have been more advantageous.

Ezra Zubrow[50] has studied the effects of such relations on population densities and reproduction. His conclusion is surprising: 'a small demographic advantage in the neighbourhood of a difference of two per cent mortality will result in the rapid extinction of the Neanderthals. The time frame is approximately 30 generations, or one millennium.'[51] Here, then, is an explanation for the rapid extinction of the Neanderthals that does not depend on calculated, purposeful genocide. A small demographic imbalance will produce the same result.

We cannot leave this question of interaction without some reference to language. There is no doubt in any researchers' minds that Upper Palaeolithic people had fully modern language – that is, they were able to create arbitrary sounds with meanings, to manipulate complex grammatical constructions, to speak about the past and the future, to convey abstract notions, and to utter intelligible sentences that had never before been put together. What is at issue is whether the Neanderthals also had fully modern language or whether they had a more rudimentary type of proto-language.[52] Another point of contro-versy is whether proto-language evolved gradually or suddenly – 'catastrophically' – into complex modern language.[53]

These are hotly debated questions, but they need not impede our discus-sion; we do not have to answer them before we can move on to issues concerning Upper Palaeolithic art. Still, they are intriguing. Because I accept that language is closely related to social complexity – in broad evolutionary terms, the more complex the social relations of a species, the more complex its language and communication systems – I am inclined to accept that the Neanderthals had a comparatively simple form of language. This notion may be difficult for us to grasp because their language would have been compatible with a type of consciousness different from ours (Chapter 4).

To what extent Neanderthals would have been able to communicate lin-guistically with *Homo sapiens* people is a moot point that researchers have insufficiently explored. I think that there would have been the possibility of certain kinds of linguistic communication that did not presuppose fully modern consciousness on the part of the Neanderthal auditors.[54] The in-coming Aurignacians brought modern language with them;[55] the Neanderthals may have learned to understand at least something of what they were saying and thereby even to have improved their own linguistic skill to a certain extent – as they did their flint-knapping. The Neanderthals' *potential* for language may have been greater than their social environment had so far required. Verbal communication between the two communities would there-fore have been possible at a fairly straightforward, day-to-day level – perhaps the Neanderthals learned to speak a kind of 'pidgin-Aurignacian' – but the Aurignacians would have found it impossible to convey notions that the Neanderthal mind simply could not entertain.

So far we have considered social networks, demographic patterning and communication. Can we go further in our investigation of Neanderthal and *Homo sapiens* interaction?

What Neanderthals did not borrow

At this point we need to break down the comprehensive, ragbag word 'art' and to distinguish between different kinds of visual arts (song, dance and myth-telling do not concern us at the moment). We need to distinguish between those kinds of art that can interact to produce viable new forms and those that cannot evolve into other types. Fundamentally, I argue that an art form such as body decoration could not have evolved into the making of two-dimensional images of animals on cave walls.

The use of red ochre and a range of body adornments were, I argue, kinds of art that the Neanderthals were able to imitate. In some circumstances they may have literally acquired Aurignacian items of decoration by exchange or stealth.[56] These kinds of art are closely related, and none places more intellectual or cognitive demands on the user than any other; they all presuppose the same range of cognitive abilities. Further, they may have 'interbred': one kind may have spawned another, or at least have influenced the form of another. But we cannot leave the matter of body adornment there.

An important point that has received insufficient attention is that the stone tool types and technologies that the Neanderthals took over were probably used for the same practical purposes as the *Homo sapiens* people used them – cutting meat, scraping bone, preparing skins, and so forth. Was this also true of body adornment? To answer that question, we need to note that body decorations are not simply 'decorations', the fruit of personal whims; on the contrary, they signify social groups and status. 'The surface of the body…becomes the symbolic stage upon which the drama of socialisation is enacted, and body adornment…becomes the language through which it is expressed.'[57] Social identity changes through life: people move from adolescence to adulthood, from unmarried to married, from child-bearing to post-child-bearing, from unrelated to related-by-marriage status. There are also different contexts within a single stage of life: the presentation of self at a major ritual occasion differs from that of daily life. Body adornments are sensitive to these changes, and people change them to signal their social role-of-the-moment. Death is but one social context; researchers do not suppose that the elaborate adornments found in some Upper Palaeolithic burials were worn in everyday life.

If body decoration signalled social identity, it is interesting to note a feature on which Randall White comments. Although the Aurignacians in southern Germany were making portable statuettes and carvings of animals, they did not, generally speaking, make much use of representational art as body adornment. Instead, they used parts of actual animals in a metonymical way, that is, part of the animal stood for the whole. Beads were made from bones and teeth. Moreover, many of the animals whose teeth were used for necklaces and pendants were carnivores – felids and canids. As White says, 'It is surely more than just a coincidence that animals that hunt other animals were singled out for use in social display by the most dangerous predator of all.'[58] This function of body decoration may well have had validity in the Aurignacian, but, as we shall .

see in subsequent chapters, it would be wrong to see hunting as a purely economic, subsistence activity: it was probably also associated with the
procurement of supernatural power. I return to the concept of a supernatural
realm in a moment.

What, then, could borrowed body adornment have signified in Neanderthal
society? It is highly unlikely that the Neanderthals recognized the same range
of social distinctions as did *Homo sapiens* people and that the items of decoration would have signified exactly the same thing in both societies; Neanderthal
social structure was surely different from *Homo sapiens* social structure. If
body decoration did signify social distinctions among late Neanderthals, they
were not the same distinctions as identical items signified in *Homo sapiens*
communities. That being so, it may be misleading to speak of 'borrowing'
because the word covertly implies similar functions. If the items meant something different to the Neanderthals – they may have signified no, or very
different, social distinctions among the Neanderthals – it was only the
'outward show' that was taken over. The Neanderthals were, in some sense,
pretending to be *Homo sapiens*.

By contrast to body decorations, representations – pictures or carvings – of
animals and human figures are kinds of art that the Châtelperronian
Neanderthals did not take over (Fig. 21). This is a sharper and more informa-
tive distinction than researchers have allowed: whatever the Neanderthals may
have done that suggests they had some sort of symbolic faculty, there is no evidence that they made pictures and carvings. This distinction suggests that we
are now dealing with a radically different kind of art: body-painting, for
example, did not evolve into image-making (Chapter 7). Image-making
demands mental abilities and conventions of a different, more 'advanced',
order.

As we have seen, an altogether different kind of art, or perhaps one should
say 'symbolic behaviour', is the burial of selected dead with grave goods con-
sisting of rich body decorations, beads, pendants, and other artefacts.
Although beads and so forth may have been placed in graves, no one can argue
that the notion of burial grew out of body decorations. Nor could there have
been any evolutionary relationship between graves and pictures – in either
direction. They are distinctly different kinds of 'art'.[59] An important point to
remember is that some Upper Palaeolithic burials are so rich in grave goods
that the items must have been contributed to the burial by a much wider social
circle than an individual family. Such burials point to wider social networks
and attendant symbolism than those of the Middle Palaeolithic.[60]

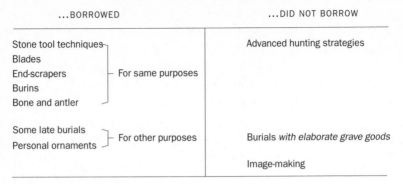

21 *What the Châtelperronian Neanderthals borrowed and did not borrow from their* Homo sapiens *neighbours.*

Why, then, did the Neanderthals ignore the images *and* the elaborate burials of *Homo sapiens* life? Their selective borrowing raises key questions about society and human consciousness. I argue that elaborate, highly ritualized burial and the making of representational pictures and carvings had, at that time though not necessarily in later periods of human history, two important points in common – even though they are radically different kinds of art.

First, as instances of material culture, body adornment and burial were both associated with the expression and construction of a type of hierarchical, or at least differentiated, society that was not simply based on age, sex and physical strength. For the Neanderthals, this kind of society was – literally – unthinkable. They probably groped to understand why Aurignacians showed respect and deferred to certain people who, as far as the Neanderthals could see, were physically weak. As I have suggested, types of body decoration and ornaments were sporadically absorbed into late Neanderthal culture, but perhaps only to lend a superficial resemblance to their more astute and complex Aurignacian neighbours.

My second point is more fundamental and will lead on to the substance of later chapters. I suggest that the type of consciousness – not merely the degree of intelligence – that Neanderthals possessed was different in important respects from that of Upper Palaeolithic people, and that this distinction precluded, for the Neanderthals, both image-making and elaborate burial. Because of the neurological structure of their brains and the type of consciousness that that structure produced, Neanderthals were unable to

– remember and entertain mental imagery derived from a range of states of consciousness (introverted states, dreaming, altered states, etc.),
– manipulate and share that imagery,
– by such socializing of mental imagery, conceive of an 'alternative reality', a 'parallel state of being' or 'spirit world' so memorable and emotionally charged that it had a factuality and life of its own,
– recognize a connection between mental images and two- and three-dimensional images,
– recognize two- and three-dimensional representations of three-dimensional things in the material world,[61] and
– live in accordance with social distinctions that were underwritten by degrees of these abilities and differential access to types of mental imagery.

True, the Neanderthals evidently had mental images of what their tools should look like, though not as precise or flexible as those of Upper Palaeolithic people. They could also understand the purposes that those tools served. But the kind of mental image that enabled them to do all this was, I argue, of an altogether different kind from the type that can be translated into a representation of, say, an animal, and compared with other people's mental imagery to create an 'alternative reality'. Neanderthal mental imagery was, I suggest, closely linked to motor skills – such as the series of manual actions that produced a flint tool of the desired shape. Physical action activated mental imagery and, to a limited extent, *vice versa*.

The more complex Upper Palaeolithic mental imagery could be independently entertained and subtly manipulated. It could also be extended to find expression in, or to be perceived as parallel to, two-dimensional representations of three-dimensional things. Indeed, Aurignacian people could achieve all six of the abilities I have listed. Neanderthals could comprehend neither the Aurignacians' representational images nor the purposes of their burials. How, they may have asked, can those few marks on a cave wall possibly call to mind a real, live, huge, active bison? (Later, I argue that the Aurignacian images probably represented something even more incomprehensible to the Neanderthal mind.) What could these Aurignacians possibly mean when they talk about the 'spirit' of a dead person going to a 'realm' where there are other 'spirits'? Why do Aurignacians place items associated with living, individual people in graves with the bodies of people whose lives have ended?

What are the implications of these points? I suggest that, in Upper Palaeolithic communities, representational art and elaborate burial practices were both associated with different degrees and kinds of access for different categories of people to 'spiritual' realms (that is, realms of mental imagery) and, as such, had a common foundation in a type of consciousness that the Neanderthals lacked. That, I argue, is the reason why Neanderthals neither borrowed nor mimicked them. It was not merely that they were insufficiently intelligent (though that may well have been true) but that they had a different kind of consciousness. Fully modern human consciousness, by contrast to that of the Neanderthals, includes the ability to entertain mental images, to generate mental images in various states of consciousness, to recall those mental images, to discuss them with other people within an accepted framework (that is, to socialize them), and to make pictures. How did these abilities and lack of abilities affect the Aurignacians' and the Neanderthals' conceptions of their own identities?

From the point of view of the Aurignacians, the ability to form, entertain and manipulate mental imagery in social contexts, to conceive of a spiritual realm and to prepare the dead for that realm were practices that they brought with them when they moved into western Europe, as the early statuettes and burials found in eastern and central Europe imply. They must have realized that the Neanderthals did not have these abilities: they must have seen that, whatever else the Neanderthals may have been able to copy, this was something that they just could not manage. The exploitation of a particular kind of consciousness and mental imagery for social concerns thus became, for the Aurignacians, a major distinguishing feature of their society vis-à-vis their Neanderthal neighbours. That their possession of it would have engendered a sense of superiority over the Neanderthals and coloured their relationships with them are inescapable conclusions that researchers have not explored.

Moreover, it seems likely that the Aurignacians would have gone further and actively cultivated those characteristics of their lives and thought that set them apart from and 'above' the Neanderthals. Especially in competitive circumstances towards the end of the Châtelperronian, they would have developed those distinctions that were closely associated with social control within their own communities and with subsistence effectiveness that was dependent on such control. The oldest representational art (the Swabian statuettes) does not appear in the earliest levels of the Aurignacian but somewhat later.[62] This delay is understandable. After initial contact, and perhaps a wary stand-off, the two species would have needed time to develop relations of various kinds. Some, but not all, of these relations may have been linked to growing population density and competition for specific resources. It was only when inter-species relations reached a certain level of intimacy that the Aurignacians found it necessary to escalate the making of representational art out of their existing mental imagery; the images that they made were, in part, statements about their social dominance and helped to entrench that dominance. Image-making thus reflected and played an active role in the evolution of social relations right from the beginning.

The Neanderthal point of view must have been entirely different. They had lived in western Europe for 160,000 years or more, and in that time they had successfully honed their relationship with their environment as best they could with their mental capacity. During the period from about 60,000 to 40,000 years ago, they developed regional variations and micro-adaptations: their development had not ground to an absolute halt; their culture was not terminally moribund. Then between 45,000 and 35,000 years ago they had to cope with the new arrivals. They were now participating in a new world of social relations, something with which they had never had to contend before. The new challenges were not environmental, like the ones with which they had previously managed to cope. Now their surroundings contained more complex *Homo sapiens* social communities and, especially threatening to their way of life, various forms of symbolism that pointed to a more efficient way of life that they could not emulate. These new, challenging components were beyond their ken. They could successfully imitate some components of Aurignacian life, such as stone tool-making; there were aspects, such as body adornment, that they could mimic without being able to take over their full meaning; and then there were kinds of Aurignacian behaviour – elaborate burials, beliefs about a spirit world, and image-making – for which they were not mentally equipped. Their deficiency can be traced not so much to inferior intelligence as to their particular kind of consciousness (Chapter 7).[63]

I believe that it was a conflictual scenario of social divisions, perceptively prefigured by Max Raphael, that was the dynamic behind the efflorescence of Upper Palaeolithic art. When Laming-Emperaire and Leroi-Gourhan developed the mythogram component of Raphael's ideas at the expense of his social emphasis, they led Upper Palaeolithic art research down a functionalist avenue, one that emphasizes the 'beneficial' effects of image-making by claiming that images facilitated extended inter-group co-operation, intra-group cohesion, information-exchange, the resolution of binary oppositions, and so forth. The reality was, I argue, more complex and much less comfortable. It was not 'beauty' or an 'aesthetic sense' that was burgeoning at the beginning of the Upper Palaeolithic but rather social discrimination. Art and ritual may well contribute to social cohesion, but they do so *by marking off groups from other groups* and thus creating the potential for social tensions. It was not co-operation but social competition and tension that triggered an ever-widening spiral of social, political and technological change that continued long after the last Neanderthal had died, indeed throughout human history.

A wider focus

So far, we have focused on the well-documented region of western Europe and, as a result, have been able to see the Transition as being triggered by the arrival some 45,000 years ago of anatomically modern Aurignacian people who brought with them complex social structures, sophisticated, planned hunting, diverse symbolic behaviour and, of course, image-making. The sud-denness with which this new package appears in western Europe and the comparative speed with which it replaced the old Neanderthal way of life are certainly striking. Small wonder then that writers speak of a 'Creative Explosion'[64] or, on a grander scale, of the 'Human Revolution'.[65] They are right to do so. But only if they are geographically specific and explicitly ignore evidence from Africa and the Middle East. In these regions we find precursors of the 'Creative Explosion', but the overall picture looks much less explosive. It is in Africa that we must seek the earliest evidence for the 'Human Revolution'.

The more extreme proponents of the 'Human Revolution' theory argue that modern human behaviour is a 'package deal' and that it appeared everywhere about 50,000–40,000 years ago. They ascribe this apparent sudden change to species-wide neurological changes coupled with the advent of fully modern language.[66] This view results from too tight a focus on the west European evi-dence. Sally McBrearty and Alison Brooks, in a critical review of a much wider sweep of evidence that embraces, especially, the African continent, comment:

There is a profound Eurocentric bias in Old World archaeology that is partly a result of research history and partly a product of the richness of the European material itself. The privileging of the European record is so entrenched in the field of archae-ology that it is not even perceived by its practitioners.[67]

To achieve a less biased account of the west European Transition we need to distinguish between what we may see as (a) anatomically modern features of the human body and (b) behaviourally modern features of human life. The first of these two concepts is the easier to define: we need only examine recent human skeletons and agree on which features and measurements are the ones that distinguish them from much older specimens (though this is easier said than done). The second concept is more controversial. Archaeologists have derived their notion of modern human behaviour, that is, behaviour associated with anatomically modern human beings, from the west European evidence. Consequently, they formulate lists to characterize modern human behaviour, such as the following:[68]

- abstract thinking, the ability to act with reference to abstract concepts not limited in time or space,
- planning depth, the ability to formulate strategies based on past experience and to act upon them in a group context,
- behavioural, economic and technological innovation, and
- symbolic behaviour, the ability to represent objects, people and abstract concepts with arbitrary symbols, vocal or visual, and to reify such symbols in cultural practice.

Given the west European evidence, this list seems reasonable enough. But, as its compilers point out, it is unreasonable to expect all early anatomically modern populations to have expressed these characteristics in exactly the same way. All early *Homo sapiens* communities did not, for instance, make bone tools, eat fish and use paint to make images in caves.[69]

The importance of this point becomes clear when we turn to the African evidence for the emergence of modern human anatomy and behaviour. Because our principal interest lies elsewhere, I summarize this evidence and avoid the detail of human fossil types, dates and dating techniques, site names, differences between what is known in Africa as the Middle Stone Age and the European Middle Palaeolithic, stone artefact typologies, demographic patterning within Africa, highly specific internal debates, and much else – fascinating and important though all these issues are.[70]

Although there is still some residual opposition, as well as a good deal of refining that needs to be done, researchers today generally accept the 'Out of Africa' hypothesis. They believe that the fossil evidence shows conclusively that the precursors of anatomically modern human populations evolved in Africa and left the continent in two waves. This hypothesis explains why western Europe was occupied by anatomically archaic Neanderthals for thousands of years before the *Homo sapiens* communities made their way west from the Middle East and through eastern Europe. One view of this second exodus from Africa is that the anatomically modern populations that left Africa did not have fully modern behaviour and acquired it only some 40,000 to 50,000 years ago.

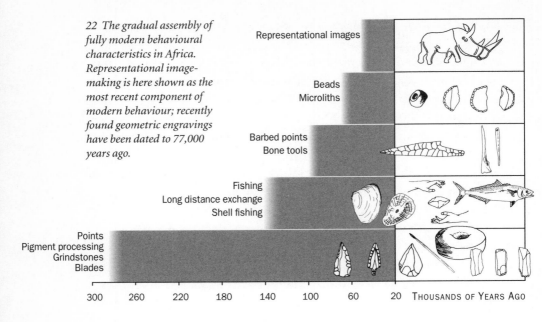

22 The gradual assembly of fully modern behavioural characteristics in Africa. Representational image-making is here shown as the most recent component of modern behaviour; recently found geometric engravings have been dated to 77,000 years ago.

Representational images

Beads
Microliths

Barbed points
Bone tools

Fishing
Long distance exchange
Shell fishing

Points
Pigment processing
Grindstones
Blades

300   260   220   180   140   100   60   20   THOUSANDS OF YEARS AGO

The African evidence challenges this crucial point. It now seems that the shift to behavioural modernity started in Africa as long as 250,000 to 300,000 or more years ago.[71] It is also clear that we should speak not of 'modern human behaviour' but of 'modern human behaviours'. Modern behaviour did not appear suddenly as a complete package; in this sense, there was no 'revolution'. The four characteristics of modern behaviour I listed above manifested them-selves in various ways and appeared at different times and in widely separated places in the African archaeological record (Fig. 22).[72] For instance, the making of blades and pigment processing using grindstones date back to 250,000 years ago. Long-distance exchange and shellfishing started about 140,000 years ago. Bone tools and mining are about 100,000 years old. Ostrich eggshell bead-making started between 40,000 and 50,000 years ago, but present evidence suggests that the species of art that we call representational images may date back to between only 30,000 and 40,000 years ago. Most astonishing of all is the recent find that Chris Henshilwood and his colleagues made in the southern Cape cave known as Blombos. A piece of ochre, carefully engraved with crosses with a central and a containing line has been dated to approximately 77,000 years before the present (Pl. 6). Though not a represen-tational image, this is now the oldest dated 'art' in the world. It shows indisputable modern human behaviour at an unexpectedly early date. While there may be some debate about the details of all this evidence, it now seems clear that modern human behaviour was appearing piecemeal in Africa before the Transition in western Europe.[73]

Change in the behaviour of the earliest African anatomically modern human communities was episodic, and contact between those scattered groups probably intermittent. These two conditions resulted in what McBrearty and Brooks call 'a stepwise progress, a gradual assembling of the modern human adaptation'.[74] It is therefore critical that 'the Middle to Upper Palaeolithic Transition in Europe not be confused with the origin of *Homo sapiens*'.[75] The African evidence shows that, far from any concept of a revolution, innovations were *ad hoc* and their dissemination was sporadic. Western Europe was a special case, a *cul-de-sac* which saw an efflorescence of certain components of modern human behaviour.

There was, therefore, an 'Upper Palaeolithic Revolution', a 'Creative Explosion', in one sense but not in another. To be sure, there was a comparatively sudden burst of symbolic activity, but that explosion was not universal, nor was it an indivisible 'package deal'. The idea that all the different kinds of art and fully developed symbolic behaviour suddenly appeared in western Europe may be termed the 'Creative Illusion'.

This cautionary note does not diminish the importance of what happened in western Europe; it merely places those events in a wider perspective, one that opens up new lines of explanation. If the modern mind and modern behaviour evolved sporadically in Africa, it follows that the potential for all the symbolic activities that we see in Upper Palaeolithic western Europe was in existence before *Homo sapiens* communities reached France and the Iberian Peninsula. This pre-existing potential means that we should not seek a neuronal event as the triggering mechanism for the west European 'Creative Explosion'. With what possibilities are we left? It seems to me that the answer must lie in social circumstances. As I have argued, this means we must investigate the role of art in social conflict, stress and discrimination. We should pick up the story where Max Raphael left it. We need to eschew functionalist explanations that, under the silent influence of Darwin's ideas of natural selection, reiterate in one way or another the supposedly beneficial effects of image-making, the ways in which image-making is said to have contributed to a harmonious society. Instead of following this (I suggest facile) route we need to explore the role of images and the complex social processes of image-making in circumstances of social conflict. Far from lying at the root of a 'pure, higher aesthetic sense', image-making, linked to religion, was, much more murkily, born in and facilitated the formation of stratified societies as we know them today.[76]

  Having come to a better understanding of the specific role of western Europe in the larger scheme of things, we can now focus in a more informed way on the enigma of Upper Palaeolithic art. The first issue that we need to address is the distinction between human intelligence and consciousness and the ways in which this distinction helps to clarify what was happening to the Upper Palaeolithic human mind in the caves of western Europe. Why did people penetrate into those dark passages and chambers and fashion images that even today make us hold our breath as they overwhelm us in the interplay of light and darkness?

CHAPTER 4

The Matter of the Mind

The previous chapters brought us from the nineteenth-century discovery of human antiquity to present-day enquiries into the curious interaction of two species of *Homo* during the Middle to Upper Palaeolithic Transition in western Europe. We saw that, although modern human behaviour of the kind practised by the first *Homo sapiens* communities to reach western Europe was put together piecemeal in Africa and the Middle East, something rather special happened in the European *cul-de-sac*. Circumstances peculiar to that region created an illusion of the sudden appearance of a package deal of symbolic activity:

- refined stone-tool technology that went beyond the purely functional to signal group identity,
- body adornments that conveyed information about personal and group identity,
- elaborate burial of certain dead,
- fully modern language, and
- the making of images.

I also began to argue that this behavioural package, however slowly and sporadically it may have been assembled in Africa, presupposes a kind of human consciousness that was alien to the Neanderthals and that permits conceptions of an 'alternative reality'. We now need to investigate theories of how human intelligence evolved through the millennia, but we also need to go further and consider the role of human consciousness. We stand on the threshold of a new kind of enquiry that is concerned with the human mind, not just with stones and bones, the material remains of human activities. At this point, some archaeologists begin to feel uneasy: what they deride as 'palaeopsychology' is, for them, anathema.

Their discomfort derives from too rigid a devotion to what are, I believe, restrictive methods of research. Indeed, enquiry into the nature of Upper Palaeolithic mind and consciousness demands further consideration of methodology. We need a method different from the comparatively simple one we used in discriminating between the early hypotheses about the purposes of

Upper Palaeolithic image-making, such as sympathetic magic and the supposed existence of a prehistoric mythogram. The criteria that we employed for evaluating hypotheses remain important, but we need to go beyond them. As soon as we move, as we began to do in Chapter 3, from fairly restricted fields of evidence to much broader considerations of human consciousness, we need to explore neuropsychology – the study of how the brain/mind works – in addition to technology, the archaeology of prehistoric settlement patterns, economic activity, and the other components of early human life with which we have so far been principally concerned. This widening of interest means that we now have to accommodate a new strand of evidence.

Strands of evidence

The intertwining of numerous strands of evidence is a method of constructing explanations that philosophers of science recognize as being closer to what actually happens in daily scientific practice than the formal, sequential testing of hypotheses, the method about which researchers frequently talk. Alison Wylie,[1] herself a philosopher of science, has advocated this 'cabling' method in archaeology. To illustrate the difference between 'cabling' and other kinds of argument she points out that some arguments are like chains: they follow link after logical link; if one link fails through lack of evidence or faulty logic, the whole argument breaks down (Fig. 23). This is a difficulty that faces researchers who tackle the kind of enquiry that we are pursuing. Archaeology is, almost by definition, the quintessential science of exiguous evidence. We have to devise ways of getting around the gaps that – understandably enough – punctuate the entire sweep of the archaeological record.

Wylie points out that, in practice, archaeologists overcome this problem by intertwining multiple strands of evidence. The value of this method is that each of the strands is, in its own way, both sustaining and constraining. These two characteristics of evidence require a word of explanation.

23 Two types of argument. (Left) Cable-like arguments that intertwine a number of strands of evidence. (Right) Chain-like arguments that proceed link by link. Cable-like arguments are sustainable even if there are gaps in some strands.

A strand is *sustaining* in that it may compensate for a gap in another strand. For example, the archaeological record itself may not suggest an explanation for a particular feature discovered in an excavation (say, a cramped stone structure), but the ethnographic record of small-scale societies around the world may well suggest an explanation (people seeking contemplative solitude are known to have built similar structures). If a certain human activity in a hunter-gatherer community in one part of the world led to physical evidence similar to the archaeological discovery, the same relationship between activity and material record *might* have occurred in a hunter-gatherer settlement in the deep past. Having been enlightened by ethnography, a researcher can return to the archaeological record (perhaps at the same time exploring some other strand of evidence) to search for any data hitherto unnoticed that may support or contradict the ethnographic hint. The ethnographic evidential strand, along with other kinds of evidence, may thus help to 'cover' a gap in the archaeological strand.

The 'cabling' method is useful in another way as well: it is *constraining* in that it restricts wild hypotheses that may take a researcher far from the archaeological record. An archaeologist may, for instance, think that a severe drought led to the abandonment of a human settlement in a climatically marginal environment, but palaeo-climatic evidence (another strand that depends in part on the analysis of ancient pollen) may show that no such drought occurred.

This is the method that researchers adopt – whether they acknowledge it explicitly or not – when they cast around for hints as to what may have been happening to the human brain/mind during the Transition. They look for strands of evidence beyond the archaeological record itself. Some turn to the study of apes and chimpanzees and the ways in which they can, or cannot, learn to communicate; they are, after all, our nearest hominid relatives. Other researchers explore the construction of artificial intelligence, and the ways in which scientists are trying to build thinking machines. Others study how children learn and acquire language in the hope that that process may in some ways parallel the way in which the human species learned to think and use language. Still others examine the brains/minds of mentally impaired or brain-damaged people in the hope that their fragmentary minds may cast some light on an early stage in the evolution of the human mind. None of these approaches has, at least to my way of thinking, contributed much to our understanding of how the human brain/mind came to be as it is today. They are fascinating in their own right, but apes are not frozen ancestors of human beings; children do not have the brains of archaic human beings; damaged brains are damaged anatomically modern brains not precursors of modern brains. Finally, even if scientists were able to construct a machine that would function just like a human brain, it would not *be* a brain and would therefore not assist us in explaining the evolution of the human brain. This may seem an unduly cavalier dismissal of much valuable research. It is not that I totally reject all this work; I just feel that we can proceed with our investigation of Upper Palaeolithic art without exploring all these controversial avenues.

The brain/mind problem

Some common, frequently used words are extraordinarily difficult to define. We have noted the problem of defining 'art'. 'Consciousness' is another such word. We all know what it means – until someone asks us to define it. One of the sources of this difficulty is that consciousness is a historically situated selection and evaluation of mental states from a wide range of potential states. It is not a universal, timeless 'given'. As before in this book, I side-step the tedious task of attempting to define the slippery word in a formal way. Instead, I allow an understanding of the word to emerge from a series of observations.

Two things we do know are, one, that the brain/mind evolved, and two, that consciousness (as distinct from brain) is a notion, or sensation, created by electro-chemical activity in the 'wiring' of the brain. These two observations guide much of the following discussion.

Enlarging on the first of these points, we can say that the brain/mind did not suddenly appear *ex nihilo*. The origins of the human brain/mind must lie deep in the past. Moreover, the beginnings of the brain/mind must have been shaped by conditions of survival that, in our modern Western society, no longer exist. That being so, we need to turn to Darwin and his insights into the mutability of species and the effects of natural selection – and, of course, also to more recent evolutionary theory that builds on Darwin's well-laid foundation.

The second observation is rather different and requires more comment. If we are speaking of evolution, we are speaking – essentially – of the human body, our physical, material make-up of bones, blood, tissue, brain matter. By contrast, mind is a projection, an abstraction; it cannot be placed on a table and dissected as can a brain. Nor, it seems, can mind be placed on a philosophical table and defined and described. Indeed, the age-old mind/body problem continues to niggle despite the ingenuity of generations of philosophers.

The issue is most famously associated with René Descartes (1596–1650), a

French-born thinker who lived most of his life in Holland. In view of the issues I discuss later, it is worth noting that Descartes said that he derived his ambition of designing a new philosophical and scientific system not from rational, lucid thought but from a series of dreams. That contradiction derived from the duality of his thinking. On the one hand, he developed philosophical and scientific theories that were rooted in rigid mathematics and the material world. On the other, his system was posited on the existence of a divine, benevolent creator. Out of this contradiction grew his well-known 'Cartesian dualism' that proposes the existence of two radically different kinds of substance: material substance (rocks, trees, animals and the human body) and 'thinking substance' (the human mind, thoughts, desires). From this duality arises a notion that the 'self' (more or less what we are calling consciousness) is something non-material and that it in some way operates the brain (which is material), rather as a puppeteer manipulates a puppet. The English philosopher Gilbert Ryle (1900–76) summed up this notion in his famous phrase 'The Ghost in the Machine'. Descartes's idea persists in what is now called 'attributive dualism', the doctrine that psychological phenomena cannot be reduced to a physical foundation. Whilst there is some sense in this kind of opposition to a reductionist explanation of mind, I believe that any persuasive explanation must refer to the form and functioning of the brain, the matter of the mind. The ghost hidden in the machine is a cognitive illusion created by the electro-chemical functioning of the brain.

That said, we have to admit that, despite the current plethora of studies of human consciousness, we still do not know how the functioning of the brain produces human consciousness. We do have a much better understanding of what happens in the brain than we did 20 years ago, even though, as Ian Glynn points out in his elegant and erudite book, *An Anatomy of Thought*, much remains mysterious.[2] More pessimistically, there are those who argue that the problem will never be solved. For them, consciousness is like religion: if you have it, you cannot study it. Put another way, our cognitive abilities do not allow us to understand our cognitive abilities. It may be true that, if you have religion, you cannot study it, but it is a false analogy to go on to argue that our consciousness prevents us from understanding our consciousness. The fascinating issues of consciousness, self-awareness, introspection, insight and foresight remain, but, like other fields of great interest to which I have referred, they are not the destination of our present enquiry. Fortunately, we can circumnavigate them and examine the debate that surrounds relationships between brain, mind and the earliest art.

Minds and metaphors

When we speak of the brain, we are on fairly solid ground. We can literally dissect a brain and find left and right hemispheres, the cortex, the hippocampus, synapses, neurotransmitters, and so forth. But, when we come to attempt the same kind of process with the mind and consciousness, we are forced to adopt a different procedure altogether. Inevitably, or so it seems, we are obliged to use metaphors and similes: we have to compare what we imagine to be the human mind to something simpler and something with which we are familiar. So the mind may be thought of as a blank slate on which, from birth, information is written by a process of learning. Or we may think of it as a sponge, soaking up knowledge, retaining it, and then squeezing it out again. Or, much more popularly today, we may think of the mind as a computer that has hardware (its neural make-up, which some like to call 'wetware') and software (the programmes that make it work). Some computers are more powerful than others: they can store more information and perform more complex tasks. So the minds of early hominids were like simple computers; ours are more powerful. A newer and increasingly influential metaphor, one that we shall examine in more detail, is that of a Swiss army knife, an instrument that contains a number of blades and gadgets, each designed to perform a specialized task.

It is important to remember that all these understandings are no more than metaphors: they have no foundation in physical evidence. The various components of a computer, for instance, are not paralleled by physical, discrete parts of the brain that can be dissected in the same way that a computer can be dismantled; the brain with its intricate neural pathways is more complex than that. This is a very real problem. Some metaphors are more attractive than others for a variety of reasons: not only are some more evocative, even more emotive, than others; in addition, some spawn sub-metaphors that seem to correspond to components of the mind that we are trying to explain. So it is that a computer's hard drive may be likened to our memory; the keyboard to our organs of perception; the screen to modes of expression. When this sort of thing happens we may feel that we are indeed explaining the phenomenon of mind. But we are not. We are merely playing with words that have no correspondence in the material world in which the brain exists.

With these caveats in mind, we can turn to the most recent and widely discussed explanation for the Middle to Upper Palaeolithic Transition and the two metaphors of mind on which it is built – Swiss army knives and cathedrals. How did these engaging metaphors come to provide so attractive an explanation and yet one that, I argue, misses the point?

Ecclesiastical Luddites

Most archaeologists agree that something drastic must have happened to earlier forms of the human mind to account for the west European evidence of the Transition, whether that change in mind took place in the Middle East and Europe or, as I have argued, principally in Africa. How else, they ask, can one explain the comparatively sudden appearance of an abundance of body decoration, burials and art? Point taken – at least in part. That is why some of these archaeologists turn to evolutionary psychology for insights into the stages through which the human mind evolved through the millennia of prehistory and up to its present state.[3] They believe that they can bring their knowledge of the archaeological record into a mutually explanatory relationship with the stages of mental development that evolutionary psychologists propose. This research programme is certainly attractive, and the premise of mutual illumination between disciplines is surely valid.

Steven Mithen, an archaeologist at Reading University in England, is the most influential and thorough explorer of the relationship between the two disciplines. His ideas are comprehensively and clearly set out in his book *The Prehistory of the Mind: A Search for the Origins of Art, Religion and Science.*[4] He (together with his evolutionary psychologist mentors) is principally concerned with intelligence and *different kinds* of intelligence. Without wishing to downplay the obvious significance of intelligence, I emphasize later the equal importance of consciousness.

I refer to different kinds of intelligence because the issue at the heart of evolutionary psychology is whether intelligence is a single, general-purpose 'computer' or a set of 'computers', each dedicated to a specific purpose. Evolutionary psychologists believe that the second of these propositions is the more likely because studies of non-human animal behaviour have shown that what is learned in one domain often cannot be transferred to another: there is little or no 'transfer of training'. Evolutionary psychologists therefore speak of 'mental modules', 'multiple intelligences', 'cognitive domains', and 'Darwinian algorithms'.[5] The notion denoted by these phrases is perhaps most easily understood if we glance at one of Noam Chomsky's ideas. He pointed out that children's ability to learn complex language at an early age is probably in some way 'wired into' the human brain/mind.[6] Other kinds of intelligent behaviour, such as facility with numbers, may be learned later – and less perfectly. There are therefore types of intelligence. Moreover, loss of facility in one domain, say language, perhaps through trauma, does not necessarily mean lack of ability in discerning social relations or in relating to the material environment: people who lose the power of speech can still move around without bumping into furniture.

The next key notion is 'accessibility'. By this, evolutionary psychologists mean contact, or interaction, between mental modules. They argue that anatomically modern people have better interaction between modules than other animals. We are therefore able to perform more complex behaviours that extend across domains. Rather than a highly modular intelligence, we have a *generalized intelligence*. Researchers believe that the mental modules responsible for domain-specific behaviours are situated in specific neural circuits in the brain and that accessibility between them is achieved by neural pathways.

We need not examine all the variations of these fundamental propositions. Instead, we can move on to see what mental modules Mithen identifies and how he believes the generalization of these modules explains what happened at the Transition.

He proposes four mental modules:
- social intelligence,
- technical intelligence,
- natural history intelligence, and
- linguistic intelligence.

For instance, anatomically archaic people (who did not have generalized intelligence) could learn multi-stage procedures for making stone artefacts (technical intelligence), but this degree of complexity could not spill over into elaborate kinds of social relations (social intelligence). Indeed, he argues that there was little interaction, or accessibility, between intelligence modules prior to the Transition. The minds of archaic people were like Swiss army knives: they comprised a set of gadgets each dedicated to a specific task.

To illustrate an extension of this point, Mithen invokes a second beguiling metaphor, that of a cathedral (Fig. 24). The central nave represents general intelligence. Ranged around the nave are four chapels, each dedicated to one of the four mental modules. Prior to the Transition, there was little or no traffic between the chapels, though the possible linking power of rudimentary language in the Middle Palaeolithic should be taken into account. Then, at the Transition, there was a wave of vandalism that led to the demolition of the walls between the individual chapels and between them and the nave. This

24 Steven Mithen's cathedrals of intelligence: (above) integrated intelligence that permits interaction between 'chapels'; (below) modular intelligence with little accessibility between 'chapels'.

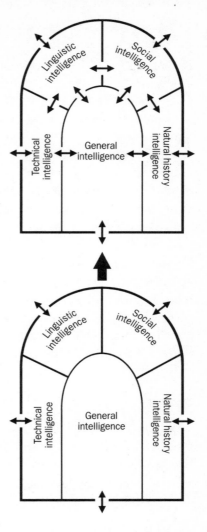

demolition allowed the transfer of intelligence from chapel to chapel and the enlargement of the central nave of general intelligence. The vandal that directed the destruction was fully modern language. The metaphor of language breaking down walls may be especially appropriate because, as researchers such as Chomsky[7] and Bickerton[8] have argued, the emergence of fully modern language must have been fairly sudden and not a gradation of barely discernible steps (though when this happened and what its immediate effects were remain to be determined).

At this time of neurological demolition, new mental abilities became viable. For instance, metaphorical thought became possible as a result of traffic between chapels. People could think of, say, social relations in terms of natural history intelligence – thus totemism was born: people could speak of human groups as if they were animal species. Similarly, anthropomorphism (the ascription of human characteristics to animals) was achieved by traffic from social intelligence through to the chapel of natural history: animals became like people. Then, too, for the comparatively complex subsistence strategies of the Upper Palaeolithic there had to be traffic between technical intelligence and natural history intelligence. Improved hunting equipment (technical intelligence) was of no use without integrating it with knowledge of the environment in which it was to be used and the behaviour of the animals to be hunted (natural history intelligence). All in all, human-environment interactions were transformed by this new mode of generalized intelligence.

Ingeniously, Mithen uses cathedral vandalism to explain the appearance of not only better adaptations, but also art at the Transition. He begins by proposing four cognitive and physical processes (not to be confused with the four intelligence modules):

– making visual images,
– classification of images into classes,
– intentional communication, and
– attribution of meaning to images.[9]

He then points out that the first three abilities are found in non-human primates. The fourth is the key ability, and it, Mithen argues, is found only in hominids. Yet, even though hominids such as the Neanderthals had it, visual symbolism arose, or at any rate flowered, only at the Transition (some researchers argue for an earlier date for the first signs of symbolic behaviour). So, what happened? Prior to the Transition, intentional communication and classification were probably sealed in the social intelligence chapel, while mark-making and the attribution of meaning, which both implicate material objects, were probably ensconced in chapels of non-social intelligence. At the Transition, accessibility between chapels made art possible by allowing intentional communication to escape into the domain of mark-making.

Some reservations

Evolutionary psychology as a sub-discipline has its critics.[10] Unfortunately, there is a muddying of the waters with political correctness. Some critics find that the tenets of evolutionary psychology are uncomfortably close to free-market economics, which they abhor. That observation has some support, but any scientific proposition must be accepted or rejected on rational grounds, not on its perceived social consequences.

This is a point that I bear in mind as I briefly consider Mithen's evolutionary psychology explanation for the origin of the human mind and art: it is attractive, but I believe that it has weaknesses and that it leaves some important points outstanding.

First, despite the considerable ingenuity of evolutionary psychologists, the explanation is heavily dependent on mental modules inferred, very largely, from animal and human behaviour. How can we be sure that pre-*sapiens* hominids had the four intelligence modules that Mithen postulates? To what extent are these modules inferred by modern human minds from modern human behaviour? Indeed, is it possible to infer modules from behaviour?

Secondly, we have no direct information on the possible modularity of ancient minds. As a result, evolutionary psychologists are free to invent historical trajectories that move repeatedly between modularity and access between modules for as much as 100 million years.[11] Thirdly, it is not clear how a species could break down the walls between chapels, at least in neurological terms. Would the creatures have to 'grow' new neural pathways, or would they simply have to learn to use ones they already had? Fourthly, the prominence of metaphors in Mithen's discourse keeps us at a remove from the realities of human neurology, that is, from the matter of the mind. There is a tendency to develop the argument by exploring the metaphors rather than by coming to grips with realities. At times it is not clear whether the argument is being prosecuted entirely in a metaphorical realm. Technological innovations that involve non-invasive three-dimensional imaging of living brains are, however, beginning to test supposed connections between particular types of behaviour and specific brain locations.[12]

These four reservations are sources of concern, but they do not entirely eliminate the possibility that intelligence may indeed be modular in some way. Either way, we can proceed with our enquiry because I argue that we need to go beyond intelligence, whether it is modular or not.

My fifth reservation takes up this point. It concerns what I see as too exclusive an emphasis on intelligence. Intelligence is what researchers use when they study human origins and all the other puzzles of science. Whilst they allow intuition and unexplained flashes of insight a role in the solving of scientific problems, ideas so acquired must, they rightly insist, be subjected to rational evaluation.[13] As a result of this essentially Western view, one that explains the invention of the radio and makes space travel possible, they regard rational intelligence, as they themselves experience it, as the defining characteristic of human beings. They therefore explain everything that early people achieved in terms of evolving intelligence and rationality – of becoming brighter and smarter. As they see it, early people were becoming more and more like Western scientists. This is what we may call 'consciousness of rationality'.

Consciousness: neurological and social

The problem here is that the emphasis on intelligence has marginalized the importance of the full range of human consciousness in human behaviour. Art and the ability to comprehend it are more dependent on kinds of mental imagery and the ability to manipulate mental images than on intelligence. We must see consciousness as much more than the interaction of intelligence modules to create generalized intelligence. Mithen deals briefly with consciousness, but the way in which he does it is steeped in the general scientific emphasis on intelligence. Drawing on Nicholas Humphrey's[14] work, he highlights 'reflexive consciousness'. This phrase means not only being aware of our physical selves and our own thought (introspection), but also an ability derived from our social intelligence module: being able to predict the behaviour of others – in a sense, to read their minds. The adaptive value of this kind of consciousness is clear. But it is also clear that what is being described is part of highly valued Western problem-solving techniques.

What we have here is a case of our knowledge of the past being entrenched in present-day values and practices. In this instance, the social constructivist position (Chapter 2) clearly has some merit. What constitutes consciousness for us at our particular position in history informs our investigation and knowledge of the past. Catherine Lutz[15] identifies a number of features that are considered integral to our own Western, twenty-first-century consciousness. These features include an absence of emotion in problem-solving, objectivity, linear thought, and sustained attention spans: 'Consciousness so construed is seen as fundamentally good and important.'[16] These features of consciousness as it is conceived in the West come out clearly in Lutz's review of the historical definitions of consciousness listed in the *Oxford English Dictionary*.[17] But when she moves on to consider consciousness as it is conceived in non-Western societies, the inadequacy of her method is exposed. She regards consciousness as something entirely constructed in social discourse and thus without neurological, 'hard-wired' foundations.[18] In this, she (together with the many others who follow similar approaches) comes close to Descartes's separation of mind from body. Despite her wish to rise above the received norms of her own Western society, she falls prey to a current academic aversion to any reference to the neurological basis of consciousness or behaviour. Other components of consciousness, such as Descartes's dreams, are therefore considered aberrations and suppressed in formulations of what constitutes human consciousness. As we shall shortly see, consciousness is not entirely a construct. Rather, it derives from historically specific responses to and categorizations of a shifting neurological substrate.

For an initial illustration of this dialectic between social construction and neurological foundations I turn to the medieval concept of consciousness. It was different from present-day concepts, even though it had to make sense of the same neurological foundation. Medieval people valued dreams and visions

1 One of the large aurochs bulls that were painted in the Hall of the Bulls in Lascaux. The curious way in which the ear has been positioned is peculiar to Lascaux. A 'broken' sign has been placed on the animal's forequarters. It is comparable to one of the signs in the Shaft (Plate 28); its repetition points to the conceptual unity of the cave.

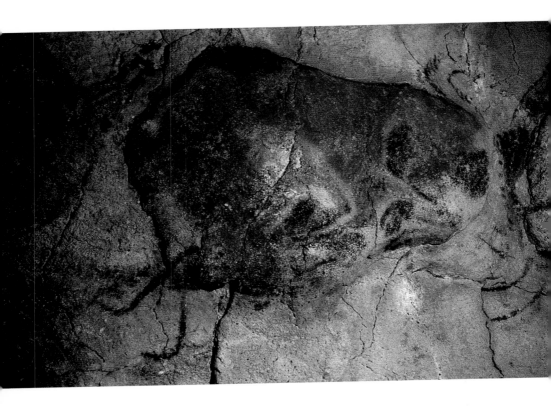

2 (Above) A curled-up bison painted on the ceiling of Altamira. The form of the animal has been 'squeezed' into the shape of a boss of rock that hangs down from the ceiling. There are others like it in Altamira. There was an interaction between the shape of the rock and the image-maker.

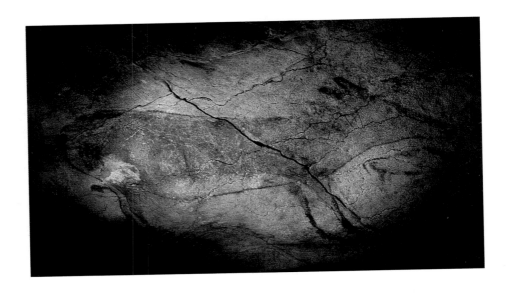

4 and 5 (Left and below) Two 'masks' painted in the Horse's Tail, the deepest passage in Altamira. This is another instance of interaction between physical features of the cave and images. The two 'masks' seem to peer out of the wall as the visitor turns at the end of the passage and begins to leave the cave. It is hard to say if these are the faces of animals or human beings. Either way, they suggest mysterious 'presences' in the caves watching those who venture into the underworld.

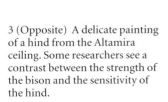

3 (Opposite) A delicate painting of a hind from the Altamira ceiling. Some researchers see a contrast between the strength of the bison and the sensitivity of the hind.

6 (Left) The world's oldest 'art' (77,000 years old) comes from Blombos Cave on the southern coast of South Africa. A regular pattern was engraved on the ground edge of a small piece of ochre. Researchers debate whether this important find suggests fully modern minds, language and symbolism at an unexpectedly early date.

7 (Below) Rock engravings in the semi-arid Karoo, the part of southern Africa where Wilhelm Bleek and Lucy Lloyd's San teachers lived. These engravings were made by the 'scratched' technique.

8 (Above) A southern African San rock painting of an eland antelope. The image was made by the shaded polychrome technique that depicts the animal in remarkable detail. The eland was the San trickster-deity's favourite creature: it was a powerful, resonant symbol with many associations.

9 (Right) A southern African San polychrome rock painting of an antelope-headed figure that wears a white kaross (skin cloak). Note the blood falling from its nose; it indicates that the 'being' is a San shaman who has entered an altered state of consciousness and thus travelled to the spirit world where people assume animal features.

10 A piece of quartz lodged in a crack in a rock in Sally's Rockshelter in the Mojave Desert, North America. Shamans believed that quartz contained a supernatural essence and afforded contact with the spirit world that lay behind the rock face.

11 Rock art that was made as part of North American girls' puberty rituals and found in southern California. The zigzags, closely associated with such rituals, probably derive from geometric imagery wired into the human brain and activated in altered states of consciousness. Researchers have found that shamans, who controlled altered states, supervised such rituals.

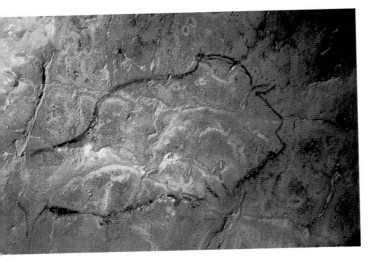

12 A painting of a bison in the Salon Noir, Niaux. It shows how Upper Palaeolithic images seem to 'float' on the walls of the underground chambers, an effect that is here enhanced by an absence of hoofs. Though a simple outline, the image catches the vast power of the bison.

13 A more detailed painting of a bison in the Salon Noir, Niaux. Here the sense of free 'floating' is suggested by the animal's 'hanging' hoofs; it does not appear to be standing on the ground. Some researchers believe that such animals may be depicted lying on their sides, but the position of the tail and other features make this unlikely.

as sources of knowledge vouchsafed by God. Hildegaard of Bingen (1098–1179), for example, believed that her visions revealed not just God's personal instructions to her but also the material structure of the universe: she did not distinguish between religious revelation and 'science'. Indeed, the contact with the deity that dreams and visions were believed to afford was considered a *defining trait* of human beings, a function of the divine spark that animals lacked, even if it was something to which not everyone aspired. Today this kind of mental state is generally shunned and is not considered a valuable component of human consciousness. No one in the West is likely to be elected to high political office on a ticket of a blinding, personal, divine revelation – or, for that matter, be consecrated as Archbishop of Canterbury. Yet the paradox remains: the large 'esoteric' sections of bookshops show that 'non-scientific' thinking is alive and well, and people still pray, meditate and consult priests and psychics. It is just that, today, altered states are marginalized in the conduct of affairs of state, scientific endeavour, and even within mainstream religion. What today constitutes acceptable human consciousness – the 'consciousness of rationality' – is therefore an historically situated notion constructed within a specific social context but founded on the neurology to which I now turn. It is not simply a function of interacting intelligences.

The spectrum of consciousness

I shall use a metaphor (inevitably!) to clarify aspects of the notion of consciousness. I hope that this metaphor will expose some serious lacunae in the ways in which archaeologists (and others) consider human consciousness and, more specifically, in what it was like to be human during the Transition. The contemporary Western emphasis on the supreme value of intelligence has tended to suppress certain forms of consciousness and to regard them as irrational, marginal, aberrant or even pathological and thereby to eliminate them from investigations of the deep past.

As long ago as 1902, the influential American psychologist William James, who successively taught physiology, psychology and philosophy at Harvard, noted that what we think of as normal, waking consciousness is only one type of consciousness (though, as we shall see, it too is not a unitary state), 'whilst all about it, parted from it by the filmiest of screens, there lie potential forms of consciousness, entirely different'. He added: 'No account of the universe in its totality can be final which leaves these other forms of consciousness quite disregarded.'[19] More recently, Colin Martindale, a cognitive (rather than evolutionary) psychologist, has re-emphasized the point that studies of the mind have concentrated too much on rational states. He argues:

We need to explore altered states of consciousness as well as normal, waking consciousness. We need to understand the 'irrational' thought of the poet as well as the rational thought of the [laboratory] subject solving a logical problem…. We need to investigate the historical evolution of ideas in the real world as well as how concepts are formed in laboratory situations. Finally, since people are not computers, we must ask how emotional and motivational factors affect cognition.[20]

Martindale is by no means alone in this view, yet archaeologists persist in ignoring all but the 'consciousness of rationality'. The important point is that consciousness varies: we must not forget Descartes's dreams and Hildegaard's visions. Whether we ourselves value such experiences or not is irrelevant: they are an unavoidable part of being human, and, if we ignore their potential effects during the Transition and the Upper Palaeolithic itself, we must expect to produce no more than a partial explanation. I therefore suggest that we follow Martindale and think of consciousness not as a state but as a continuum or, the metaphor I favour, as a spectrum.

Two points about the colour spectrum are worth noting. First, in a spectrum cast by a prism on a sheet of white paper the colours grade imperceptibly into one another, yet there is no doubt that, say, red is different from green, and green is different from violet.

Secondly, we know that the Western notion that the colour spectrum comprises seven colours (red, orange, yellow, green, blue, indigo and violet) is not a given. Other cultures and languages designate and name different segments of the colour spectrum; that is, they divide up the spectrum differently. For instance, the Standard Welsh word *glas* denotes hues ranging from what in English is called green through blue to grey. By contrast, the Ibo word *ojii* denotes a range of hues from grey through brown to black. Why, then, do we think of the spectrum as comprising seven colours, when other cultures acknowledge fewer? It was Isaac Newton who decided on the seven colours. Having poor colour vision himself, Newton asked a friend to divide up the spectrum. When the friend obliged and split it into six colours, Newton insisted on seven colours because of the significance of the number seven in Renaissance thought, and, as Newton himself said, seven corresponded to 'the seven intervals of our octave'. Newton therefore asked his friend to add indigo to the spectrum, it being a popular dye at that period.[21]

Bearing these two points in mind, I now introduce the spectrum of consciousness. I first describe the states that Martindale[22] identifies between waking and sleeping. Thereafter, I consider a partly parallel trajectory and further states. According to Martindale's view, as we drift into sleep we pass through:

 – waking, problem-oriented thought,
 – realistic fantasy,
 – autistic fantasy,
 – reverie,
 – hypnagogic (falling asleep) states, and
 – dreaming.

It should be noted that Martindale has imposed these six stages on a spectrum of states. Other researchers may find it useful to propose fewer or more stages.

In waking consciousness we are concerned with problem-solving, usually in response to environmental stimuli. When we become disengaged from those stimuli, different kinds of consciousness begin to take over. First, in realistic fantasy we are oriented to problem solving. We may, for instance, run through a possible social strategy that we plan to use in a forthcoming interview and assess possible outcomes. These realistic fantasies grade into more autistic ones, that is, ones that have less relevance to external reality. In what Martindale calls reverie, our thought is far less directed, and image follows image in no narrative sequence. Then reverie shades into hypnagogic states that occur as we fall asleep. Sometimes hypnagogic imagery is extraordinarily vivid, so vivid that people experience what are called hypnagogic hallucinations: they start awake and believe that their imagery of, say, someone entering the room was real. Hypnagogic hallucinations may be both visual and aural.[23] Finally, in dreaming, a succession of images appears, at least in recall, as a narrative.[24] Actually, we add much of the narrative structure as we recall the imagery. During REM sleep (rapid eye movement sleep that precedes deep sleep) random neuronal activity produces mental imagery. As we all know, this imagery is sometimes bizarre: images transmute into different ones, and we experience sensations of flying, fleeing, and falling, together with attendant emotions.

Concentrating on the first part of this sequence, the neuropsychologist Charles Laughlin and his colleagues[25] speak of 'fragmented consciousness'. They point out that during the course of a day we are repeatedly shifting from outward-directed to inward-directed states. Sometimes we are fully attentive to our environment; at other times we withdraw into contemplation and are less alert to our surroundings. This is simply an inherent feature of the way in which our nervous system functions. There is evidence that our normal waking day comprises cycles of 90 to 120 minutes of moving from outward-directed attention to inward-directed states.[26] As I have observed,[27] some societies regard inward-directed states as pathological, others see them as indicative of divine afflatus, while still others pay little attention to them.

Such is the spectrum of consciousness from shifting wakefulness to sleep. We must now consider another trajectory that passes through the same spectrum but with rather different effects (Fig. 25). I call it the 'intensified trajectory': it is more profoundly concerned with *inward-direction* and *fantasy*. Dream-like, autistic states may be induced by a wide variety of means other than normal drifting into sleep. One of these means is sensory deprivation, during which a reduction of external stimuli leads to the 'release' of internal imagery. Normal subjects, isolated in sound-proof, dark conditions report hallucinations after a few hours.[28] They also experience what Martindale calls 'stimulus hunger': they crave and focus on even the smallest, most trivial stimulus. Comparable sensory deprivation is part of many Eastern meditative techniques. Devotees are required to shut out as much of their environment as possible and to concentrate on a single focal point that may be a repeated mantra or a visual symbol. Then, too, audio-driving, such as prolonged drumming, visual stimulations, such as continually flashing lights, and sustained rhythmic dancing, such as among Dervishes, have a similar effect on the nervous system. We also need to mention fatigue, pain, fasting and, of course, the ingestion of psychotropic substances as means of shifting consciousness along the intensified trajectory towards the release of inwardly generated imagery. Finally, there are pathological states, such as schizophrenia and temporal lobe epilepsy, that take consciousness along the intensified trajectory. Hallucinations may thus be deliberately sought, as in the ingestion of psychotropic substances, or they may be unsought, as in many of the other modes of induction that I have mentioned.

This second trajectory has much in common with the one that takes us daily into sleep and dreaming, but also differences. Dreaming gives everyone some idea of what hallucinations are like. For most modern Westerners, dreams lack the intensity of hallucinations, but earlier Western values (and those of many other societies) tended to take dreams seriously and to rescue them from the oblivion of forgetfulness.[29] Perhaps one could say that the difference between the two spectra is a matter of degree rather than kind. I draw a distinction between the two trajectories because it is useful for the argument I am developing.

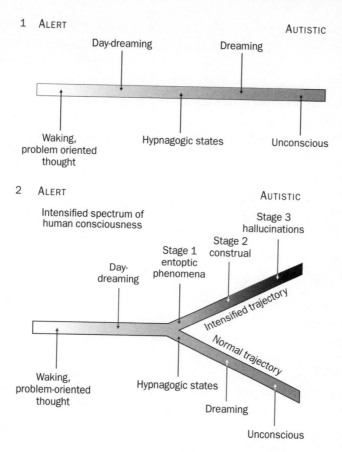

25 *The two spectra of consciousness: (1) 'normal consciousness' that drifts from alert to somnolent states, and (2) the 'intensified trajectory' that leads to hallucinations.*

The states towards the far end of the intensified trajectory – visions, and hallucinations that may occur in any of the five senses – are generally called 'altered states of consciousness'. The phrase can apply equally to dreaming and 'inward' states on the normal trajectory, though some people prefer to restrict its use to extreme hallucinations and trance states. By now it will be obvious that this commonly encountered phrase is posited on the essentially Western concept of the 'consciousness of rationality'. It implies that there is 'ordinary consciousness' that is considered genuine and good, and then perverted, or 'altered', states. But, as we have seen, all parts of the spectrum are equally 'genuine'. The phrase 'altered states of consciousness' is useful enough, but we need to remember that it carries a lot of cultural baggage.

It is essential to note that all the mental states that I have described are generated by the neurology of the human nervous system; they are part and parcel of what it is to be fully human. They are 'wired into' the brain. At the same time, we must note that the mental imagery we experience in altered states is overwhelmingly (though, as we shall see, not entirely) derived from memory and is hence culturally specific.[30] The visions and hallucinations of an Inuit person living in the Canadian snowfields will be different from the vivid intimations that Hildegaard of Bingen believed God sent to her. The Inuit will 'see' polar bears and seals that may speak to him or her; Hildegaard saw angels and strange creatures suggested by scripture and the medieval wall paintings and illuminations with which she was familiar. The spectrum of consciousness is 'wired', but its content is mostly cultural.

A neuropsychological model

The concept of consciousness that I have outlined will explain many specific features of Upper Palaeolithic art. In this, it is unlike other explanations (such as art-for-art's-sake or information-processing) that provide overall, blanket understandings that could apply to virtually any images. But, if we are to attempt to cross the neurological bridge that leads back to the Upper Palaeolithic, we need to look more closely at the visual imagery of the intensified spectrum and see what kinds of percepts are experienced as one passes along it. We can identify three stages, each of which is characterized by particular kinds of imagery and experiences (Fig. 26).[31]

In the first and 'lightest' stage people may experience geometric visual percepts that include dots, grids, zigzags, nested catenary curves, and meandering lines.[32] Because these percepts are 'wired' into the human nervous system, all people, no matter what their cultural background, have the potential to experience them.[33] They flicker, scintillate, expand, contract, and combine with one another; the types are less rigid than this list suggests. Importantly, they are independent of an exterior light source. They can be experienced with the eyes closed or open; with open eyes, they are projected onto and partly obliterate visual perceptions of the environment. For instance, the so-called fortification illusion, a flickering curve with a jagged or castellated perimeter and a 'black hole' of invisibility in the centre, may, with a movement of the head, be positioned over a person standing nearby so that his or her head vanishes in the black hole (Chapter 5). This particular percept is associated with migraine attacks and is therefore well-known to sufferers from that condition. Such percepts cannot be consciously controlled; they seem to have a life of their own.[34] Sometimes a bright light in the centre of the field of vision obscures all but peripheral images.[35] The rate of change from one form to another seems to vary from one psychotropic substance to another[36] but it is generally swift. Laboratory subjects new to the experience find it difficult to keep pace with the rapid flow of imagery, but, significantly for the understanding I develop in following chapters, training and familiarity with the experience increase their powers of observation and description.[37]

Writers have called these geometric percepts phosphenes, form constants and entoptic phenomena. I use *entoptic phenomena* because 'entoptic' means 'within vision' (from the Greek), that is, they may originate anywhere between the eye itself and the cortex of the brain. I take this comprehensive term to cover two classes of geometric percepts that appear to derive from different parts of the visual system. *Phosphenes* can be induced by physical stimulation, such as pressure on the eyeball, and are thus entophthalmic ('within the eye').[38] *Form constants*, on the other hand, derive from the optic system, probably beyond the eyeball itself.[39] I distinguish these two kinds of entoptic phenomena from *hallucinations*, the forms of which have no foundation in the actual structure of the optic system. Unlike phosphenes and form constants, hallucinations include iconic imagery of culturally controlled items, such as animals, as well as somatic (in the body), aural (hearing), gustatory (taste) and olfactory (smell) experiences.

The exact way in which entoptic phenomena are 'wired into' the human nervous system has been a topic of recent research. It has been found that the patterns of connections between the retina and the striate cortex (known as V1) and of neuronal circuits within the striate cortex determined their geometric form.[40] Simply put, there is a spatial relationship between the retina and the visual cortex: points that are close together on the retina lead to the firing of comparably placed neurons in the cortex. When this process is reversed, as following the ingestion of psychotropic substances, the pattern in the cortex is perceived as a visual percept. In other words, people in this condition are seeing the structure of their own brains.

In Stage 2 of the intensified trajectory, subjects try to make sense of entoptic phenomena by elaborating them into iconic forms,[41] that is, into objects that are familiar to them from their daily life. In alert problem-solving consciousness, the brain receives a constant stream of sense impressions. A visual image reaching the brain is decoded (as, of course, are other sense impressions) by being matched against a store of experience. If a 'fit' can be effected, the image

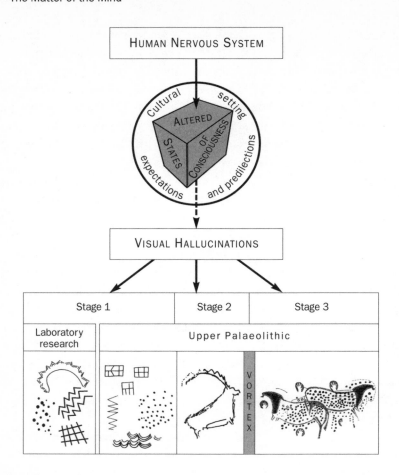

26 *The neuropsychological model. How the functioning of the human nervous system is shaped by the cultural circumstances of people experiencing altered states of consciousness.*

is 'recognized'. In altered states of consciousness, the nervous system itself becomes a 'sixth sense'[42] that produces a variety of images including entoptic phenomena. The brain attempts to decode these forms as it does impressions supplied by the nervous system in an alert, outwardly-directed state. This process is linked to the disposition of the subject. For example, an ambiguous round shape may be 'illusioned' into an orange if the subject is hungry, a breast if he is in a state of heightened sexual drive, a cup of water if the subject is thirsty, or an anarchist's bomb if the subject is fearful.[43]

As subjects move into Stage 3, marked changes in imagery occur.[44] At this point, many people experience a swirling vortex or rotating tunnel that seems to surround them and to draw them into its depths.[45] There is a progressive exclusion of information from the outside: the subject is becoming more and more autistic. The sides of the vortex are marked by a lattice of squares like television screens. The images on these 'screens' are the first spontaneously produced iconic hallucinations; they eventually overlie the vortex as entoptic phenomena give way to iconic hallucinations.[46] The tunnel hallucination is also associated with near-death experiences.[47]

Sometimes a bright light in the centre of the field of vision creates this tunnel-like perspective. Subjects report 'viewing much of their imagery in relation to a tunnel…[I]mages tend to pulsate, moving towards the centre of the tunnel or away from the bright light and sometimes in both directions.' One laboratory subject said, 'I'm moving through some kind of train tunnel. There are all sorts of lights and colours, mostly in the centre, far, far away, way, far away, and little people and stuff running around the [walls] of the tube, like little cartoon nebishes, they're pretty close.' Siegel found that among 58 reports of eight kinds of hallucinations, this sort of tunnel was the most common.[48]

Westerners use culture-specific words like 'funnels, alleys, cones, vessels, pits [and] corridors' to describe the vortex.[49] In other cultures, it is often experienced as entering a hole in the ground. Shamans typically speak of reaching the spirit world via such a hole. The Inuit of Hudson Bay, for instance, describe a 'road down through the earth' that starts in the house where they perform their rituals. They also speak of a shaman passing through the sea: 'He almost glides as if falling through a tube.'[50] The Bella Coola of the American Northwest Coast believe such a hole is 'situated between the doorway and the fireplace.'[51] The Algonkians of Canada travel through layers of earth: 'a hole leading into the bowels of the earth [is] the pathway of the spirits.'[52] The Conibo of the Upper Amazon speak of following the roots of a tree down into the ground.[53] Such reports could easily be multiplied. The vortex and the ways in which its imagery is perceived are clearly universal human experiences, and the descriptions of them that I have given will play a key role in subsequent chapters.

Stage 3 iconic images derive from memory and are often associated with powerful emotional experiences.[54] Images change one into another.[55] This shift in iconic imagery is also accompanied by an increase in vividness. Subjects stop using similes to describe their experiences and assert that the images are indeed what they appear to be. They 'lose insight into the differences between literal and analogical meanings.'[56] Nevertheless, even in this essentially iconic stage, entoptic phenomena may persist: iconic imagery may be projected against a background of geometric forms[57] or entoptic phenomena may frame iconic imagery.[58] By a process of fragmentation and integration, compound images are formed: for example, a man with zigzag legs. Finally, in this stage, subjects enter into and participate in their own imagery: they are part of a strange realm. They blend with both their geometric and their iconic imagery.[59] It is in this final stage that people sometimes feel themselves to be turning into animals[60] and undergoing other frightening or exalting transformations.

These three stages of the intensified spectrum of consciousness are not ineluctably sequential. Some subjects report being catapulted directly into the third stage, while others do not progress beyond the first. The three stages should be seen as cumulative rather than sequential.

Harnessing the brain

The implications of what I have so far said for an understanding of the Transition are clear and different from those implied by studies that concentrate on intelligence. All anatomically modern people of our own time and of the Transition have, or had, the same human nervous system. They therefore cannot, or could not,

– avoid experiencing the full spectrum of human consciousness,

– refrain from dreaming, or

– escape the potential to hallucinate.

Because the *Homo sapiens* populations of that period were fully human, we can confidently expect that their consciousness was as shifting and fragmented as ours, though the ways in which they regarded and valued the various states would have been largely culturally determined. Moreover, they were capable of passing along both the trajectories that I have described, though the content of their dream and autistic imagery would have been different. As we shall see, we cannot say exactly the same of the Neanderthals. We therefore have a neurological bridge to the Upper Palaeolithic, but probably not to the Middle Palaeolithic.

Furthermore, all societies are obliged to divide up the spectrum of consciousness into (probably) named sections, even as they divide up the colour spectrum in one way or another. Human communities are not viable without some (possibly contested) consensus on which states will be valued and which will be ignored or denigrated. Bluntly put, madness is culturally defined: what counts as insanity in one society may be valued in another. States that occasion embarrassment and are ignored in one society may be cultivated in another. But, despite such cultural specifics, the nervous system cannot be eliminated: all people experience dreaming on the first trajectory, and all have the potential to experience the states characteristic of the autistic trajectory. And they experience them in terms of their own culture and value system; this is what has been called the 'domestication of trance'.[61]

The ubiquity of institutionalized altered states of consciousness is borne out by a survey of 488 societies included in Murdock's *Ethnographic Atlas*.[62] Erika Bourguignon, who carried out this survey, found that an overwhelming 437, or 90 per cent, of these societies were reported to have 'culturally patterned forms of altered states of consciousness'.[63] She concluded that 'the *capacity* to experience altered states of consciousness is a psychobiological capacity of the species, and thus universal, its utilization, institutionalization, and patterning are, indeed, features of cultures, and thus variable.'[64] The materials from which the *Ethnographic Atlas* was compiled were, however, not always reliable, and the definition of altered states employed was too narrow. For example, sub-Saharan Africa is shown to have a comparatively high percentage of societies from which altered states are said to be absent. Yet we know that this is not the case. All sub-Saharan societies do recognize the importance of altered states, though they may not be as overtly institutionalized as in other parts of the world. Dreams, for instance, play a prominent role in these societies. It seems, then, that Bourguignon's '*capacity*' should be changed to 'necessity', if the full range of altered states is recognized and the ways in which they may be institutionalized are seen as highly variable.

Because there is no option but to come to terms with the full spectrum of consciousness, people of the Upper Palaeolithic must not only have experienced the full spectrum; they must also have divided it up in their own way and so created their own version of human consciousness.

This italicized paragraph encapsulates two vital steps in my argument. Although many Westerners today recognize the intensified trajectory for what it is and do not attach profound significance to its imagery, this 'sceptical' attitude is not, nor has been, universal.

For an instance of a non-Western attitude, I turn to the Tukano people of the Colombian northwest Amazon Basin and glance briefly at the stages of their *yajé*-induced visual experiences.[65] *Yajé* is a psychotropic vine that occurs in numerous varieties. The Tukano speak of an initial stage in which 'grid patterns, zigzag lines and undulating lines alternate with eye-shaped motifs, many-coloured concentric circles or endless chains of brilliant dots'

(Fig. 26).[66] During this stage they watch 'passively these innumerable scintillating patterns which seem to approach or retreat, or to change and recombine into a multitude of colourful panels'. The Tukano depict these forms on their houses and on bark and explicitly identify them as elements of their *yajé* visions. Geraldo Reichel-Dolmatoff, who worked for many years with the Tukano and other peoples of the Amazon Basin, demonstrated the parallels between what the Tukano see and draw and the entoptic forms established independently by laboratory research. Comparable but greatly elaborated and formalized designs come from 'eye spirits' to the Shipibo-Conibo shamans of eastern Peru during *ayahuasca*-induced hallucinations. These designs are believed to have therapeutic properties and to be closely associated with songs that are 'engraved in the shaman's consciousness': song and design become one.[67]

In a second stage recognized by the Tukano there is a diminution of these patterns and the slow formation of larger images. They now perceive recognizable shapes of people, animals, and strange monsters. They see '*yajé* snakes', the Master of the Animals who withholds animals or releases them to hunters, the Sun-Father, the Daughter of the Anaconda, and other mythical beings. The intense activity of this stage gives way to more placid visions in the final stage. It seems clear that the Tukano first and second stages correspond to our Stages 1 and 3 respectively.

Here, then, we have an instance in which people take hold of the possibilities of the intensified trajectory – they harness the human brain – and believe that they derive from their visions insights into an 'alternative reality' that, for them, may be more real than the world of daily life. This is a worldwide experience. Indeed, ecstatic experience is a part of all religions – as I have pointed out, people have to accommodate the full spectrum of consciousness in some way.

Amongst hunter-gatherer (and some other) communities the sort of experience that the Tukano describe is called 'shamanism'. The word derives from the Tungus language of central Asia.[68] Today this is a disputed word.[69] Some researchers feel that the term has been used too generally to be of any use and that it should be restricted to the central Asian communities of its origin. Although I appreciate the point that these writers make, I and many others disagree. We believe that 'shamanism' usefully points to a human universal – the need to make sense of shifting consciousness – and the way in which this is accomplished, especially, but not always, among hunter-gatherers. The word need not obscure the diversity of worldwide shamanism any more than

'Christianity' obscures theological, ritual and social differences between the Russian Orthodox, Greek Orthodox, Roman Catholic and the many Protestant Churches. Nor does 'Christianity' mask the changes that have taken place in those traditions over the last two millennia. Too intense a focus on differences is in danger of losing sight of the wood.

Because I use 'shamanism' frequently in subsequent chapters, I give a brief outline of what I take the word to mean when I use it to refer to ritual specialists in hunter-gatherer societies. Our ultimate goal is the Upper Palaeolithic when all people were hunter-gatherers, so we need not consider broader manifestations of shamanism, sometimes alongside and integrated with other religions.

- Hunter-gatherer shamanism is fundamentally posited on a range of institutionalized altered states of consciousness.
- The visual, aural and somatic experiences of those states give rise to perceptions of an alternative reality that is frequently tiered (hunter-gatherers believe in spiritual realms above and below the world of daily life).
- People with special powers and skills, the shamans, are believed to have access to this alternative reality.
- The behaviour of the human nervous system in certain altered states creates the illusion of dissociation from one's body (less commonly understood in hunting and gathering shamanistic societies as possession by spirits).

Shamans use dissociation and other experiences of altered states of consciousness to achieve at least four ends. Shamans are believed to

- contact spirits and supernatural entities,
- heal the sick,
- control the movements and lives of animals, and
- change the weather.

These four functions of shamans, as well as their entrance into an altered state of consciousness, are believed to be facilitated by supernatural entities that include:

- variously conceived supernatural potency, or power, and
- animal-helpers and other categories of spirits that assist shamans and are associated with potency.

In listing these ten characteristics of hunter-gatherer shamanism I have excluded features that some writers consider important, if not essential, for the classification of a religion as shamanistic. I do not, for instance, link shamanism to mental illness of any sort, though some shamans may well suffer from epilepsy, schizophrenia, migraine and a range of other pathologies. Nor do I stipulate the number of religious practitioners that a shamanistic society may have; some societies have many, others very few. Some shamans wield political power, others do not. Nor do I stipulate any particular method or methods for the induction of altered states of consciousness. Still less do I attend to diverse concepts of the soul, spirit and subdivisions of the tiered cosmos.

In addition, I wish to emphasize the diversity of altered states of consciousness. If we focus, as some writers have done, too much on the word 'trance' and imagine 'altered states' to be restricted to deep, apparently unconscious conditions, we shall miss the fluidity of shamanistic experiences, and even fail altogether to notice the presence of altered states of consciousness in religious practices.[70] The Saami shamans of Lapland and northern Scandinavia, for instance, receive visions and experience out-of-body travel in a variety of states. These range from a 'light trance' in which shamans are still aware of their surroundings but in which spirit helpers none the less appear and in which they can heal the sick and perform divinations. The spirits also appear to Saami shamans in 'ordinary' dreams. Then in 'deep trance', the shamans lie as if dead; in this condition, their souls are believed to have left their bodies and to have travelled to the spirit realm. In all three states, shamans are believed to have direct contact with the spirit realm. The anthropologist Anna-Leena Siikala took Arnold Ludwig's study of altered states of consciousness as a starting point for her study of Siberian shamanism. She found that the so-called 'ecstatic experience' of shamans is far broader than is commonly imagined.[71] These instances may be readily multiplied around the world. It is therefore essential to keep the full spectrum (or, as I have presented it, spectra) of consciousness in mind when we consider religious expressions that fall under the rubric of shamanism.

Just which stages of altered consciousness are emphasized and highly valued depends on the social context of an expression of shamanism. Some societies, such as the Tukano, place considerable value on Stage 1 entoptic phenomena; others virtually ignore Stage 1 and seek out Stage 3 hallucinations. In whichever stage, and also in hypnagogic hallucinations, shamans learn to increase the vividness of their mental imagery and to control its content. Novices learn to do this by 'actively engaging and manipulating the visionary phenomena'.[72] Allied to this engagement is 'guided imagination', a form of imagination that goes beyond what we normally understand by the word: in

Siikala's phrase, it consists in 'setting aside the critical faculty and allowing emotions, fantasies and images to surface into awareness'. Amongst those 'fantasies and images' are beings and episodes from myths that the novice has been taught and that concern the 'making' of a shaman and the structure of the universe that he or she will traverse in spiritual travel; such images 'are frequently used…as a means of achieving sensations and experiences of the other world'.[73] The shamanistic mind is a complex interweaving of mental states, visions and emotions. We must beware of stipulating some naively simple altered state of consciousness as *the* shamanistic state of mind.

I am not alone in emphasizing the importance of making sense of altered states of consciousness in the genesis of religion. Peter Furst, then a research associate of the Harvard Botanical Museum, wrote, 'It is at least possible, though certainly not provable, that the practice of shamanism…may have involved from the first – that is, the very beginnings of religion itself – the psychedelic potential of the natural environment.'[74] Without stressing the use of psychotropic plants to alter consciousness, James McClenon sums up the matter: '[S]hamanism, the result of cultural adaptation to biologically based [altered states of consciousness], is the origin of all later religious forms.'[75] And Weston La Barre came to the same conclusion: '[A]ll the dissociative "altered states of consciousness" – hallucination, trance, possession, vision, sensory deprivation, and especially the REM-state dream – apart from their cultural contexts and symbolic content, are essentially the same psychic states found everywhere among mankind; …shamanism or direct contact with the supernatural in these states…is the *de facto* source of all revelation, and ultimately of all religions.'[76]

Before we proceed to examine the evidence from Upper Palaeolithic western Europe in the light of what this chapter has set forth about the human brain/mind and the genesis of religion, I describe two shamanistic societies that made rock art – the San of southern Africa and the Native American groups of California. In both cases we have a considerable amount of information on their beliefs. We do not have to indulge in the blind (and often wild) guessing that is frequently associated with the study of rock art. These two case studies widen our understanding of how the working of the brain can be harnessed in hunting and gathering societies. They also present further key features of shamanism that are relevant to Upper Palaeolithic art.

CHAPTER 5

Case Study 1:
Southern African San Rock Art

On 21 June 1874, a /Xam San man by the name of Diä!kwain opened a window on his people's beliefs and religion (Fig. 27). Looking at a copy of a rock painting, he said that it depicted a *!khwa-ka xorro*, and the people associated with it were *!khwa-ka !gi:ten*. The exclamation and slash marks in these words represent the 'clicks' characteristic of San languages, sounds that Westerners find extremely difficult to pronounce. I return to Diä!kwain's /Xam San words in a moment, for they encapsulate the very essence of San religion.

Diä!kwain was speaking to Wilhelm Heinrich Emmanuel Bleek, a German linguist who had gone to southern Africa to prepare a grammar of the Zulu language.[1] After a short spell in the British Colony of Natal, where the Zulu people live, Bleek moved to Cape Town, but before he did so he learned of the 'Bushmen', as the San were then called, who lurked in the fastnesses of the high Drakensberg Mountains. As a linguist, he was intrigued by what he heard about their language, but he was unable to make contact with them.

Soon after arriving in Cape Town he discovered that there were San men incarcerated in Cape Town gaols. They were not from the Drakensberg, but from the central parts of what was then the Colony of the Cape of Good Hope. They spoke of themselves as the /Xam, a name for which Bleek could find no translation. At once he abandoned his Zulu research and set about trying to learn

27 Diä!kwain, one of Wilhelm Bleek and Lucy Lloyd's /Xam San teachers. He holds his flute and hat.

the /Xam San language, but he soon found that prison conditions were not conducive to successful study. Later, he managed to persuade the Governor of the Cape Colony to release some of the prisoners into his care, and they moved to the Bleek home in a Cape Town suburb.

They made no attempt to escape. On the contrary, they welcomed the opportunity to teach Bleek their language and folklore. They realized that their way of life, their language, their religion, and indeed their whole population were threatened by colonial expansion. When their terms of penal servitude expired, some voluntarily remained on in the Bleek household to continue with their teaching; others arranged for their families to join them from their ravaged homeland (Pl. 7). They wanted the world to know the truth about them, their beliefs and the comparatively undisturbed lives they had lived up until a couple of decades before they were arrested for what the colonial authorities deemed crimes. None of the southern San communities still pursues the old way of life and speaks the old languages; they have been absorbed into other groups or marginalized.

To facilitate his work, Bleek devised a phonetic script that could cope with the difficult clicks and other strange sounds of the San languages. There are many San languages, most of them mutually unintelligible; we shall encounter some of them later. With his co-worker, Lucy Lloyd (who was also his sister-in-law), Bleek mastered the /Xam San language. While he devoted himself to the study of grammar and phonetics and started to compile a /Xam dictionary, Lloyd took down by dictation verbatim accounts of /Xam personal histories, daily life, rituals, beliefs and myths. These transcriptions are in the now-extinct /Xam language, for the most part together with line-by-line, literal English translations. All in all, Bleek and Lloyd amassed 12,000 pages of texts – an accomplishment that affords us unparalleled insights into the /Xam people's lives. Most of this material remains unpublished.[2] It has been indispensable in my work on San rock art.

The people with whom the Bleek family worked had all encountered the white settlers who were expanding farther and farther into their land and, as they advanced, destroying the vegetation of those semi-arid plains and devastating the vast herds of game that had formerly roamed freely. But their parents had lived there before the arrival of the whites, and they were repositories of their ancestral folklore. Both the people who came to Cape Town and their parents made stone artefacts, hunted with bows and arrows, and knew how to use deadly poison to compensate for the limited effectiveness of their puny arrows. They were a Stone Age, hunting and gathering community.

Possessors of potency

Bleek and Lloyd knew that the San made rock paintings (pictographs) and engravings (petroglyphs), though neither of them had been able to visit any of the sites where, in those days, recently made paintings glowed resplendently and engravings had been freshly cut into the rock (Pls 7, 8, 9).[3] They had seen a few rather poor copies, but these had not prepared them for the fine, full-colour ones that a geologist, George William Stow, was making. A batch of these reached Cape Town in 1875.[4] Bleek was delighted to see them. 'They are,' he wrote, 'of the greatest possible interest, and evince an infinitely higher taste, and a far greater artistic faculty, than our liveliest imagination could have anticipated.'[5] He added that their publication would 'effect a radical change in the ideas generally entertained with regard to the Bushmen and their mental condition.' The colonists' low opinion of the San was roundly contradicted by the unparalleled delicacy, minute detail, fine shading, accurate draughtsmanship, and infinite variety of their rock art.[6]

Bleek was quick to show Stow's copies and others made by Joseph Millerd Orpen, the British Resident in the eastern parts of the Cape Colony, to his /Xam teachers. He realized that he stood on the threshold of breathtaking insights into the mysteries of San religion: 'An inspection of these pictures, and their explanation by Bushmen has only commenced; but it promises some valuable results, and throws light upon many things hitherto unintelligible.'[7] Sadly, Bleek died later that year, so he was unable to seek further explanations. But Lucy Lloyd continued the work until her death in 1914. Thereafter, Bleek's daughter, Dorothea, took over (though without the benefit of /Xam teachers) until her death in 1948. Both of them recognized the importance of San rock art.

Amongst the 'many things hitherto unintelligible' were beliefs about *!gi:ten* (sing.: *!gi:xa*), one of the words that Diä!kwain used when he responded to copies of rock paintings that Orpen had made in the southern Drakensberg. The first syllable of the word, *!gi:*, means 'supernatural potency', a kind of 'electricity' that /Kaggen, the /Xam trickster-deity, gave to humankind and that resides in the great animals, especially the eland, the largest of all African antelope.[8] The second syllable, *xa*, means 'full of'. A *!gi:xa* was thus a person, male or female, who was filled with supernatural potency. Lloyd translated the word as 'sorcerer'. We must remember that she knew nothing about world shamanism, shifting human consciousness or the neurology of hallucinations; nor did she ever see /Xam *!gi:ten* performing their rituals. Today, *!gi:xa* is sometimes given as 'medicine man' or 'medicine woman', but I believe that the now inter-nationally used word 'shaman' is an appropriate translation and that it moreover highlights the universal aspects of the San *!gi:ten*.[9]

In the 1950s, some 75 years after Bleek's death, the Marshall family began serious, informed anthropological work amongst the Ju/'hoan (!Kung) San, who live in the Kalahari Desert of Namibia and Botswana, some 1,200 km (750 miles) to the north of the region where the /Xam had lived and speak a differ-ent language from that of the /Xam. After World War II, Laurence Marshall, an American industrialist, took his wife, Lorna, and his children, John and Elizabeth, to the Kalahari Desert of southern Africa. Lorna became a leading ethnographer;[10] Elizabeth wrote the sensitive and influential book *The Harmless People*;[11] John made a series of outstanding ethnographic films, including 'N/um Tchai', a startling record of the San 'medicine dance'.[12] The family has ever since been deeply involved in caring for the San in times of escalating change.[13]

Lorna Marshall and her daughter Elizabeth found that the Ju/'hoansi believed in the effectiveness of people whom they called *n/om k"ausi* (sing.: *n/om k"au*). Today we know that *n/om* is the Ju/'hoan equivalent of *!gi:*, and that *k"au* means 'possessor' or 'owner'. *N/om k"au* is thus the Ju/'hoan equiva-lent of the /Xam word *!gi:xa*. About half the men in any San camp are shamans and about a third of the women.

We can now turn to the cosmos in which San shamans operated – and in the Kalahari still do. The San believe in a spiritual realm that is inhabited by God, members of his family, his vast herds of animals, spirits of the dead who shoot 'arrows of sickness' into people, and strange monsters, including Diä!kwain's *!khwa-ka xorro*, to which I shall come in a moment. It is the task of San shamans to activate their supernatural potency, to cause it to 'boil' up their spines until it explodes in their heads and takes them off to the spirit realms – that is, they enter a state of trance at the far end of the intensified trajectory.

For the San, this sort of trans-cosmological travel takes place at a 'medicine', 'healing' or 'trance' dance, in dreams or at a 'special curing' when only a few people may be present.[14] The great dance is the central religious ritual of the San. All people – men, women, children and visitors – attend the dance. Everyone is healed by the laying on of hands, for people may have arrows of sickness in them without being aware of it. In the Kalahari today, shamanistic dances conform to a standardized pattern, though southern rock paintings suggest that there were a number of forms farther to the south (Fig. 28).

The present-day pattern is circular. In the middle is a fire, a source of potency. Around it, the women sit in a tight circle, shoulders touching. They sing and clap the intricate rhythms of 'medicine songs' that are believed to contain potency. Outside the women's circle, the men dance in another circle. They stamp the rhythm of the dance and accentuate it with the swishing sound of their dance rattles that they tie around their calves. They carry fly-whisks made from animal tails to flick away arrows of sickness; they use whisks only in the dance. While the dance proceeds, children play around, sometimes hilariously mimicking the shamans in trance. No one seems to find this mixing of what we may see as 'sacred' with 'secular' activities in any way disruptive or disrespectful.

28 Two southern African rock paintings of San 'medicine dances': (Below) Five men wearing antelope-eared caps dance in the bending-forward posture that is occasioned by painful contractions of their stomach muscles; they support their weight on dancing sticks. To the left and right women clap the rhythm of a powerful 'medicine song' that intensifies the men's altered state of consciousness.

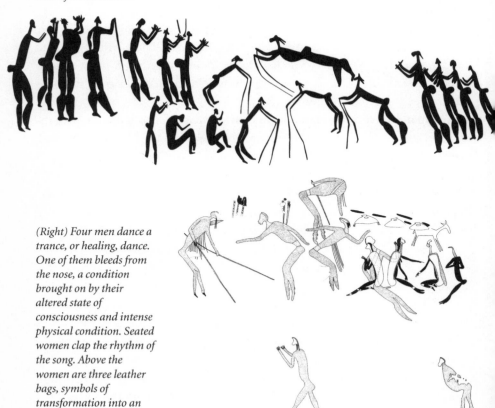

(Right) Four men dance a trance, or healing, dance. One of them bleeds from the nose, a condition brought on by their altered state of consciousness and intense physical condition. Seated women clap the rhythm of the song. Above the women are three leather bags, symbols of transformation into an animal.

The San do not use hallucinogens; instead they induce an altered state of consciousness by intense concentration, audio-driving, prolonged rhythmic movement, and hyperventilation (swift, shallow breathing). During the dance, female shamans sometimes rise from their circle around the fire and join the men with more graceful steps and gestures. Dances begin lightheartedly, but gather intensity until the night is filled with the sounds of the songs and the cries of the shamans. When large numbers of people are present, and especially if a sizeable animal has been killed, the San may dance a few times a week; at other times of the year, when the bands are smaller, they dance less frequently.

If such a dance floor were to be preserved as a fossilized land surface, it would pose problems for archaeologists of a distant future. They would find the central hearth, some scuffing of the sand where the women sat, the deep circular rut formed by the men's dancing feet, and all this would, perhaps, suggest some sort of formalized, ritual activity. But then they would find children's footprints weaving in and out of the pattern, and living areas close by. If these future archaeologists were to view their find in terms of strictly formalized 'religious' activity, they might well conclude that the pattern they had unearthed was no more than the remains of some, perhaps puzzling, secular living space.

Yet, for the San, the dance is unquestionably their most important religious ritual.[15] Certainly, for the shamans, this is a serious and often terrifying business. Sometimes, if they are unable to control their 'boiling' potency, they fall to the ground cataleptic, their bodies rigid. The /Xam people told Bleek and Lloyd that, when a shaman falls down trembling violently, 'lion's hair' grows on his back. Transformation into a lion or some other animal is a key part of San spiritual experience. 'Great' San shamans, who have learned to harness their potency, are able to move around laying hands on people so that they can draw sickness from them and into their own bodies; then, with a wild shriek, they expel it through a 'hole' in the back of the neck. The sickness then returns to the spirits of the dead, who sent it in the first place.

When San shamans enter a deep trance, they sometimes suffer a nasal haemorrhage (Fig. 28; Pl. 9). In the past, the /Xam smeared this blood on their patients in the belief that its odour would keep sickness at bay. Odour was believed to be a vehicle for the transference of potency.

In deep trance, the shamans' spirits are believed to leave their bodies through the top of the head. They may then travel to other parts of the country to find out how friends and relatives are faring, or they may go to God's house, where they plead for the lives of the sick.

In the Kalahari of today, San shamans may become famous, and people summon them from great distances to perform curings, but they do not enjoy any special material privileges. They hunt or gather plant foods along with everyone else. At best, they may expect a small gift for a successful healing; the same seems to have been the case for the nineteenth-century /Xam.

A significant change is, however, taking place in parts of the Kalahari where the land now belongs to farmers and the San are required to settle as serfs on the farms. The anthropologist Mathias Guenther[16] has found that, in such circumstances, there are fewer shamans, and they become itinerant, moving from farm to farm to perform their rituals. They then begin to emerge as political leaders who express the longings of the settled and impoverished communities. Thomas Dowson,[17] an archaeologist who has studied rock art in the Drakensberg Mountains of South Africa, argues that something similar happened when the people of that region were forced into an ever-decreasing area by the advance of both white and black farmers. This emergence of powerful shamans from what was until then an essentially egalitarian society is reflected in the art by the appearance of exceptionally large human figures with marked facial features and other distortions that point to their being shamans.[18]

Despite linguistic and other differences between the /Xam and the Ju/'hoansi, they and other San groups all share a common religious foundation.[19] At the centre of that foundation are relations with the spirit world, the great trance dance, and the activities of shamans. This point can hardly be overemphasized. The American anthropologist Megan Biesele, who has enjoyed a life-long association with the Ju/'hoansi San and speaks their language fluently, comments,

Though dreams may happen at any time, the central religious experiences of the Ju/'hoan life are consciously, and as a matter of course, approached through the avenue of trance. The trance dance involves everyone in society, those who enter trance and experience the power of the other world directly, and those to whom the benefits of the other world – healing and insight – are brought by the trancers.[20]

Revelation through trance is central, not just in the sense that it is part of 'religion', but in that all aspects of life are caught up in it. For the San, and for other shamanistic societies as well, shamanism is not an optional add-on to daily life: rather, it is the essence of all life. Biesele comments on this point:

Two other rituals involving dance and celebrating 'production' and 're-production', the boys' hunting initiation and the Eland dance for a girl at her first menstruation, have close connections to these main themes of the folklore and are also linked through them to the great curing [shamanistic] dance.[21]

Moreover, three important related concepts, *!aia* (trance), *n/om* (supernatural potency) and *n!ao* (a power related to the weather, childbirth and hunting), should be 'used as reference points in the analysis of Ju/'hoan folktales'.[22] Trance experience therefore permeates folktales and myth.[23] The same may be said of San rock art.

Images of another world

The Abbé Henri Breuil, the French authority on Upper Palaeolithic art whose influence in the first half of the twentieth century I noted in earlier chapters, visited South Africa on a number of occasions and indeed spent some of the years of World War II at the University of the Witwatersrand in Johannesburg. Largely, but not entirely, under his influence, San rock art came to be regarded as art for art's sake or as the trappings of hunting magic: the then-current interpretations of Upper Palaeolithic art were uncritically imported into southern Africa. He was also committed to finding evidence for early European penetration into the African continent. For him, Europe was the cradle of art. His most enduring endeavour in his pursuit of diffusion from Europe was his identification of an image in Namibia as depicting a young woman of Minoan or Cretan origin. He thus initiated the misleading myth of the 'White Lady of the Brandberg'. Today we know that even a cursory examination reveals that the figure is male and that, fine though it is, it is simply an ordinary San rock painting.

But, chiefly, researchers thought of southern African rock art as simple pictures of a simple life-style made by simple, childlike people. Neither Breuil nor any of the later South African workers paid much attention to the Bleek and Lloyd records or to those that were coming to hand from the Kalahari. In the 1870s, Bleek had concluded that San rock art was 'a truly artistic expression of the ideas that most deeply moved the Bushman mind, and filled it with religious feelings'.[24] This doughty statement challenged head-on the colonial view that the San had no religion whatsoever, indeed that they were mentally so stunted that they could not conceive of a god in the Christian sense of the word. But Bleek's insight was smothered by colonial notions of the San as treacherous, primitive people who had no sensitivity and certainly no spiritual experiences.

The situation changed in the late 1960s and the 1970s when some South African researchers turned to the ignored Bleek and Lloyd Collection and began to take an interest in the research being conducted by the Marshall family in the Kalahari.[25] At first, I found all this San ethnography impenetrable: it was not easy to see how I could relate it to the rock art images.

Then there was a breakthrough. I realized that the ethnography – the San myths and their own explanations of specific images – did not explain the art in any direct sense. Even San people's comments on specific rock paintings, such as the invaluable ones that Orpen[26] garnered, did not provide the simple answers for which researchers were hoping. On the contrary, both the ethnography and the art require explanation because *both* are permeated and structured by a set of metaphors and by San notions of the cosmos, which I discuss in detail shortly. Much of the painted and engraved imagery, even that which appears most 'realistic', is shot through with these metaphors and shows signs of having been 'processed' by the human mind as it shifted back and forth along the spectrum of consciousness.[27] The same metaphors necessarily structured the explanations of images that San people provided. The San explained the images in their own terms, not in the language of anthropologists.

To illustrate how metaphor, mind, image, society and cosmos coalesce – a central theme of this book – I describe the San cosmos and spiritual realms. I argue that, at this fundamental level, the working of the universal human nervous system is a principal informing agency. The relevance of this discussion to west European Upper Palaeolithic art will become increasingly apparent as I distinguish between experiences that derive from the human nervous system and those that are culturally contributed and are therefore specific to the San.

A cosmos in the brain

San religion is built around belief in a tiered universe. As do other shamanistic peoples throughout the world, the San believe in a realm above and another below the surface of the world on which they live.

Concepts of a tiered universe are, of course, not restricted to shamanistic religions. Heaven above, Hell below, and the level of anxious humanity in between appear in one form or another across the globe. Why should this be so? In the materiality of daily life there is, after all, no evidence whatsoever of hidden spiritual realms above and below. The answer to this question is, I argue, to be found in a set of widely reported mental experiences. These reports come not only from laboratory experiments but also from an extremely broad range of shamanistic (and other) societies. The experiences fall into two categories: those that are taken to relate to an underworld, and those that are interpreted as relating to a realm in the sky above (Fig. 29).

In discussing the underworld, we may group underground and underwater experiences. In Chapter 4, I described the sensation of passing through a vortex, or tunnel, as subjects move along the intensified spectrum and into Stage 3 of deeply altered consciousness. Tunnel experiences also occur in dreams and near-death experiences. Often there is a bright light at the end of the tunnel. As we saw, Siegel[28] notes that the first iconic images appear on the sides of this enclosing vortex. Here, I suggest, is the reason why so many peoples around the world believe in passing underground to a subterranean realm. The notion has its origin in altered states of consciousness and then becomes part of socially transmitted culture so that even those who have never experienced the far end of the intensified trajectory accept the beliefs.

At the same time, subjects often experience sensations of inhibited breathing, distorted vision, sounds in the ears, difficulty in moving, weightlessness, and a sense of being in another world. These sensations are frequently interpreted as being underwater. Both underground and underwater travel are widely reported shamanistic experiences.[29]

It is important to remember that these experiences are the result of the way in which the human brain and nervous system are neurologically constructed

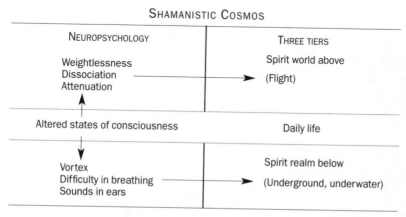

29 *The tiered shamanistic cosmos and its generation in altered states of consciousness. Beliefs in upper and subterranean realms derive from the 'wiring' and functioning of the human brain.*

and the ways in which they operate electro-chemically in altered states of consciousness. To this extent, the experiences are universal. The *precise* ways in which they are rationalized are culturally situated and hence differ in some ways from society to society: some people speak of entering caves, others of following the roots of a tree, and still others of going down animal burrows, rather like Alice. Similarly, and depending to some extent on the environment in which people live, others speak of diving into the sea or deep pools.

Both underwater and underground experiences seem to be reflected in Coleridge's poem 'Kubla Khan: or, A Vision in a Dream'. Having taken opium as an anodyne, the poet fell into 'a profound sleep, at least of the external senses', during which time he experienced vivid imagery. Having been interrupted in the urgent task of writing down his recollections of his vision by the now-famous man from Porlock, he found he could later remember little 'with the exception of some eight or ten scattered lines and images'. Out of these he fashioned 'Kubla Khan', including the following lines from near the beginning of the poem:

> Where Alph, the sacred river, ran
> Through caverns measureless to man
> Down to a sunless sea.[30]

However they are interpreted, the fundamental sensations of being underground or underwater remain universal: they are the most obvious, most logical explanations for the effects created by the behaviour of the nervous system in altered states. An 'introcosm' is projected onto the material world to create a cosmology.

We can now turn to records of San beliefs to see, in their own words, how they respond to the sensations I have described.

Both underground and underwater experiences are evident in an account of a shamanistic journey that K"au Giraffe, a Ju/'hoan San shaman, gave Megan Biesele.[31] He began by saying that his 'protector' (or 'animal helper') and Kaoxa (God) came and 'took' him.

We travelled until we came to a wide body of water…Kaoxa made the waters climb, and I lay my body in the direction they were flowing. My feet were behind, and my head was in front…Then I entered the stream and began to move forward…My sides were pressed by pieces of metal. Metal things fastened to my sides. And in this way I travelled forward, my friend…And the spirits were singing.

After reaching the spirit world, Kaoxa taught K"au how to dance and told him that his protector, the Giraffe, would give him potency. Then, suddenly, K"au finds himself once more underwater:

But I was under water! I was gasping for breath, I called out, 'Don't kill me! Why are you killing me?' My protector answered, 'If you cry out like that, I'm going to make you drink. Today I'm going to make you drink water…' The two of us struggled until we were tired. We danced and argued and I fought the water for a long, long time…

Then, my friend, my protector spoke to me, saying that I would be able to cure. He said that I would stand up and trance. He told me that I would trance. And the trancing he was talking about, my friend – I was already doing it… Then my protector told me that I would enter the earth. That I would travel far through the earth and then emerge at another place.[32]

Here the underground and underwater experiences are mixed. But we can see how the San understand the universal experiences of altered states. Struggle, fear, the idea of death, gasping for breath, constricting pressure on the sides of the body, they are all present.

Another type of sensation also derives from the structure and functioning of the human nervous system. Subjects experience weightlessness and a sensation of rising up that is often associated with attenuation. They feel that they are looking down on their surroundings and that their limbs and bodies are exceedingly long. Throughout the world, these experiences are, understandably enough, rationalized as floating and flying. The most obvious explanation of these sensations is that the subject is flying through the air. Shamanistic flight is, of course, as widely reported as underground journeys.[33]

As with the underground experience, travel through the sky also appears in K"au Giraffe's account. He spoke of ascending to the sky:

When we emerged [from the ground], we began to climb the thread – it was the thread of the sky! Yes, my friend. Now up there in the sky, the people up there, the spirits, the dead people up there, they sang for me so I can dance.[34]

Taken together the neurologically generated experiences of travelling underground and flying are, I argue, the origin of notions of a tiered cosmos. This is, I believe, the best explanation for so universally held beliefs that have no relation to the material experience of daily life. Such beliefs were not inferred from observations of the natural environment. Nor did they easily and swiftly diffuse from a single geographically located origin because they made excellent sense of the world in which people lived. Rather, they are part of the in-built experiences of the full spectrum of human consciousness.

Both underground and flying experiences are represented in San rock art. A few instances must now suffice to show how San cosmos and art are inseparable.[35]

Cosmos and art

Figure 30 shows a deep fold, or crack, in the rock face that has been smeared with black paint. Rising up out of the fold and the paint are seven figures; it is as if the paint is acting as a solvent that makes the crack in the rock face more permeable. The best preserved, on the left, has a clear eland head; four smaller figures comprise only necks and heads, the rest of their bodies being apparently 'behind' the rock face. The nasal blood of trance falls from one of the heads. Close to the head of the eland-figure is a bunch of at least ten flywhisks, far more than one would expect to see together in daily San life. Surrounding the eland-figure are eight fish, two eels and two turtles. The painter here has managed to suggest both underground and underwater experiences: the figures rise from inside the rock, that is, from underground, and they are associated with underwater creatures.[36] Indeed, water often seeps through cracks as well as through joint and bedding planes in the walls of rock shelters.

These are by no means the only paintings that seem to emerge from behind the rock face: animals, people and 'monsters' all do so. Then there are painted lines that represent the 'threads of light' that San shamans say they climb when they go up to God's house in the sky.[37] Often painted in red and fringed with tiny white dots, these 'threads' appear to weave in and out of the rock face. It seems that the walls of rock shelters were thought of as a 'veil' suspended between

30 A southern African San rock painting showing figures emerging from a deep cleft in the rock face that has been smeared with black paint. The fish, eels and turtles symbolize the 'underwater' experience of shamans in an altered state of consciousness. The unrealistically large bunch of flywhisks relates to the trance, or healing, dance. One of the small human heads emerging on the right bleeds from the nose, an indication of trance states.

this world and the spirit realm. Shamans passed through this 'veil', sometimes following the painted 'threads of light', and, on their return, brought with them revelations of what was happening in the world beyond. We do not have any evidence to suggest that *only* shamans painted, but it seems likely that it was the shamans themselves who painted images coming through into the world of the living and visions of the transformations they experienced in the spirit world.[38] Nor do I imply that shamans painted while in trance; the images are too delicate, too fine to have been executed by the trembling hand of a trancer. Rather, San shamans were manifesting, or re-creating – perhaps re-living – their experiences of the supernatural realm while in an alert state.

In this way, the painters actualized the tiered cosmos and their journeys through it. I argue that the three levels were not merely conceptual: they were manifest in the rock shelters. The painted images of another world made sense because of their location on the 'veil', the interface between materiality and spirituality. The rock wall on which paintings were placed was not a *tabula rasa* but part of the images; in some ways, it was the support that made sense of the images. Art and cosmos united in a mutual statement about the complex nature of reality. The walls of the shelters thus became gateways that afforded access to realms that ordinary people could not visit – but they could glimpse what it was like in that realm as painted images filtered through and shamans, such as K"au Giraffe, described their journeys.

The next set of images (Fig. 31) includes what Diä!kwain called a *!khwa-ka xorro*.[39] Literally translated, this phrase means 'large animal (*xorro*) of the rain (*!khwa*)'. The /Xam San spoke of the rain as if it were an animal. A rain-bull was the thunderstorm that roared and destroyed the people's huts; the rain-cow was the gentle, soaking rain. The columns of rain that fall from beneath a thunderstorm were called the 'rain's legs', and the rain was said to walk across the land on its legs. Shamans of the rain (*!khwa-a !gi:ten*) were believed to catch a rain-animal beneath the surface of a waterhole and to lead it through the sky to the territories of their own people. There they cut and killed it so that its blood and milk (if it was female) would fall as rain. The parched ground would thus be renewed, sweet grass would spring up, and herds of antelope would be attracted. //Kabbo, one of Bleek and Lloyd's teachers who was himself a rain-shaman, expressed the joy of long-awaited rain:

I will cut a she-rain which has milk, I will milk her, then she will rain softly on the ground, so that it is wet deep down in the middle. Then the bushes will sprout and become nicely green, so that the springbok come galloping...they will feel that they

31 A southern African rock painting of a rain-animal surrounded by transformed, winged San shamans. Note the number of zigzags, probably representations of entoptic phenomena.

can leap about, because the she-rain has fallen everywhere for she means to make all places wet.[40]

Surrounding the rain-animal in Figure 31 are six highly transformed shamans. The central one has two flywhisks protruding from its neck. It and others appear to have wings, the individual feathers being painted. 'Underwater' is thus represented by the rain-animal, which was captured beneath the surface of a waterhole, and 'flying' is represented by the wings and feathers. The human figures and the rain-animal are also intimately associated with zigzags, as one would not be surprised to find in Stage 3 visions. It will be recalled that, in Stage 3, geometric entoptic imagery is peripheral to, or integrated with, iconic imagery (Chapter 4). Like so many other San rock paintings and engravings, these images provide a vivid glimpse of the inner experiences of long-dead shamans. Even today, they exercise an uncanny, fascinating impact on viewers.

The trans-cosmological leading of a rain-animal from beneath the water and up into the sky is explicitly shown in Figure 32. A rain-animal is walking

32 A San rock painting depicting a rain-animal making its way from underwater (the fish to the right) to the sky (the birds on the left). Eventually shamans of the rain will, in their trance hallucinations, kill it so that its blood will fall as rain.

along a line that extends horizontally (the gap in the line to the left may be a result of fading). On the right, whence the rain-animal comes, is a shoal of fish; on the left, where the rain-animal is heading, is a flight of birds. The tiered cosmos and the mediation of that cosmos by the way in which the shamans of the rain cause the rain-animal to move from below to above is graphically depicted by representing creatures (fish and birds) that are associated with sensations wired into the human nervous system and triggered by certain altered states of consciousness.

The imagery that I have so far introduced derived from the far end of the intensified trajectory of altered consciousness (though some of it is also experienced in dreaming). We have thus been dealing with the imagery of what I called Stage 3. We can now turn to the more subtle, more arcane, imagery of Stages 1 and 2.

Construing universals

I have pointed out that the San people of southern Africa made both rock paintings and engravings. The paintings tend to be concentrated in the more mountainous edge of the escarpment that separates the interior plateau from the coastal lowlands. As we have seen, they are found in shallow rock shelters that were also living sites. There are very few deep limestone caves in southern Africa (far fewer than in western Europe), and those few that do exist seem not to have been used by the San. The engravings, on the other hand, tend to be found on the open plains of the central plateau. They were executed on flat rocks and boulders on low rises and on rock surfaces, including glacial pavements, along river beds.

Perhaps the most interesting distinction between southern African paintings and engravings is that the engravers seem to have taken far more interest in the luminous, geometric mental imagery of Stage 1 than did the painters.[41] When the painters did explore entoptic phenomena they tended to incorporate them in iconic images – which suggests that they were in fact dealing with the residual entoptic imagery of Stage 3 (Fig. 31).

Sometimes among the engravings one finds images that conform closely to the kinds of entoptic phenomena established by laboratory research (Fig. 33). At other times, the zigzags and other geometric forms are associated with images of animals. Both isolated and integrated entoptic

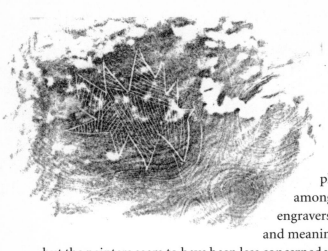

33 An old copy made by the (no longer practised) rubbing technique of a southern African rock engraving of an entoptic phenomenon. The pointed shape is comparable to that experienced by migraine sufferers.

phenomena are common amongst engravings. The engravers seem to have placed value and meaning on entoptic phenomena, but the painters seem to have been less concerned with them. We do not know why there was this difference in emphasis between painters and engravers.

Stage 2, construal of an entoptic form as an object, is of particular interest among the paintings, for it shows how San shamans grappled with and made sense of neurological universals. Figures 34–39 illustrate how the San process of construal took place in relation to a specific entoptic phenomenon.[42]

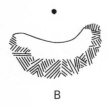

On the left are three variations of the navicular (boat-shaped) entoptic phenomenon (A–C), sometimes known as the 'fortification illusion'; its form has been established by laboratory research.[43] This is the scotoma frequently experienced by migraine sufferers.[44] In its more elaborate form, this percept comprises two elements: an outer arc characterized by iridescent flickering bars of light or zigzags, and, within the arc, a lunate area of invisibility – a 'black hole' that obliterates veridical imagery. Beyond the area of invisibility is the centre of vision, marked by the dots in Figures 34 A–C. This is one of the mental images that San shamans (and, in certain circumstances, others as well) would have 'seen'. We know without a shadow of doubt that the San frequently entered trance states; moreover, we can be sure that they had the neurological potential to see the same entoptic phenomena as every one else. But how did they understand, or construe, them?

A

B

C

34 Three versions of the navicular entoptic phenomenon, as established by Western laboratory research.

35 A–C Three fairly simple San rock paintings of the same entoptic phenomenon. In the past, these paintings were mistaken for depictions of boats bringing ancient Western mariners to southern Africa.

A

Figure 35 shows what I call 'minimally construed' versions, as they appear in southern African rock art: these rock paintings are formally close to the 'fortification illusion', as established by laboratory research. In the past, these and similar paintings were mistaken for depictions of boats. As with the engraved entoptic phenomena, we do not know what the San understood them to mean.

B

Figure 36 shows a more elaborate construal of the related entoptic phenomenon that appears as shimmering, nested U-shapes. A set of five catenary curves, it depicts honeycombs as they appear in the wild – often, it should be added, in rock shelters.[45] The painter has even added minutely drawn bees in

C

red, each with a pair of white wings. Some researchers have taken such paintings to be unproblematic depictions of things in the real world and assumed that the San painted them because they liked honey – which indeed they still do. But we have already seen enough of San rock art to doubt simple, 'narrative' interpretations. Two strands of evidence – neuropsychological and ethnographic – explain why some rock painters construed their navicular visions in this way.

First, and as I have pointed out, altered states cause all the senses, not just sight, to hallucinate. A common aural experience is a buzzing or humming sound.[46] Like entoptic phenomena themselves, such aural experiences are open to a variety of construals. The Amahuaca shamans of the Amazon Basin, for example, interpret the humming sound they experience while in trance as the calls of frogs, crickets and cicadas;[47] other people construe it as wind, trickling water or rain.[48] In southern Africa it seems that some San linked this aural experience to their simultaneous, shimmering visual hallucinations of navicular entoptic phenomena, and thus believed that they were both seeing and hearing bees swarming over honeycombs.

36 Rock painting of the navicular entoptic phenomenon construed as honeycombs with bees. In the wild southern African honeycombs take this form.

This view is supported by the ethnographic evidential strand which, I soon found, offers a clue as to the meaning that these painted images may have held for San viewers. The Ju/'hoansi San consider bees to be messengers of God and to have a great deal of potency.[49] They like to dance when the bees are swarming because they believe that they can harness 'bee potency'. They also have a 'medicine', or trance dance, song called 'Honey'. They do not, of course, actually dance in a swarm of bees, but it is easy to understand how the sight and sound of a glittering, insistently humming swarm could not only be associated with an altered state of consciousness but could, moreover, contribute to conditions that induce or intensify an altered state. I therefore argue that some shaman-artists construed their combined visual and aural experiences as visions of powerful and emotionally charged symbols – bees and honey. The neuropsychological and ethnographic strands thus combine with features of the art itself to suggest a component of San shamanistic belief and practice that could not be ascertained from one strand only.

Figure 37 takes us even further into the spiritual experiences of the San and shows another way of construing the navicular entoptic phenomenon. We now need to distinguish more clearly between the flickering outer arc and the inner area of invisibility of the navicular entoptic phenomenon. Here we see how some shaman-artists construed the outer arc: arranged clockwise around the arc are six antelope heads facing the viewer, the profiles of two eland, and twelve antelope legs. Within the curve are the extremely faded remains of some earlier, now indecipherable, images and a cloud of white dots. The general form of this painting parallels the simpler forms shown in Figures 35 A–C, but the flickering zigzag or denticulate margins have been replaced by a 'fringe' of antelope legs and other elements.

This construal may have been suggested to the painters by what must have been a fairly common sight, one that is, I believe, depicted in the elegant painting shown in Figure 38. Six buck are massed one behind the other; all 24 legs of the six buck are shown. For those shamans who were believed to have the

37 *The navicular entoptic phenomenon. Here the flickering outer curve has been construed as flashing antelope legs. Eland emerge from the form. At the top, some eland heads are shown facing the viewer.*

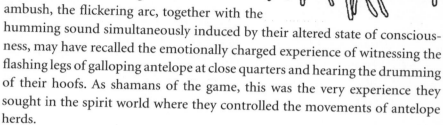

38 A San rock painting of six small antelope. The way in which their legs are painted helps to clarify the rock painting in Fig. 37.

power to guide antelope herds towards the waiting hunters' ambush, the flickering arc, together with the humming sound simultaneously induced by their altered state of consciousness, may have recalled the emotionally charged experience of witnessing the flashing legs of galloping antelope at close quarters and hearing the drumming of their hoofs. As shamans of the game, this was the very experience they sought in the spirit world where they controlled the movements of antelope herds.

For a final example of how the navicular entoptic phenomenon was construed, I turn to Figure 39. It links up with what I have already said about the 'veil'. Here we have a red and white navicular form, on the outer edge of which are five white zigzags. In this painting, a San shaman-artist has closely approached Western laboratory subjects' representations of the flickering arc as zigzags. Two therianthropic (part-animal and part-human) figures emerge from the inner arc and so recall the figures emerging from the deep crack in the rock in Figure 30. One is covered with white dots, some of which spill over beyond the outline of its body. Emerging from the backs of both therianthropes are flywhisks, again more than one would expect to see in real life.

Disappearance into an area of invisibility and transformation into an animal are associated with entry into the vortex that leads to deep trance. In a nineteenth-century San myth,[50] /Kaggen, himself a shaman, descended three times into the ground and emerged at a different place each time. After the third leg of his subterranean journey, he came up transformed into a large bull eland.

39 A complex construal of the navicular entoptic phenomenon. Note the peripheral zigzags and the two transformed figures emerging from the area of invisibility.

It seems that some painters took the area of invisibility within the arc of the navicular entoptic phenomenon to be an entrance into the spirit world and a gateway to transformation; in this way the area of invisibility paralleled the vortex.

Again, art, cosmos and spiritual experience coalesced. The San fused the 'abstract' experiences of altered states with the materiality of the world in which they lived. Perhaps most strikingly, this fusion is seen in the way in which the painted 'threads of light' are identical in widely separated rock shelters: the uniformity of the width of the line and the spacing of the white dots is so remarkable that some researchers have felt that all the depictions of the line must have been made by a single painter, though we know that this cannot have been so. It is as if there is only one 'thread' that links all the shelters: the shamans thus constituted a network of extra-corporeal travel that united distant communities and that was manifest in the people's living places.

Now we may ask: if the rock face had significance as the tangible interface between two realms, what of the paint that was placed on it and how was paint-making and painting-making linked to painting-viewing?

Technology, potency and social relations

Today, it is easy to think of paint as a merely technical substance, something that one purchases at a hardware store. But I have already hinted that, for the San, paint had special powers in that it could 'dissolve' the rock face and allow images of the other world to slip through. That being so, it is not surprising to find that the manufacture of paint was but one part of a complex ritual chain that included the making and viewing of images. Image-making was not an isolated event.

To show how this chain of operations was socially situated, I identify four stages in the 'social production and consumption' of San rock art images.[51] In doing so, I take up ideas developed by André Leroi-Gourhan, who early in his career coined the term *chaîn opératoire* in discussions of the manufacture of stone artefacts; other, more recent, researchers have taken his ideas further.[52] We need to situate technology in a social matrix. Artefacts, including rock art images, are made in a social arena. That is to say, individual people drew on a known 'chain of operations', not in isolation, but in the flux of social relations, and, as Max Raphael would have pointed out, those relations were frequently conflictual.

STAGE 1: ACQUISITION OF IMAGERY

There were at least four contexts in which San shamans acquired insights into the spiritual world:
- the trance dance,
- special curing rituals,
- viewing rock art, and
- dreams.

Each of these contexts was associated with two related oppositions that people could exploit to create or sustain social and political divisions:
- society : the individual
- socially sanctioned visions : novel, unexpected visions that altered states of consciousness inevitably produce

It is in these oppositions that we see a principle that will assume prominence in later chapters: the unavoidable process of coming to terms with the full spectrum of human consciousness has to be agreed on by most members of a community; without such agreement, ordinary life is impossible. Further, the ways in which only certain people are allowed to experience the far end of the intensified trajectory are socially governed.

During a San trance dance, everyone agrees that the shamans will receive revelations, travel to other parts of the country, and move into the spiritual levels of the cosmos. This agreement sets the shamans apart from ordinary people who do not have their abilities. Society comprises those who 'see' and those who do not 'see' – 'seers' and 'receivers'. This distinction tends to be reinforced by the way in which shamans share visions. During the course of a dance, one shaman may draw the others' attention to what he or she can see, perhaps a number of spirit-eland standing in the semi-darkness beyond the light of the fire. The others look in the direction indicated, and then they too see the same visions. There is thus a sharing of insights that makes for commonality of visions and a bond of shared experiences among shamans.

At the same time, there are forces pulling in the opposite direction. No matter how powerful the informing social influences may be, the human brain in an altered state of consciousness always produces novel, or aberrant, hallucinations. In all societies, most people ignore these sports of the human nervous system because they are seeking specific kinds of visions that will make them feel part of a social group. But some people seize on hallucinatory novelties and then present them to others as specially privileged insights that set them above others or, more agonistically, challenge the whole social structure. In this way, the tension between socialized and idiosyncratic mental imagery presented San shaman-artists with an opportunity to establish their social positions by manipulating, within socially accepted parameters, certain classes of mental imagery. Moreover, it seems certain that this negotiation of identity was facilitated by painted imagery: the powerful re-creations of visions could not be gainsaid.

The second context in which San shamans achieve insights is known as a special curing and is conducted for an individual who is especially ill. One or two shamans may enter trance without the women's singing and clapping. Under these circumstances, a shaman may 'see' into the body of a patient and discern the cause of illness – perhaps an arrow of sickness. Some shamans become renowned for their special curing abilities and may be summoned from afar to cure a sick person. Their special abilities set them apart from other shamans.

The third context, the viewing of rock art, probably also gave shamans insights which could become part of their own experiences in altered states. People tend to hallucinate what they expect to hallucinate. There was, therefore, probably a recursivity between rock art images and visions: visions were painted on the rock walls, and then these paintings prompted people to see similar visions. As a result, rock art probably exercised a conservative, stabilizing effect on the range of mental imagery that shamans experienced.

The role of individual shamans is also evident in the ways that they understand dreams, the fourth and most personal of all contexts in which they obtain visions. New medicine songs may be received in dreams and passed on to other shamans; even a non-shaman may receive a medicine song and pass it on to a shaman who will be able to use it.[53] One remarkable group of images shows two sleeping eland, each

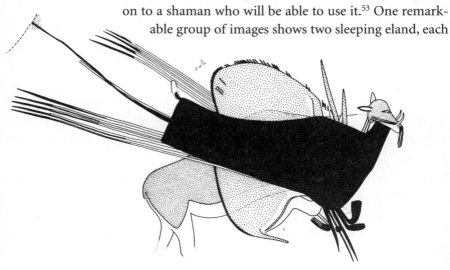

apparently superimposed by a hunting bag transformed into a flying creature (Fig. 40).[54] The sleeping eland represent dreaming shamans and the rest of the imagery shows the transformations they experienced. Interestingly, one of Bleek's San teachers was nicknamed '//Kabbo', the /Xam word for 'dream'. He was a !gi:xa and made rain while in a 'dream'.

STAGE 2: THE MANUFACTURE OF PAINT

In the early 1930s, Mapote, a Sotho man who, at the end of the nineteenth century, had learned to paint with San in their rock shelters, explained to Marion How, wife of a district commissioner in Lesotho, how the San made paint.[55] It was a remarkable and illuminating occasion. First, he said that San painters greatly desired a special type of red haematite pigment known as *qhang qhang*: it glistened and sparkled and could be found only in the high basalt mountains. Painters therefore had to undertake a 'pilgrimage' to the towering heights of the Drakensberg if they wished to use this pigment. The Sotho people themselves believed that it would protect them from lightning. Mapote said that a woman had to heat the *qhang qhang* out of doors at full moon until it was red hot. It was then ground between two stones until it was a fine powder. The production of red pigment was thus, at least at certain times, a collective enterprise. As men and women collaborated in the trance dance, so too did they co-operate in the making of paint.

Then the ground *qhang qhang* was mixed with a highly significant medium – the blood of a freshly killed eland. *Qhang qhang*, said Mapote, was the only pigment mixed with eland blood. As How points out, this suggests that certain kinds of painting took place only after a successful eland hunt. In the early 1980s, an old woman of San descent, who was living just south of the Drakensberg and whose father had been a shaman-artist, explained that, on certain occasions, a young girl accompanied the San hunters.[56] By simply 'pointing' at an eland the girl could 'hypnotize' it and lead it back to the camp. The old woman explained that eland blood contained potency and that it was therefore mixed with the paint. Her words and actions suggested that a painting made with eland blood was a kind of reservoir of potency. As we watched,

40 (Opposite) A sleeping, curled-up eland, one of a pair of almost identical images painted next to one another. Superimposed on it is a hunting bag (made of antelope skin) transformed into an animal-headed being. The eland's ears and horns are visible above its shoulder hump back. The blood of trance falls from its nose. Note the 'streamers' that are painted to represent sectioned, link-shaft arrows. Three flywhisks, men's accoutrements of the trance dance, and a digging stick weighted with a bored stone (used by women to call up spirits) emerge from the creature's chest.

she danced in the rock shelter and turned to the paintings that her father had made so long ago. She lifted her hands and said that power would flow into her. Clearly, for the San, rock paintings were far more than mere pictures.

STAGE 3: THE MAKING OF ROCK PAINTINGS

The delicate workmanship and sureness of line that are evident everywhere in southern Africa suggest that it is unlikely that all shamans painted. At some times and in some places, the making of rock paintings may have bestowed a privileged status on those who possessed the necessary skills.[57] As I have pointed out, it does not seem likely that shamans painted while in deep trance. More probably, they painted while in a 'normal' state of consciousness, recalling their vivid glimpses of the spirit world and making power-filled images of those visions. Probably, too, the very act of painting assisted in the recall, recreation and reification of otherwise transient glimpses of spiritual things: painters are not automatic photocopying machines who exactly reproduce mental images. Like Wordsworth's observation on poetry, San rock art should be seen as powerful emotion recollected in tranquillity.

Unfortunately, we do not know if this fixing of visions on the 'veil' was accompanied by rituals or how a shaman-artist prepared him- or herself for the task. Perhaps, like the dance in which visions were acquired, this fixing of visions was also considered an appropriate occasion for the singing of medicine songs to strengthen the shamans in their work. Whatever the case, it seems unlikely that San painters were anything like the detached ascetics of the Western Romantic fiction.

STAGE 4: THE USE OF SAN ROCK PAINTINGS

Once made, many San images continued to perform significant functions, but there is unfortunately little ethnographic information on what precisely happened to these potent images after they had been made.

As we have seen, the old woman who lived south of the Drakensberg said that people were able to draw potency from some of the images. She also said that, if a 'good' person placed his or her hand on a depiction of an eland, the potency locked up in the painting would flow into that person, thus giving him or her special powers. To demonstrate how this was done, she arranged my fingers so that my entire hand was on a depiction of an eland. As she did so, she cautioned that, if a 'bad' person did this, his or her hand would adhere to the rock and the person would eventually waste away and die.

The importance of touching, and not merely looking at, rock paintings is confirmed by patches of paint that were placed on the walls and ceilings of rock shelters and then rubbed smooth.[58] It is not clear what the patches were rubbed with, but the smoothness of the rock, particularly in the centre of the patches, is often easily discerned. Numerous paintings of human figures and animals have also been touched and the paint smeared to create blurred 'haloes' around the images. Similarly, the making of positive handprints was probably closely associated with ritual touching of the rock rather than with the making of 'pictures' of hands.[59] San paintings were not merely looked at: they were also touched.

As time went by, certain rock shelters acquired more and more potency as the images piled up, one on top of another; the paintings in a rock shelter were never 'complete'. The most densely painted rock shelters were probably regarded as places of exceptional personal or group power.[60] Historical records suggest that certain large, strikingly painted rock shelters were associated with specific San 'chiefs' who began to emerge during the final decades of their traditional way of life.[61]

When viewed or touched by people from within a San community, painted images would have reinforced or challenged social relations between San individuals and various groups: one had either been to the spirit world or one had not; some people could touch the images; for others, it would have been prudent to refrain from touching them. When people from outside the San community were present, for whatever reasons, images that would otherwise have been divisive may, for the San, have performed a unifying role in the face of the contestation implied by the outsiders. That is why it is necessary always to situate the images in the production-consumption 'chain of operations' as precisely as possible. One must not isolate the images from the 'chain' and treat them as no more than cyphers of a code waiting to be cracked.

Many meanings

So far I may have given the impression that *all* San images 'said' the same thing and that the shamanistic view of the making and using of San rock art is monolithic and insensitive to nuances of meaning. Nothing could be further from the truth.

Paintings of eland, for example, referred also to the Eland Bull Dance that is performed at a girl's first menstruation, to a boy's first-kill rituals during which he is scarified with eland fat, and to marriage ceremonies when a bride is anointed with eland fat.[62] Generally, eland fat symbolized all that is good, fertile and protecting. The eland as a symbol was therefore multi-faceted. But, if one seeks painted contexts that explicitly depict, or otherwise explicitly refer to, these other connotations of eland, one finds few, if any. Most of the images refer explicitly, in one way or another, to the spirit world. They are, after all, inscribed on the 'veil' between the material and the spiritual realms. Still, it seem likely that the other resonances of the eland were present as a penumbra that lent richness and extra power to the images.[63] San rock art therefore had many meanings and referred allusively to varied ritual contexts and human beings' place in the cosmos. Nevertheless, the polysemy of the art was not diffuse and completely untrammelled: the images were part of, and built into, the tiered cosmos. They spoke primarily of that cosmos and the special people who had the ability to traverse it. The making and viewing of them was woven into the shifting social fabric of San communities.

Above all, I have tried to spell out some of the complexity of San image-making. I began with the ways in which San people (indeed, all people) made sense of the functioning of the human nervous system in its spectrum of states of consciousness and, in doing so, constructed a tiered cosmos. Access to the spiritual levels of this cosmos was restricted to those who had mastered the techniques of what the San still call *!aia*, and what we understand as states at the far end of the intensified trajectory. Image-making, conducted within the parameters of the tiered cosmos, was intimately implicated in the spiritual levels of the cosmos *and* in the material world of rock shelters and waterholes. Art and the physical environment, as the San understood it, were inseparable. The chain of operations, of which image-making was but one link, was both materially and socially constituted: image-makers were necessarily implicated in shifting social relations. During the final decades of the San's tenure of their ancestral lands, the old social structures crumbled, and individuals and inter-est groups began to deploy images in new ways as they built up new social identities and distinctions.

CHAPTER 6

Case Study 2:
North American Rock Art

For a second case study of shamanistic rock art, I turn to North America – which is just about as far from southern Africa as it is possible to go. There is no possibility of interaction between the two regions, or diffusion of religious beliefs from one to another: North American shamanism is related to the circumpolar and Siberian expressions; southern African San shamanism is a distinct expression.

North America is a vast continent, and there are many Native American traditions and language groups. In this short chapter, I adopt a limited, generalized approach to this diversity and, whilst acknowledging significant differences between regions and cultural groups, concentrate by and large on commonalities between communities living in the far west and Great Basin. In taking this generalized approach, I am following a long history of American anthropological research; for a century, the cultural unity of the far west has been recognized. The region comprises three closely related 'culture areas', as defined by Alfred Kroeber, the early North American anthropologist who worked at the University of California.[1] The differences between these three areas are mostly adaptive and related to subsistence, rather than to belief. It is also in these regions that the most recent and illuminating rock art research is being done. It could be argued that this geographical focus is, in some ways, an unsatisfactory compromise, but limited space necessarily entails summary. Still, by adopting this approach, I am able to concentrate on aspects of North American rock art that are germane to the principal themes of this book.

In Chapter 5, I made a number of key points concerning
   – the neurological origin of the tiered shamanistic cosmos,
   – rationalizations (flying and underwater and subterranean travel) of the
      universal sensations of altered states of consciousness,
   – the manifestation of visions on rock surfaces,
   – the integration of belief, vision and cosmos, and
   – the social impact of 'fixed' visions.

I need not repeat those fundamentals here. Instead, I proceed directly to the ways in which the points I made in the southern African case study resurface in an examination of North American rock art.

Historical setting

A comparison of the ways in which rock art research has been conducted in southern Africa and North America reveals parallels and differences deriving from the methodological approaches that researchers adopted on the two continents. Unlike in southern Africa, those in North America never really doubted that much (to be sure, not *all*) of the continent's hunter-gatherer rock art was in some way associated with shamanism.[2] So many Native American foraging communities practised, or had practised, forms of shamanism that the implication seemed inescapable. But that was not the whole story.

Although there was, in North America, no west European influence in the person of the Abbé Henri Breuil, as there was in southern Africa, there was a long-established tradition of hunting-magic explanations, perhaps as part of a form of shamanism but more commonly in isolation from broader conceptions of religion, myth and society.[3] We need not consider the various forms of the hunting-magic explanation: recent researchers have shown them to be inadequate and lacking in ethnographic support.[4]

Nor need we dwell on the widespread belief that North American rock art was concerned with astronomical beliefs and that the sites themselves monitored the passing of the seasons. It is true that astronomical beliefs permeated Native American cosmology and that some celestial phenomena were apparently depicted in rock art. But the idea that sites were used for solstice observations is ethnographically unsupported. As the American archaeologist David Whitley[5] points out, studies of putative alignments are based on 'counting the hits and ignoring the misses'. The occasional sites that seem to support the argument are probably random.

Rather than pursue these and other explanations that have no ethnographic foundation, it will be more profitable to move on to writers who recognize the importance of Native American beliefs, rituals and ways of life. As Whitley wisely remarks, 'we will always be on firmer interpretive ground when we use indigenous voices, directly or indirectly, to guide us in our understanding of this traditional art'.[6] To be sure, Lévi-Strauss hit the nail on the head when he wrote: 'Against the theoretician, the observer should always have the last word, and against the observer, the native.'[7]

North American ethnography

At the beginning of the 1970s, Thomas Blackburn began to explore an early twentieth-century North American ethnographic collection, though not with the specific aim of explaining rock art. From the outset, he set his face against the 'obfuscating verbiage of structuralist approaches to oral narratives'.[8] Instead of seeking sets of binary oppositions, as Lévi-Strauss did in his monumental and somewhat intimidating study of North and South American myths, Blackburn was interested in elucidating 'the fundamental issue of the interrelationships between oral narratives and other aspects of culture'.[9] This is, of course, the methodological approach that southern African researchers adopted when, in the late 1960s, they sought connections between the Bleek and Lloyd nineteenth-century ethnography and rock art images.

For Blackburn, John Peabody Harrington took the place of Bleek and Lloyd. Harrington was an ethnologist and linguist who was born in 1884; he died in 1961. During his colourful life he amassed vast quantities of material from virtually every North American linguistic group. The Smithsonian Institution, which was his employer for many years, collected his records after his death. Most of the material remains unpublished. Blackburn was not able to comb through all the over 400 large boxes in the Smithsonian; instead he concentrated on Harrington's work with the Chumash, who lived on the west coast of North America in the vicinity of present-day Santa Barbara. Harrington had begun work with the Chumash in 1912. Like Bleek and Lloyd, he became conversant with the indigenous language.

Blackburn noticed that 'magic and the supernatural play a prominent role in most of the [Chumash] narratives'.[10] This is exactly what we find in the Bleek and Lloyd Collection. Indeed, any dichotomy between the natural and the supernatural is likely to be a Western imposition on traditional hunter-gatherer communities. Another, related, parallel is also important. Blackburn found that the 'Chumash universe...consists of a series of worlds placed one above the other. Usually three such worlds are described'.[11] This is, of course, the tiered shamanistic cosmos that I described in Chapter 4 and, in Chapter 5, identified amongst the San. Again like the San, the Chumash recognized shamans of various types; they performed the kinds of tasks that I listed in Chapter 4. As a result of his reading of Harrington's notes, Blackburn concluded that Chumash rock art was the work of shamans.[12] From there, it was but a short step to take up Geraldo Reichel-Dolmatoff's work with the Colombian Tukano (Chapter 4) and to find parallels between Chumash geometric rock art images and the entoptic phenomena of the first stage of altered consciousness.[13] Other North American writers followed suit; they included Klaus Wellmann,[14] Werner Wilbert[15] and, especially, Ken Hedges of the San Diego Museum of Man.[16] This work was not restricted to the Chumash: evidence for the depiction of shamanistic visions was found across the American Plains and the West.

The neuropsychological work that Blackburn triggered undoubtedly set the stage for major advances in North American rock art research, but a methodological problem remained; the study of North American rock art did not, at first, blossom as one might have expected it to. As Blackburn rightly pointed out, the principal challenge is to demonstrate links between the ethnography and other components of culture – including rock art. What was needed was a sustained, detailed, persuasive intertwining of three evidential strands: the imagery itself, ethnography, and neuropsychology. This task has been notably achieved by David Whitley.[17] He is today the most prolific, perceptive and innovative writer on North American rock art.

Whitley has shown that the old notion that North American ethnography is silent on the all-important question of who made rock art is incorrect. Earlier writers had either missed the sometimes subtle and metaphorical references or had simply been loath to spend the time necessary to explore the ethnography. The clues were there, waiting to be discerned. Dealing with the Columbia Plateau region alone, James Keyser and Whitley[18] list 19 references in ethnographic reports to an association between rock art and shamanistic vision quests (solitary sojourns during which a person seeks a vision of a power-giving animal) and nine to shamans themselves making rock art. Similar evidence exists for other parts of the continent, especially in the west.

Without going into all the complex details of Native American indigenous religions in this part of the continent, I now focus on those components that are relevant to an understanding of rock art.[19]

Vision quests

Southern African San shamans do not seek out places for personal isolation to contact a spirit helper: they obtain their visions in sleep or during a trance dance. By contrast, vision questing is fundamental to native North American shamanistic religions, but not all vision quests are undertaken by shamans. As we shall see, people who are not shamans do, in some communities, seek power-bestowing visions in the same ways that shamans do. For an initial example, I turn to Åke Hultkranz[20] who has described vision questing among the Wind River Shoshoni, a community who still live in some of their ancestral territories in the Wind River Valley and the Grand Teton, Wyoming. There is therefore a direct historical relationship between them and the rock art of that region.

At first, Hultkranz argued that power-bestowing visions were originally obtained in dreams, and that institutionalized vision quests were a later development. Subsequently, he accepted the evidence gathered by other ethnographers and agreed that vision questing has considerable time depth.[21] Either way, the belief that visions may be obtained in dreams or during vision quests is not restricted to the Shoshoni: it is widespread in North America, and the Shoshoni example is typical of the general practice.

The principal aim of a vision quest is to 'see' a spirit animal that will become the quester's animal-helper and source of his power. Amongst the Shoshoni, a suppliant desiring a vision mounts his horse and rides up into the hills where there are already rock art images. He washes, and clothed in only a blanket he lies down on a ledge below the images. His vision is induced by fasting, enduring cold and lack of sleep, and smoking hallucinogenic tobacco. Some reports say that it may take three or four days before a vision comes to the suppliant – if at all. It is hard to tell if the vision comes when the quester is awake or dreaming.[22] Sometimes tobacco was smoked just prior to sleep: drug-induced hallucinations would thus be experienced during sleep.[23] People may also experience spontaneous waking visions.

Significantly, the Shoshoni use the word *navushieip* to denote both dreaming and waking.[24] This is also true of other groups, such as the Yokuts.[25] Their divisions of the spectrum of consciousness thus accord dreaming the same status as waking for the reception of information. (In some parts of North America 'waking visions' are, however, discounted.) The dreams in which spirits appear are more vivid than other dreams; the Shoshoni say that they hold your attention and you cannot awake until they are over. Visions may be mercurial: for instance, a 'lightning spirit' may appear as a body of water, then like a human being, then like an animal. Often frightening animals come to threaten suppliants, and they must brave them if their power-giving spirit animal is to appear. During visions, questers feel that they leave their bodies – the sensation of out-of-body travel.

Throughout North America, this travel often involves entering a hole in the rock, passing though a tunnel, evading various monsters and seeing a spiritual personage, the Master of the Animals, and his creatures. After receiving power, the shaman may emerge from a different place, sometimes via a spring. Whitley remarks, '"Entering a cave" or rock was a metaphor for a shaman's altered state; therefore, caves (and rocks more generally) were considered entrances or portals to the supernatural world.' He adds that flight and entering a cloud were further metaphors for shamanistic travel. During vision quests, North American shamans sometimes bled from the nose and mouth.[26] The parallels with the southern African accounts of extra-corporeal, hallucinatory travel are arresting. Entry into the rock, movement through a tunnel, encounters with spirits and animals, emergence elsewhere through water, flight, and nasal haemorrhaging are experiences common to both continents.

Some ethnographic reports indicate that Native American people believed that rock art images were made, not by the quester, but by spirits, commonly named as 'water babies', 'rock babies', or 'mountain dwarves'. These spirits were especially powerful shamans' spirit helpers; they could be seen only in an altered state of consciousness. A shaman was so intimately identified with his spirit helper that, as Whitley[27] points out, to say that a rock art image was made by a 'rock baby' was the same as saying that the shaman himself made it. To illustrate this point Whitley cites Harold Driver:[28] a Native American informant told Driver that rock art sites were created by shamans who 'painted their spirits (*anit*) on rocks "to show themselves, to let people see what they had done". The spirit must come first in a dream.'[29]

Maurice Zigmond[30] found that, amongst the Kawaiisu of south-central California, it was believed that a spirit named Rock Baby dwelt in the rock and made rock paintings. If one returned to a rock art site and found that more images had appeared since one's previous visit, they were said to be the handiwork of Rock Baby. If one touched a rock painting and then rubbed one's eyes, sleeplessness and death could result. The images thus possessed inherent power, rather like those in southern Africa: they were not merely pictures.

As early as the 1870s, J. S. Denison reported that a Klamath man told him that rock paintings 'were made by Indian doctors [shamans] and inspired fear of the doctor's supernatural power'.[31] Similarly, a 1900 report records that, among the Thompson, 'rock paintings were made by noted shamans',[32] and in the 1920s Glenn Ranck found that '[o]ne night a Wishram medicine man [shaman] used an unseen power to paint a pictograph during the night. He was found in a trance at the foot of the pictograph the next morning'.[33] Such reports could be multiplied many times over: the link between North American shamans and rock art is indisputable. But that realization is only the beginning – not the end – of research.

Vision quests were not one-off affairs. Shamans usually repeated quests throughout their lives. They believed that their power could be increased in this way. When a shaman had received a vision in a dream, he awoke and concentrated on it so that he would not forget it. At dawn he went into the hill to experience more dreams. When he had received sufficient revelations, he entered his 'shaman's cache' to converse with his spirit helper.

Shamans' caves

The term 'shaman's cache' was coined by Anna Gayton to denote Yokuts rock art sites;[34] other Californian groups used the terms 'doctor's cave', 'spirit helpers' cave', and 'shaman's medicine house'. These caches were located in rock shelters or, where there are no shelters, on low ridges. The word 'cache' was suggested by the presence at these places of a shaman's paraphernalia – his ritual costumes, talisman bundles, feathers and other accoutrements. The rock shelters were commonly embellished with rock art images.

In California, it seems that cache sites were individually owned and could be passed down from generation to generation. In the Great Basin, on the other hand, sites were used by many shamans. Some sites in this region became renowned for their power, and shamans still journey great distances to seek visions at them, sometimes from as far away as northern Utah.[35] The principal motif in this area is the bighorn sheep, which was a spirit helper for rain shamans.

The actual cache was believed to be *inside* the rock, which would open to admit the shaman. Yokuts people said that the openings were invisible to non-shamans, no matter how carefully they searched for them.[36] Not surprisingly, it was through such openings that vision questers entered the spiritual realm. Gayton, who worked among the Yokuts in the 1930s, described a vision quest at a cache:

When a man had dreamed sufficiently [in preparation for receiving power], all the animals of his moiety gathered on a hill near a cache. The man was there too, and the animals opened the [site], telling him to enter. He stayed in there for four days. No one knew where he was, and often people went in search of him. While he was in the [site] the animals told him what to do. They gave him songs and danced with him all night. They gave him his regalia: 'this just appeared on him, nobody knew where it came from...' At the end of four days, the animals sent him out....[37]

Just how the experience of entering the rock may be generated became evident to the American archaeologist Thor Conway when he was at a

Californian rock art site known as Salinan Cave:

Red and black paintings surround two small holes bored into the side of the walls by natural forces. As you stare at these entrance ways to another realm, suddenly – and without voluntary control – the pictographs break the artificial visual reality that we assume…. Suddenly, the paintings encompassing the recessed pockets began to pulse, beckoning us inward. The added effects – a nighttime setting, firelight, shadows dancing on the walls, and the resonation of aboriginal chanting – could induce even more profound experiences.[38]

It is highly probable that those San paintings that seem to thread in and out of the walls of rock shelters similarly came to life and drew shamans through the 'veil' into the spirit realm.

Other reports show that a shaman's cache site was also spoken of as *mawyu-can* – 'whirlwind place' – because a shaman's ability to fly was sometimes called 'whirlwind power'. Among some groups the word for whirlwind was a synonym for spirit helper. In Sequoia National Park, in the southern Sierra Nevada, a rock art site was known as *pahdin*, which means 'place to go under', a reference to passing underwater and drowning.[39]

Comparison of these reports with K"au Giraffe's account (Chapter 5) of how his helper came and took him underground and underwater, how he was taught to sing special songs, and how he experienced the presence of many animals reveals parallels that could be multiplied if we had the space to examine other North American reports – and, indeed, reports from elsewhere in the world. It is possible to discern in such accounts specific rationalizations of experiences generated by the neurology of the human brain in altered states of consciousness. I can think of no other way to explain the similarities: they are the product of the universal human nervous system in altered states of consciousness, culturally processed but none the less still recognizably deriving from the structure and electro-chemical functioning of the nervous system.

Puberty ceremonies

So far, I have focused on shamanistic visions. North American rock art is, however, also associated with another kind of vision quest. Among the Quinault of Puget Sound, boys made rock paintings of mythical water monsters that they saw in visions.[40] In southern California, too, puberty ceremonies culminated in rock painting. During the southern California rituals, boys and girls learned religious and moral truths and correct behaviour. They also ingested hallucinogens, jimsonweed for the boys and tobacco for the girls. At the climax of the rituals the initiates took part in a race to a designated rock. The winner of the race was believed to enjoy longevity. After the race, the initiates made rock art images on the rock. Shamans supervised both the boys' and the girls' rituals.

The girls' images comprised red geometric designs that included diamond chains and zigzags; both were said to represent rattlesnakes, culturally sanctioned spirit helpers for girls (Pl. 11). These designs corresponded to ones painted on the girls' faces. Whitley found that the last such ceremony took place in the 1890s.[41]

The boys' initiation rituals had ceased earlier in the nineteenth century and are less well documented. Nevertheless, it seems that they followed the same pattern as the girls' ceremony and also culminated in rock painting. One early account suggests that the boys' motifs included circles, nested curves, and a human figure (Fig. 41).[42]

41 Western American rock art made as part of boys' puberty rituals. The images differ from those made by girls in their puberty rituals.

A key aspect of these rituals is that the boys and girls focused on different entoptic phenomena. Both sexes would have had the neurological potential to see the full range of entoptics, and we may be fairly certain that the boys' entoptic forms would have flashed in and out of the girls' visions, and *vice versa*. But the guidance given by the shamans who were conducting the rituals encouraged each sex to focus on what were considered to be its appropriate images. The same gender distinction in motif-use is evident in baby cradle-board headcover designs; it was widely sanctioned and recognized.[43]

Again we see that the neuropsychological approach does not in any way suggest a mechanistic link between mental and painted images. Cultural interventions select items from the full repertoire of potential mental images, and this selection process takes place within a social community: the spectrum of consciousness is simply one of the raw materials that society uses to construct itself through the intervention of individuals.

Whitley points out that these puberty ceremonies were part and parcel of a shamanistic belief system. As I have noted, the ceremonies were overseen by powerful shamans who interacted with the initiates during their drug-induced trances to ensure that they experienced the culturally approved visions. Moreover, the initiates received spirit helpers during these rituals and then painted them on the rocks.

These parallels between the puberty rituals and vision quests explain why some researchers distinguish between 'shamanic' and 'shamanistic'.[44] For them, 'shamanic' denotes the behaviour and experiences of shamans; 'shamanistic', on the other hand, denotes a broader range of behaviour, as, for example, the role of shamans in some North American puberty rituals. It could be said that the San trance dance is 'shamanic' and the girls' Eland Bull Dance is 'shamanistic'. At the Eland Bull Dance, an old shaman mimes the mating behaviour of an eland bull, while the women mime that of eland cows. At the climax of the dance, the eponymous antelope is said to run up to the dancers. They are afraid, but the shaman taking the role of the eland bull reassures them: he says that this is a 'good thing' come from god.[45] The appearance of the spirit eland is thus 'shamanistic' rather than specifically 'shamanic'.

Metaphors in the brain

This brief overview does not take account of local variations in North American rock art motifs that may have had somewhat different, though probably related, meanings. Certainly, researchers should always guard against seeking similarities at the expense of dissimilarities. Yet the general association of much North American rock art with shamanistic visions should not be ignored. It provides a foundation for considering local variants. Moreover, the indisputable depiction of visions in North American (and San) rock art is clearly relevant to our exploration of Upper Palaeolithic art: the people who made North American (and southern African) rock art and those who made Upper Palaeolithic art had the same nervous systems.

As I have pointed out, some North American archaeologists have appreciated the value of multiple evidence and have begun to intertwine the ethnographic and neuropsychological evidential strands – with striking results. Whitley in particular has systematically applied the neuropsychological model (Chapter 4) to North American rock art.

He has shown that seven of the Stage 1 entoptic forms are present in the Great Basin rock art and elsewhere (grids, parallel lines, swarms of dots, zigzags, nested catenary curves, filigrees and spirals).[46] Moreover, he has found evidence for all three stages of transition along the intensified trajectory of altered consciousness.[47] It will be recalled that in Stage 1 subjects see entoptic phenomena; in Stage 2 they construe them as important objects; in Stage 3 they experience and participate in fully developed hallucinations, though entoptic elements may persist peripherally or integrated with visions of animals and people. Whitley reiterates an important point that Dowson and I made when we first formulated the neuropsychological model in 1988:[48] 'Without this model, features of the art (such as the common association and juxtaposition of geometric and representational motifs) would remain enigmatic'.[49] He also notes that the close fit between the motifs suggested by the model (and derived from laboratory conditions) and those of the rock art provides an independent 'scientific test of the rock art's ethnographic interpretation – its origin in altered states of consciousness'.[50]

Taking this sort of comparison as a starting point, Whitley discusses the widely reported ways in which the visual, somatic and aural effects of altered states are construed in North America. He concludes that there is a 'shamanistic symbolic repertoire' that includes hallucinations of

– death/killing,
– aggression/fighting,
– drowning/going underwater,
– flight,
– sexual arousal/intercourse, and
– bodily transformation.

42 The killing of a bighorn sheep was associated with rain-making. When a shaman killed a sheep, he was, in effect, killing himself.

In this list, Whitley gathers together the ways of rationalizing altered states of consciousness that we have already discussed in earlier chapters and adds important new ones (Figs 42, 43). I briefly consider each in turn and note some parallels with the southern African San.

As in southern African San religion and art, so, too, in North America shamans are sometimes said to 'die' when they enter trance. 'A shaman's activities as a sorcerer, or his own conscious act of entry into the supernatural world, were a kind of "killing".'[51] Moreover, when a Numic rain shaman made rain he was said to have killed a bighorn sheep. That is, he killed himself because he was a bighorn sheep in the supernatural realm. Perhaps most interestingly, well over 95 per cent of the bighorn sheep engraved across the Mojave Desert have large, upraised tails – unlike the real animals which have small, pendant tails (Fig. 42). A bighorn sheep raises its tail in two circumstances: death and defecation. It therefore seems likely that virtually all the engravings of bighorn sheep depict dead or dying animals. Similarly, in southern Africa, many eland are depicted dead. When he was speaking to Joseph Orpen, the San man Qing said that the shamans were 'spoilt' – that is, they 'died' – at the same time as the elands and that it was the dances that caused this to happen to both men and antelope. Finally, in North America, nasal bleeding was commonly associated with physical death and entry into the spirit world, as it was in southern Africa.

The notion of aggression and fighting, Whitley's second metaphor, is clearly related to the death metaphor. An association of fighting with North American shamans is, for instance, suggested by the Yokuts term *tsesas* which means spirit helper, shaman's talisman, and stone knife.[52] Moreover, among some south-central California groups the words for *shaman*, *grizzly bear*, and *murderer* were interchangeable.[53] The potential violence of trance experience was manifest in the battles and fights that were sometimes seen by shamans in trance. In Native California rock art, people are shown shooting a symbolic arrow at others, and dangerous animals, such as rattlesnakes and grizzly bears, are painted at many sites. Most importantly, shamans are depicted bristling with weapons – bows, arrows, atlatls, spears and knives. In southern Africa comparable paintings of fights have been interpreted as records of bands defending their territories against invaders. But the San did not defend territories. Close inspection of these depictions often reveals details that indicate that the fight is actually taking place in the spirit realm.

Thirdly, drowning and passing underwater are themes that crop up in many North American shamans' narratives. In the art, the experience is referred to by images of aquatic spirit helpers. They include water-striders, frogs, toads, turtles, beavers and swordfish (Fig. 43 D). Turtles were sometimes thought of as doors to the spirit world. We have seen that, in southern Africa, depictions of fish and eels often suggest subaquatic locations.

Fourthly, supernatural flight is ubiquitous in North American shamans' narratives. In the art, shamans are depicted wearing quail feather topnots (Fig. 43 A). The quail was associated in a number of ways with shamans. For instance, the bowl used to prepare infusions of jimsonweed was called 'quail', and the Master of the Animals, whom shamans visited, was clothed in a quail feather cape.[54] Shamans are also depicted with birds' feet (Fig. 43 B, C). Sometimes, quails and other birds were depicted, often sitting on shamans' heads. Whitley also argues that concentric circles, frequently associated with shamanistic figures, allude to flight and signify that he was a 'concentrator of power'.[55] In southern Africa, flight and birds are similarly often associated with images of shamans.[56]

Fifthly, sexual arousal is an important theme that Whitley adds to the list. In North America, supernatural power was associated with sexual potency, and shamans were believed to be especially virile. Rock art sites were symbolic vaginas, and entry into

43 North American rock art images depicting shamanistic experience: A Flight; the figure wears a quail topknot; B and C Winged flight; D Underwater; a salamander swimming around a saltwater kelp plant; E Transformation of a shaman into a rattlesnake; rattlesnake shamans cured snake bites and controlled snakes.

the wall of a rock art site was thus akin to intercourse. Sexual arousal and penal erections are associated with both altered states of consciousness and sleep. In southern Africa, a great many figures are ithyphallic. This feature has generally – and rather vaguely – been taken to refer to 'masculinity', but the painted contexts of the figures seems to confirm that, as in North America, sexual arousal was a metaphor for altered states of consciousness.

Bodily transformation, Whitley's last metaphor, is so common in both North America and southern Africa that it hardly needs further comment. On both continents, shamans fuse with animals and experience bodily distortions (Fig. 43E).

This list of metaphors – or rationalizations of altered states of consciousness – presents a mixture of somatic, aural, visual and mental experiences associated with trance. The similarities that I have outlined show that fundamental neurological events can be variously interpreted, but also that these events are nevertheless likely to be seen in certain ways. Underlying all these shamanistic experiences is the concept of supernatural power and the ways in which it can be harnessed in altered states of consciousness.

Quartz and supernatural power

One of the most fascinating findings to emerge from recent North American rock art research concerns a link between the way in which engravings were pecked, or hammered, into the rock and a manifestation of supernatural power. To demonstrate this link, Whitley and four of his associates focused on a Mojave Desert site known as Sally's Rock Shelter. They found that pieces of quartz were scattered around the engraved rocks; they had been used as hammer-stones. Unmodified white quartz cobbles, approximately 12 cm (5 in) long, were also wedged in cracks between boulders (Pl. 10). It is common to find offerings of beads, sticks, arrows, seeds, berries and special stones at vision quest sites.

This is by no means the only rock art site associated with quartz; the stone is widely associated with shamanism. For instance, Bob Rabbit, the last known Numic rain-shaman, used quartz crystals in his weather-control ceremonies, and crystals were believed to be inhabited by spirits.[57] More specifically, reports show that shamanistic vision questers in the Colorado Desert 'would break up white quartz rocks, believing that the high spiritual power contained within these would be released to enter his or her body'.[58] The scatter of quartz fragments at Sally's Rock Shelter apparently resulted from this practice.

The reason for the practice of breaking open quartz seems to be that, when quartz stones are rubbed together, they generate a bright, lightning-like light. Triboluminescence, as this characteristic is known, became a manifestation of supernatural power. Although striking quartz against basalt in the act of making an image will not activate triboluminescence, the scatters of quartz fragments found at rock art sites suggest the importance of the mineral as intrinsically containing power. Here is another instance of rituals that were performed at rock art sites.

Images in society

An important point that emerges from this discussion and from Chapter 5 is that the insights of shamans are accepted by their communities. People who have never moved to the end of the intensified spectrum none the less believe in a tiered cosmos, accept that shamans are able to travel between its levels, and respect rock images (whether they are allowed to see them or not) as material-izations of supernatural visions or dreams. Why are people so compliant? There are a number of reasons. For one, they have had some glimpse, some inkling, of the spirit world in their own dreams. In the absence of any knowl-edge of human neurology, dreams provide them with personal, indeed incontrovertible, evidence for the existence of a spiritual realm. This spirit world may be the preserve of the shamans, but it can unnervingly invade the minds of ordinary people. The whole of society is thus drawn into the shamanistic way of seeing things. Shamanism is not simply a component of society: on the contrary, shamanism, together with its tiered cosmos, can be said to be the overall framework of society.

In this context, we can enquire what impact rock art images had on Native North American communities. As yet, this is a line of research that has not been much followed in North America, though Whitley has explored the social role of shamanism and rock art in the western Great Basin.[59] As we have seen, he has shown that killing a bighorn sheep was a metaphor for making rain. When the people of this region moved into an economy based on seed-gather-ing, rain-making assumed even more importance. This shift, Whitley argues, must be seen in the context of two systems of inequality: men over women, and shamans over non-shaman males. Rock art, Whitley argues, was impli-cated in efforts to maintain gender asymmetry and in the growing political organization of the region. Parallels with the roles of shamans and their rock art in southern Africa, especially during the socially turbulent times of the colonial period, are evident enough. Rock art becomes an instrument of social discrimination, as Max Raphael long ago argued was the case during the west European Upper Palaeolithic.

One of the most striking social differences between southern African and North American shamanism concerns secrecy. In southern Africa, the San are generally open about their beliefs. After shamanistic journeys to the spiritual realm and to other places on the level on which people live, shamans recount their experiences to everyone: all men, women and children are permitted to listen – indeed, everyone is eager to find out what is going on in the spiritual world. As Wilhelm Bleek and Lucy Lloyd found in the nineteenth century, and as I and many anthropologists working in the twentieth- and twenty-first-century Kalahari Desert have found, the San are eager that everyone should know what they believe and experience. When I was in the Kalahari, some of the old Ju'/hoansi told Megan Biesele to check what I was writing down: they wanted the world to know everything.

By contrast, much shamanistic activity in North America was conducted in secrecy. The degree of secrecy varies from group to group. Working in 1948 among the Shoshoni, Hultkranz found that, although they were more open about their religious beliefs and experiences than the Plains Indians, they were reluctant to disclose the details of their visions except to close kin and friends.[60] In the past, they also initiated hunts. Places where Shoshoni shamans obtain their visions are considered to be powerful, filled with spirits and best avoided. The Shoshoni were formerly nomadic, and sacred places are therefore scattered throughout their territory: there was a network of sacred places across the landscape.

North American shamans conducted their vision quests in remote places, far from ordinary social relations. Rock art sites were believed to be protected by supernatural powers, swarms of insects, and mysterious lights.[61] If they were close to settlements, they were avoided by all who were not shamans. This seclusion set shamans apart, physically and symbolically, from ordinary people. They were reluctant to speak about what they 'saw' at these isolated places or to reveal the identity of their spirit helpers.[62] This secrecy built up an aura of fear: people not only respected shamans, they also feared them. Knowledge is power. In the 1870s, Denison noted that Klamath shamans' rock paintings 'inspired fear of the doctor's supernatural power'.[63] Indeed, shamans had the ability to bring harm to people who disobeyed them or failed to observe religious rules. The images remained as incontrovertible signs of the shamans' awesome power.

The sites themselves, the shamans' caches, were perceived as places of great wealth by people who were not shamans. They emphasized the riches as well as the danger of such places. Whitley points out that non-shamans' perceptions of caches 'probably resulted from the tension between shamans and non-shamans, based on perceived material wealth, potential malevolence, and the sexually predatory nature of some shamans'.[64] In this way, the material manifestations of shamans' activities – rock art images and shamans' caches – played a role in establishing social relations and making them appear part of the natural order of things. Beliefs about the power of the images, backed up by peoples' own dreams, made the shamans' powerful positions in society appear inevitable. By making powerful images derived from the spirit world, shamans were creating and establishing their social positions: they knew that the images would have the effect on others that they did in fact have. As with the San, North American rock images thus continued to play a role after they were made.

When Anna Gayton explored the relationship between Yokuts and Mono chiefs and shamans, she found a system of alliances between secular and spiritual authority.[65] A chief could increase his wealth by a close relationship with a shaman, and the shaman, in turn, could claim the protection of his chief. Wealth derived largely from the annual mourning ceremony; rich people who declined to contribute to this occasion stood in danger of spiritual attack from the chief's shaman. Conflict, sometimes internecine, between descent lineages also implicated both chiefs and shamans. Religion was certainly not separated from politics and jockeying for power.

Was this kind of relationship, together with the continuing social impact of rock art images long after they had been made, also true, we may now ask, of the hidden, subterranean images of Upper Palaeolithic western Europe? Was Upper Palaeolithic religion also implicated in political affairs? To begin to answer this question, we need to take a step back to the Middle to Upper Palaeolithic Transition and think about the circumstances in which human beings began to make pictures in the first place.

CHAPTER 7

An Origin of Image-Making

Case studies, such as the two in Chapters 5 and 6, greatly enrich our understanding of the ways in which human beings not merely cope with but also actively exploit the full spectrum of shifting consciousness. Ethnography puts flesh and life on the skeleton – the framework – that neuropsychology provides. But even the two studies that I have presented show that simple, one-off ethnographic analogies may be decidedly misleading. The solitary vision quest, for instance, that is so important in North American shamanism is absent from its southern African San counterpart, and this difference points to different social relations between shamans and their communities.

Above all, we see that intelligence is no doubt important. But it is in the ways in which people understand shifting consciousness that cosmology, experiences of cosmology, concepts of supernatural realms, and art all come together. When we move to the Upper Palaeolithic, there is, of course, no ethnography, and we have, as it were, to re-arrange our evidential strands.

Interlocking change

Perhaps the most striking feature of the west European Upper Palaeolithic, one on which many writers comment, is a sharp increase in the rate of change. Compared with the preceding Middle Palaeolithic, a great deal happened in a comparatively short time. We have noted greater diversity in the kinds of raw materials used for artefact manufacture, the appearance of new tool types, the development of regional tool styles, socially and cognitively more sophisticated hunting strategies, organized settlement patterns, and extensive trade in 'special' items. Even more striking is the explosion of body decoration, elaborate burials with grave goods, and, of course, portable and parietal images. It is clear that all these areas of change were interdependent – they interlocked. They were not a scatter of disparate 'inventions' made by especially intelligent individuals; rather, they were part of the very fabric of a dynamic society. At the same time, archaeological evidence suggests that they did not interlock in the sense that they constituted an indivisible package (Chapter 3). The west

European Upper Palaeolithic was certainly not a period of social, technological and conceptual stasis. There can be no doubt that significant, all-
embracing change was at last on the march.[1]

An implication of this new dynamic is that the Upper Palaeolithic was a
period of *social diversity*, a time when social distinctions and social tensions
proliferated and came to be the driving force within society.

If we are to seek a driving mechanism for the west European 'Creative
Explosion', it must be in social diversity and change. This means that we need
to consider the *divisive* functions of image-making. In doing so, we distance
ourselves from earlier functionalist explanations, such as art for art's sake,
sympathetic magic, binary mythograms, and information exchange, all of
which see art as contributing to social stability. Instead, we follow up and
develop Max Raphael's ideas. It was he who said that Upper Palaeolithic communities were 'history-making peoples *par excellence*';[2] he realized that their
art was not simply an idyllic expression of contentment, an efflorescence of a
'higher' aesthetic sense, but rather an arena of struggle and contestation.

To understand how image-making could be born in social contestation I
return to the notions of consciousness that I developed in earlier chapters and
introduce two new concepts: fully human and pre-human consciousness.

Consciousness and mental imagery

I have pointed out that the making of images of animals and people could not
have developed out of, say, body painting. The notion that an image is a scale
model of something else (say, a horse) requires a different set of mental events
and conventions from those that perceive the social symbolism of red marks
on someone's chest. Body decoration did not evolve – could not have evolved –
into image-making. Art historians have given much attention to the ways in
which graphic imagery is perceived as commensurate with mental imagery
and objects in the world; scale, perspective, and the selection of distinguishing
features are just some of the ideas that they discuss. Whilst these notions help
to explain how people today interpret a pattern of lines on a surface as an
image of something other than itself, they do not explain how people first
came to believe that such marks could call to mind a bison, a horse or a woolly
mammoth – if indeed they did.

As may be expected, the Abbé Henri Breuil held strong views on the question of the origins of art. All his ideas were based on the innatist position. In
Chapter 2, we saw some of the limitations of the notion that human beings

have an innate artistic drive and that this characteristic of their minds leads, almost forces, them to make pictures. Breuil called this supposed urge 'the artistic temperament with its adoration of Beauty'.[3] But he also tackled the problem in more practical terms, wondering how people first thought of making representational images. One of his suggestions was that images evolved from masks, though exactly how this could have happened he did not say. A more influential notion of his was that people suddenly discerned the outline of, say, a horse in natural marks on the wall of a rock shelter. At once, they realized that they could make such marks themselves – and not only of horses but of other animals as well. Breuil also pointed to the so-called 'macaronis', arabesques and meanders that Upper Palaeolithic people made with their fingers in the soft mud on cave walls. In amongst these apparently idle loops and marks, according to Breuil, people discerned parts of animals and realized that they could make pictures in this way. Then, alongside natural marks and 'macaronis', Breuil placed handprints and argued that these marks in some way evolved into representational images of animals, though exactly how and what the intermediate stages were he did not explain.

Then there is the short-cut explanation for the origin of image-making that does not require pre-existent marks or 'macaronis'. Suddenly, some exceptionally intelligent person simply invented picture-making. At once, the idea caught on, and others started making their own images of animals. French archaeologists and cave art specialists Brigitte and Giles Delluc sum up this position:

Around 30,000 years ago, in the Aurignacian, at the beginning of the Upper Palaeolithic, someone or some group in the Eyzies region invented drawing, the representation in two dimensions on the flat of the stone of what appeared in the environment in three dimensions.[4]

There are serious problems with all these still-popular and widely published explanations. First, the evidence of the caves suggests that 'macaronis' were not the first wall markings; they were made throughout the Upper Palaeolithic. Secondly, the explanations are often couched in the plural: '*people* suddenly discerned…' But what is really meant here is that especially bright *individuals* (as the Dellucs allow) here and there in western Europe invented imagery or spotted a resemblance between the natural marks or 'macaronis' and an animal and then told others about it. But why did an individual examine marks and 'macaronis' so closely if he or she did not have some prior expectation of what might be found in them? Even allowing for the effectiveness of a chance, serendipitous glance of a twenty-first-century Westerner at, say, damp marks on a wall, we must say that one cannot 'notice' a representational image in a mass of lines unless one *already has* a notion of images. And such a notion must be *socially* held; it cannot be the exclusive property of an individual.

There is good reason for coming to this conclusion. Indeed, Breuil himself relates a tale that counts against his own explanation. He says that Salomon Reinach, the writer who early on propagated the idea of sympathetic magic, found that a Turkish officer whom he met when he was a student in Athens was incapable of recognizing a drawing of a horse 'because he could not move round it'.[5] Islam, of course, forbids the making of representational images. Being a Muslim, the officer was entirely unfamiliar with representational pictures.

The anthropologist Anthony Forge discovered the same sort of thing when he was working amongst the Abelam of New Guinea. He found that these people make three-dimensional carvings of spirits and also paint bright, two-dimensional, polychrome spirit motifs on their ritual structures. Although the motif itself is essentially the same in both cases, the two-dimensional versions arrange the elements in different ways; for example, the arms may emanate from beneath the noses of the figures whereas the three-dimensional carvings have the arms in the usual place. Why do the Abelam not find this difference strange? The answer to this question is that neither the three- nor the two-dimensional versions are representations: they do not show what the spirits look like; rather they are avatars of the spirits. 'There is no sense,' Forge found, 'in which the painting on the flat is a projection of the carving or an attempt to represent the three-dimensional object in two dimensions.'[6] The paintings are not meant to 'look like' something in nature, as we so easily assume.

As a result of their understanding of the non-representational nature of painting, the Abelam had difficulty in 'seeing' photographs.[7] If they were shown a photograph of a person standing rigidly face-on, they could appreciate what was shown. But if the photograph showed the person in action or in any other pose than looking directly at the camera, they were at a loss. Sometimes Forge had to draw a thick line around the person in a photograph so that people could retain their 'seeing' of him or her. This is not to say that the Abelam are inherently incapable of understanding photographs. Forge managed to teach some Abelam boys to understand the conventions of photographs in a few hours, but up until his tuition, 'seeing' photographs was not one of their skills. As Forge puts it, 'Their vision has been socialized in a way that makes photographs especially incomprehensible.'[8]

'Seeing' two-dimensional images is therefore something that we learn to do; it is not an inevitable part of being human. How, then, could Upper Palaeolithic people 'see' images in the convolutions of 'macaronis' unless they already had a notion of such imagery?

Despite this (to my mind insuperable) difficulty, writers have persisted in trying to get around the problem because they can conceive of no other way in which people could have stumbled upon the notion of two-dimensional images on cave walls. The most ingenious – and complex – attempt has come from the art historian Whitney Davis.[9]

Davis fully understands the fundamental problem of assuming that, in dealing with the earliest Aurignacian images, we are in fact dealing with *images*. As Forge succinctly puts it when writing about the Abelam, 'We must beware of assuming that they see what we see and *vice versa*.' This is the crux of the matter. Then, too, Davis rightly rejects the notion that an evolving 'aesthetic sensibility' led to image-making.[10] But he finds no option other than (a) to proceed as if Upper Palaeolithic images were representations of things in real, material life and (b) to assume that two-dimensional image recognition evolved inevitably.

At the risk of over-simplifying his work, we can say that, although he rejects the origin of images in 'macaronis', he argues that people made random 'marks', even during the Middle Palaeolithic. But, at first, they did not adopt a 'seeing-as' approach to their handiwork; that is, they did not see the marks as representing something else. If we allow this idea of random scratches, where do we go from there? It is at this point that it seems to me that Davis's line of reasoning is stymied. He writes:

Continually marking the world will continually increase the probability that marks will be seen as things. Eventually very complex clusters of marks – it does not matter whether they are intentionally clustered or just happen to be seen together – will result in occasional perceptual interpretations of marks as very complex things, such as the closed contours of natural objects. The manufacture of marks on surfaces and all manner of other activities, from body ornament to building, potentially add marks and colour patches to the world. In sum, the emergence of representation is the predictable logical and perceptual consequence of the *increasing elaboration of the man-made visual world* [Davis's emphasis].[11]

As James Faris, in a comment on Davis's argument, pointed out, the art historian is saying that the discovery of image-making in random lines was inevitable.[12] Given long enough, people just *had* to tumble to the potential of image-making. Davis has substituted inevitability for serendipity. Faris made another key point when he asked: 'Why *these* images rather than, say, plants or small animals, and why not suns or snakes or faces…?' In other words, why this particular motivic vocabulary of bison, horses, aurochs, mammoths, and so forth? Although there are parietal images of, for instance, hyenas, owls and fish, they are very rare indeed. There must therefore have been presuppositions in the Upper Palaeolithic minds; they were 'looking for' certain things and not others. However we explain the origin of the conventions of representation, we are left with the key thought that a vocabulary of motifs existed in people's minds *before* they made images. They did not begin by making a wide range of motifs – anything an individual image-maker may have wished to draw – and then focus on the limited range of motifs. Why? The inevitabilist argument begs this awkward question.

Finally, even if all this were to have happened and some clever Upper Palaeolithic people did 'invent' two-dimensional imagery, society at large would need to have had some reason for wanting to make more images, and, moreover, images from the predetermined vocabulary. It follows that images must have had some pre-existing, shared value for people, first, for them to notice them at all, and, secondly, to want to go on making them. That is, images of a specific set of animals must have had some *a priori* value for people to take any interest in them. A chicken or egg problem, if there ever was one, but, as we shall see, it takes us to the heart of the matter.

How, then, did people invent two-dimensional images? We seem to have reached an impasse in our attempts to answer this question. The difficulty, however, lies more with the question itself than our ability to answer it. It presupposes a specific type of answer – the wrong type of answer.

In short, people did *not* invent two-dimensional images of things in their material environment. On the contrary, a notion of images *and* the vocabulary of motifs *were part of their experience* before they made parietal or portable images.

To explain this apparently contradictory yet, I believe, crucial point we need to return once more to the spectrum of human consciousness and see how it came to assume the form that it now has and that it had for *Homo sapiens* at the beginning of the Upper Palaeolithic.

The neurobiology of primary and higher-order consciousness

In some sense, consciousness is the last frontier. If researchers wish to go boldly (the famous Star Trek split infinitive is indefensible) where no one has gone before, consciousness is a favoured launch-pad to fame. Consciousness is the struggle of the moment, and there is no shortage of protagonists. It is not my purpose to review so complex and disputatious a field. Instead, I turn to the researcher whom I consider most relevant to our more modest quest to understand Upper Palaeolithic image-making.

Gerald Edelman won the 1972 Nobel Prize for his work in immunology. Then he reached out for the prize of 'consciousness explained'. Soon after winning the Nobel Prize, he began to see that recognition in the brain was rather like recognition in the immune system. He is now Director of the Neurosciences Institute and President of the Neurosciences Research Foundation.[13] To study the origins of consciousness, he realized, one had to combine a study of the anatomy of the brain with Darwin's theory of natural selection. He therefore wholeheartedly embraced the belief that mind and consciousness are the products of matter, the matter that we call brain. There is no place in his work for Descartes's dualism. Nor is there room for pessimism: he rejects the notion that you cannot use consciousness to explain consciousness – that the task is too difficult. Consciousness has evolved biologically and can therefore be explained biologically. The dense neural link-ups in the brain are not like a programmed computer, nor like the chapels of a cathedral, with or without interconnections, nor like a Swiss army knife; they are more open-ended than any of these similes suggest.

Still, there is a lacuna in Edelman's work. Let me say at once that it is by no means a fatal flaw, and later I try to fill it within the framework that he has developed. The problem is that he concentrates on the 'alert' end of the spectrum of consciousness and overlooks the autistic end. But, as I say, this is a deficiency that can be rectified – and he has himself supplied the tools for the job.

When it comes to discriminating between acceptable and non-acceptable hypotheses, Edelman is explicit: he realizes that researchers must make their methodological criteria plain – as I have tried to do at a number of points in this book. Rightly, I believe, Edelman insists that any explanation of consciousness must be based on observable phenomena and be related to the functions of the brain and body. If an explanation is to be based on evolution, an anatomical foundation is essential. That is to say, an explanatory theory of consciousness must propose 'explicit *neural* models' that explain how consciousness arose during evolution. Moreover, any explanation must advance 'stringent tests for the models it proposes in terms of neurobiological facts'. Finally, the explanation must be 'consistent with presently known scientific observations from whatever field of enquiry and, above all, with those from brain science'.[14] Edelman is here summarizing some of the criteria for evaluating hypotheses that I noted in Chapter 2.

But what is the basic neurology of the brain? All neurobiologists accept that the fundamental cell type in the brain is the neuron. Neurons are connected to other neurons by synapses. These connections are facilitated by the generation of neurotransmitters, chemical substances that allow electrical impulses to cross over from one neuron to another. The cerebral cortex, the outer 'skin' of the brain, contains as many as ten billion neurons. This complexity is daunting. Yet it is out of complex interactions between the billions of neurons that consciousness arises.

Next, we need to distinguish between the limbic system and the thalamo-cortical system. Both are made up of neurons, but they differ in their organization. The limbic system is concerned with fundamental, non-rational behaviours: appetite, sexual behaviour and defensive behaviour. It is extensively connected to many different body organs and the autonomic nervous system. It thus regulates breathing, digestion, sleep cycles, and so on. The limbic system evolved early to regulate the functioning of the body. By contrast, the thalamocortical system evolved to make sense of complex inputs from outside the body. It comprises the thalamus, a central brain structure that connects sensory and other brain signals to the cortex, and the cortex itself. The thalamocortical system developed after the limbic system and became intimately linked to it.

If we do full justice to Edelman's ideas, we shall have no space over to discuss Upper Palaeolithic image-making. Let us therefore move on to Edelman's identification of two kinds of consciousness: primary consciousness and higher-order consciousness.

Primary consciousness is experienced to some degree by some animals, such as (almost certainly) chimpanzees, (probably) most mammals, and some birds, but (probably) not reptiles. This is how Edelman defines primary consciousness:

Primary consciousness is a state of being aware of things in the world – of having mental images in the present. But it is not accompanied by any sense of a person with a past and future... [Primary consciousness depends on] a special reentrant circuit that emerged during evolution as a new component of neuroanatomy... As human beings possessing higher-order consciousness, we experience primary consciousness as a 'picture' or a 'mental image' of ongoing categorized events... Primary consciousness is a kind of 'remembered present'... It is limited to a small memorial interval around a time chunk I call the present. It lacks an explicit notion or a concept of a personal self, and it does not afford the ability to model the past or the future as part of a correlated scene.

An animal with primary consciousness sees the room the way that a beam of light illuminates it. Only that which is in the beam is explicitly in the remembered present; all else is darkness. This does not mean that an animal with primary consciousness cannot have long-term memory or act on it. Obviously it can, but it cannot, in general, be aware of that memory or plan an extended future for itself based on that memory... Creatures with primary consciousness, while possessing mental images, have no capacity to view those images from the vantage point of a socially constructed self.[15]

Before pointing out the relevance of this sort of consciousness to the Transition, I give Edelman's summary of higher-order consciousness. It is the kind of consciousness that *Homo sapiens* possesses:

Higher-order consciousness involves the recognition by a thinking subject of his or her own acts or affections. It embodies a model of the personal, and of the past and future as well as the present... It is what we as humans have in addition to primary consciousness. We are conscious of being conscious... How can the tyranny of the remembered present be broken? The answer is: By the evolution of new forms of symbolic memory and new systems serving social communication and transmission. In its most developed form, this means the evolutionary capacity for language. Inasmuch as human beings are the only species with language, it also means that higher-order consciousness has flowered in our species...

[Higher-order consciousness] involves the ability to construct a socially based selfhood, to model the world in terms of the past and the future, and to be directly aware. Without a symbolic memory, these abilities cannot develop... Long-term storage of symbolic relations, acquired through interactions with other individuals of the same species, is critical to self-concept.[16]

As I have said, Edelman explains the evolution of higher-order consciousness in neurobiological terms, but we need not consider all the details here. Higher-order consciousness sits, as it were, on the shoulders of primary consciousness. Simply put, the development was enabled by the evolution of enormously complex re-entry neural circuits in the brain. These circuits created more efficient kinds of memory. Indeed, the difference between primary consciousness and higher-order consciousness is that members of the species *Homo sapiens*, the only species that has it, can remember better and use memory to fashion their own individual identities and mental 'scenes' of past, present and future events. This is the key point.

It is also true that fully modern language is a *sine qua non* for higher-order consciousness. A corollary to this observation is that language makes possible auditory hallucinations: it is only with language that 'inner voices' can tell people what to do. In this way, visual hallucinations acquire a new dimension: they speak to those who experience them. Not only do shamans 'see' their animal spirit helpers; the spirits also talk to them.

When did this transition from one kind of consciousness to another take place? Edelman believes that higher-order consciousness evolved rapidly, though he does not hazard an estimate in years. In fact, relatively few gene mutations are required to bring about relatively large changes (new memory and re-entry circuits) in the brain. But Edelman refuses to be drawn on just when the change took place.

The Middle to Upper Palaeolithic Transition reconsidered

For the purposes of my argument, and bearing in mind the recent research that I outlined in Chapters 3 and 4, I believe it is reasonable to assume that higher-order consciousness developed neurologically in Africa before the second wave of emigration to the Middle East and Europe. The pattern of modern human behaviour that higher-order consciousness made possible was put together piecemeal and intermittently in Africa. Now the jigsaw pieces of previous chapters begin to fall into place. It seems likely that fully modern language and higher-order consciousness were, as Edelman argues, linked: it is impossible to have one without the other. This is a point that some researchers into the origins of language do not appreciate. When we speak of the acquisition of fully modern language, we are in effect also speaking of the evolution of higher-order consciousness.

In sum, in western Europe at the time of the Transition, the Neanderthals, descendants of the first out-of-Africa emigration, had a form of primary consciousness and the *Homo sapiens* communities had higher-order consciousness. This hypothesis clarifies a number of puzzling issues.

First, it explains why the Neanderthals were able to borrow certain things from their new neighbours but not others. Because their consciousness and form of language were essentially confined to 'the remembered present', Neanderthals could learn how to make fine blades but they could not conceive of a spirit world to which people went after death. Nor could they conceive of social distinctions that depended on categorizations of generations, past, present and future. Elaborate burials with grave goods were therefore meaningless, though immediate burial may not have been. Carefully planned hunting strategies that foresaw the migration of herds at particular times and places and required complex planning were also impossible. All in all, social hierarchies that extended beyond the immediate present (in which strength and gender ruled) were beyond their ken. They could learn some things but not others. As Edelman describes it, primary consciousness seems to fit what we know about the Neanderthals.

Secondly, and perhaps even more significantly, the shift from primary to higher-order consciousness facilitated a different experience and socially agreed apprehension of the spectrum of human consciousness. Improved memory made possible the long-term recollection of dreams and visions and the construction of those recollections into a spirit world. Simultaneously, the wider range of consciousness afforded a new instrument for social discrimination that was not tied to strength and gender. This is the part of the picture that Edelman does not consider in any depth, though he wonders if what he calls the abandonment of higher-order consciousness is what mystics seek.[17] Mystics are people who exploit the autistic end of the spectrum of consciousness not only for their personal gratification but also to set themselves apart from others.

Sleep, dreaming and the activity of the brain in altered states of consciousness are part and parcel of the electro-chemical functioning of the neurons. Dreaming takes place during 'rapid eye movement' (REM) sleep. This state occurs for about one and a half to two hours during a good night's sleep. It seems that all mammals experience REM sleep and probably dreaming; reptiles, which have a more primitive nervous system, do not. A human foetus at 26 weeks spends all its time in REM sleep. It therefore seems probable that dreaming is something that came about when, during evolution, the early limbic system became fully articulated with the evolving thalamocortical system.

Some researchers believe that dreaming is what happens when sensory input to the brain is greatly diminished: the brain then 'freewheels', synapses firing more or less at random, and the brain tries to make sense of the resultant stream of images. Be that as it may, we still need to ask if sleep is of any value to people and certain animals; if it is not, why did it evolve? After all, chances of survival in a hostile environment are reduced by sleep. The answer is that, in deep sleep, the brain manufactures proteins at a faster rate than during waking. Proteins are essential for maintaining the functioning of cells, including neurons, and in sleep, the human body builds up a reserve of proteins.[18] Sleep (together with the dreaming that takes place in REM sleep, the prelude and postlude to deep sleep) is therefore *biologically*, rather than psychologically, important, and the brain evolved in such a way as to facilitate sleep for good biological reasons. There was no evolutionary selection for dreaming as such – only for the manufacture of proteins. Dreaming is a non-adaptive, but not maladaptive, by-product. The content of the dreams themselves is not significant. Yet people have always felt it necessary to 'explain' dreams, be it as voices of the gods or invasions by devils. More modern dream analysis by Freudians and Jungians is simply a contemporary way of giving meaning to dreams. It is, in the strict sense of the word, a modern *myth* that tries to make sense of a human experience that does not require that sort of explanation.

Now, as I have pointed out, it seems that dogs and other animals dream. This can be determined by observing their behaviour and by EEG studies.[19] But – and this is the key point – they do not remember their dreams, nor do they share their dreams. With only a limited form of primary consciousness at their disposal, we can now see why this must be so, whether they have a simple form of communication or not. Human beings, on the other hand, can remember their dreams and are able to converse with one another about them. They are thus able to socialize dreaming: people in a given community agree, more or less, what dreaming is all about.

This point again brings us back to the spectrum of human consciousness. People have no option but to socialize the autistic end of the spectrum. They place value on some of its experiences in accordance with socially constructed concepts about dreaming. This is also true of states on the intensified, induced trajectory – visions and hallucinations. These experiences are possible because, with higher-order consciousness, people are able to remember them and, with fully modern language, to speak about them. Dreams and visions are thus inevitably drawn into the socializing of the self and into concepts of what it is to be human, concepts that change through time.

By this argument, *Homo sapiens* could dream, as we understand the term, and speak about dreams, but Neanderthals could not: they, with their particular level of primary consciousness, could not remember their dreams, though they must have passed though periods of REM sleep. Nor could they apprehend visions, even if some *Homo sapiens* neighbours showed them how to induce altered states of consciousness, and, even if they managed to enter an altered state (which they probably could do), they would have had no significant recollection of what happened during it.

It was, I argue, this distinction between *Homo sapiens* and Neanderthals that was a pivotal factor in the relationships between the two species and in triggering and driving the efflorescence of image-making that started at the Transition and, long after the Neanderthals had gone, spiralled through the rest of the Upper Palaeolithic. *Homo sapiens* communities saw that they had an ability that Neanderthals did not have: Neanderthals were congenital atheists. *Homo sapiens'* more advanced ability in this mental arena may have made it important for them to cultivate the distinction by (in part) manifesting their visions as two- and three-dimensional images.

How, then, does this understanding answer the question with which this chapter began? How did human beings come to realize that marks on a plane surface or a carved three-dimensional piece of bone could stand for an animal?

Two-dimensional images

The answer lies partly in the ability to recall and socialize dreams and visions and partly in a specific characteristic of the visual images experienced in altered states of consciousness.

In the late 1920s, Heinrich Klüver found that both the entoptic elements from what I have called Stage 1 altered consciousness and the iconic mental images of animals and so forth from Stage 3 seem to be localized on walls, ceilings or other surfaces.[20] This is a common experience and these images have been described as 'pictures painted before your imagination'[21] and as 'a motion picture or a slide show'.[22] Klüver also found that images (what are called 'after-images') recurred after he had awakened from an altered state and that they too were projected onto the ceiling.[23] These afterimages may remain suspended in one's vision for a minute or more. Reichel-Dolmatoff confirmed this experience: the Tukano see their mental images projected onto plane surfaces, and, as afterimages, they can recur in this way for several months.[24] We thus have a range of circumstances in which mental images are projected on to surfaces 'like a motion picture or slide show'. It can happen while a person is actually in an altered state, or it can happen, unexpectedly, as uncalled-for afterimages, flash-backs to earlier altered states of consciousness.

Once human beings had developed higher-order consciousness, they had the ability to see mental images projected onto surfaces and to experience afterimages. Here, I suggest, is the answer to the conundrum of two-dimensional images. People did not 'invent' two-dimensional images; nor did they discover them in natural marks and 'macaronis'. On the contrary, their world was already invested with two-dimensional images; such images were a product of the functioning of the human nervous system in altered states of consciousness and in the context of higher-order consciousness.

Because communities need to reach some sort of consensus about the full spectrum of consciousness, including altered states, and come to some understanding of the significance of moving along it, they would already have developed a set of socially shared mental images, which were to become the repertoire of Upper Palaeolithic motifs, long before they started to make graphic images. This prior formulation explains why the repertoire of motifs seems to have been established right from the beginning of the Transition in western Europe (though emphases within the repertoire changed through time and space).[25] There was not a period during which individuals made whatever images they wished, followed by a period of more restricted socialized imagery. Nor is there any evidence for an early phase of random mark-making. In any event, image-*making* is not an essential feature of a shamanistic society: for instance, the San communities that today live in the Kalahari Desert (and have lived there for millennia) do not have a tradition of painting. There are no rocks in that sandy waste on which they could make images. Yet, despite a measure of idiosyncrasy, they do have a repertoire of animals that they 'see' in trance and a limited number of experiences that they expect to have in the spirit world. It is the entertaining and socializing of *mental imagery* that is fundamental to shamanistic societies. The imagery does not have to be expressed graphically.

How, then, did people come to make representational images of animals and so forth out of projected mental imagery? I argue that at a given time, and for social reasons, the projected images of altered states were insufficient and people needed to 'fix' their visions. They reached out to their emotionally charged visions and tried to touch them, to hold them in place, perhaps on soft surfaces and with their fingers. They were not inventing images. They were merely touching *what was already there*.

The first two-dimensional images were thus not two-dimensional representations of three-dimensional things in the material world, as researchers have always assumed. Rather, they were 'fixed' mental images. In all probability the makers did not suppose that they 'stood for' real animals, any more than the Abelam think that their painted and carved images represent things in the material world. If we could be transported back to the very beginning of the Upper Palaeolithic so that we could compliment a painter on the 'realism' of his or her picture, I believe we should have been met with incredulity. 'But,' the painter might have replied, 'that is *not* a real bison: you can't walk around it; and it is too small. That is a "vision", a "spirit bison". There is nothing "real" about it.' For the makers, the paintings and engravings *were* visions, not representations of visions – as indeed was the case for the southern African San and the North American shamans (Chapters 5 and 6).

I do not argue that people 'fixed' their projected visions while in a *deeply* altered state of consciousness. If the vision seekers were cataleptic or 'unconscious', they could not have made images on the walls of caves. But, as we have seen, there are states in which one can move around and relate to one's surroundings, even though one is seeing visions. Vision seekers would have been able to reach out to visions while they were in lighter states, experiencing after-images, or, having shifted to a more alert state, they were trying to reconstitute their visions on the surfaces where they had seen them floating.

Further support for this view comes from Upper Palaeolithic parietal images themselves: they have a number of characteristics in common with the imagery of altered states of consciousness. For instance, the parietal images are disengaged from any sort of natural setting. In only a very few cases (e.g., Rouffignac Cave) is there any suggestion of what might possibly be a ground line (a natural stain on the rock wall): there is no suggestion of the kind of environment in which real animals live – no trees, rivers, or grassy plains. Moreover, Upper Palaeolithic parietal images have what Halverson perceptively called their 'own free-floating existence'. They are placed 'without regard to size or position relative to one another'.[26] These characteristics are exactly what one would expect of projected, fixed, mental images that accumulated over a period of time. Mental images float freely and independently of any natural environment.

The impression of floating is sometimes enhanced by two further characteristics. Often, Upper Palaeolithic parietal images of animals have no hoofs; the legs terminate open-endedly in a way that suggested to some early researchers that the image-makers were depicting animals standing in grass that concealed their hoofs – but, of course, no grass is ever shown (Pl. 12). Other researchers have suggested that the animals may be depicted as dead, but more often than not they are clearly alive. It is more reasonable to suppose that the absence of hoofs implies an absence of 'standing'. Then, too, when hoofs are depicted, they are sometimes in a hanging, rather than standing, position (Pl. 13). In Lascaux and other sites, hoofs are depicted to show their underside, or hoofprint. The combined effect of these features is particularly powerful in the Axial Gallery at Lascaux, where the images seem to float up the walls and over the ceiling, thus creating a tunnel of floating, encircling images (Chapter 9), or in the densely engraved panel in the Sanctuary at Les Trois Frères (Fig. 44) .

This is not to say that all Upper Palaeolithic depictions are images fixed in altered states of consciousness or while experiencing afterimages. Once the initial step had been taken, the development of Upper Palaeolithic art probably followed three courses. One stream continued to comprise mental imagery fixed while it was being experienced. A second stream derived from recollected mental imagery: after recovering from the experience, people tried to reconstitute their visions by closely examining the surface on which they had floated. They not only looked closely at the rock wall or ceiling; they also felt its contours and protu-

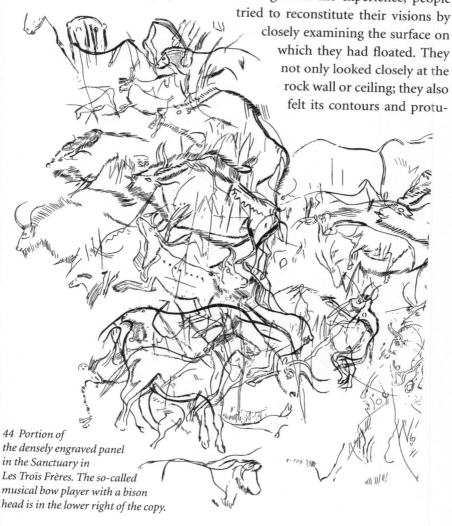

44 Portion of
the densely engraved panel
in the Sanctuary in
Les Trois Frères. The so-called
musical bow player with a bison
head is in the lower right of the copy.

berances. Sometimes, they needed only to add a few lines, perhaps legs and an underbelly, to complete the vision/image that was, for them, inherently *in* the rock surface. A third stream derived from contemplation of the graphic products of the first two streams and the realization that someone who had never experienced an altered state could duplicate them. Many shamans believe that spirit animals, the ones that they see in their visions, also mingle with herds of real animals; there was therefore a link between spirit and real animals. In some cases, large depictions of animals, whether real or spirit animals, were communally produced: although one person may have been responsible for deciding on the subject matter and, perhaps, the general outline, a number of people co-operated to make the image.

These momentous steps were taken during a time of social change and differentiation. Higher-order consciousness allowed a group of people within a larger community to commandeer the experiences of altered consciousness and to set themselves apart from those who, for whatever reasons, did not have those experiences. The far end of the intensified spectrum became the preserve of those who mastered the techniques necessary to access visions. Although all people have the neurobiological potential to enter altered states of consciousness, those states are not socially open to all.

The spectrum of human consciousness thus became an instrument of social discrimination – not the only one, but a significant one. Its importance lay in the way in which the socializing of the spectrum gave rise to image-making. Because image-making was related, at least initially, to the fixing of visions, art (to revert to the broad term) and religion were simultaneously born in a process of social stratification. Art and religion were therefore socially divisive.

At first glance, one may be alarmed by such a grim thought and conclude that, because art and religion did not contribute directly to social cohesion in an all-embracing, functionalist way, they would not have lasted long. On the contrary, it was the very social discriminations that the process of dividing up the spectrum created that drove society forward. Social divisions are not necessarily maladaptive; indeed, they facilitate complex social adaptations to environments.

Three-dimensional images

I have dealt extensively with two-dimensional imagery because our interest is primarily in Upper Palaeolithic parietal art and the use that the people of that time made of the caves. We must, however, also consider three-dimensional imagery, the portable art that I described in Chapter 1.

The earliest three-dimensional imagery was found in Aurignacian strata in southern Germany.[27] The pieces come from open rock shelters, not deep caves. Radiocarbon dates for the four sites are as follows:

Vogelherd	31,900–23,060 years ago
Hohlenstein-Stadel	31,750 years ago
Geissenklösterle	35,000–32,000 years ago
Stratzing	31,790–28,400 years ago

Until the 1994 discovery of the Chauvet Cave (approximately 33,000 years ago), these were the oldest dated pieces of Upper Palaeolithic art (Fig. 45). Most of the pieces are about only 5 cm (2 in) long, though an especially striking therianthropic figure with a lion's head from Hohlenstein-Stadel is just over 29 cm (11½ in) high (Fig. 46). Nearly all the pieces were carved from mammoth ivory, the only exception being made from mammoth bone. The ivory came from the centre of mammoth tusks; the harder outer ivory was used for projectile points. The pieces were carved with stone tools, but subsequent polishing removed most traces of the carving process. Joachim Hahn, the German archaeologist who has studied the pieces in detail, believes that the polishing was done with hide or wet limestone. His experiments suggest that it must have taken about 40 hours to make the Vogelherd horse, the most widely illustrated piece (Fig. 45, top).[28]

At Vogelherd, the statuettes were found in two strata (there were as many as ten occupation floors), but in only two locations, one above the other, an observation that suggests considerable continuity of site use. In addition to the statuettes, the sites yielded pierced ivory *bâtons de commandement* (decorated long bones with a hole at one end that have been interpreted as symbols of political power), perforated fox canines and ivory pendants, as well as stone endscrapers and burins, but the various kinds of items were not mixed indiscriminately. At Vogelherd, the statuettes were well away from a stone flaking area outside the cave and from an activity area within the rock shelter; at Stadel, the statuettes were far inside the shelter; at Geissenklösterle, they were on the fringe of two artefact concentrations.[29] Although some of them were clearly used as pendants, this sort of spatial separation suggests that they were not part of daily, mundane activities. Hahn concludes that the rock shelters were used as caches, or storage sites, in an inhospitable landscape. He may well be right, and it is hard not to recall the caches of North American shamans.

The Aurignacian sites, or areas within them, may also have been special places, entrances to a spiritual realm.

The species represented by the statuettes include

4 felines,

4 mammoths,

3 anthropomorphs,

2 bison,

1 bear, and

1 horse.[30]

The faunal remains found in the same rock shelters as the statuettes come from a much wider range of species – 21 in all; the image-makers focused on a limited bestiary.[31] Although the small number of pieces makes generalizations hazardous, Hahn concluded: 'As in wall art, animal species represented in mobiliary art do not simply mimic the relative proportions of animal species in the faunal assemblages from the sites.'[32] Other criteria than simply food were operating in the selection of species for statuettes. By the Magdalenian, portable art embraced a wider range of animal motifs than parietal art.

Significantly, the set of species selected is similar to that found throughout Upper Palaeolithic parietal art. But, within the overall Upper Palaeolithic bestiary, the Aurignacian carvings place an unusually marked numerical emphasis on felines (though one must bear in mind that only a small number of pieces are known). This emphasis is particularly interesting in view of the comparatively large number of parietal images of felines found in Chauvet Cave, an Aurignacian site that was more or less contemporary with the southern German statuettes.[33] Was there, at this time, a fairly general shamanistic concern with felines, and indeed other apparently dangerous animals, that was in some way modified over time? Judging from the presently available evidence that seems to have been the case.

Further, the hoofs or paws of the statuettes are hardly represented, a feature that recalls numerous parietal images. None of the Aurignacian sites in southern Germany has parietal art, but one of the portable art excavations (Geissenklösterle) yielded a piece of multicoloured, painted limestone.[34] At this site, the statuettes came from the upper Aurignacian strata and the painted stone from the lower.

The evidence is too slight to make confident generalizations. Nevertheless, we need to ask: how can we account for the appearance of both two- and three-dimensional art at the beginning of the Upper Palaeolithic? There is no evidence that one evolved out of the other. Are two distinct scenarios required to explain the two types of art, or can they both be explained by a single set of generating factors?

In answer to this question, I argue that the same neurological mechanism that explains the genesis of two-dimensional imagery also explains the origin of three-dimensional statuettes. How could this have been? The mental imagery that the nervous system projects in altered states of consciousness is not exclusively seen on two-dimensional surfaces. On the contrary, people in deep altered states of consciousness also see small, three-dimensional halluci-nations. If, as I have argued, the world of (some) people in Upper Palaeolithic communities was invested with images even before they started 'fixing' them on cave walls, those images would have been three- as well as two-dimen-sional.

Next we must recall that the repertoire of animal motifs must have been established, in broad terms, *before* people started making parietal images. An established, restricted repertoire must also have been present before Aurignacians in southern Germany started making statuettes. Even as an explanation for the origin of two-dimensional imagery had to be consonant with a pre-existing repertoire of animal motifs, so, too, does an explanation for the earliest three-dimensional images. Moreover, apart from internal numeri-cal emphases, those repertoires were similar in broad terms. This means that early Upper Palaeolithic people believed a set of animal species to have certain properties or meanings that made them special. The diverse evidence that I discussed in previous chapters strongly suggests that those properties and meanings included the supernatural potency that animal helpers gave to shamans and, further, that could be harnessed to accomplish various tasks, and the zoomorphic persona that shamans assumed when they went on out-of-body travel to the subterranean or upper spirit worlds or to other parts of the landscape. From these premises, we may assume that fragments of those animals, such as ivory, teeth and antlers, were believed to possess related essences and powers, an assumption that has abundant ethnographic support (Chapter 9).

Now let us return to one of the aspects of parietal image-making that I noted earlier. The images were not so much painted onto rock walls as released from, or coaxed through, the living membrane (rather than 'veil' if we think of the bowels of the earth) that existed between the image-maker and the spirit world. In some instances, natural features of the rock stood for parts of the animals. I argue that this fundamental principle probably also applied to the making of three-dimensional images: the carver of the image merely released what was already inside the material. This is, of course, a well-known principle that sculptors in various cultures, including the Western tradition, speak about. Aurignacian three-dimensional image-makers, from their point of view, may therefore not have superimposed meaning (an image) on the otherwise meaningless pieces of ivory that they were handling; rather, they released the animal essence from within the fragments of animals. As we shall see in Chapter 9, many shamanistic communities believe in the regeneration of animals from bones. It need not follow that only lions could be carved from lion bones or only horses from horse bones; hunter-gatherer bestiaries, or symbologies, are more fluid than that. As we have seen, mammoth ivory was the favoured raw material for the statuettes.

The way in which these beliefs about animal power and fragments of animals could have come together with small, three-dimensional hallucinations of animals is clear. Under certain social circumstances, which may have varied from time to time and place to place, certain people (shamans) saw a relationship between the small, three-dimensional, projected mental images that they experienced at the far end of the intensified spectrum and fragments of animals that lay around their hearths. Remember that the set of significant species was already established, shared, spoken about, seen in visions and dreamed about. Subsequent cutting, scraping and polishing released the symbolic animals from within the pieces of ivory so that they became three-dimensional, materialized visions. The portable animal statuettes were therefore far more than decorative trinkets: they were reified three-dimensional spirit animals with all their prophylactic and other powers.

We have now moved some distance from the underworld of the caves and are in the open rock shelters that the Aurignacians occupied daily. It is therefore not surprising that, in later periods of the Upper Palaeolithic, when portable art became more various than present evidence suggests it was during the Aurignacian, a wider range of species came to be represented than the more limited set of motifs that we find in the specific, fixed contexts of cave walls. Portable art came to be made in more varied circumstances and contexts than the restricted circumstances established by the underground locations of parietal images. As with the three streams of image-making that flowed from initial fixed-vision parietal images, so with portable art a wide range of animal symbolism came to be associated with tool embellishments and socially significant body adornment of various kinds.

In all cultures, selected animals acquire spectra or sets of associations and meanings, not a single one-to-one meaning. It may well be that a carved three-dimensional pendant of a horse did not encode exactly the same segment of that species' range of meaning as did a painting of a horse in a deep cavern. The context of an image focuses attention on one segment of its spectrum of associations. But the 'subterranean' focus of meaning would have been present in the background as a penumbra that imparted extra power to the pendant.[35] We saw in the San case study that shamans were involved in hunting: they were believed to guide antelope into the waiting hunters' ambush.

This is not what is generally understood by 'hunting magic', but it goes some way towards explaining why, say, horses were engraved on spear-throwers. Spirit horses may well have been some shamans' animal helpers; that is why they appear fixed on the subterranean membrane. At the same time, associating a horse image with a spear-thrower may have highlighted more general associations of success and power in hunting. Similarly, the meaningful spectra of some species did not extend from portable art to the nether world: they are therefore not depicted in cave art.

A comparable fluidity is evident in the geographical distribution of Aurignacian art: it seems not to have been a universal component of the Aurignacian technocomplex. There were centres of Aurignacian art in central France, the Pyrenees, and farther east in the Middle and Upper Danube Basin. Elsewhere there are many Aurignacian sites with comparable preservation, but no art.[36] Again we note that the making of representational images was not an inevitable part of the Transition. Certain social circumstances were required for image-making.

A step towards understanding those circumstances is facilitated by a closer examination of the Aurignacian statuettes (Fig. 45). Hahn[37] found that the horse from Vogelherd is in the

45 Some of the Aurignacian statuettes recovered at Vogelherd. The small horse has a chevron carved into its smooth surface; other statuettes are marked by curves, crosses and dots.

posture that a stallion adopts to impress its females. The bear from Geissenklösterle is in an aggressive upright position. The two Vogelherd lions, with their triangular, backward-pointing ears are in the 'tense open-mouth' posture of a lion defending its kill. Both the Stadel lioness head and the one from Vogelherd also seem to be in an alert state.[38] This ethological evidential strand leads Hahn to argue that the statuettes encoded notions of power and strength.[39] But what sort of power and strength?

Thomas Dowson and Martin Porr answer this question in their own examination of the postures of the animals represented.[40] They conclude that the statuettes were associated with an early form of shamanism: 'entering an altered state of consciousness is often considered a dangerous activity' and 'shamans have to be strong and powerful to…perform the work they do'. To support this interpretation, Dowson and Porr point to the therianthropic statuette from Hohlenstein-Stadel, with its human body and feline head (Fig. 46). As they rightly say, transformation into an animal is an integral part of shamanism. In providing social and conceptual contexts for the statuettes, they note the comparatively segregated locations in which the objects were found and suggest that Aurignacian shamans may have performed their tasks in relative seclusion, though the statuettes' use as pendants also suggests that they had a public significance.

Given the set of beliefs that I have now outlined, it is not difficult to see that the origin of three-dimensional images was not markedly different from that of two-dimensional images; the same generating principles applied to both. The earliest Upper Palaeolithic image-making was all underpinned by the same conceptual foundations.

A new threshold

The title of this chapter was circumspectly chosen. I have been concerned with one origin of image-making, that which took place during the west European Transition. The explanation that I have outlined for that particular instance does not preclude multiple independent origins elsewhere and at other times – once, that is, higher-order consciousness

46 *The Hohlenstein-Stadel therianthrope. It is part human, part lion, and stands approximately 30 cm (12 in) high.*

had evolved. Image-making did not originate in only one place and then diffuse throughout the world. The circumstances in other times and places may not have been identical to those that I have described for the west European Middle to Upper Palaeolithic Transition. They remain to be demonstrated, not merely asserted. There is nothing mechanistic about my explanation. But it nevertheless highlights certain universals in human neural morphology, shifting consciousness, and the ways in which people have no option but to rationalize and socialize the full spectrum. As we know from our own times, the ways in which people name and place value on segments of the spectrum is open to contestation. Indeed, it seems likely that within a given society the rationalizing of the spectrum will always be divisive and contested.

The picture of the Transition that we have begun to build up has resolved a number of long-standing and seemingly intractable problems. We can now understand much better the kind of relationship that must have obtained between Neanderthals and the in-coming *Homo sapiens* communities. We can glimpse a kind of relationship that is different from anything we can possibly experience in the world today. We can also begin to comprehend why Neanderthals managed some activities but not others.

Importantly, we can begin to see social stirrings in the *Homo sapiens* camps, stirrings that were related to the socializing of the autistic end of the spectrum of higher-order consciousness and to image-making. Humanity was on the threshold of new kinds of social discrimination. In subsequent chapters we explore more carefully the kind of society that may have been evolving at this time and the roles that images and caves began to play.

CHAPTER 8

The Cave in the Mind

In one of the most evocative passages in Plato's *The Republic*, Socrates invites Glaucon, a devoted pupil, to envisage 'an underground cave-dwelling, with a long entrance reaching up towards the light'.[1] In this cave are fettered prisoners who have been in this condition since infancy and who can see only the shadows of statues and other objects that men are carrying across the entrance. These shadows fall on the wall before their fixed gaze. With no knowledge of the world beyond their cave, the prisoners, as Glaucon readily concedes, believe that they are looking at reality. If one of their number – emblematic of the philosopher – were to manage to escape and reach the light behind the source of the shadows, and then return to tell the prisoners that they are seeing mere shadows, they would not believe him.

If, Socrates continues, the benighted prisoners had a 'system of honours and commendations' and awarded prizes to the man who had the keenest eye for the passing shadows and the best memory of them, they would not wish to abandon their awards merely on the word of the one who had been up to the light. Nor would he wish to return to sharing their esteem for those who had been recipients of awards.

There is much in this rather disturbing trope that is relevant to our enquiry into Upper Palaeolithic parietal images. From our perspective, there is, however, a key point that Socrates does not make. In our version of the cave, the light streaming from above catches the prisoners themselves and throws the 'shadows' of their minds onto the wall so that they mingle with the shadows of the external objects to create a multi-dimensional panorama.

We are concerned not only with the human mind in the cave; we must also take into account the neurological cave in the mind. We are considering some of the ways in which the human mind behaved in the Upper Palaeolithic caverns, whether as a result of the sensory deprivation of the caves themselves or the many other factors that induce altered states of consciousness. Amongst those states is, as we have seen, the sensation of entering a constricting vortex and coming out on the far side into an hallucinatory realm with its own conditions of causality and transformation. This is the cave in the mind. Then, too, there is the projection of mental imagery onto surfaces. In the absence of anyone who had the kind of understanding of altered states that we have today, Upper Palaeolithic people must have believed, like Socrates's prisoners, that those images and experiences were part and parcel of 'reality', as they conceived it. This chapter explores the ways in which the cave in the mind and the topographies of geomorphological caves interlocked.

To accomplish this task, I intertwine more tightly the various strands of evidence that we have been following, and, at the same time, continue my consideration of shamanism. I began with a suspicion, an intelligent guess that writers have mooted from time to time; I now move on to confirmation of that suspicion and, in the next chapter, to an exploration of specific Upper Palaeolithic caves with well-supported hypotheses in mind. At that point, I shall consider how Upper Palaeolithic people may have awarded 'honours and commendations' to those who were skilled in discerning, remembering and 'fixing' the 'shadows' on the walls. We shall be able to see how the caves were used and, at least in general terms, why they were embellished as they were. Our evidential strands will intertwine to form a strong cable.

Hypothesis

All in all, the preceding chapters have shown that there are two major reasons for suspecting some form of shamanism in the west European Upper Palaeolithic:

There is every reason to believe that the brains of Upper Palaeolithic *Homo sapiens* were fully modern. They therefore experienced dreams and had the potential to experience visions. Further, they had no option but to reach some common understanding of what dreams and visions were and what they meant. By contrast, combined neurological and archaeological evidence suggests that Neanderthals, like other mammals, had the neurological potential to experience dreams and hallucinations, but not to remember them in any significant way, to act upon them, or to use them as a basis for social discrimination.

Secondly, we have noted the ubiquity among hunter-gatherer communities of what we call shamanism. Not being concerned with societies that combine elements of shamanism with other religions, I listed what I take to be the principal features of hunter-gatherer shamanism (Chapter 4). Whatever differences exist between them, and they are doubtless numerous, hunter-gatherer societies throughout the world have ritual functionaries who exploit altered states of consciousness to perform the tasks that I noted in our general discussions and in the two case studies.[2] I argue that the widespread occurrence of shamanism results not merely from diffusion from a geographical source area, such as central Asia – though the first people to enter North America doubtless took tenets of shamanism with them. Rather, we should note the ancient, universal, human neurological inheritance that includes the capacity of the nervous system to enter altered states and the need to make sense of the resultant dreams and hallucinations within a foraging way of life. There seems to be no other explanation for the remarkable similarities between shamanistic traditions worldwide.

Taken together these two points – antiquity and ubiquity – make it seem likely that some form of shamanism was practised by the hunter-gatherers of the west European Upper Palaeolithic. That ancient expression of shamanism would in all probability not have been *identical* to any of the historically recorded types of shamanism, but it would have had comparable core features – hence the value of both ethnographic case studies and neuropsychology. Nor does it seem likely that Upper Palaeolithic shamanism was static and unchanging through the 30,000 and more years of the Upper Palaeolithic and across the whole of western Europe. But, as the analogy that I drew with Christianity implies (Chapter 4), change does not mean total overthrow, and Upper Palaeolithic *shamanisms* were probably subsumable under the general rubric of 'shamanism'.

Our suspicion seems well-founded enough to be called a hypothesis. As we intertwine evidential strands, we can move on to consider other kinds of support for that hypothesis and to see what puzzling features of Upper Palaeolithic art it explains.

Animals and 'signs'

One of the most baffling features of Upper Palaeolithic art is the co-occurrence of geometric motifs with images of animals: sometimes they are adjacent, sometimes superimposed. Some panels, such as the Apse in Lascaux[3] or the Sanctuary in Les Trois Frères,[4] are so densely covered with both representational and geometric images that some relationship between the two types seems inescapable. What could that relationship be?

We have seen that representational imagery could not have evolved out of geometric or 'macaroni' marks: the non-representational marks are not feeble early attempts at image-making. What, then, about the suggestion that the two types of image derive from two distinct, parallel, probably complementary, graphic systems?[5] Some researchers think that the relationship between geometric and representational images may have been akin to that between text and diagrams in a book: each says the same thing but by means of different conventions.

The answer is in fact more straightforward. As we have seen, in certain altered states, the human nervous system produces both geometric and representational imagery. The two kinds of imagery are not exclusively sequential, each obliterating its predecessor; in Stage 3, they are experienced together. Their intimate association in shamanistic art throughout the world therefore comes as no surprise. Indeed, we can go a step further. The behaviour of the human nervous system in altered states resolves the postulated dichotomy between geometric and representational imagery that has formed the foundation for all classifications of Upper Palaeolithic art hitherto devised. Contrary to these classifications, both types of image are representational: they both represent (by way of complex processes) mental imagery, not (at least initially) things in the material world.

That is not the end of the matter. When the neuropsychological model (Chapter 4) is applied to Upper Palaeolithic imagery we find *all* stages represented. This model was an initial attempt to get a better hold on Upper Palaeolithic art, one that went beyond general assertions and unsupported ethnographic analogies. It has, however, become much misunderstood: there is more to the model than entoptic phenomena. It is incorrect to refer to the hypothesis as the 'entoptic explanation' or the 'entoptic theory', as numerous writers do. Indeed, clear depictions of entoptic phenomena are rare in Upper Palaeolithic cave art, as indeed they are in southern African shamanistic rock paintings (as opposed to engravings where they are more numerous). Both Upper Palaeolithic people and San rock painters were more concerned with Stage 3 hallucinations than with Stage 1 entoptic phenomena. What is significant is that there are Upper Palaeolithic images referable to *all three* stages of the model, and this strengthens the argument for a connection with the mental imagery of altered states. We find entoptic forms (Stage 1), construals (Stage 2), and transformations and combinations of representational and entoptic imagery (Stage 3).[6] The proportions of imagery ascribable to each of the stages varied from time to time and place to place.

But we also find Upper Palaeolithic 'signs' that do *not* conform to any of the known entoptic types. Figure 47 shows some of these non-entoptic motifs. Amongst them are 'claviforms', vertical lines with a bulge on one side, and 'tec-

47 Not all Upper Palaeolithic signs conform to the shapes of entoptic phenomena as established by laboratory research. These include so-called claviforms and hut-shaped tectiforms.

tiforms', hut-like motifs. This distinction is a major step forward because it helps us to address the non-entoptic 'signs' and how these relate to animal motifs from a different point of view from that which we adopt when we examine the entoptic elements. Because meaning is not inherent in but rather assigned to entoptic imagery (and indeed to all imagery) in specific cultural contexts, we do not know what the 'signs' of Upper Palaeolithic art meant to the people of the time. The Cro-Magnons of western Europe were not South American Tukano, so we cannot transfer the meanings that Reichel-Dolmatoff discovered those Amazonian people ascribed to their geometric mental images to the Upper Palaeolithic paintings and engravings.

Whether we shall ever be able to crack the meanings of the entoptic and non-entoptic signs remains to be seen; I am not irredeemably pessimistic on this point. At present we can at least say that *some* of them are similar to entoptic forms. Those motifs are, as far as their origin rather than their meaning is concerned, explicable in terms of altered states of consciousness. They therefore fit the overall pattern suggested by the hypothesis that Upper Palaeolithic parietal art was shamanistic.

Caverns measureless to man

Another highly puzzling characteristic of Upper Palaeolithic imagery is also clarified by our hypothesis, and, moreover, clarified in such a way as to lead us on to further, more detailed, questions and answers. The heuristic potential of the hypothesis is thus revealed: it does not ring the curtain down on research, but encouragingly leads on to further questions.

The characteristic to which I now refer is the placing of images in deep, often small, underground contexts to which no light penetrates and which people seem to have seldom visited. These locations are connected to larger chambers, also in total darkness, in which a number of people could have gathered to view the images and to perform other activities. Then there are the images in the open air and in the entrances to caves; these are well-lit. The way in which the images trail from the level of daily life into underground caverns and then on into spaces that in some cases can be reached only by negotiating hazardous, labyrinthine subterranean passages suggests that parietal art was a cultural product that linked the tiers of the Upper Palaeolithic cosmos. In Lévi-Straussian terms, one could say that Upper Palaeolithic parietal art mediates, or forms a connecting link between, the two elements of an 'above-ground:below-ground' binary opposition.

This inference means that to speak of Upper Palaeolithic shamanism is to make a statement about cosmology, not just about religious belief and ritual, as if such matters were epiphenomena and therefore of no great importance to our understanding of Upper Palaeolithic life. All life, economic, social and religious, takes place within and interacts reciprocally with a specific conception of the universe. It cannot be otherwise. As we saw in previous chapters, the shamanistic cosmology is conceived, in the first instance, as comprising two realms, the material world and a spiritual realm. Often, the spirit world is immanent, interdigitating with the material world as well as separate from it. At the same time, these two realms are conceived of as subdivided and layered, the more socially complex the shamanistic society, the more tiered the subdivisions of the cosmos. There is not one, monolithic 'shamanistic cosmos'. We also saw that universal, neurologically 'wired' sensations of flying and passing through a constricting tunnel probably gave rise to these conceptions.

I now argue that entry into Upper Palaeolithic caves was probably seen as virtually indistinguishable from entry into the mental vortex that leads to the experiences and hallucinations of deep trance. The subterranean passages and chambers were the 'entrails' of the nether world; entry into them was both physical and psychic entry into the underworld. 'Spiritual' experiences were thus given topographic materiality. Entry into a cave was, for Upper Palaeolithic people, entry into part of the spirit world. The embellishing images blazed (possibly in a fairly literal sense) a path into the unknown.

We can go a step further. Altered states of consciousness not only create notions of a tiered cosmos; they also afford access to, and thereby repeatedly validate, the various divisions of that cosmos. The tiered shamanistic cosmos and 'proof' of its reality constitute a closed system of experiential creation and verification. Even people who, for whatever reasons, did not have access to the far end of the intensified trajectory or to the caves themselves, were still able to verify the structure of their cosmos through the more evanescent glimpses of another realm that their dreams afforded them. That they could fleetingly and imperfectly glimpse the creatures and transformations of the spirit world was, for them, evidence enough that the shamans could actually visit it and return with detailed accounts of it. Such people were like Socrates's prisoners who were able to talk to each other but who merely confirmed each other's view of the passing shadows.

The Upper Palaeolithic subterranean passages and chambers were therefore places that afforded close contact with, even penetration of, a spiritual, nether tier of the cosmos. The images that people made there related to that chthonic (subterranean) realm. Images were not so much taken underground – pictures of the world above lodged in people's memories – and placed there; they were both obtained and fixed there. The hallucinatory, or spirit, world together with its painted and engraved imagery, was thus invested with materiality and precisely situated cosmologically; it was not something that existed merely in people's thoughts and minds. The spiritual nether world was *there*, tangible and material – and some people could empirically verify it by entering the caves and seeing for themselves the 'fixed' visions of the spirit-animals that empowered the shamans of the community and also by experiencing visions, perhaps even in those underground spaces.

Moreover, image-making did not merely take place in the spirit world: it also shaped and incrementally created that world. Every image made hidden presences visible. There was thus a fecund interaction between the given topography of the caves, mercurial mental imagery, and image-fixing by individuals and groups; through time, the images built up and modified the spiritual world both materially (in the caves) and conceptually (in people's minds). The spirit world, like the social world above, was to some degree malleable; people could engage with it and to a certain extent shape it. In most cases, this shaping took the form of adding new images to those already there or starting to create a new panel altogether. But, in some rare cases, there seem to have been attempts at removing images already there. In the Cosquer Cave, for instance, hand-prints were deeply scored across, as if to cancel them, and in Chauvet it seems that images may have been removed by scraping the surface.[7]

A living support

This understanding of the caves as the entrails of the nether world brings me to another feature of Upper Palaeolithic parietal art that is difficult to explain outside of the shamanistic hypothesis. As we have seen, one of the best-known and most consistent features of Upper Palaeolithic art is the use that image-makers made of features of the rock surfaces on which they placed their images. Almost every cave contains instances, and numerous writers have commented on the puzzle that they present.[8] Here are a few examples over and above those to which I have already referred; they lead, cumulatively, to an important conclusion about the seemingly 'dead' cave walls.

Upper Palaeolithic images are sometimes placed so that a small, apparently insignificant nodule or protuberance forms the eye of an animal. Some of the nodules are so insignificant that one suspects that they were identified and selected by touch rather than by sight. In the dim light of flickering lamps, fingers lightly exploring the walls discovered a nodule, and the mind, prepared for the discovery of animals, took it to be an eye. In some cases, touch may have aided the recall, or reconstitution, of a visionary animal. Having experienced a vision in deep trance or as an afterimage, a vision seeker in a more alert state carefully felt the wall for indications of where the spirit animal was.

On a larger scale, a natural rock at Comarque seems to have suggested a remarkably realistic horse's head, complete with nostrils and mouth (Fig. 48).[9] An engraver merely completed and added details to the form. Then, too, human figures occasionally also make use of natural features of the rock. At Le Portel, for example, two red outline human figures are painted so that stalagmitic protuberances become their penes (Pl. 15).[10]

A particularly illuminating and well-known example is at Castillo (Cantabria) where a depiction of a bison has been painted to fit the rough surface of a stalagmite: the artist discerned the back, tail and hind leg in the shape of the rock (Fig. 49). Significantly, this meant that he or she would have to depict the animal in a vertical position.[11] But this does not seem to have mattered. On the contrary, the resultant image exemplifies one of the differences between mental imagery and the animals of the material world outside the cave that, in the nature of things, normally walk or stand in a horizontal position. The Castillo artist was not trying to depict an animal as anyone may see it outside the cave; rather, he or she was reconstituting a 'floating' vision. As we saw in Chapter 7, Upper Palaeolithic images seem to 'float' on the rock; when they are anchored by some feature of the surface, they are not necessarily in a realistic posture.

48 Partly natural and partly sculpted, this rock form represents a horse's head. (Comarque, Dordogne.)

49 *A few lines were added to the natural form of a stalagmite in Castillo, Spain, to produce an image of a vertical bison.*

50 *(Below) This hole in the rock wall of the Salon Noir, Niaux, resembles a deer head seen face-on. Upper Palaeolithic people added antlers to the natural shape to enhance the appearance of a deer's head looking out of the wall.*

So far, I have described depictions that present lateral views of animals. By contrast, in the Salon Noir at Niaux an artist added antlers to a hole in the rock that, viewed from a certain angle, resembles a deer head, as seen from the front (Figure 50).[12] At Altamira, Upper Palaeolithic people created a similar effect in the Horse's Tail, the deepest part of the cave: natural shapes in the rock have been transformed by the addition of painted eyes and, in one case, a black patch that may represent a beard.[13] Visitors who reach the end of this narrow passage and

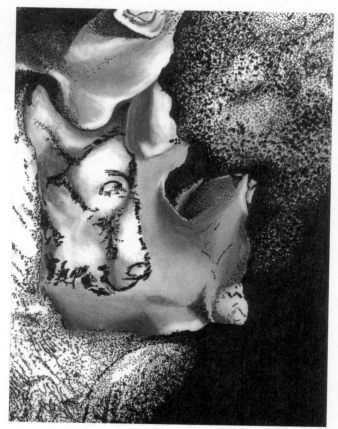

51 A horse's head painted on a flint nodule projecting from the wall of Rouffignac, Dordogne, gives the impression of the animal being inside the rock.

then turn to leave the cave are confronted by faces apparently peering from the rock walls (Pls 4, 5). A similar effect was created in Gargas, in the foothills of the Pyrenees.[14] Perhaps even more remarkable is a horse's head painted in Rouffignac (Fig. 51). Here the head has been depicted on a flint nodule that juts out from the wall; the rest of the animal's body seems to be 'inside' the wall.

The effect created by these and many other images is of human and animal faces looking out of the rock wall. The figures are not merely painted onto the surface; they become part of the cave itself, part of the nether realm. In this way, human intervention changed the significance of the topography. What could that significance be?

We saw in the North American case study that shamans go on a vision quest, usually in a remote isolated place, sometimes a high cliff-top, sometimes a cave, to fast, meditate and induce an altered state of consciousness in which they 'see' the animal helper that will impart the power requisite for shamanistic practice.[15] The evidence that I have assembled in this and previous chapters, especially that pertaining to small, hidden niches in the Upper Palaeolithic caves, suggests that *one* of the uses of the caves was for some sort of vision questing.[16] Certainly, the sensory deprivation afforded by the remote, silent and totally dark chambers, such as the Diverticule of the Felines in Lascaux and the Horse's Tail in Altamira, induces altered states of consciousness.[17] In their various stages of altered states, questers sought, by sight and touch, in the folds and cracks of the rock face, visions of powerful animals. It is as if the rock were a living membrane between those who ventured in and one of the lowest levels of the tiered cosmos; behind the membrane lay a realm inhabited by spirit animals and spirits themselves, and the passages and chambers of the caves penetrated deep into that realm.

This suggestion recalls the experience of Barbara Myerhoff, an anthropologist who worked among the Huichol people of northern Mexico. After having ingested the hallucinogenic plant peyote, she 'sat concentrating on a mythical little animal.... The little fellow and I had entered a yarn painting and he sat precisely in the middle of the composition. I watched him fade and finally disappear into a hole.' So-called yarn paintings are made by sticking coloured yarn onto an adhesive surface; they frequently depict hallucinatory experiences and mythical concepts. Entering depicted imagery in this manner was probably also part of Upper Palaeolithic and southern African shamanistic experience.[18]

A tangible 'other world'

This explanation extends to another enigmatic feature of the embellished caves: the various ways in which the walls of numerous caverns were touched.

In some sites, such as Cosquer Cave, near Marseilles, the entrance to which was inundated by the rising sea-level at the end of the Ice Age, so-called finger-flutings cover most of the walls and parts of the ceiling, even beyond head height (Pl. 14). People trailed two, three or four fingers through the mud on the cave walls wherever the surface was malleable. Above the now-submerged entrance passage that leads to Cosquer, the finger marks are several yards up and their making must have required rudimentary ladders.[19] Indeed, at Cosquer the only parts of the cave not covered with finger-flutings are those without the soft mud film that is made by the weathering of the limestone.[20] The cross-sections of some of these flutings, 2–3 mm deep, suggest that they might not have been made with fingers but with some sort of instrument, perhaps the tip of a flint blade with nicks that left striations, though such marks may have been left by fragments of stone carried along by the fingers or by broken fingernails.

The patterns so created are rectilinear, curving or zigzagged; some were gone over twice, so we can be sure that they were not entirely random – the shapes mattered. For us, they recall some of the entoptic elements, but there is more to it. In Cosquer, the finger-flutings form a background to the images, which are, in every case, executed on top of them. In one instance, however, a group of two red handprints are also overlain by finger-flutings. The handprints and the flutings in Cosquer therefore seem to constitute a temporal group of markings.

This sort of treatment of cave walls was more widespread in the west European Upper Palaeolithic than is usually allowed; perhaps researchers find finger-flutings rather boring compared with images of animals and therefore tend to ignore them. A detailed and valuable study was, however, undertaken by Michel Lorblanchet, a French archaeologist who has studied the rock art of the Lot Département of France. In the Pech Merle Cave, he found as many as 120 sq. m (1,290 sq. ft) of finger markings: 'Almost all the clay walls that are accessible without too much difficulty bear these markings.'[21] Most marks seem to have been made by adults, though two bands of lines were clearly executed by two small hands, either of a woman or an adolescent. The second of these possibilities may be supported by a dozen or so footprints of an adolescent or big child on the floor of Pech Merle.[22]

Lorblanchet found that representational images were integrated into a number of the apparently random finger-flutings, though he rightly rejected any suggestion that simple finger marks evolved into depictions.[23] Still, his interest centred on recognizable images rather than the 'macaronis' themselves. As a result, he saw the practice of finger-fluting as associated with creation mythology, 'bringing forth creatures from the void and the inextricable'. But finger-flutings appear without representational images often enough to suggest that they had their own significance.

This conclusion is borne out at Hornos de la Pena, in Spain. Here the flutings are more restricted in distribution than in Cosquer or Pech Merle: in one place, a finger-traced 'grid' surrounds and appears to issue from a natural cavity (Pl. 16).[24] In another remarkable treatment of cave walls at Hornos de la Pena, cavities in the walls were filled with mud and then punctured, apparently with fingers or sticks.[25]

In Cosquer, the treatment of the surfaces was taken further than finger-flut-ings. In some locations, sizeable areas were scraped with a tool of some sort as if people wanted to collect the soft, sticky clay; no attempts were made to scrape hard surfaces.[26] There is next to no sign in the cave of the quantities of clay that must have been removed from the walls; unless it was deposited in the now-flooded areas, it was therefore carried out of the cave. Red clay was also scraped out of fissures and seemingly removed from the cave. Although one cannot be absolutely certain because of the flooding, it seems that the clay was valued for some purpose, whether for body decoration, the manufacture of paint, or decoration of skin clothing we cannot tell.

On the question of the meaning of finger-flutings, Peter Ucko, Director of the Institute of Archaeology, London, remarks, 'it is…inconceivable to us today to understand the nature of such action.'[27] Jean Clottes and Jean Courtin also remain puzzled by finger-fluting. They ask: 'What could their purpose be, except to mark the presence of people in the depths of the earth – to take pos-session of these places, as mysterious as they are frightening, where for all we know no one before them had dared to venture?'[28] I defer answering this crucial question until after considering what I believe to be a related form of human activity in the caves.

Hands-on experience

Indeed, the evidence of finger-fluting places us in an advantageous position to consider in a new way one of the most talked-about features of Upper Palaeolithic art – handprints. In some respects, researchers have studied hand-prints in the same way that they have considered finger-fluting and 'macaronis': even as they looked for recognizable images amongst the flutings, they have been interested in the *image* of the hand rather than the act of making it. Chapters 5 and 6 showed that there is reason to believe that an image itself and the act of making it are simply parts of a longer chain of oper-ations entailing social action and beliefs.

As we saw in Chapter 1, handprints are of two kinds: positive and negative. Positive prints were made by placing paint on the palm and fingers and then pressing the hand against the rock wall. Negative prints were made by placing the hand against the rock and then blowing paint over the hand and the sur-rounding rock; when the hand was removed, an image of a hand remained.

A fascinating variation on handprints has been found in the Chauvet Cave. Here, there are two panels of what, from a distance, appeared to be large red dots. Eventually, when researchers were able to move closer to the rock wall without disturbing the Upper Palaeolithic surface beneath their feet, they found that the dots are in fact palm-prints. Paint was placed in the hollow of the palm and then slapped against the rock; here and there one can see a trickle of paint falling from the print and the fainter imprints of fingers. On the left side of each print there is a slight notch left by the gap between the thumb and the first finger; they are all right-hand prints. So far, the technique is unique to Chauvet.[29]

If we take into account what we have already noted about the shamanistic tiered cosmos and the rock wall as a membrane between people and the subterranean spirit world, we must consider the act of making the prints as important as (possibly more than) the resulting shape of a hand. To be sure, the handprint may well have signified the presence of a particular person, as is often suggested – an ancient 'Joe was here' – but the fact that a whole panel in Chauvet seems to have been made by a single person diminishes this possibility, at least for that instance. Further, if a handprint indicates the presence of a particular person, we need to ask about the circumstances in which it was made. People had to carry paint into the depths of the caves: handprints were not made on the spur of the moment. Why would people want to have their handprints in the deep caves?

Again, it seems that the answer to this question has more to do with touching the rock surface than with image-making. In the case of negative prints, the paint was applied in such a way that it completely covered the entire hand, and sometimes part of the forearm as well, together with the surrounding rock (Fig. 52). The hand thus 'disappeared' behind a layer of paint; it was 'sealed into' the wall. In the case of positive prints, the paint was a mediating film that connected the hand to the rock. We have seen that paint should not be

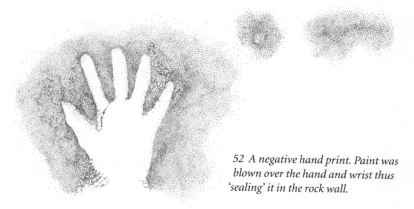

52 A negative hand print. Paint was blown over the hand and wrist thus 'sealing' it in the rock wall.

regarded as a purely technical substance (Chapter 5); it probably had its own significance and potency. Perhaps it was a kind of power-impregnated 'solvent' that 'dissolved' the rock and facilitated intimate contact with the realm behind it.

The importance of Upper Palaeolithic paint as a significant substance is borne out by the Chauvet palm-prints. In one panel there are 48 prints; in the other there are 92. The size and anatomical characteristics of the prints suggest that each panel was made by one person, possibly a youth or a woman, but the two panels were not painted by the same person. The panel of 48 dots seems to have been initiated by a clear, full handprint to the left; the palm-prints were added, but care was taken to ensure that they did not overlap the original handprint. The panel of 92 prints has no full handprint; the 'ghosts' of fingers, when visible, appear to be fortuitous. Paint was evidently not added to the palm for each print because some have a thinner film of paint in the centre of the palm. But the trickle of paint falling from some prints seems to me to suggest that the action was designed, at least in part, to place a fair quantity of red paint on the rock, so much that it occasionally trickled down the rock face.

In other caves, such as Enlène, there are small dots and strokes of paint in the Galerie du Fond – no images, just the red marks (Fig. 1). As their placing in this deep, out-of-the-way location shows, the marks could not have been made by accident. Here the mere presence of even a small quantity of paint on the rock seems to have been important. The placing of paint, a highly charged substance, on the 'membrane' was a significant act.

The act of blowing paint onto the rock also requires careful consideration, lest we imagine that it was no more than a technical operation. Lorblanchet, who had considerable anthropological experience in Australia, investigated the blown handprints and images in the Pech Merle cave in the light of what he had learned about Aboriginal painting techniques. As part of his work in France, he undertook to try to replicate the complex 'spotted horses' panel in Pech Merle, which includes six negative handprints (Pl. 19). He found that the handprints were added around the two horses after they had been completed. There can be little doubt that the handprints here are integrally related to the representational horse images; together, they constitute a meaningful 'composition'.

He also found that parts of the horses themselves were made by blowing paint onto the rock. To replicate the process of blowing he used charcoal:

I put the charcoal powder in my mouth, chewed it, and diluted it with saliva and water. The mixture of charcoal and saliva extended with water forms a paint that adheres well to a cave wall…. To reproduce [the handprints], I used both my hands, but I found it easier to use my left hand with its back against the wall to make what appear to be prints of my right hand.[30]

A poison-control centre in Paris warned Lorblanchet not to experiment with manganese dioxide, one of the pigments that Upper Palaeolithic artists used, because he would 'risk serious health problems' if he accidentally swallowed it.

Standing in front of the Upper Palaeolithic 'spotted horses', and contemplating them for a long time, I noticed a point of interest. I found that my hands comfortably and simultaneously fitted the two black prints over the back of the right-hand horse (I did, of course, take care not to allow my hands to touch the rock). I also found that the rock between these two prints bulged out slightly so that it came close to my mouth. At this point, the rock is stained with a red haze of paint that may have come from the mouth of a person standing exactly where I was and with both hands placed on the rock. As I stood there, my body was close to the image of the horse; I was almost embracing the horse, and my face was inches away from the 'membrane'.

Although Lorblanchet believes that each handprint in this panel was made separately and that the uniform size of the prints suggests that they were made by only one person, I do not believe his conclusions are inescapable. The lowest handprint, for instance, must have been made by the right hand of someone lying prone on the rock floor of the cave; the print is so low that the person's wrist and forearm must have been in contact with the floor. From this position, it would have been difficult, though perhaps not impossible, for the prostrate person to blow the paint onto his or her own hand. It seems probable that the blowing of the paint need not have been done by the person who was holding his or her hand(s) against the rock but by another, perhaps one could say 'officiating', person. It is also possible that more than one person took part in the paint-blowing; a small group of people may have taken turns in the paint-blowing process. This kind of co-operative mode of making at least some of the prints seems to be confirmed by an instance in Gargas, where the hand and forearm of a child were held against the rock by an adult, whose grip on the child's arm can be seen; it was not the child who was blowing the paint.

As a result of his experience of making a replica of the 'spotted horses' panel, Lorblanchet concluded:

The method of spit-painting seems to have had in itself exceptional symbolic significance to early people. Human breath, the most profound expression of a human being, literally breathes life onto a cave wall. The painter projected his being onto the rock, transforming himself into the horses. There could be no closer or more direct communication between a work and its creator.[31]

We can now return to the questions posed by finger-fluting. If we allow that Upper Palaeolithic people believed that the spirit world lay behind the thin, membranous walls of the underground chambers and passages, the evidence for finger-fluting, handprints and much otherwise incomprehensible behaviour can be understood in rational, if not absolutely precise, terms. In a variety of ways, people touched, respected, painted and ritually treated the walls of caves because of what they were and what existed behind their surfaces. The walls were not a meaningless support. They were part of a highly charged context, a context that, I now argue, provides the earliest evidence that we have for one of the archetypal religious metaphors.

Darkness and light

Sometimes an undulation in the rock surface becomes the dorsal line of an animal if one's light is held in a specific position; an artist simply added legs and some other features to the shadow. There is a particularly fine example at Niaux where an undulation in the rock has been used to suggest a bison's back (Pls 17, 18). The distinctively humped dorsal line is clear when a light source is held to the left of and slightly below the image. Like the bison at Castillo (Fig. 49), this Niaux animal is positioned vertically in order to exploit the natural feature of the rock. Similarly, the head of the right-hand 'spotted horse' at Pech Merle is suggested by a natural feature of the rock, especially when the source of light is in a certain position – also to the left of the image. In this case, the artist distorted the painted horse's head, making it grotesquely attenuated; the rock shape itself is more realistically proportioned than the painted head within it. It is as though the rock suggested 'horse', yet the artist painted not a naturalistic horse but a deliberately, though only partially, distorted horse, perhaps a 'spirit-horse', recognizable as to species but clearly not 'real'. This technique of using shadows to complete a depiction is more common than is usually supposed:[32] people used the insubstantial interplay of moving shadows to seek power and create images of that power.

In these instances, the sought-after animal was not simply 'discovered' in the convolutions of the rock. It was created by human intervention *and* an interaction between two elements, light and darkness. Leaving the world of light and entering the dark, subterranean realm, the image-maker, or makers, carried a lamp or torch. This flickering flame was something that questers had to master and which, the evidence suggests, they used for further revelations.

An important reciprocality is implied by these images born of light and shadow. On the one hand, the creator of the image holds it in his or her power: a movement of the light source can cause the image to appear out of the murk; another movement causes it to disappear. The creator controls the image. On the other hand, the image holds its creator in its power: if the creator or subsequent viewer wishes the image to remain visible, he or she is obliged to maintain a posture that keeps the light source in a specific position. If the viewer tires and as a result lowers the light, the image seems to retreat into the realm behind the membrane. Perhaps more than any other Upper Palaeolithic images, these 'creatures' (creations) of light and darkness point to a complex interaction between person and spirit, artist and image, viewer and image. There was a great deal more to Upper Palaeolithic cave paintings than pictures simply to be looked at: some of the images sprang from a fundamental metaphor.

This conclusion is supported by some of the lamps found in the caves. The controlled use of fire dates back more than half a million years, but the use of fire in lamps started at the beginning of the Upper Palaeolithic; lamps were an invention of *Homo sapiens*. Most of the known examples come from France; lamps from Spain, Germany and farther east are rare. Sophie de Beaune and Randall White, archaeologists who undertook a detailed study of Upper Palaeolithic lamps, concluded that lamp-producing communities were restricted to a particular region.[33] This, as we have seen, is also the region of prolific cave art.

Most lamps were simply rough pieces of stone with natural hollows that could contain the tallow; wicks were made of lichen, moss, conifers and juniper. They did not produce a very bright light. De Beaune and White estimate that as many as 150 lamps would be required to provide accurate colour perception of images along a 5-m (16-ft) long panel; each lamp would have to be placed about 50 cm (20 in) from the wall. So many lamps in one place seems unlikely. Lamps were therefore probably usually supplemented by torches made from Silvester pine. But in caves where only lamps were used viewers would have experienced the paintings and engravings very differently from the way we do today with harsh electric lamps that penetrate every recess. With small tallow lamps, only limited portions of a wall could be seen at any one time, and, as de Beaune and White put it, 'The illusion of animals suddenly materializing out of the darkness is a powerful one.'[34]

Some lamps were clearly 'special'. One of these was discovered in La Mouthe (Dordogne), where, early on, excavations demonstrated the antiquity of Upper Palaeolithic cave art (Fig. 8). It is a beautifully shaped, shallow stone bowl. On the underside, there is an engraving of an ibex head with large curving horns. Though not as common as depictions of horses, bison and reindeer, ibexes were engraved on the walls of La Mouthe in close association with other species.

Another example, this one from Lascaux, is also fashioned from sandstone, but it has a 'handle' (Fig. 52). It is engraved with a central line that runs the length of the handle. Towards one end of the line there are, on one side, four separate marks and, on the other side and towards the other end of the line, a set of similar incisions. Such signs occur on the walls in all parts of Lascaux, along with depictions of animals. Most of these are painted, though one in the remote Diverticule of the Felines is engraved. This lamp was found at the bottom of the 'Well', an area of the cave I discuss in the next chapter.

The imagery on both these lamps thus relates to the parietal art of the caves in which they were found. At first glance, one may suppose that the imagery on the lamps is there merely for decoration. But what I have so far noted about the shamanistic cosmos, the relations between some images and light, and the significance of entering the entrails of the underworld are all points that suggest there was more to light and lamps than simple utility. Both the animals and the geometric motifs were, in some way, related to the light:darkness metaphor.

It is, of course, quite possible that the genesis of the binary light:darkness metaphor took place before people ventured into the caves. Day and night might well have been a much earlier generating circumstance, each having its own connotations. Once created, the metaphor was probably extended to embrace and inform beliefs about the caves and the nether world. Indeed, it

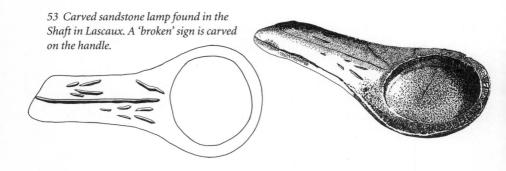

53 Carved sandstone lamp found in the Shaft in Lascaux. A 'broken' sign is carved on the handle.

seems probable that, during the Upper Palaeolithic, the great binary metaphor became a vehicle for multiple meanings that might have included notions of life and death, good and bad, though in formulations probably different from those that have run through the Western tradition down to the present day.

Numerous writers have discussed the metaphors by which we live, the ones that give meaning and orientation to our lives, that structure the ways in which we react to the world around us and to other people.[35] Light and darkness constitute one of those metaphors. But, unlike many others of more recent origin, light:darkness can be traced back to the Upper Palaeolithic.

An echo from the opposite wall

Light and darkness and the other characteristics of Upper Palaeolithic art that I have considered have focused on the visual. But, in altered states of consciousness, *all* the senses hallucinate. It is this complexity that gives visions and hallucinations such overwhelming impact.

Socrates made this point when he developed his notion of bound prisoners in a cave. He suggested that, if those carrying the objects across the entrance to the cave were to speak and there was 'an echo from the opposite wall', those in the cave would believe 'that the voice came from the shadow passing before them'.

In shamanistic belief, images and visions are not silent: they speak, make animal sounds and communicate. For instance, a Greenlandic Inuit shaman seeking spirit helpers went to an entrance into a glacier. After calling on the spirits, he heard a voice telling him to enter the 'under-ice' world. There, in the darkness, he encountered a growling bear.[36]

Sound also plays a prominent role in the *Banisteriopsis*-induced trances of the Peruvian rain forest Cashinahua:

I heard armadillo tail trumpets and then many frogs and toads singing. The world was transformed. Everything became bright…. I came down the trail to a village. There was much noise, the sound of people laughing. They were dancing kacha, the fertility dance.[37]

Here, the shaman's trance experience includes sounds of various kinds. It is common to find that shamans hear not only the sounds of musical instruments, spirit people and spirit animals, but those animals also speak to them, give them instructions and teach them songs. Some of these sounds derive from neurologically induced aural sensations which shamans interpret in culturally specific ways; others, those that include comprehensible statements, are more properly hallucinations.[38] To these 'inner sounds' must be added those made by people to accompany rituals and mental experiences.[39] There is evidence that Upper Palaeolithic people had the means to make 'music'. More than two dozen so-called 'flutes' have been reported, but it is not always clear if the holes in these hollow bones were made to facilitate the sounding of different pitches or if they are simply the result of the bone having been bitten by animals. But some are convincing, and it appears that people used hollow bones to make sounds.[40] Whether the sounds so produced could be called music or whether they were imitations of animal sounds we do not know.

Another type of sound was evidently made by 'bull-roarers', flat pieces of bone, antler or wood that were attached to a cord and swung round and round to produce a powerful humming sound. A particularly fine example, covered with geometric decorations and rubbed with red ochre, was found at La Roche de Birol in the Dordogne.[41] Such instruments were also used by the southern African San to imitate the sound of bees swarming; bees were, for them, a significant source of supernatural potency. We do not know what Upper Palaeolithic people believed about the sounds emitted by bull-roarers, but, if they were used in subterranean chambers, the effect must have been awe-inspiring.

To my mind, the oft-cited 'musical bow player' in the Sanctuary at Les Trois Frères is somewhat less convincing (Figs 1, 44). This bison-headed figure seems, at first glance and in numerous illustrations, to be holding a bow to his face. Closer inspection of the whole panel reveals so many apparently random lines amongst the tangle of figures that the bow-playing interpretation becomes tenuous. Finally, we need to notice that a number of caves contain evidence for stalactites, especially of the undulating 'drapery' kind, having been struck, though we cannot always be sure that this was done during the Upper Palaeolithic. These stalactites emit a deep booming sound when struck. In the Réseau Clastres (Fig. 2) in the foothills of the French Pyrenees, they have been struck by someone standing on the far side; someone entering the cave with only a lamp or burning torch would not easily see the percussionist, and the sound would swell and resonate from the darkness in enveloping waves.

The effect of rhythmic sound, especially drumming and chanting, is widely recognized as a means of contacting the world of spirits.[42] The literature on this point is indeed vast. One has only to think of the sounds of clapping and dancing rattles fixed around the ankles that cause potency to 'boil' in San shamans and to carry them off to the spirit world. Elsewhere, shamans are intimately associated with drums. Amongst Siberian shamans, the tiered cosmos is represented on drums along with creatures that inhabit the various levels.[43] On one drum the horizontal levels were crossed by a perpendicular line 'which the shaman called *kiri* (bowstring) and which was supposed to serve him as orientation when he was going on unknown roads or flying on his drum to the spirits.'[44] This 'bowstring' is what anthropologists call the *axis mundi*.

Amongst the Siberian Tuvas, a clan ritual was performed to 'enliven' a shaman's drum: in this ceremony, the process was regarded as 'taming and training the horse',[45] thus emphasizing the point that the drum was the shaman's 'vehicle' to the spirit world. In northern Siberia, the shaman's drum may represent a reindeer, the hide of which is used in the making of the drum. The shaman was said to ride the reindeer-drum to the spirit world; drums were 'animals in their own right as well as makers of sounds'.[46]

The drum is also called a boat. As Anna-Leena Siikala of Joensuu University, Finland, a long-time student of Siberian shamanism, explains:

Calling a drum a boat is also more than an expression of figurative language. Mythical images or metaphoric expressions are often understood as a real manifestation of the signified. The drum-boat, for example, can be visualised and sensed as a real object in visions and shaman songs.[47]

The American anthropologist Michael Harner sums up the effect of persistent drumming: 'The steady, monotonous beat of the drum acts like a carrier wave, first to help the shaman enter the SSC [Shamanic State of Consciousness], and then sustain him on his journey.'[48] This is not a flight of fancy. Like so much else of what I have discussed, there is a material, neurological, not merely psychological, basis for widespread shamanistic beliefs. Research has shown that low-frequency drum-beats produce changes in the human nervous system and induce trance states, which, of course, include sensations of out-of-body travel.[49] There is thus a neurological explanation for the shamanistic use of drums.

Working on the altogether reasonable hypothesis that some sort of musical or rhythmic activity probably took place in Upper Palaeolithic caves, researchers have investigated the acoustic properties of various chambers and passages.[50] Findings suggest that resonant areas are more likely to have images than non-resonant ones. The implication is that people performed rituals involving drumming and chanting in the acoustically best areas and then followed up these activities by making images. An extension to this suggestion is that depictions of felines are placed (for unexplained reasons) in non-resonant chambers. All in all, the hypothesis is interesting but, I feel, ultimately unpersuasive. For instance, a comparison of the highly decorated Axial Gallery with the much less elaborate Diverticule of the Felines in Lascaux is misleading. They are not both 'narrow dead-end tunnels'.[51] The Axial Gallery is much larger than the Diverticule of the Felines, which can accommodate only one person and then in a prone position. Then, too, the recent discovery of feline images in a deep but large chamber in Chauvet will require investigation. The factors that governed the placing of images were far more complex than resonance alone, and included the way in which the topography of a cave was conceived and the locations where specific kinds of spiritual experiences were encouraged. Still, we need not doubt that resonance and echoes added to the effect of subterranean Upper Palaeolithic rituals. The caves, if not the hills, were *alive* with the sound of music.

What are the effects of music on someone in an altered state? Westerners, having ingested LSD, expressed the experience like this:

I lay quietly and listened to the music…then my vision commenced to change a little…and slowly the music seemed to absorb all my consciousness…. It seemed to me as though the music and I became one. You do not hear it – you are the music. It seems to play in you…. As the music started, I suddenly felt a great lifting from within. Then outer space became alive. The music carried me and flowed through me…I felt much larger than normal and more elongated in my limbs.[52]

Barbara Myerhoff had a comparable experience after she ingested peyote. She became intensely and blissfully conscious of passing vehicles. 'With great delight I began to notice sounds, especially the noises of the trucks passing on the highway outside…. My body assumed the rhythm of the passing trucks, gently wafting up and down like a scarf in a breeze.'[53]

If that is the effect of music and rhythmic sound on Westerners, what would it have been on Upper Palaeolithic people? Would animal sounds, for instance, have led to a feeling of oneness with the animals? Did sound aid transformation into an animal? 'You are the music.' It is, of course, difficult to answer such questions, but, given the universality of the human nervous system, it seems likely that these Western reports throw some light on what it must have been like to enter an Upper Palaeolithic cave, to experience altered states and to hear music and emotive sounds.

The cumulative effect

Socrates's simile of a cave inhabited by prisoners bound so that they can see only shadows is a more dramatic presentation of the insights that he offered in the previous section of *The Republic*. Immediately preceding his development of the cave simile, Socrates asked Glaucon to think of a line divided into four sections that represent states of mind: at the top end is intelligence, next is reason (understanding), next is belief (faith) and at the lower end of the line is illusion (imagining).[54] This conceit is uncannily like the spectrum of consciousness that I have outlined. Upper Palaeolithic people moved along Socrates's line as do twenty-first-century people, though it would be good to think that we do not occupy the lower, illusory, end of the line as extensively as they did. The mind in the cave and the cave in the human mind cannot be separated; they are keys to subterranean Upper Palaeolithic parietal art.

The combined effect of the underground spaces, altered states of consciousness, mysterious sounds, the interplay of light and darkness, and progressively revealed, flickering panels of images is, in one sense, easy to imagine, but, in another sense, the impact of such multi-sensory experiences on Upper Palaeolithic people probably exceeded anything that we can comprehend today. We enter the caves with our minds at the top end of Socrates's line; their minds were working with faith and illusion. Nor can we fully reconstruct the rituals that must surely have been performed in the cold, silent and dimly lit chambers and passages. Nor can we say what each and every image and geometric sign meant to the people who saw them or were told about them.

Yet, if we see the caves as entities, as natural phenomena taken over by people, and try to place them in a social context, as Max Raphael urged, we can begin to sense something of the role that they must have played in Upper Palaeolithic communities. Rather than attempt to generalize the exceedingly diverse caves into a rigid, imposed 'structure', as André Leroi-Gourhan did, we need to take them individually and try to discern the various ways in which each was used by a community of people – not just by individuals for the making of individual images. It is to this essentially sociological task that I turn in the next chapter.

CHAPTER 9
Cave and Community

One of the most demanding challenges to understanding Upper Palaeolithic art, especially parietal art, is to go beyond generalities to the empirical specifics of images and caves. As we saw in Chapter 2, there has been an uneasy tension between generality and particularity. With structuralist explanations, the tendency has been towards generalities. On the other hand, present-day empirical work goes to the other extreme. Researchers now abjure generalization and explanation (which must, of course, include some generalization) in favour of what they see as objective data-collection.

Rather than think in hard-line structuralist terms and focus on the animal species depicted, as Leroi-Gourhan and others have done, I consider a congeries of aspects of Upper Palaeolithic parietal art as I try to come to grips with specific caves:

– the ways in which images were made,
– the spaces in which they were made,
– the social implications of how and where images were made, and
– how modes of execution, meaningful spaces and social relations all interacted within a shamanistic, tiered cosmos.

In adopting this multi-component approach, I take up the position that Max Raphael initiated but did not develop. In short, we need to consider the exploitation of the varied topographies of caves from a social perspective. In doing so, I identify what I call 'activity areas', spaces in which people behaved in what they considered appropriate ways and in which they performed rituals relevant to those parts. It was communities of people, not just random, isolated individuals, who used the caves. There must have been shared notions about what the caves were and what counted as appropriate activities to perform in them. There was therefore some sort of 'structure', some set of beliefs about the caves, but it was not inexorably superimposed on the caves by unthinking automatons. Rather, the beliefs were a malleable resource on which individuals and groups of individuals drew and which they consciously manipulated when they embellished the caves.

The argument that I explore in this chapter acknowledges two dialectic relationships:

1   between, on the one hand, cosmologies and beliefs in people's minds and, on the other, the shapes of the caves;
2   between social structure and the topographies of the caves.

I use the word 'dialectic' (in the sense of progressive, interactive unification of opposites) because I wish to move away from the purist structuralist notion of a fixed mental structure that people impose on the world. Instead, I argue that the uses that people made of the caves did not merely reflect the structure, or structures, of diversifying Upper Palaeolithic society. Rather, the caves were active instruments in both the propagation and the transformation of society. As the anthropologist Tim Ingold puts it, 'Culture is not a framework for *perceiving* the world, but for *interpreting* it, to oneself and others.'[1] How this could be will become apparent as I proceed.

From the outset, it is essential to remember that the 'shamanistic explanation', that I built up in previous chapters, and that I now use as the foundation for an exploration of specific caves, should not be taken to be a monolithic invariable that obscures temporal, geographical, social and iconographic diversity. On the contrary, it is (or should be) a tool for uncovering diversity, not for concealing it. To demonstrate the heuristic potential of the explanation I contrast the ways in which Upper Palaeolithic people exploited different caves. They explored and adapted each cave in accordance with its peculiar topography[2] and in terms of the particular shamanistic cosmology and social relations that prevailed at that time and place. There were probably Upper Palaeolithic 'shamanisms', rather than one immutable, monolithic religion.

To illustrate these points, I contrast two caves in the Dordogne that are believed to be of approximately the same age but that have vastly different topographies – Gabillou and Lascaux. We shall see similarities and also dissimilarities between them that point to different kinds of social relations within the societies that embellished them and thus to different 'shamanisms'.

Gabillou

Gabillou, a cave that overlooks the Isle River near the small town Mussidan in the Dordogne, is a fairly simple initial example of how the distribution of imagery within caves may be understood in terms of the shamanistic explanation.

Not long after the discovery of Lascaux in 1940, workmen were enlarging a cellar beneath a modern house when they found an entrance to a tunnel; it had been blocked by a medieval wall. The area had also been part of a quarry. Alerted by the discovery of Lascaux, a bricklayer was on the look-out for Upper Palaeolithic art – and he was not disappointed. In the late 1940s, Jean Gaussen, a local doctor and enthusiastic prehistorian acquired the property. The owner, one of Gaussen's patients, had been having a long wrangle with his tenants, who refused to leave, and who denied Gaussen access to the site because they perceived him as a friend of the owner. Exasperated, the owner sold the house to Gaussen at a very reasonable price. Gaussen thus bought the site without having seen it. The tenants were immediately content to let him into the cave. Once their dispute with the original owner had thus come to an abrupt and, from their point of view victorious, end they left amicably within three months.

Visitors caused a little damage in the narrow tunnel soon after its discovery, but Gaussen at once put a stop to that. Through his concern, the cave has been well preserved. It has never been open to tourists, and Gaussen, who died in 2000, never allowed more than two, or at most three, visitors at a time to enter the narrow tunnel. I am greatly indebted to the late Dr Gaussen for allowing me and my companions three extensive visits to the site.

Because early Magdalenian deposits were found inside and outside of what is now the entrance, Gabillou is believed to date from the early part of that period; it was thus contemporary with Lascaux.[3] Unlike many caves that ramify into complex interlinked passages, chambers and small *diverticules*, Gabillou comprises only an entrance chamber, that was probably at least partially open to natural light during the Magdalenian, and a single slightly sinuous tunnel that extends from the entrance chamber for approximately 30 m (100 ft) (Fig. 54).[4]

Several researchers, including Gaussen, excavated the cave. The first investigator, Gaston Charmarty, found eight lamps on the surface of the tunnel, a horse molar and several pieces of bone. Subsequently, Gaussen himself excavated the tunnel and found a further 10 lamps, a stone hammer, a rock plaquette with traces of paint, and 20 flint flakes or blades, one of which was covered on both sides with red ochre.

THE ENTRANCE CHAMBER

Unfortunately, the entrance chamber was partially destroyed when the cellar was first constructed. Apparently, the builders were unaware of the images. As far as we can tell from what remains of them, the chamber was embellished with paintings and also with 'simpler' engravings. The species represented

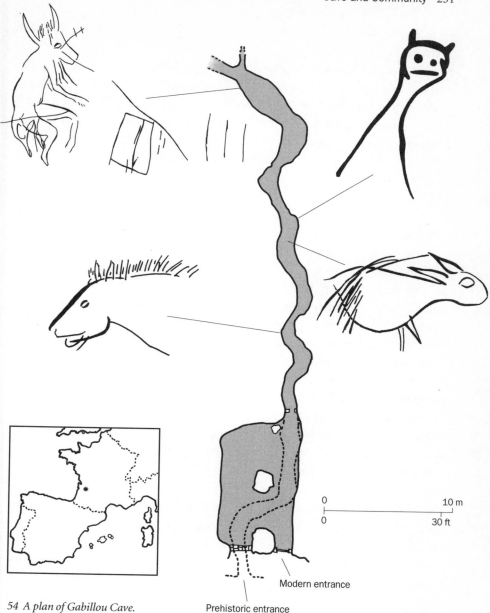

54 A plan of Gabillou Cave.

Modern entrance

Prehistoric entrance

include two deer, a bird, a horse, and bison; there are also now-unidentifiable marks. Some of these images are on projections from the ceiling, the reason why they escaped destruction during the modern centuries when the space was occupied. Because of poor preservation, it is impossible to say how many images were originally in the entrance chamber. Images exist wherever the old surface is preserved.

The space is today large enough to accommodate a fair number of people, and the distribution of images on the ceiling and on the wall near the entrance to the tunnel suggests that this was also so in Magdalenian times, though it is hard to establish the exact Upper Palaeolithic dimensions. It does not seem to have been large enough to have made a commodious living site; perhaps there was a living area outside the entrance. We cannot tell.

THE TUNNEL

The floor of the tunnel that leads off from the entrance chamber was considerably lowered by excavations; the excavators painted a line on the walls to indicate the ancient surface. Originally, the tunnel contained a fine clay filling 1.2 to 1.5 m (3 ft 11 in–4 ft 11 in) deep. During the Magdalenian, visitors to the passage were obliged to go on hands and knees, and movement was restricted. Indeed, only one person at a time would have been able to crawl along the tunnel with any ease; two people would, especially at narrow points, have been impossible. The images must have been made by people sitting or lying down. They do not extend below the former level of the floor surface.

In the tunnel, preservation is excellent. Beautiful engraved images of horses, aurochs, bison, 'monsters' and a remarkable hare are strung out along virtually its entire length, though they tend to concentrate in bays in the wall. Most were made by only a few deft engraved strokes in the soft rock; even a fingernail could produce an engraved line, but most of the lines seem to have been made with an implement with a wider point.

There are no elaborately painted images in the passage, although there do appear to be patches of red ochre that may be the remains of paint. The Abbé Breuil believed that the engravers 'took care to show certain characteristic details so as to make the attitude of the animal more exact…The rest of the figure seems to have been intentionally neglected as it took secondary importance in the mind of the artist.'[5] He also argued that the many engraved lines that overlie a number of the images were 'magical strokes'.[6] I return to such lines when I consider Lascaux.

A considerable number of the images are fitted into inequalities in the rock – or, as I argue, extracted from suggestive features of the surface. The nose of one animal is neatly shaped around a small boss of rock. At least one image is engraved so that it is clearly coming out of the rock face. Then, too, some few red-painted images were executed after the engravings. At the end of the tunnel, an engraved horse is superimposed by a painted one. The painter used the mane and part of the head of the earlier image, but the breast of the later image is new.

This kind of participation in already-existing images is characteristic of parts of Lascaux. Other parallels with Lascaux include: quadrilateral grid signs, a distinctive way of painting the hoofs of animals, and the presence of a claviform at the end of the tunnel in Gabillou (there are numerous examples in Lascaux). 'Broken signs', that is, lines with detached, short side additions, also occur in both sites. Finally, the trick of draughtsmanship of leaving a gap between an animal's leg and the body, apparently to show depth, is found at both sites. As many researchers believe, large Lascaux and the smaller Gabillou were probably used by people belonging to a single social network, a point to which I return.

Magdalenian Gabillou

Because of its good preservation, the quality of the images and its contemporaneity with Lascaux, Leroi-Gourhan[7] regarded Gabillou as 'one of the most important French caves'. In order to make sense of the images and the cave in terms of his mythogram, he had to postulate not one but two sanctuaries. The first, he claimed, comprised the entrance chamber, its 'end' being marked by two felines and a 'horned personage' near the beginning of the tunnel. The end of the second sanctuary – and the tunnel itself – was marked by another feline and 'horned personage'. Within these two postulated sanctuaries, the horse/bison theme was 'taken up over and over again'.[8]

If we abandon any attempt to plot the distribution of motifs and instead examine the cave from the point of view of contrasting human activity areas, we find that the relative sizes and shapes of the two parts of the cave suggest a significant distinction.

Communal rituals could have taken place in the entrance in the presence of images now only fragmentarily preserved: there is space for a number of people. The remains here of simpler engraved images show that the area was not exclusively reserved for one kind of activity. Because we cannot date individual images, we must also allow that the two kinds of image may reflect changes through time in the uses to which the entrance chamber was put. This part of my interpretation must remain tentative because of the destruction of so much of the entrance.

The situation in the tunnel is clearer. Throughout its length, it was, I argue, used by individual vision questers who, isolated from the community in a restricted space, made comparatively swiftly executed engravings. Questers passed through three spatial stages and in doing so crossed two thresholds: first, they left the outside world for the entrance chamber and communal, preparatory rituals; then they left that space to penetrate more deeply into the underworld, the tunnel replicating – and possibly inducing – the mental vortex that leads to vivid visions. In the depths, they individually sought the visions of altered states that would guarantee them supernatural power, and then they either fixed those visions as they were experiencing them or reconstituted them after returning to a more normal level of consciousness (Fig. 55). Amongst those visions were the 'monsters' of Gabillou: weird creatures with long necks (Fig. 54).[9] As Ann Sieveking remarks, they are comparable to those at the end of Pergouset in the Lot district of central France, another long tunnel cave. She entertains the possibility that they may have derived from drug-induced visions.[10]

Finally, transformed mentally and socially by their experiences, questers returned to the level of daily life where they were regarded as those who had traversed the cosmos and had thereby acquired abilities not possessed by everyone. They entered into new kinds of social relations with other members of their community. Every time the cave was used, social divisions were dramatized: the many outside, probably the few in the entrance, and even fewer in the depths, face to face with the creatures of the nether world.

Paralleling those social divisions were segments of the spectrum of consciousness. Although deeply altered states could, of course, be experienced outside the cave or in the entrance chamber, it seems likely that a more delimited distribution would have been insisted upon, if not actually achieved: 'true', mentally and socially transforming visions could be obtained only in the

CAVE		
Outside	Entrance chamber	Tunnel
SOCIAL RELATIONS		
Whole community	Select group	Individual questers
CONSCIOUSNESS		
Alert/dreams	Full spectrum	Autistic end of spectrum

55 *A highly generalized summary of space, society and consciousness in Upper Palaeolithic caves.*

underworld. As our two ethnographic case studies suggest, dreams and visions experienced on the level of daily life were probably considered to be mere glimpses of what was possible in the cave. In this way, a group of people within the community, and with the community's general consent, linked the cave to the spectrum of consciousness to create social divisions, not the only ones, but significant ones. The topography of the cave thus paralleled narrowing social divisions – a form of hierarchy – and underwrote them with varied mental experiences, access to which was controlled. The cave itself and the experiences of shifting consciousness were thus implicated in the fashioning of social structure that was not founded entirely on brute strength, age or gender, though those discriminating factors probably played some role.

We should not suppose that this pattern of space and consciousness was rigidly observed. People, being the individuals that they are, always blur divisions. We should therefore not be surprised to find some swiftly made, personal, fixed images in large chambers where there are, principally, communally constructed images. What I propose is a generalization, a pattern that emerged as caves were explored and adapted, and as people used them over extended periods. The ways in which such explorations and adaptations changed over time remain to be studied. Nor is it likely that people moved through the caves while in states of deeply altered consciousness: the journeys are often hazardous enough for someone in a fully alert state. Deep, visionary states would have been incompatible with negotiating the passages and chambers and would have been achieved in specific places.

Returning to specifics, we can draw two further inferences from the distribution of images in Gabillou. The first concerns the few who had access to the tunnel. It is important to note that they did not, by and large, crowd and superimpose their images on one another, though they could have done so if they wished; certainly, there are no dense clusters of images such as we shall encounter in Lascaux. This kind of separation between images probably paralleled social relations between shamans. By and large, it seems that questers aimed for individuality: they did not want their own spirit helpers' images to be mixed up with those of other shamans.

The second inference derives from the most convincing therianthrope (part human, part animal figure), the so-called 'sorcerer of Gabillou', that is at the very end of the tunnel (Fig. 54). (Another two so-called 'sorcerers' are certainly anthropomorphic, but I am unconvinced that they are therianthropic.) At the end, the tunnel turns slightly to the left and the image is on the wall facing the visitor. It is in a striking, confrontational position. The image is a bison-headed human figure with a tail. Its form implies that it is not simply a masked person. The bent legs of its posture suggest that it may be dancing, though this may be a tenuous inference. A line extends from its mouth to the right where it crosses a fairly deep cleft in the rock and then brushes the top of a quadrilateral grid sign and extends beyond it.[11]

The deep, terminal position of this therianthrope was probably significant: its remote location is comparable with that of the therianthrope in the depths of Les Trois Frères that dominates the Sanctuary (Chapter 1, Time-Byte I) and with the figure in the Shaft in Lascaux, which I describe in a moment. Its association with a grid motif, a form found elsewhere in Gabillou and also in Lascaux, links representational images with signs, though in this case the representational component is, of course, not 'naturalistic'. As we saw in earlier chapters, both the therianthrope and the grid could have derived from the deep level of autistic consciousness that I labelled Stage 3.

Before we leave Gabillou, I sum up the key points of its topography and imagery. Seen from a social perspective, the topography of Gabillou divided a (probably select) group of people who occupied the entrance from those individuals who crawled into the tunnel and made swiftly executed images. (This does not, of course, mean that images were made every time people entered the tunnel.) Communal activities – dancing and choral chanting, for instance – may have been possible in the entrance but certainly not in the tunnel. In addition, one must allow the possibility that a still larger group of people was not allowed even into the entrance chamber.

Art, religion and social discrimination were thus intricately interwoven. Here are the seeds that grew into the sort of society we know today with its cross-cutting social differentiations. How did the people of Gabillou regard the 'seers' who had penetrated the tunnel and had experienced visions? We cannot say in exact terms, but Coleridge probably captured something of their awe in poetic imagery:

> And all should cry, Beware! Beware!
> His flashing eyes, his floating hair!
> Weave a circle round him thrice,
> And close your eyes with holy dread,
> For he on honey-dew hath fed,
> And drunk the milk of Paradise.

We can now contrast this 'simple' cave with the more complex topography and imagery of Lascaux, where we can identify multiple activity areas.

Lascaux

Lascaux, the most famous of all Upper Palaeolithic caves, is situated on the left bank of the Vézère River near the small town Montignac. For just over two decades after its discovery, it was open to visitors, and tens of thousands trooped through every year. It is said that over a million people passed through the cave in the first 15 years. In 1963, when a growth of micro-organisms caused by the presence of so many people was discovered, the cave was closed to visitors, an action that was essential but which caused shopkeepers and hoteliers in Montignac considerable distress. Today, the cave remains closed to the general public, but an astonishingly accurate replica of two parts of it has been constructed nearby, and this affords visitors an excellent experience of what the cave itself is like, physically, visually and atmospherically. Lascaux II, as the replica is known, was opened in 1983 – and Montignac revived.

Modern visitors to Lascaux I are so overwhelmed by the beauty, size and startling preservation of so many of the images thronging the walls that 'scientific' appraisal is apt to be silenced. A prominent American archaeologist, who was granted 20 minutes in the cave, told me that the first half of his allotted time was rather wasted because, overcome by the wonder of it all, he viewed the art through a curtain of tears. Such is the impact of Lascaux.

However one looks at it, Lascaux strongly gives the impression of having been a much-used and highly structured cave. Soon after the end of World War II, when archaeologists could begin to study it in earnest, this quality excited Laming-Emperaire's structuralist interest.[12] Surely, she and many others felt, Lascaux holds the keys to major mysteries – if only we can spot them.

To do so, researchers need to study not only the comprehensive publications on the site but also the cave itself. They need to visit the cave repeatedly and to spend more than the 20 minutes or so that are normally allowed those who are fortunate enough to be admitted at all. I am therefore deeply grateful to the authorities charged with the preservation of Lascaux for permitting me generous access and for valuable discussions with them. At present, Norbert Aujoulat is conducting a reappraisal of the imagery: his meticulous work and expert photography are bringing to light much that was formerly unknown.[13]

Lascaux is customarily divided into seven sections (Fig. 56):

- The Hall of the Bulls
- The Axial Gallery
- The Passage
- The Apse

– The Shaft
– The Nave
– The Diverticule of the Felines

I now give a brief description and interpretation of each of these sections. This should not be seen as anything like a complete inventory of every image; that would require a book to itself. To guide my discussion, I expand concepts that I developed in earlier chapters and in my account of Gabillou. I also introduce a distinction between 'composed' and 'confused' parts of the cave and argue that it points to different human activity areas.

THE HALL OF THE BULLS

When the young discoverers of the cave slid down the sink hole, it was in this chamber that they found themselves, though the first images that they noticed were in the Axial Gallery. Although the Upper Palaeolithic entrance to Lascaux may not have been in exactly the same place as the hole that Marcel Ravidat and his friends used, it must have been close by; this is the part of the cave that is nearest to the surface. Most

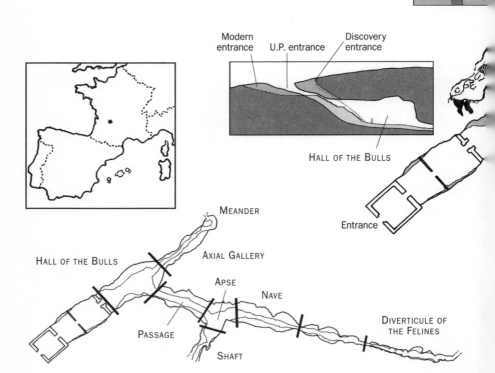

researchers now believe that the ancient entrance was blocked by a rock fall, not dissimilar to the one that exposed the entrance so many millennia later. Although there may have been other means of access that are now blocked, there seems to be little doubt that the Hall of the Bulls was the first section of the cave that Upper Palaeolithic visitors encountered; it would certainly have been the most accessible. There was probably a widening passage some 18 m (60 ft) long that led from the outside world down to the Hall of the Bulls. Dim light may have penetrated this far, though it would have been insufficient for image-making.

The Hall of the Bulls is a large, roughly elliptical chamber measuring some 9 m (29 ft 6 in) across the painted section.[14] When the cave was discovered, parts of the floor were covered by pools of water. Breuil, who was summoned within days of the discovery, ill-advisedly drained them by making holes through the floor to a

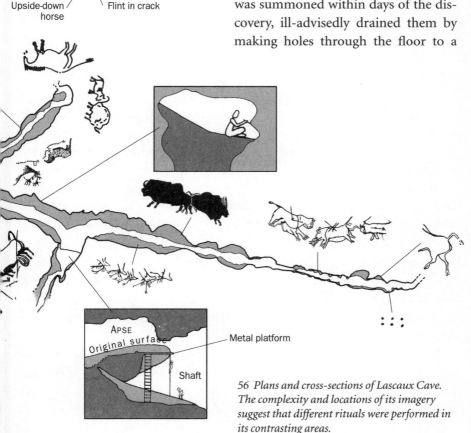

56 *Plans and cross-sections of Lascaux Cave. The complexity and locations of its imagery suggest that different rituals were performed in its contrasting areas.*

lower level and allowing the water to drain away – and to carry with it valuable archaeological remains. The lower cave system has not been explored, but it is generally believed that it was inaccessible to Upper Palaeolithic people. While archaeologists were trying to excavate the site, workmen were inexorably digging away deposits to prepare the cave for tourists. All in all, it was a highly unsatisfactory situation.

The upper walls of this large chamber are covered with white calcite that gives a glistening appearance and that has contributed to the preservation of the paintings. In parts, though, the calcite has flaked off. Some flaking took place in prehistoric times, for a couple of images extend onto the flaked surfaces.

The part of the Hall of the Bulls farthest from the entrance is covered by two converging cavalcades of animals (Pl. 21). This is one of the few instances in which a natural feature, here a brown ledge about 1.5 m (5 ft) above the present floor, seems to provide a vague ground line for some (by no means all) of the images. Apart from a small, incomplete horse, the first image that a person entering the cave comes across is the approximately 2-m (7-ft) long so-called Unicorn (Pl. 20). The appellation is inappropriate for a number of reasons, not least being the fact that, if it has horns at all, it has two; they slope forward from its head. The creature has a pendulous belly and six oval shapes painted on its upper back. Some researchers see a resemblance between its head and a bearded human head. Brigitte and Gilles Delluc, who have studied the cave extensively, believe that the Unicorn has 'the body of a rhinoceros, the withers of a bear or bison, the head and spots of a big cat, the tail of a horse'.[15] It is certainly a puzzling image, especially as the species of the other images in the cave are easily identified; its form is not the result of poor draughtsmanship.

The outlines of two horses are within the body of the creature. In front of the fantasy animal are seven more horses, not all of them complete. Then there is the head and forequarters of a huge bull, or aurochs. A large red horse with black mane and head has its ears pricked in an alert state. Many of the images here and throughout the cave have been integrated with folds and ridges in the rock wall, indeed so many that it is impossible to mention them all: the images fuse with the 'membrane'.

In front of the nose of the right-facing aurochs is the central part of the frieze: four, possibly five, small red deer stags, facing left. Some of them have unnaturally complex antlers. Above these deer is a partial horse, facing right and with its ears pricked; the painter took care not to allow it to impinge on other images. Part of its back is emphasized by a natural hollow in the rock.

14 Finger-fluting in soft mud on the walls of the Cosquer
Cave, the entrance to which was flooded when the level of the
Mediterranean rose at the end of the Ice Age. People touched
every part of the chamber's walls, even above head height,
and left these patterns in the malleable surface. Touching was
clearly an important part of whatever rituals took place in the
cave. An image of a horse was placed on top of the fluting.

15 (Left) An accretion on the wall of Le Portel has an anthropomorphic figure drawn around it so that the accretion becomes the figure's erect penis. A similar instance a few metres away confirms that this use of the wall of the cave was not accidental.

19 (Opposite below) The two Spotted Horses and surrounding hand prints in Pech Merle Cave. The head of the horse on the right is less realistic than the natural shape of the rock into which it is fitted. The lowest handprint suggests that the person was lying prone on the floor of the cave when it was made.

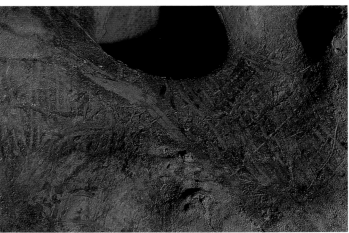

16 (Above) A grid drawn with fingers in the mud around a natural hole in the wall of Hornos, Spain. It is as if the pattern is flowing out from behind the rock surface.

17 and 18 (Above and right) Light and shadow playing over a natural rock formation in the Salon Noir, Niaux, suggests the distinctive dorsal line of a bison in a vertical position.

20 (Below) The so-called Unicorn (it actually has two horns) is the first major image in the Hall of the Bulls in Lascaux. Some researchers believe that the pendant belly suggests that the creature is pregnant. It has a number of oval shapes painted on its body. It is the first of a line of animals that face away from the entrance and towards the opening to the Axial Gallery.

21 (Opposite above) The entrance to the Axial Gallery, Lascaux, is beneath the cavalcade of animals in the Hall of the Bulls. The opening can be seen straight ahead in this photograph. To reach the Axial Gallery, a visitor has to pass beneath, and almost through, the huge, impressive animals.

22 (Opposite below) The Roaring Stag with its impressive antlers is on the right-hand wall, near the beginning of the Axial Gallery, Lascaux. The line of dots below the animal extends from a quadrilateral sign on the left to a jutting piece of rock on the right.

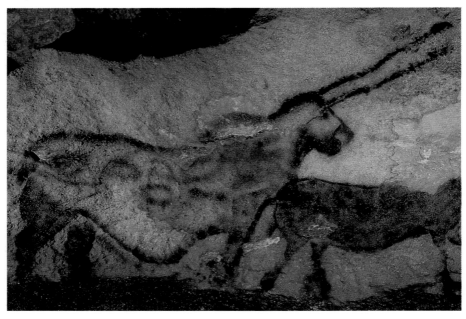

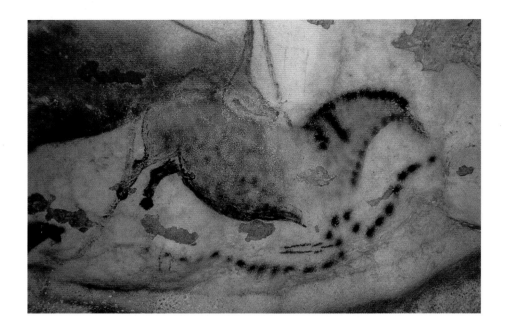

23 (Above) A tawny horse and dots to the left of the Roaring Stag in the Axial Gallery, Lascaux. The line of dots may be a continuation of those beneath the Roaring Stag (Plate 22). The image was made by the technique of blowing paint onto the wall of the cave.

24 (Right) Pieces of bone were thrust into cracks in Enlène, one of the Volp Caves. They suggest another Upper Palaeolithic way of 'treating' the meaningful walls of the caves.

25 (Above) A tooth of the now-extinct cave bear was placed in a niche in the Chamber of the Lion in the Les Trois Frères Cave, which leads off Enlène.

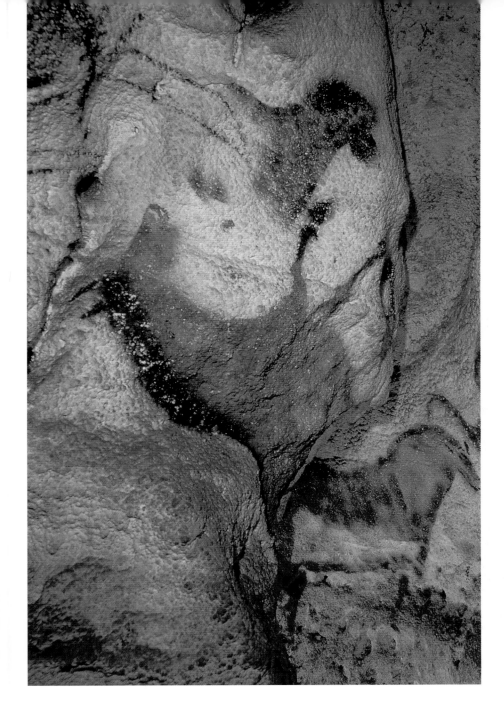

26 The Falling Horse is in the Meander at the end of the Axial Gallery, Lascaux. Curving around a pier of rock, it is one of the most striking images of Upper Palaeolithic art. Other images shown here include a horse on the far wall of the passage and, on the extreme right, the raised tail of a bison. Ochre-covered flint artefacts were found in a niche in the wall opposite the Falling Horse.

27 Two partly overlapping bison were painted in a natural hollow in the cave wall near the end of the Nave, Lascaux. The way in which they are painted and the curved surface suggest that the bison are coming out towards – and around – the viewer.

28 The images in the Shaft, Lascaux, are perhaps the best known and most debated Upper Palaeolithic cave paintings. Those shown here include a rhinoceros with raised tail, the outline figure of a man (the only one in Lascaux), a wounded bison and an outline bird on top of a staff.

Then, facing the animals that are coming in from the left, are three huge aurochs bulls advancing from the right; the largest is 5.5 m (18 ft) long, the other two not much less. There are the less distinct remains of three aurochs moving in the opposite direction to these bulls; they are in a lower part of the panel and may date from an earlier period than the large animals. Laming-Emperaire remarks that the hindquarters of the first of these bovids 'are outlined by a horizontal protuberance of the rock, and when viewed in a slanting light the flank and bony rump stand out in remarkable relief'.[16] This effect is destroyed by the electric lighting that has been installed in the cave. In a dark area below the second bull there is a small image of a bear, the head, ears and back of which are formed by a natural ridge in the rock. It is a brown bear, not one of the larger, now-extinct, cave bears. The bear tends to blend with the black belly-line of the aurochs; this makes it rather difficult to see. It seems that the claws of the bear that protrude below the black of the aurochs were touched up with darker paint.

Some parts of some of the animals in the Hall of the Bulls were painted by means of the blowing technique. Horses' manes are examples, but, more interestingly, at least one of the large aurochs has its nose fashioned by blown paint. One of the aurochs also has a line painted in its open mouth that may represent the tongue or an emanation of 'breath'. Just which images were made, or partially made, by the blowing technique is a line of research that will be followed up in the future.

In addition to the animals, there are some signs, though fewer than elsewhere in the cave. They include nine short, red parallel and right-angled marks and dots above the snout of the last of the right-facing bulls, and two 'broken signs' in the right-hand section that comprise a central line and separated segments. There are also sets of black dots and lines.

The highest parts of the frieze are some 4 m (13 ft) above the floor. The image-makers must have constructed some means of reaching that high up. When one thinks of the 5½-m (18-ft) long aurochs on the right, it becomes clear that the painters must have constructed a large platform or a series of smaller movable platforms made, probably, of tree trunks lashed together with rope. Serious, planned labour was needed before the work of painting could start.

That the paintings in the Hall of the Bulls were carefully 'composed' seems inescapable. But more can be said. The sheer size of the images suggests that they were communally made. People must surely have co-operated in the preparation of paint, construction of scaffolds, outlining the huge images, and then the application of the paint, even if one, or a few, highly skilled people directed the work. The space available in the Hall of the Bulls would have readily facilitated such co-operative labour. In addition, the chamber would have permitted a large number of people to view the images and to perform various rites, of which no evidence now remains. Such activities may well have included dancing, music and chanting. This is the only part of Lascaux that could have accommodated a large number of people. The Hall of the Bulls may therefore be regarded as a 'vestibule' and thus be comparable to the poorly preserved entrance to Gabillou.

The Axial Gallery

The composed nature of the frieze in the Hall of the Bulls is evident in the way that it accommodates the entrance to the Axial Gallery (Pl. 21). This gallery leads off the far left side and may in some limited sense be considered an extension of the Hall of the Bulls. Its entrance is between the second and third aurochs. These two images were positioned to allow for the entrance, which arches up between them; one leg of the right aurochs folds into the entrance to the Axial Gallery. Entering the Gallery thus entails passing beneath – and through – the cavalcade of animals in the Hall of the Bulls. Having done so, one is no longer standing back and looking at a procession of monumental images: one is now among them.

As in the Hall of the Bulls, the walls here are covered with sparkling calcite. In prehistoric times people would have been able to walk upright through the gallery, though the floor is now lower than it was. The remains of scaffolding have been found; it was used to reach the higher parts of the walls and ceiling. The Axial Gallery is richly decorated with images that extend over the ceiling: visitors to the Axial Gallery feel entirely surrounded by wonderful, vivid paintings. As is the case with the Hall of the Bulls, it is clear that the scaffolding and images were made by co-operating people in an alert state of consciousness. I select a few images that are especially significant for our enquiry.

On the right wall, just inside the entrance are the head, neck and back of a large black stag with open mouth; it is known as the Roaring Stag (Pl. 22). Stags lift their heads and roar in this posture during the rutting season at the end of winter. Mario Ruspoli, in his photographic study of the cave, suggests that this image should be seen in association with two butting ibexes and a male horse chasing a mare in other parts of the cave; all these images, he says, are indications of the rutting season.[17] That the stag is emitting a sound was probably significant in terms of multisensory experiences in the cave: sound is implied by the image. Perhaps people participating in rituals imitated the roaring sound; some may have interpreted their aural hallucinations as the roaring of stags. If we take ethnographic evidence into account, we must allow that the painted and engraved animals of Upper Palaeolithic art probably also 'spoke' to people in auditory hallucinations. Intense, concentrated viewing of 'fixed' spirit animals, may, in the subterranean conditions of sensory deprivation, have triggered parallel hallucinations, Stage 3 visions that involved all the senses and imparted messages and truths to awed recipients.[18]

Beneath the Roaring Stag is a line of black dots that terminates at a quadrilateral sign that is probably earlier than the dots.[19] A little farther to the left is a tawny horse with a black mane, legs and underbelly; it faces towards the stag (Pl. 23). Beneath the horse is a line of dots that appears to be a continuation of the dots beneath the stag, though whether they were made at the same time is debatable. The dots associated with the horse have two noteworthy features. First, they seem to disappear behind a boss in the rock and then emerge again beneath the stag. Secondly, the line of dots bends up and back again so that it suggests the front legs of the horse. Signs and representational images thus combine, as the neurological model shows they indeed do in deeply altered consciousness.

At the end of the Axial Gallery is a section known as the Meander. It is of great interest. At this point the gallery is narrower than at its entrance, and on the left is a 'pier' of rock that juts out to create a tight, semicircular space. Past and behind the 'pier', the passage swings to the left and becomes so narrow that further progress is soon impossible. On the calcite of the left-hand wall at this point are a number of small horses and branching signs.

On the opposite wall are a bison and two horses; they appear to be coming out of the narrow tunnel behind the 'pier' (Pl. 26). The bison is of particular interest: it has its tail raised, a point to which I return later, and its penis is shown. The horse deepest in the tunnel is also remarkable. Its eye is formed by a small circular hole 5 cm (2 in) deep. Laming-Emperaire writes, 'Perhaps this hole inspired the artist to place the animal's head at this point.'[20] Here is another instance in which touch and sight may have combined in the detection and creation of images.

Painted on the curved 'pier' itself is the Falling Horse, a miracle of Upper Palaeolithic draughtsmanship (Pl. 26). The horse is upside down, its head towards the entrance of the gallery, its legs in the air. As Laming-Emperaire rightly says, 'The impression of a horse falling into space is vividly conveyed.'[21] Here, the passage is only 90 cm (3 ft) wide, and visitors have to turn sideways in order to slip into the space. To see the entire image of the Falling Horse, one has to crouch down in the Meander and move around the rock. The whole horse cannot be seen at once: complete viewing implies movement around the 'pier'.

Naturally enough, the Falling Horse has excited much interest and comment. Some researchers consider that it depicts a horse tumbling over a cliff during a hunt or corralling.[22] The various strands of evidence that I have so far intertwined suggest that this literal reading is unlikely. To explain the significance of the Falling Horse, we need to retreat back along the Axial Gallery and then turn to look down as much of its length as we can.

From farther back, we see that the gallery slopes downwards: the Meander is in fact some 9 m (30 ft) lower than the threshold where the gallery leaves the Hall of the Bulls. The Axial Gallery distinctly leads deeper into the nether world than the Hall of the Bulls. At the same time, the way in which the images swirl around and over the ceiling of the Axial Gallery recalls the neurologically generated vortex with its surrounding images that leads into the deepest stage of altered consciousness and the most vivid hallucinations. This impression is strikingly heightened by the Falling Horse turning over at the focus of the vortex. The Axial Gallery, carefully planned and communally executed, is, all in all, a remarkable evocation of the neurological vortex. As I have argued, physical entry into the subterranean passages was probably seen as equivalent to psychic entry into deeply altered states of consciousness. This parallelism is nowhere better seen than in the Axial Gallery.

In addition to being the focus of the vortex – a point of breakthrough – the Meander is special in another way. Its floor was originally 1 m (3 ft 3 in) lower than that of the far end of the Axial Gallery. The Abbé André Glory, who excavated areas of Lascaux and copied many of the engravings, found that the earth at this point contained ochre and the remains of flint knapping. Opposite the Falling Horse, he made an even more notable discovery: three flint blades were thrust into a small niche in the wall; they showed signs of use, but they were also covered with red paint.

This find recalls the prehistoric person in Time-Byte I who carried the tooth of a cave bear through the low, narrow passage that leads to Les Trois Frères, and then placed it in a niche in the small chamber with engravings of lions. In Enlène itself, where there are no parietal images but many engraved plaquettes, hundreds of small pieces of bone were thrust into cracks in the rock (Pls 24, 25).[23] In addition, larger pieces of bone were deeply planted into the ground by the first people who used the cave; the bones were subsequently covered by later deposits. Further examples from Upper Palaeolithic caves could be cited.

People placed objects of various kinds *into* the walls and floors of caves. Small pieces of animals clearly had significance, a point that supports my explanation for the origin of three-dimensional images (Chapter 7). If, as I have argued, people saw the walls as a 'membrane' between themselves and the spirit world, they were performing a two-way ritual. They were drawing (in two senses) spirit animals through the 'membrane' and fixing them on the surface; they were also sending fragments of animals back through the 'membrane' into the spirit world. In these instances, one may possibly discern some sort of restitution ritual: two-way traffic between this world and the spirit world. The Upper Palaeolithic people who entered these spaces were behaving in terms of a pact between the powers of the nether realms and the community that they represented and on behalf of whom they acted. The powers of the underworld allowed people to kill animals, provided (in some expressions of Upper Palaeolithic shamanism) people responded in certain ritual ways, such as taking fragments of animals into the caves and inserting them into the 'membrane'.

There is ethnographic support for these suggestions. In shamanistic societies throughout the world bone has special significance and is associated with spirit. For instance, the Huichol of Central America believe that the spirit, or soul, of a person lodges in the top of the head and in the bone that grows over the fontanel in the months after birth. The Iroquois of North America have a development of this idea that may throw some light on what was happening in Enlène (Time-Byte I). Their word for 'burned bones' (*uq-sken-ra-ri*) also means 'the soul as "animated skeleton", or ghost'.[24] In the Salle des Morts, some 160 m (525 ft) from the Enlène entrance, people kindled fire with wood and then used bone as the chief combustible material. Vast quantities of bone were brought into the cave: the stench must have been overpowering.[25] Around the world, notions of a skeletal soul and rebirth from bones are expressed ritually. The Warao of Venezuela, for example, place fish bones into the walls and thatch of dwellings in the belief that this display of respect will lead to new fish being born; fish and animals, like people, are believed to have souls.[26] Such instances are paralleled in many shamanistic societies. I do not wish to imply *identical* practices among Upper Palaeolithic communities, but the notions of soul/bone and revitalization of bones in the underworld are eminently compatible with the west European subterranean evidence.

In the case of the paint-covered flints in the Lascaux Meander, we seem to have a variation on this theme that brings us back to the symbolic importance of technology. Paint is not merely 'paint'. It had supernatural properties and significances that facilitated the apprehension and fixing of visions. In the Meander there is a suggestion that stone artefacts also, at least in certain circumstances, meant more than simply 'tools'. Indeed, there are numerous other instances in Upper Palaeolithic caves in which stone tools were evidently treated in special ways and associated with the walls of the caves. There is, for example, the ochre-covered blade that Gaussen found in the Gabillou tunnel. Stone tools, as most researchers now recognize, had social significance, and their special treatment in Upper Palaeolithic caves was one manipulation of that significance. Whatever that significance may have been, it was being deliberately associated with the spirit world.

Already, we can see that the parts of Lascaux suggest different kinds of activities. Numerous people probably congregated in the Hall of the Bulls for a range of rituals. All of these rites may not have been related to vision questing; some may have been associated with economic and political relations between comparatively far-flung communities that came together at Lascaux at certain times.[27] Vision questing was but one of the functions of the caves. Nor was the whole cave necessarily traversed every time people entered it. In the very nature of the topography, fewer people were able to enter the downward sloping Axial Gallery and the terminal Meander/vortex. Then someone, in a very restricted space next to the Falling Horse, placed paint-covered stone tools in the cave wall.

Both the Hall of the Bulls and the Axial Gallery are composed areas: people co-operated to produce patterns of images that evoked particular kinds of responses. In the other parts of Lascaux, we begin to encounter different evidence that suggests 'confused' *pot-pourris* of images.

THE PASSAGE

If one is standing in the Hall of the Bulls, the entrance to the Axial Gallery is on the left, highlighted by the great frieze. Far less noticeable is the entrance to the Passage. It is over to the right, below the feet of the last large aurochs. It is almost as though the composition of the frieze was designed to draw attention away from the Passage and to direct it to the Axial Gallery.

During the Upper Palaeolithic, the entrance to the Passage was much smaller than it is now. Photographs taken in 1940 show how inconspicuous it was.[28] People entering it had to crouch down. Its floor is lower than that of the Hall of the Bulls, and there is no calcite; the walls are softer and far less even.

Especially the left-hand wall of the Passage has been repeatedly painted and engraved. Over and over again images were added, one on top of the other, some painted, some engraved, and some executed by both techniques. Unfortunately, the Passage conducted a slow draught for many millennia, and as a result the images are poorly preserved. As Laming-Emperaire remarks, the passing of human beings through this narrow area may, even in prehistoric times, have contributed to the destruction of the images.[29]

There are images of horses, aurochs, and ibex heads. This was an area of 'confusion' in which image-makers did not hesitate to place their handiwork over that of other people; in that way, it is in direct contrast to the 'composed' Hall of the Bulls and the Axial Gallery. This characteristic is even more pronounced in the next section of the cave.

THE APSE

The Apse is a comparatively small, domed chamber on the right of, and a little higher than, the Passage. The walls are harder than those in the Passage, and this has contributed to the better preservation of the engravings found here. There are also a few paintings. Most of the walls and the ceiling are so dense with engravings that it is difficult to decipher them. The copying of these images was one of the great achievements of Upper Palaeolithic art research. The Abbé Glory undertook the daunting task, and his copies are published in *Lascaux inconnu*.[30] Since then, Norbert Aujoulat has returned to the Apse and has found even more engraved lines than Glory detected.

The complexity of the Apse is indeed astonishing (Fig. 57). There are crowded images of horses, bison, aurochs, ibexes, deer and a possible wolf and a lion, though these seem doubtful to me. Many of the images have 'hanging' hoofs that are sometimes interpreted as a graphic device to show the hoof to better advantage. There are also large numbers of partially depicted animals, especially heads. This is another instance of 'confusion', clearly something different was happening here from what was taking place in the 'composed' Hall of the Bulls and the Axial Gallery. The impression of confusion arises from uncoordinated participation by many people, probably over a long period.

To complicate matters further, large numbers of engraved lines cut across the images. In one instance, just above the opening that leads straight down to the Shaft, a natural seam in the rock has been cut across by a long line of independent short strokes. This sort of occurrence shows yet again that the rock face was not a neutral *tabula rasa*: it had its own significance and needed to be 'respected', or 'acknowledged', in its own right.

As with 'macaronis', the engraved lines have not attracted much study.

Although there are many single lines, most appear in parallel sets, some straight, some curving. Some seem to be hatching between two parallel lines; others are a series of much shorter strokes lined up one after the other. The sets themselves frequently cross over one another. Far from being uncontrolled, the individual lines within the sets usually avoid crossing one another. Although they give an overall impression of being random, perhaps even destructive of existing imagery, they are in fact carefully executed, ordered additions to the panels.

Can such additions to panels of representational images be explained in terms of 'art'? Probably not. They are, however, explicable in terms of the explanation I have been developing. They probably represent *participation* in a panel of spirit animals set on the living 'membrane' between realms. Individuals who did not (at any rate at that time) make representational images of visions could nevertheless participate in the experience of the spirit world in other ways. Many of the sets of lines may, of course, have been made by people who had earlier made the images and were now re-participating in the experience of the 'membrane'. In doing so, they *cut* or *scored* the 'membrane',

57 Dense engravings in the Apse in Lascaux. Images and apparently random lines are piled one on top of another in a dense confusion.

perhaps to allow power to seep through to them. The sets of parallel lines, then, represent attempts by individuals to access supernatural power and to participate in ways that we do not fully understand in religious experience.

Although we may see the results of such activity as confused, that was the effect that people were content to create. Perhaps it was not so much in a visual sense – that they valued 'confused' panels for aesthetic reasons – but because 'confusion' represented the spatially focused access of numerous people to religious experience. These cut marks are thus comparable to handprints (Chapter 8). Although the resultant visual effect doubtless had significance, it was the ritual act of their making that was of principal importance.

In amongst the representational images in the Apse are many grid, branch and other signs. One of the grids in the Nave has been exceptionally closely scored with lines that fill its segments in different directions. I return to grids in the next section of the cave. There are also funnel-shaped clusters of converging engraved lines.[31] It was one of these that Breuil famously, but unconvincingly, likened to a 'French Guinea black sorcerer clad from head to foot in a disguise of plaited fibre'.[32] It was this kind of slick, one-to-one ethnographic parallel that persuaded Leroi-Gourhan to attempt to abandon all ethnographic evidence. Similar but more curved engraved forms in the Apse have been interpreted as 'huts', but the same reservations concerning simplistic ethnographic analogies apply.

If my explanation of the engraved lines as cuts across the 'membrane' be accepted, we can see that these so-called 'sorcerers' simply comprise sets of cut lines that converge and relate to the narrowing vortex that leads to a focal point at which the 'membrane' is actually penetrated. This suggestion is eminently compatible with the overall view that Upper Palaeolithic art was implicated in various shamanistic rituals that took people into the subterranean spirit realm and through the 'membrane'.

Before considering the mysterious chamber below the Apse, I return to the Passage and its continuation.

THE NAVE

After having crawled through the Passage, Upper Palaeolithic visitors came to the junction between it and the Apse, which is on the right. At this point the chamber widens and the ceiling is much higher: it would now have been possible for them to walk upright again. Straight ahead of them, the level of the floor fell away into the Nave.

This part of the cave is less densely embellished than the Passage. Here the ceiling is high (5.5 m or 18 ft), and the 25-m (81-ft) long chamber slopes quite steeply downwards. The walls of the Nave are smoother than those of the Passage, and there is some calcite. The images are all above a ledge that is at floor height where the Nave begins, but that is soon above head-height as one moves through the chamber. The visitor thus drops down below the images. Lamps and pigments were found on the ledge. Bone remains show that people ate here as well, though whether they did so while they were making the images or whether they came here subsequently for other purposes is not clear. The bones found in the Nave and elsewhere in Lascaux came largely from young reindeer, yet there is only one reindeer image in the cave; it is engraved in the Apse. The Lascaux people were not painting their diet.

Once inside the Nave, we leave behind the 'confusion' of the Passage and the Apse and again enter a more 'composed' area, though one with its own characteristics. Here there are monumental images of horses, bison, and the line of deer heads that has been dubbed the 'Swimming Deer'. But the ways in which the images were made suggest that this space was by no means equivalent to the Hall of the Bulls or the Axial Gallery. There are more 'additions' and 'participations' than we find in those two sections – but the impression of order remains.

Many of the images have been both painted and engraved, some repeatedly. This applies to the quadrilateral grids that are numerous in this part of the cave and that seem to link Lascaux to Gabillou. Some of the grids have been outlined and painted a number of times; the individual segments of the grids are in some cases coloured differently (Fig. 58). Participation in their significance by renewal (even though the original does not seem to have been especially faded) was clearly an important ritual. It is tempting to see these quadrilateral signs as formalized, elaborated representations of the grid-shaped entoptic phenomenon to which people ascribed meanings now lost to us.

Participation is also evident in the head of one of the horses that has been outlined five times and its mane four times. This reworking of images, something we do not find nearly as much in the Hall of the Bulls and the Axial Gallery, suggests repeated returns to specific images and participation in their already-existing meaning. Probably, going over existing images of powerful spirit animals was one way, in a complex system of rituals, of accessing transforming power and experience by imprinting the outline of the spirit animal on one's mind. Some of the images are also cut across with lines that have been interpreted as spears. Whether they are or are not spears, they represent another sort of participation in the imagery comparable to what happened in the Apse.

58 A painted and engraved grid in the Nave in Lascaux. The image was renewed, a feature that suggests its lasting significance.

The additions and re-workings do not destroy the impression that we are once more in an area of planned, balanced imagery. This characteristic is especially noticeable in the last panel on the left wall. Two splendid male bison are shown back to back, their rumps overlapping (Pl. 27). Their tails are raised in a manner that recalls the bison at the end of the Axial Gallery and that suggests anger and arousal. This composition has been interpreted as an early achievement of the kind of linear perspective that is usually associated with the Italian Renaissance. This is an attractive conclusion, but the images were probably not recording a three-dimensional 'scene' from life outside the cave, as the perspective explanation implies. We should rather bear in mind what we noted about the difficulty in 'seeing' two-dimensional images and extrapolate our inferences to the notion of perspective. There is not simply one 'correct' way of representing perspective: Eastern artists, for example, often adopt an approach very different from the converging sight-lines of Western art. The Renaissance artists did not discover a 'truth' that, by a stroke of ingenuity and brilliance, was foreshadowed by a couple of Upper Palaeolithic image-makers.

This kind of art-historical approach tends to obscure significant inferences with a cloak of Western conventions and concerns.[33] It is of more interest to note that the two bison are placed in a hollow bay in the rock wall: they seem to be issuing forth, tails raised, from inside the rock. The curve of the rock, not visible on the page of a book, enhances the sense of the bison charging towards the viewer. As we have seen, they are by no means the only examples of animals painted so that they appear to be coming out of clefts in the rock face; photographers who, understandably enough, try to avoid any distortion of images, often miss this feature.[34] Emergence from the 'membrane' is, I suggest, the kind of 'perspective' that would have been intelligible to Upper Palaeolithic artists who believed that a spirit realm filled with powerful animals lay just behind the rock wall.

The bisons' raised tails have been plausibly interpreted as suggesting bulls intimidating one another in the rutting season; indeed, one of them seems to be shedding its winter coat, as the species does at the end of spring. This is another instance in which ethology (the study of animal behaviour) becomes an evidential strand, though not in a simple, straightforward way. We need to ask: what, *in the context of the nether world*, could this depiction of aggressive behaviour mean? If the animals are issuing from the hollow, as I argue they are, their belligerent posture may have been associated with the fear that shamans experienced when, at the climax of their quest, they faced their spirit animals: they had to maintain a stoic disposition in the face of such danger if they wished to acquire power. Perhaps the aroused bison bulls prepared Magdalenian vision questers for terrors that lay ahead in the next section of the cave, the Diverticule of the Felines. Perhaps even merely passing by this 'picture' required courage, as, in flickering lamp light, the two bison sprang forth at one. If indeed we are here dealing with perspective, it is, as Michael Kubovy pointed out for the Italian Renaissance, not simply the discovery of the 'correct' way to represent space but rather a 'symbolic form' that created in the viewer a deeply religious response.[35]

The intimidating pair of bison are the last images in the Nave. Perhaps this was a second but somewhat different 'vestibule', a ritual space preparatory to the Diverticule of the Felines. From that point the passage narrows sharply and the hazardous route to the Diverticule of the Felines begins.

THE DIVERTICULE OF THE FELINES
The character of the cave changes markedly as one leaves the Nave. One is soon on all fours making one's way through a narrow tunnel. Then comes an area of soft clay walls. Eventually, one reaches the Diverticule of the Felines where one has to lie

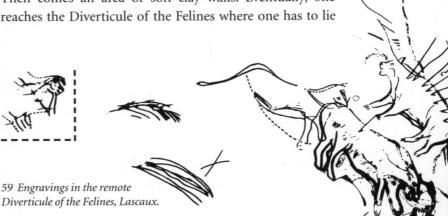

59 Engravings in the remote Diverticule of the Felines, Lascaux.

down or crouch. Despite its remoteness, this section of Lascaux is filled with many images.

The motifs include the eponymous felines, aurochs, a horse seen face-on, a bison with raised tail, ibexes, some dots, grid 'signs', branching signs with the lateral parts separated from the central shaft (Fig. 59), and sets of parallel lines. The felines, possibly as many as eight, seem to be so-called cave lions, a type of *Panthera leo* without manes that occurred in small prides in Ice Age Europe.[36] One has its ears back and its mouth open in the posture I noted in connection with the early Aurignacian statuettes. One of the lions has lines emanating from its mouth and anus. Its tail is extended and apparently lashing. The mouth lines have been interpreted as representing an angry growl, the rear ones as indicating that the creature is marking its territory with urine. Perhaps both oral and anal lines should be seen as emanations of spirit, essence or power.[37] The terminal dots are six in number and painted in black in two rows of three. As we shall see, a similar set of dots is in the Shaft beneath the Apse.

A horse tooth was found in this chamber, as well as pieces of bone, a considerable quantity of pigment and, most remarkably, a piece of hard clay bearing an imprint of rope seven millimetres in diameter and made of plant fibres. The storing of pigment in this remote spot may have reinforced or conserved the power of the substance. But why would someone carry a horse tooth this far underground? Again, we recall the cave bear tooth in Les Trois Frères and the paint-covered flints in the Meander. People were taking special objects of various kinds into the underworld and deliberately leaving them there.

All in all, it seems that people did not visit the Diverticule of the Felines often; the walls are soft and there would be more prehistoric damage than there is if people had crawled there frequently. Although some of the engraved animals are tech-

nically the equal of those in other parts of Lascaux, it does seem that they were, for the most part, made comparatively swiftly. Together with the numerous 'cut marks' and parallel lines, the engraved animals and the painted sections of this small, remote chamber suggest an extremity of experience as well as of topography. If there were vision quest niches in Lascaux, this was surely one of them. Long separated from the communal, mind-orienting viewing of the great images in the Hall of the Bulls, possibly having performed other rituals in the Axial Gallery, the Passage and the Apse, and having passed the Cerberus-like paired bison, it was here, in the extreme depths, that questers came face to face with visions of power and made personal contact with the spirit realm.

THE SHAFT

One section of Lascaux remains to be discussed – the Shaft. The opening to this deep well – in France it is known as the 'Puits' – is at the back of the Apse; over it, on the curved wall and ceiling of the Apse are engravings that include a grid and claviforms. The young discoverers of the cave descended the 16 or so feet into the Shaft by means of a rope; their exit proved more difficult, but Ravidat was eventually able to haul the others out. Today, the original projection of hard clay has been removed, and there is a metal platform and manhole; one now descends by means of a ladder fixed to the wall.

The Shaft is the most enigmatic section of Lascaux. First, there is some debate as to whether it was part of Upper Palaeolithic Lascaux or whether it belongs to another cave altogether. Many researchers today accept that it was indeed part of Upper Palaeolithic Lascaux. They point out that arguments from style (for example, the human figure in the shaft is in a 'stick' style not found elsewhere in the cave) are unreliable. More positively, they note that 'broken signs' appear on the beautiful lamp that was found in the Shaft (Fig. 53), on the wall of the shaft, and also on the walls of other parts of Lascaux: they are characteristic of the whole cave. Then, too, the raised tails and series of dots seem to be associated with other 'end' areas of the cave. Finally, quantities of clay from the upper parts of the cave were found in the archaeological strata in the floor of the Shaft. It seems that it was brought down by Upper Palaeolithic people as they descended by means of a rope. On the other hand, none of these points is conclusive, and we must allow that the Shaft may have been part of another cave that was related to Lascaux and that it was reached via another entrance, now blocked. Either way, it is an area of great interest. In what follows, I take the widely-held view that the Shaft was indeed part of Upper Palaeolithic Lascaux.

60 A seashell made into a pendant. It was found at the bottom of the Shaft in Lascaux.

The finds in the floor of the Shaft are of particular significance. Following Breuil's initial excavation in 1947, Glory undertook more refined work in 1959. True, one must allow that some other parts of Lascaux were dug out before archaeological work could be carried out, but, even conceding this reservation, it seems that the large number of objects, in addition to quantities of pigment, found in the Shaft suggests that Upper Palaeolithic people deliberately left them there. Amongst these finds were many lamps, including the shaped and decorated one. It was found just below the tail of the rhinoceros image. Its presence in the Shaft suggests something more than the practical provision of light. The exact number of much cruder lamps found here is not known because some of them cannot now be located, but it seems that two dozen would not be too high an estimate. In 1951, charcoal from one of these lamps was dated to 17,500 ($\pm$ 900) years before the present. Glory noticed that the lamps had been turned over so that the charcoal side faced the ground, perhaps because the people who left them there wished to extinguish them. In addition to the lamps, there were numerous flint blades and ivory spears decorated with 'broken signs' (central lines with detached side marks). There was also a seashell from the 200-km-distant Atlantic coast, stained with red ochre and perforated so that it could be used as a pendant (Fig. 60). The floor area of the Shaft is so limited that the space could not have been occupied by many people at one time; nor could it have been used for any mundane activities, such as artefact manufacture or food preparation.

Descent from the lip of the profoundly embellished Apse would, in terms of shamanistic cosmology, have been seen as venturing down to a deeper level of the cosmos – as would also have been the case in the sloping Axial Gallery and Nave, though not as dramatically as in the Shaft. Indeed, it is hard not to conclude that the Shaft was a special 'end' area, a narrow cleft to which people went, where they conducted some sorts of rituals, where they deliberately abandoned objects, such as the spears which would have no utilitarian function in a deep cave, and from which they returned having extinguished the light that had guided them there. In some cases, lamps may have been thrown down the Shaft after the users had climbed up from the depths.

But what of the images in this remarkable area? They too are exceptional.

On one wall there is the partial image of a black horse. Opposite it is the most discussed group of all Upper Palaeolithic images (Pl. 28). To the left is a rhinoceros, the underbelly of which is sketchily drawn. It has a raised tail, and beneath the tail are two rows of three black dots each. The similarity between these dots and those in the Diverticule of the Felines is unmistakable. Beyond a slight curve in the rock wall is the famous man and bison. The bison was drawn around a darker, ochrey patch of rock that extends in some places beyond the image and is, to my way of thinking, not especially reminiscent of a bison. An Upper Palaeolithic artist was, as in so many other instances, taking a natural formation and making an image out of it: the rather amorphous discolouration already on the wall was fashioned into an animal. The bison's head is lowered as if it is charging, and its tail is raised and bent back over its rump in anger. Its entrails seem to be hanging from its belly, and there is what appears to be a spear across its body.

In front of the bison is a black, comparatively crudely drawn ithyphallic man who appears to be falling backwards, though the angle seems to me to be more pronounced in photographs than on the rock. The most remarkable point about the man is that he has a bird's head and four-fingered bird-like hands. The avian theme is taken up by what appears to be a staff with an effigy of a bird on its top. Beneath the feet of the man is a 'broken sign' that some writers have taken to represent a spear-thrower.

One can hardly blame researchers for concocting stories to explain what they see as a picture of a tragic incident. Usually, they claim that the man was hunting the bison; he wounded the animal (hence its entrails); it then turned on him to gore him, and he is therefore shown falling backwards. Breuil was so convinced by a slightly more elaborate version of this reading that he excavated below the panel in the expectation of finding the remains of the unfortunate hunter. He did not.

More usefully, possible shamanistic associations have been explored, the most detailed of which came from two University of Santa Barbara researchers: Demorest Davenport, a biologist, and Michael Jochim, an archaeologist who has written extensively on the Upper Palaeolithic.[38] Rightly acknowledging that it is impossible to demonstrate that the images depict a historical event, they stressed the significance of the four-fingered hands and their parallel in birds' feet. They concluded that the figure is bird from the waist up and human from the waist down. The bird on the staff is virtually identical to the man's head. Davenport and Jochim pointed out that it is 'unmistakably gallinaceous or grouse-like' and, as Leroi-Gourhan saw, resembles that carved on a spear-thrower found at Mas d'Azil, another Magdalenian site. They went further and identified the species as a Black Grouse or Capercaillie, and illustrated a contemporary Siberian shaman's *ongon*, or spirit helper, in the form of a grouse. Both the Black Grouse and the Capercaillie perform elaborate mating dances on traditional gathering places, or *leks*. Perhaps, Davenport and Jochim concluded, the shaman is being transformed into his gallinaceous spirit helper at the moment of death and his erect phallus suggests the role that some shamans play in the fertility of their communities.

Davenport and Jochim's interpretations are almost entirely acceptable. There are, however, aspects of Upper Palaeolithic art with which they were unfamiliar. First, I suggest that an image-maker fashioned a spirit bison out of the stain on the rock, thus 'fixing' a *spirit* animal. This is not a real-life tragedy. Secondly, its hoofs are shown to be cloven, and are in the position that I take to mean that the animal is not standing on the ground but rather 'floating' in spiritual space. Thirdly, I argue that the man's erection suggests death in two senses. Alan Brodrick, one of the earliest writers on Lascaux, pointed out that the erect phallus may indicate 'death by severance of the backbone'.[39] But, as we saw in the two ethnographic case studies (Chapters 5 and 6), 'death' in shamanistic thought may also mean travel to the spirit world in an altered state of consciousness. We also saw that sex is sometimes associated with shamanistic travel. Indeed, male erections are common in altered states and in sleep, and it is a peculiarly Western notion that the motif *always* stands for virility and fertility. Fourthly, 'death' is commonly a portal to shamanistic status. Shamans are said to die, to be dismembered or reduced to a skeleton, and to be resurrected with a new persona and social role.[40]

So what we have in the Shaft is not a hunting disaster; far too many points count against so simple an interpretation. Rather, we have transformation by death: the 'death' of the man paralleling the 'death' of the eviscerated bison. As both 'die', the man fuses with one of his spirit helpers, a bird. The close juxtaposition of the 'broken sign' and the similarity between such signs and the bird staff suggest that this type of sign was in some way associated with zoomorphic transformation and the bridging of cosmological levels that becoming a shaman necessitated.

It is highly probable that, as in many shamanistic societies, the metaphors of transformation into a shaman would have been woven into a myth or series of myths. But it would be naive to assume that the images in the Shaft merely 'illustrate' a myth, as pictures in a child's book may illustrate events in a fairy tale. Rather, the metaphors and images that lay at the heart of Lascaux shamanism and that structured the people's thinking were expressed in different contexts – myth and art, and probably in dance and music as well. Those who descended the Shaft did not simply view pictures: they saw real things, real spirit animals and beings, real transformations. In short, they saw through the membrane and participated in the events of the spirit realm. The paintings in the Shaft capture the essence of Lascaux shamanism in a compaction of its complex metaphors.

One final and intriguing point deserves to be mentioned. The Shaft is characterized by a very high content of naturally produced carbon dioxide. Today the carbon dioxide is pumped out of the cave, but it is still noticeable if one remains at the bottom of the Shaft for even a comparatively short time. Did, we may wonder, this high concentration of carbon dioxide induce altered states in prehistoric people?

These remarks on the Shaft conclude my examination of Lascaux. The cave has a coherence and organization that is remarkable; but it is also complex in its topography and its embellishments. No unitary explanation can cover all of Lascaux. To be sure, there is unity in that the whole ensemble of cave and embellishments is explicable in terms of a shamanistic cosmology and *diverse* explorations of a nether realm. But the precise ways in which the various contrasting parts of the cave were used and the rituals that were performed in them – ranging from vision questing to social (probably seasonal) aggregation of Upper Palaeolithic communities to shamanistic puberty rites and no doubt others as well – suggest a complex, sophisticated community with significant social distinctions that were reproduced (or challenged) every time the cave, or parts of it, were used.

Two caves: similar yet different

Broadly speaking, both Gabillou and Lascaux can be understood in terms of Figure 61, though Lascaux has more ramifications, more evidence for diverse activities and experiences. It would be rash to suggest that we can thereby infer that the people of Lascaux had a more complex social system than those at Gabillou. It is, however, possible that the sites were part of the sort of symbolically sustained social network that Clive Gamble describes (Chapter 3). People used symbols of various kinds to stand for social groups and were thus able to extend their influence and power beyond face-to-face contacts.

There is also evidence for important inter-cave diversity. 'Simple' Gabillou and 'complex' Lascaux seem to have differed in the ways in which shamans

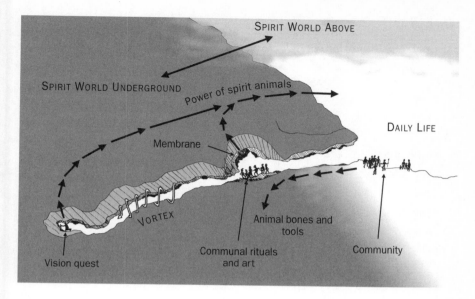

61 Diagrammatic representation of the way in which Upper Palaeolithic people used caves.

conceived of a relationship between their 'fixed' animal helpers. By and large, Gabillou vision questers preferred to keep their images separate from those of their fellows. In Lascaux, they crowded images together in the Apse as if they wished to be united with other shamans in the acquisition of a spatially concentrated power. This contrast points to somewhat different 'shamanisms', or different emphases within Upper Palaeolithic shamanism. If Gabillou was the focus of a comparatively small band, its shamans may well have wished to be independent of one another; but, if a number of groups came together at Lascaux, including the Gabillou people, shamans from all the participating groups may have wanted to integrate their visions and experiences with those of the wider community.

That those different kinds of relationships between images held implications for above-ground social relations seems likely. But all that we can conclude at present is that the caves were implicated in social distinctions and the spiralling diversity of Upper Palaeolithic societies. Exactly how subterranean image-making was manipulated by individuals is a matter I take up in the next chapter.

CHAPTER 10

Cave and Conflict

A remarkable feature of Upper Palaeolithic cave art is the persistence through a period probably longer than 25,000 years of a core of repeated animal motifs. At least in its separate elements, Laming-Emperaire and Leroi-Gourhan's mythogram is supported by empirical evidence: horse, bison, deer and aurochs are the principal themes of the art, though the proportions one to another vary considerably. To them may be added felines, the species that Leroi-Gourhan, not without reason, believed to be associated with the depths of the caves.[1] The Upper Palaeolithic was certainly not a free-for-all period during which cave artists painted whatever they fancied. Whether these persistent animal motifs retained exactly the same meanings and associations throughout the Upper Palaeolithic is another question; there were probably shifts back and forth along the spectrum of associations that each animal had.

But persistent motifs are not the whole story. Beyond the core motifs there are many species that appear far less numerously, sometimes even uniquely. Amongst the comparatively minor species are ibex, mammoth, megaceros (a large, now-extinct, deer with a humped back and spreading antlers) and reindeer. Examples of unique, or nearly unique, species are the hare in Gabillou (Fig. 54), the weasel in the Réseau Clastres (Fig. 2), and the musk ox in Chauvet (Fig. 3). There are also other exceedingly rare motifs, such as the so-called 'wounded men' that are the central topic of this chapter. What are we to make of these exceptional images?

Freedom to act

It would be impossible today to believe that Upper Palaeolithic communities were socially idyllic. In that we must concur with Max Raphael: from the Aurignacian to the end of the Magdalenian (and beyond), human beings lived in history-making communities, and that means there were social tensions and conflicts. How did individuals in Upper Palaeolithic communities challenge or subvert 'traditional' social relations and socially sanctioned art? If the hierarchy of a community was questioned, did that challenge show itself in cave art? These are questions that Laming-Emperaire and Leroi-Gourhan's structuralist approach obscured. For them, the mythogram 'thought itself' through the minds of people into art, even as Lévi-Strauss believed that binary structures thought themselves through the minds of people into specific myths.

Here I turn to the French theorist, Pierre Bourdieu, and to the English sociologist, Anthony Giddens.[2] Bourdieu's theory of practice and Giddens's related structurationist theory are particularly concerned with the resolution of the dichotomy between the individual and society, the issue that now concerns us. Bourdieu and Giddens argue that individuals are not pawns moved across an ecological chequerboard by transcendent forces, be those forces mythograms or binary oppositions. On the contrary, at least some individuals in all societies know a great deal about the ways in which their communities work and are, moreover, able to manipulate what Giddens calls the rules and resources of society to their own advantage. Such manipulation does not mean that the manipulators do not fully accept the beliefs of their community; one does not have to be an all-embracing agnostic to turn a belief system to one's own advantage. This is one of the ways in which people control, or attempt to control, the course of history.

At the same time, individuals are not completely free agents capable of doing exactly what they wish. Their actions are both enabled and constrained by the rules and resources that they manipulate. This principle is easily illustrated. If artists wish to make personal statements about their relations with the rest of the community, they are enabled to do so by a generally understood *langue* of motifs and accepted ways of deploying them. But they are, at the same time, constrained by the same *langue*: if they step too far out of line, their visual statements become incomprehensible to the people whom they wish to influence – a dilemma in which numerous twentieth-century artists found themselves. They have to tread a middle road; they have to subvert what is already there. In doing so they construct for themselves a new *persona*, or 'self', that can exist only in relation to other people's selves.

Despite the usefulness of these theoretical understandings, students of Upper Palaeolithic art have made little use of them. The role of human action, or agency, and the complex interplay between constraint and enablement in the making of Upper Palaeolithic art has not been much explored.[3] The work of intelligent human beings with personal needs and desires is, however, one of the lines of research that the shamanistic explanation of Upper Palaeolithic art opens up.

The full spectrum of consciousness and the different ways in which it can be divided up, labelled and given values is one of the resources, not of course the only one, on which individuals – and groups of individuals – can draw in the creation of their identities vis-à-vis those of others. The French philosopher Michel Foucault[4] recognized the social nature of definition when he argued that the 'normal' self, the 'normal' individual consciousness, is constituted by the various ways in which communities define and treat altered states of consciousness and madness. If there is at least one assumption about the Upper Palaeolithic that we can make confidently, it is that 'altered' consciousness and 'madness' were defined and accommodated differently from the ways in which they are in modern Western society and academia. The construction of Upper Palaeolithic 'selves', and hence the foundation of human action and social change, consequently proceeded along routes that were peculiar to that time – and that no doubt shifted somewhat during the course of the 25,000-year period.

As we saw in previous chapters, all communities *must* formulate definitions of levels of consciousness, and these definitions are constantly negotiated, that is, people jostle with one another as they establish their own *personae* and attempt to influence communal perceptions of their own and others' *personae*.[5] Claiming a segment of human consciousness as one's own particular, privileged preserve is a route to social advancement that people and groups have adopted throughout the ages. As Andrew Sherratt, the leading Oxford archaeologist, observes, any account of the European past that omits consideration of altered consciousness and its role in establishing human selves and facilitating human interaction is likely to be incomplete.[6]

Somatic hallucinations

So far in this book, I have been chiefly concerned with visual hallucinations and the part that they played in Upper Palaeolithic society and art. But, I have also noted that, when human consciousness moves to the autistic end of the intensified spectrum, all the senses hallucinate, not just vision. To understand the 'wounded men' of Upper Palaeolithic art, I now consider somatic hallucinations; these include attenuation of the body and limbs, polymelia (having extra limbs or digits), and, the one on which I focus, pricking and stabbing sensations.[7]

In this way, I again demonstrate the effectiveness of the 'cable', rather than the 'chain', method of constructing persuasive explanations. I intertwine the principal evidential strands that have provided recurrent sources of information throughout this book: the art itself, ethnography, neuropsychology and, to change the metaphor, the 'glue' that holds it all together, social theory.

Somatic hallucinations may occur in various ways and to different degrees. They may be induced by ingestion of psychotropic drugs, sensory deprivation and other extraneous factors, or by pathological conditions, such as temporal lobe epilepsy and schizophrenia.[8] They occur in various parts of the body. For instance, schizophrenics report alarming stretching of the scalp; sometimes it seems as if a fish hook is dragging the scalp as much as 30 cm (12 in) above the head.[9] Less painful somatic hallucinations are more common and occur in variously induced altered states. They include tingling, pricking and burning sensations. Although such sensations may be experienced in various parts of the body, they seem to be concentrated over the scalp, neck, shoulders, sternum, the outsides of the arms, hands and feet, stomach and the front of the upper legs. There is a difficulty in determining these locations because, in general, the sensations are ambiguously experienced, and those experiencing them sometimes find it difficult to say exactly where they are located. A schizophrenic invoked this difficulty to explain differences between her reports of physical sensations and those of other patients.[10] This potential variety facilitates individual manipulation and the personalization of experiences: if they wish, people are able to claim that their sensations are not the same as those experienced by other people.

The ratio between visual hallucinations and those in other senses may, in some instances, be affected by the cause of the altered state in which they occur. Lysergic acid diethylamide (LSD), for instance, is said to induce predominantly visual hallucinations, whereas the pathological condition of schizophrenia usually elicits a greater degree of auditory and somatic hallucinations.[11] In schizophrenia, tactile hallucinations are rarely reported independently of auditory or visual hallucinations.[12] Like LSD, psilocybin and peyote induce visual hallucinations within minutes of ingestion, but auditory hallucinations are frequently experienced as much as two hours later; other kinds of hallucinations occur only spasmodically.[13] The issue is further complicated by the observation that hallucinations experienced in one sensory modality can, by the process known as synaesthesia, be perceived in terms of another: for instance, a sensation felt on the skin (somatic) may be perceived as 'blue' (visual).[14]

Attempting to clarify the relationship between visual hallucinations and somatic hallucinations, the psychiatrist Ronald Siegel argues that there is 'an orderly progression of hallucinations from simple snow lights through geometric forms to tactile sensations'.[15] Some people, however, speak of tactile, or somatic, experiences in earlier stages than those that Siegel specifies. To clarify this apparent contradiction, it is useful to distinguish between somatic *sensations* and somatic *hallucinations*. In an early stage of altered consciousness, people may experience sensations of itching and tingling in various parts of the body. Because they do not 'illusion' these sensations they are known as pseudo-hallucinations.[16] With pseudo-hallucinations people know that the similes they employ to describe their sensations are no more than similes. In Stage 3 of altered consciousness they lose the ability to discriminate between sensory impressions coming from their environment and hallucinations. At this point, they no longer compare their physical sensations to something else; the sensations *are* what the hallucination dictates. Similes become realities.

This progression can be seen in reports given by Westerners. The anthropologist Michael Harner, for example, relates a detached, somewhat clinical, account of a physical sensation that he experienced after one cup of the South American hallucinogen *ayahuasca*: 'A hyper-excitation is felt in the body, which produces a pleasant agitation in the epiderm.'[17] Siegel, who ingested peyote while on a visit to the Central American Huichol, gives a more dramatic, but still 'objective' account, even if he does employ a metaphor: 'Another "Ping!" My skin prickled with electricity.'[18] For Westerners, electricity seems to be a ready metaphor; elsewhere, Siegel records a subject as saying that the sensations were like 'electricity running through the skin'.[19] The people experiencing these sensations were perfectly aware that they were using similes. In deeper altered states, such as chronic cocaine addiction, they are less able to distinguish between reality and somatic hallucinations. In a bizarre instance, a patient tore off his skin and, looking in the depth of his self-inflicted wound, believed he was pulling out microbes with his fingernails and with the point of a pin.[20] The modern Western setting that includes fear of contracting disease as a result of infection by invisible germs here led to the patient's attribution of his sharp sensations to the presence of microbes. In this case, the 'pleasant agitation' that Harner describes became a terrifying hallucination. Other people report 'the hallucination of small animals moving in the skin'.[21] At the same time as these people hallucinate the tingling sensation of small animals or insects on or under the skin, a condition known as 'formication',[22] they experience zoopsia (visual hallucinations of animals), thus combining two sensory modalities. In earlier chapters, we dealt extensively with zoopsia; now we see one of the ways in which it can be experienced in a multi-sensory way.

In highly charged religious contexts Westerners sometimes seem to be ambivalent about whether they are speaking in similes or not. Their statements are nevertheless clearly informed by their emotional circumstances and the sort of imagery in common use in their communities. Charismatic Christians, delighting in the ecstasy of heightened religious experience, tell of a 'gentle rain coming down on the neck and shoulders and penetrating the chest'; the sensation extends down into the legs and the middle of the back.[23] This sort of language reflects the notion of 'showers of blessing', the outpourings of divine grace for which they yearn. References to divine blessing in the form of rain are common in the Bible, written as it was in a semi-arid environment. For instance, Ezekiel,[24] with characteristic eloquence, represents the Lord as saying, 'And I will make them and the places round about my hill a blessing; and I will cause the shower to come down in his season; there shall be showers of blessing.' Clearly, this sort of imagery influences the way in which charismatic Christians interpret their somatic hallucinations. Whether they believe that the 'rain' is real or metaphorical is not entirely clear; a lack of language sophistication can lead to the suppression of 'as if' in descriptions of hallucinations.[25] Either way, these somatic experiences are a resource that individuals manipulate to achieve religious and social prominence: those who have received 'showers of blessing' are respected and admired. In some such communities there is also considerable financial reward as well.

The Western experiences that I have described range from variously successful attempts to observe one's own reactions objectively to the overwhelming experiences of religious and pathological conditions. Together, these accounts prepare for an understanding of the ways in which people in other cultures understand somatic hallucinations.

Somatic hallucinations and shamanism

Non-Western shamans who experience the same neurologically generated somatic sensations do not attempt to assess their experiences objectively. Instead, they construe them in culturally contingent ways that are often different from Western reports of 'microbes', 'electricity' or 'divine rain'. For instance, in the 1920s Isaac Tens, a Gitksan Native American shaman spoke of frequently falling spontaneously into a trance and of how, after he had undergone training, powerful chants forced themselves out of him, the phenomenon known as 'speaking in tongues' or glossolalia. Recounting one of these experiences, he said, 'The bee-hive's spirit stings my body...In my vision,

I went round a strange land which cannot be described. There I saw huge bee-hives, out of which the bees darted and stung me all over my body.'[26] The hallucination that developed out of Tens's sensations in trance was thus similar to the hallucinations of Westerners who speak of insects crawling over them. The sharpness of his somatic hallucinations, however, together with his zoopsia produced a complex multi-sensory hallucination of bees stinging him. Tens was able to use his hallucination to entrench his shamanistic status: his community accepted that he had passed through exceptional experiences.

For the Jívaro of the Amazon Basin, sharp, pricking sensations lead to a different hallucination. Jívaro shamans believe that they can keep magical darts in their stomachs indefinitely and can regurgitate them at will. These darts bear a supernatural potency that can also take the form of spirit helpers, or *tsentsaks*, that enable shamans to perform their tasks.[27] The Jívaro notion of mystical darts is developed in beliefs about *pasuks*, another kind of spirit helpers who aid malevolent bewitching-shamans by shooting their own objects into victims.[28] While in trance, curing-shamans can shoot a *tsentsak* into an eye of a threatening *pasuk*, the eyes being the *pasuks'* only vulnerable point. Apart from *tsentsaks*, there are other supernatural darts that can kill or injure people; they are called *anamuk*. They are invisible to people who are not under the influence of the hallucinogen *natemä*. In complex hallucinations, a shaman's darts sometimes take the form of animals that protrude from his skin. The darts also cover a trancing shaman's body as a protective shield.[29] The Miwok of the Central Sierra Nevada, California, held very similar beliefs. 'Poison doctors', *tu yu ku*, rubbed various kinds of poison on a pin-like stick or porcupine quill and then, by magical means, shot or threw the poisoned dart at a person who may have been as far as 80 km (50 miles) away.[30] Amongst the Jívaro and the Miwok, then, the sharpness of the pricking experienced universally during altered states contributes to beliefs about and hallucinations of pointed missiles, as well as creatures under and coming out of the skin (formication and zoopsia). Jívaro and Miwok shamans weave these experiences into accounts of their prowess and, like Tens, thus enhance their social positions. The experiences of altered states become a resource and a guarantee of special spiritual status and thereby of social standing as well.

As we saw in our North American case study, the attainment of extra-human shamanistic power and concomitant social status is frequently situated in the midst of an ordeal and an encounter with 'death'. The more horrific and painful the ordeal, the greater the prestige and power that accrue to the initiate. 'Death', suffering, excarnation (removal of flesh from a skeleton), dismemberment, transformation and rebirth are indeed common elements of shamanistic initiation.[31] Piercing is frequently a part of that experiential sequence. A Siberian Tungus shaman, for instance, told how his shaman ancestors initiated him: 'They pierced him with arrows until he lost consciousness and fell to the ground: they cut off his flesh, tore out his bones and counted them; if one had been missing, he could not have become a shaman.'[32] In a comparable account, the souls of a Siberian Buryat initiate's ancestors 'surround him, torture him, strike him, cut his body with knives, and so on'.[33] During this initiatory torture, the neophyte 'remains for seven days and nights as if dead'.[34] A Kazak Kirgiz initiate of southern Siberia spoke of spirits in heaven who cut him with 40 knives and pricked him with 40 nails.[35]

Similar reports come from southern Africa. Old K"au, a San shaman, spoke of flies clustering over his sides when he was in god's presence. There were, he said, also mambas, pythons, bees and locusts: 'When you go there, they bite you. Yes, they bite you [gestures to his legs]…Yes, they bite your legs and bite your body.'[36] The Ju/'hoansi believe that bees are vehicles for potency.[37] In southern San Drakensberg rock art bees are often depicted, sometimes on people's bodies as if they are stinging them (Fig. 62).[38] In addition, San shamans, like those of other cultures that we have considered, speak of sharp, piercing sensations. A Ju/'hoan shaman said, 'In !kia, around your neck and your belly you feel tiny needles and thorns which prick you. Then your front spine and your back spine are pricked by these thorns.'[39]

Another San construal of the pricking sensation, one that recalls the Jívaro experience, is that God himself or the spirits of the dead are shooting small, invisible 'arrows of sickness' into them. If people allow the central fire at a trance dance to die down, they say, 'God's arrows will strike us and make us painful.'[40] The heat and potency of the fire deflect the arrows. On the other hand, benign supernatural arrows are shot by an experienced shaman into a novice's stomach: 'You fire them in and fire them in until those arrows of n/um,

62 A southern African San rock painting showing bees, represented by crosses, painted on human figures.

63 A southern African rock painting of a recumbent human figure impaled and surrounded by short lines.

which are a lot like long thorns, are sticking out of your [stomach].' The informant went on to give a vivid description of how this appears: 'Your abdomen is like a pin-cushion, with arrows sticking out in all directions.'[41] Even if the researcher contributed the Western pin-cushion metaphor, this statement gives a striking impression of a St Sebastian figure.

This construal of the universal pricking sensation is represented in some San rock paintings. One shows an isolated recumbent person wearing the sort of eared cap that was associated with shamans who were said to have power over game (Fig. 63; see Chapter 5). The figure is impaled and surrounded by many short lines that are clearly not 'realistic'. The painting certainly recalls the remark about feeling like a pin-cushion. The short lines may represent arrows of sickness or, perhaps, mystical thorns, but because the figure lacks a painted context, it is difficult to say whether the 'arrows' are carrying sickness or beneficial potency.[42]

Joan Halifax summed up the suffering of shamans on behalf of their communities worldwide in the title of her book, *Shaman: the Wounded Healer.*[43] For the frontispiece she chose a photograph of an Inuit greystone, ivory and bone carving of a shaman harpooning not a seal but himself: he holds a harpoon that goes right through his body (Fig. 64). According to Halifax, this carving of a pierced figure 'captures the essence of the shaman's submission to a higher order of knowing'.[44]

This swift ethnographic overview gives us some glimpse of the ways in which shamans

64 An Inuit carving of a self-impaled shaman. Shamans submit to death in order to serve their communities.

around the world experience the pricking sensation triggered by altered states of consciousness and how they construe it into hallucinations of piercing whether by arrows, knives, nails or insect stings: I am not presenting a simple, one-off ethnographic analogy. We now have a neuropsychological and ethnographic foundation for a consideration of the Upper Palaeolithic images that are the focus of this chapter.

The 'wounded men' of Upper Palaeolithic art

Leroi-Gourhan estimated that there are only 75 anthropomorphic figures in all Upper Palaeolithic parietal art, a number that would constitute a very small percentage indeed of the (unknown) total number of images. Recent discoveries, such as the Chauvet and Cosquer Caves, have not materially affected that percentage. A stipulated proportion of human to animal images is not a crucial component of a hypothesis that an art is largely associated with ritualized altered states of consciousness. The proportion depends on the particular society: some communities seem to be principally interested in the geometric imagery of Stage 1, while other groups are more concerned with the imagery of Stage 3 – animals, monsters and beings of the spiritual levels of the cosmos. Then again, some societies focus on animals as sources of power or as helpers, while others emphasize anthropomorphic depictions of shamans and spirits.

The Upper Palaeolithic figures known as 'wounded men' occur at Cougnac and Pech Merle, two sites in the Quercy district of France. The images are of human figures with three or more lines radiating from their bodies (Fig. 65). Leroi-Gourhan places these 'wounded' figures in a larger category that he calls 'vanquished man' and in which he includes depictions of men who appear to have been knocked down by a bear or bison.[45] He thus includes the human figure in the Shaft at Lascaux. Jean Clottes and Jean Courtin, who studied the underwater Cosquer Cave, call the category '*L'Homme Tué*', the 'killed man'. They extend the category beyond the Quercy figures to include an engraved horizontal figure in Cosquer (it has a seal's head and a spear across its body);[46] and others from Sous-Grand-Lac and Gabillou.[47] All these figures are certainly associated with lines, but the lines do not seem to emanate from their bodies as clearly as they do in the Quercy examples; nor are the lines in most cases as numerous. I therefore concentrate on the Quercy figures; they constitute a clear, unambiguous group.

The sex of the Quercy figures is difficult to establish unequivocally; with the possible exception of the one shown in Figure 65 C, which may have a penis, primary sexual characteristics are not depicted. Yet, if these images are compared with those Upper Palaeolithic parietal images that are clearly female, the 'reclining women' at La Magdeleine or the profile figure at Les Combarelles, their general form seems to be male rather than female.[48] I therefore retain the current phrase 'wounded man' but add that the sex of the figures is, in any event, not crucial to my argument.

One of those at Cougnac, painted in black, is part of a larger panel.[49] It appears to be running towards the right and has three lines emerging from its lower back and buttocks (Fig. 65 A). Its torso appears to lean forward slightly, and this posture gives, at any rate to modern viewers, a sense of movement, perhaps of fleeing. The head and the upper parts of the body are not depicted. It is placed near depictions of large-horned deer (megaceri) and ibexes.[50] It is in fact painted on the lower chest of a megaceros, the throat and chest-line of which follows a natural contour of the rock. The second Cougnac 'wounded man' is part of another panel. It has seven or eight lines emerging from various parts of its body and has short arms without hands; no feet are depicted (Fig. 65 B). It bends towards the left and its bird-like head seems to be fitted into the head of a mammoth that, like the megaceros, is partially defined by the natural contours of the rock. The figure is surrounded by double applications of paint perhaps made with two fingers.[51] Below it, there is another but smaller mammoth that is partly superimposed by the larger one; to the right is an ibex. The group of images is painted near the entrance to a low side chamber that contains painted dots. One has to crouch down to enter it. Some researchers have described a third figure that they claim is the oldest; it is painted in a dark reddish colour and is said to have three lines, two in the breast and one in the back.[52] It is, however, very difficult to make out; certainly I cannot decipher it.

A further example is at Pech Merle, some 30 km (19 miles) away (Fig. 65 C). It is painted on a sloping ceiling that was formerly part of a small

65 The 'wounded men' of Quercy Upper Palaeolithic art. A and B Cougnac. C Pech Merle. The number of 'spears' impaling the figures is one of the features that suggest that these images are not realistic depictions of violent events.

diverticule in which only one or two people could fit, but the space was unfortunately opened up to allow visitors to view the images. This 'wounded man' is more erect than the others, and, like one of the Cougnac figures, has vestigial arms. It has nine lines protruding from it, but one of these may be a penis. A significant feature of this figure is that one of the so-called brace signs is painted just above it so that the right-hand 'arm' of the brace touches the back of its head. Given the ample wall space available, a connection between the figure and the sign seems to be intended. At Cougnac there is a panel of such signs. There may be eight or more of them, but some are now very fragmentary.[53] This Cougnac panel is some 35 m (115 ft) from the 'wounded men'. Nevertheless, the brace signs, like the 'wounded men', clearly suggest some sort of link between the two sites, and the way that the sign at Pech Merle touches the back of the 'wounded man's' head in turn suggests a link between these anthropomorphic figures and the enigmatic brace signs.

The bending-forward posture of one of the Cougnac figures and the slightly less bent position of another require comment. Leroi-Gourhan notes that 'an important number' of all the human figures have the body bent forward 'to about 30–45°.[54] This posture may be caused by one of the physiological effects of some altered states of consciousness. When a San man was describing the pricking of 'needles and thorns', he went on to say, 'Your [stomach] tightens into a balled fist.'[55] This painful experience causes San trance dancers to bend forward until their bodies are almost at right angles to their legs.[56] Southern African rock paintings often depict shamans in this position; sometimes they maintain balance by leaning on dancing sticks (Fig. 28).[57] Similarly, in the 'wounded men', as well as in other Upper Palaeolithic anthropomorphic figures and the Les Trois Frères 'sorcerer', this posture may represent a physical response to the prickings and contractions induced by some altered states of consciousness.[58] Again, I emphasize that this interpretation does not, of course, derive from a simple ethnographic parallel with the San.[59] Rather, it is based on what is a common physiological response that is governed, at least in part, by the human nervous system.

What sort of 'wound'?

There is one point on which all writers agree: the 'wounded men' are not easily interpreted. Clottes and Courtin, for example, believe that, without some extraordinary discovery, it will be impossible to achieve certainty, and Leroi-Gourhan concludes that the figures pose 'serious problems that we are not yet capable of resolving except through hypotheses which have little foundation'.[60] Here we again run into the old methodological problem of 'proof'. As I have pointed out, we must relinquish a desire for absolute proof and content ourselves with degrees of confidence as constituted by internal consistency, logic, and the intertwining of mutually sustaining and constraining evidential strands.

'Proof' aside, writers on the 'wounded man' figures have, for the most part, accepted that the lines depict spears, either real or magical.[61] Noel Smith, Professor of Psychology at the State University of New York, disagrees.[62] He argues that the multiple lines represent 'life forces' that link shamans to animals. 'Life forces', a generalization that Smith draws from his survey of shamanism worldwide, is an explanation that has merit, but, by itself, it seems too vague a concept to provide a firm foundation for an explanation of the Upper Palaeolithic 'wounded men'. The empirically established experiences generated by the human nervous system in altered states hold out the hope of more precision and may support, though in a different way, Smith's belief that the lines do not represent spears.

First, we must question the 'realistic' nature of the images, as we did those in the Shaft at Lascaux. The partial representation of the human body in all the examples, the possibly zoomorphic aspect of the heads of two of them, and, especially, the large number of 'spears' are features that suggest that the Quercy paintings are not literal depictions of real, violent events. We must, however, remember that our concepts of 'realism' and 'non-realism' are not universal: such notions vary because they are part and parcel of individual cultures. The words may be handy labels if loosely applied (like 'art'), but they probably obscure other and more complex notions of what may constitute 'reality'. A rigid distinction along the lines of Western concepts of what is real and what is not seems unlikely to have existed in the Upper Palaeolithic – though we should not assume unanimity on such matters, even among Westerners.

Secondly, as the neuropsychological and ethnographic evidence shows, Upper Palaeolithic people's understanding of somatic sensations and hallucinations would have been as much controlled by their cultural environment as are Westerners' or the San's. Yet, the fact that Upper Palaeolithic people were hunter-gatherers who used spears (some of which were meticulously decorated with signs and animal images) suggests that there may have been similarities between the ways in which shamans of that time and the San, Gitksan, Jívaro and Miwok shamans interpret the universal somatic sensations of altered consciousness.

Indeed, the two key factors that I have emphasized – the universality of the human nervous system and the shamanistic hunter-gatherer setting – suggest that the artists who painted the Cougnac and Pech Merle figures probably experienced the pricking sensations of trance and hallucinated them as multiple stabbings with sharp spears. So whilst the radiating lines may represent spears, they are not 'literal' spears, and the images do not record violent incidents of daily life. Rather, they represent spiritual experiences.

'Death' and the lower realm

The possible Upper Palaeolithic ritual and topographical setting of those experiences is the next question that we must address. As I have shown, beliefs in missiles of some sort that carry potency and pierce a shaman are a widespread concomitant of one of the physical experiences of some trance states. Moreover, a context in which piercing is commonly reported is shamanistic initiation. Shamans must suffer before they can heal, 'die' before they can bring life to their people. The ethnographic examples of the initiatory piercing that I cited and indeed the title of Halifax's survey of worldwide shamanism, *Shamanism: the Wounded Healer*, inevitably recall the Upper Palaeolithic images of what seem to be people pierced by spears.[63] The 'wounded men' may, I argue, represent a form of shamanistic suffering, 'death' and initiation that was closely associated with somatic hallucinations.

This interpretation can be extended by a consideration of the locations sometimes chosen for shamanistic initiations. In central Australia, an aspirant Aranda 'medicine man' goes to the mouth of a cave where he 'falls asleep'; spirits then throw invisible lances at him, piercing his neck and cutting off his head.[64] Similarly, but on the other side of the globe, a Smith Sound Inuit initiate must go to a cliff containing caves: 'If he is predestined to become a shaman, he will enter a cave…As soon as he has entered the cave, it closes behind him and does not open again until some time later.'[65]

A particularly vivid North American account of subterranean shamanistic initiation combines visual and auditory hallucinations. A 50-year-old Paviotso man wishing to become a shaman entered a cave and prayed. He tried to sleep but was prevented by strange noises – the grunts and howls of bears, mountain lions and deer. When he finally did fall asleep, he saw a healing ceremony. Then the rock split open and a 'man appeared in the crack. He was tall and thin. He had the tail feather of an eagle in his hand.' He taught the initiate how to cure.[66] This account recalls our two ethnographic case studies. Indeed,

it is readily understandable in terms of the ethnographic and neuropsychological evidence that we have considered: the cave and the vortex; auditory
hallucinations; fear; the rock as a 'membrane'; someone coming out of a crack
in the rock; hallucination of a healing ceremony; emergence from the cave
with a new *persona*. In sum, the 'death' and suffering of an initiate often
involves descent to the lowest realm of the shamanistic cosmos – and to the
furthest end of the induced spectrum of consciousness.

These and other instances of piercing and entry into caves add a further
dimension to the explanation that I propose: the 'wounded men' of Upper
Palaeolithic cave art in the Quercy district of central France may, together with
the other images, have been associated with chthonic shamanistic initiation.[67]
The neurological and ethnographic evidence suggests that, in these subterranean images, we have an ancient and unusually explicit expression of a
complex shamanistic experience that was given its form by altered states of
consciousness. That experience comprised isolation from other people,
sensory deprivation by entrance into the underground realm, possible ingestion of psychotropic substances, 'death' by a painful ordeal of multiple
piercing, and emergence from those dark regions into the light. Ritualized
altered states of consciousness and these images were thus intimately associated with the construction of social *personae* and distinctions.

We are now in a position to consider the role of human agency in the
making of the 'wounded man' images. What did people expect to achieve by
painting them?

'Wounded men' and human action

To answer this question, I note first that the 'wounded man' figures are found
in a restricted geographical area and, probably, within a comparatively
restricted period.[68] Their existence therefore points to an event, or series of
events, that took place in a particular community.

Something of the nature of those events is evident if we consider the images
in the 'traditional' Upper Palaeolithic shamanistic contexts of (a) subterranean chambers and (b) painted panels comprising depictions of animals
and signs. These two contexts, topographic and iconographic, suggest that the
'wounded man' images were associated with a social and intellectual movement that was situated within and that accepted (at least partially) the
cosmology of the time. We can go further: all novelty is a form of contestation;
it challenges received ideas and conventions. But the making of the novel

'wounded man' images was probably not an attempt to challenge the *entire* belief system and cosmology: the image-makers and their community were, after all, part of that cosmology and artistic tradition. Rather, it was probably an attempt to change the existing cosmological, social, religious and iconographic frameworks so that novel images and what they represented would be acceptable to at least some people. Cosmological, social, religious and iconographic frameworks are not immutable: they are, as Giddens puts it, resources, not fixed structures. Because people reproduce them through rituals, ordered social gatherings, images, slogans, memorized texts, and so forth, they are also malleable.

Who, then, painted the enigmatic 'wounded man' images?

It is not clear if the challenge implied by the 'wounded men' came from emergent individuals or from an interest group. In any event, the notion of an individual is complex and always molded by historical and cultural conditions.[69] Without exploring the philosophical implications of personhood, we can recall the distinction between large, complex paintings that must have been communally produced (such as those in the Hall of the Bulls and the Axial Gallery in Lascaux) and those simpler images that were probably made by individuals (such as those in the Diverticule of the Felines, also in Lascaux). As I have argued, communally produced art in large chambers was probably associated with group rituals, while smaller and more remote images may have been made by individual initiates or vision questers. The making of these personal images must have been associated with rituals that were different from those that attended the making and viewing of communal images. Although all Upper Palaeolithic individuals probably had to have some following in order to get to the point of making images in the subterranean locations, it seems likely that self-differentiating individuals played a key role in the making of the novel 'wounded man' images. Indeed, entry into caves, as well as the preparation of paint and the actual making of images, was, as we have seen, probably part of a series of interrelated, socially differentiating ritualized contexts.

Human individuality that was opposed to a dominant social and religious order is suggested by the fact that the images are not of 'otherness' – animals, animals as sources of power, visionary animal helpers and so forth. On the contrary, I argue that the 'wounded man' images are probably highly manipulated representations of the subjects themselves. In these self-images, the person him- or herself is emphasized. The distinctive 'wounded man' images were therefore probably a personal answer or challenge to the general paucity of anthropomorphic images in Upper Palaeolithic parietal art.

What that paucity meant is a difficult question. The evidence that I have put forward strongly suggests that the hegemony of animals as symbols implies that the source of supernatural power, and, in all probability, closely associated political power, lay outside the human sphere. In these depictions of (albeit transformed) human beings, we may have evidence for a challenge to the locus and control of supernatural and political power: some people were wishing to become a visible part of the interrelated symbol and power frameworks but in a new way, and this desire meant that new representations had to be fashioned out of the existing and potentially divisive religious experiences.

In mounting challenges to the *status quo* individuals adopt roles that are different from their family and economic roles. In seeking initiation as a shaman, a novice hopes to don a new *persona* that, however altruistic he or she may be, has specific social advantages that derive from beyond family relations and food production. Drawing on the dramaturgical origins of '*persona*', we must note the difficulty of separating out the fusion of man and mask; self and role become intertwined.[70] This fusion is especially closely achieved when the act of adopting a new *persona* involves altered states of consciousness, because those states are situated *within* an individual and inevitably transform an individual's conception of him- or herself; role becomes reality in the same way that simile becomes metaphor, and metaphor becomes reality.

Fusion and transformation are unusually clear in the 'wounded man' images. In one powerful motif they represent person and role, a new kind of shamanistic role made possible by a conscious, deliberate decision to highlight a distinctive and, at the same time, unrepresented component of altered states – piercing somatic hallucinations. The individuals who made the images were exploiting a particular component of altered states of consciousness and images manifesting that component to advance their own religious, social and political positions. They were presenting their religious experiences as related to, yet different from, those of others; probably, their images emphasized their personal suffering as a superior road to advancement. The challenge to the Upper Palaeolithic iconographic canon that the images constituted is therefore an example of how art, in the hands of human agents, plays an active, formative role.

From Neanderthal to conscious human action

Our enquiry into the nature and purpose of Upper Palaeolithic cave art began with the discovery of human antiquity, a startling revelation that many people found shocking – and that some still do. We then saw that a crucial threshold in human evolution was between two kinds of consciousness, not merely between moderate and advanced intelligence. Neanderthals were able to borrow only certain activities from their new *Homo sapiens* neighbours not because they were hopelessly bemired in animality and stupidity but because they lacked a particular kind of consciousness. They could entertain a mental picture of the present and, by learning processes, sense the presence of danger or reward. But they were locked into what Gerald Edelman calls 'the remembered present': without developed memory and the kind of fully modern language that must attend it, they were unable to enter into long-term planning, categorize generations and human relationships in order to initiate complex kinship and political systems, and speak of and construct mental 'scenes' of past and future times. They were almost 'there' – but not quite.

Nor could Neanderthals remember and act upon dreams and the visions of deeply altered consciousness, that inevitable component of human mental life that archaeologists have so largely ignored. Neanderthals could not therefore conceive of a spirit world; nor could they construct social and political relations founded on different degrees of access to that world. The Neanderthals' social and political distinctions were of the here-and-now and founded on sex, physical strength and age. Without fully modern consciousness and language with its developed handling of time past and time future there can be no gods.

As a result of the type of social relations that developed during the Middle to Upper Palaeolithic Transition between Neanderthal and anatomically modern communities in western Europe, mental imagery (already important in *Homo sapiens* populations, as archaeological evidence from farther to the east suggests) acquired a new and special layer of significance. A set of animals already carried (to varying degrees) symbolic meaning for west European anatomically modern communities. It now became important for those people to fix their images of another world, belief in which was one of the key traits that distinguished them from the Neanderthals.

In doing so, they created a new kind of society, a new set of social distinctions. Socialized altered consciousness, cosmology, religion, political influence and image-making (the forerunner of 'art') all came together in the sort of society that we consider fully modern. Individual people could now use esoteric resources to fashion their *personae* in relation to their fellows'. Those resources could be guarded and could thus become a controlled mechanism of social diversity, stratification and exploitation. Caves, already mentally hinted at by the experiences that fully modern neurology generated, brought the spirit realm into tangible reality. Caves, readily at hand in western Europe, where social relations between, at first, Neanderthals and *Homo sapiens* communities and, after the last Neanderthal had died, between expanding and interacting *sapiens* groups, provided controllable topographical templates for mental and social distinctions.

I have reigned in my interpretations of Upper Palaeolithic art, keeping them conservative and restricted to empirical evidence. Much more could be said about the variety of shamanistic beliefs and practices as they are recorded in transglobal ethnography. Readers of these records will repeatedly come across shamanistic activities that may well enlarge our understanding of what took place in the caves – and outside them. Sifting through the varied accounts, and through the neuropsychological literature, and tying ethnographic and neuro-logical specifics to specifics of Upper Palaeolithic art and archaeology will be a prolonged and delicate task. Some connections will prove more compelling than others, but, as I have pointed out, that is true of all archaeological expla-nations. Researchers must not allow their imaginations to run riot and thereby discredit well-supported elements: they must not permit a plethora of facile connections of the kind that early researchers proposed or an undue emphasis on a single element, such as entoptic phenomena, to swamp and by proximity weaken securely established explanations. Such cautious work will gradually uncover the changes that took place during the Upper Palaeolithic and reveal a rich temporal and geographical mosaic of human life.

Claude Lévi-Strauss spoke of myth growing 'spiral-wise' until the 'intellec-tual impulse which has produced it is exhausted'.[71] So, too, I suspect, did the Upper Palaeolithic nexus of mental states, fixed imagery, social relations, and caves, until, approximately 10,000 years ago, long after the demise of the Neanderthals, social, environmental and economic changes made it necessary for the locus of the spirit world to be built above ground, and cave art came to an end. Upper Palaeolithic religious and political leaders had painted them-selves into a subterranean corner.[72] But that is another story.

Envoi

Perhaps it would be more correct to say that the end of Upper Palaeolithic cave art was but one episode in a much longer story.

Julian Jaynes, a Princeton psychologist, tried to pinpoint the time when people recognized hallucinations for what they are. In his book, *The Origin of Consciousness in the Breakdown of the Bicameral Mind*,[1] Jaynes identifies a change in narration between the *Iliad* and the *Odyssey*. In the *Iliad*, says Jaynes, the characters have no concept of free will. They have no conscious minds; they do not sit down and think things out. It is the gods who act, who tell men what to do. The gods initiated the quarrel among men, started the war that led to the destruction of Troy, and planned the campaigns. Thus Agamemnon claims that it was Zeus and the Erinyes, 'who walk in darkness', who caused him to seize Achilles' mistress.[2] These gods were inner voices that were heard as distinctly as present-day schizophrenics hear voices speaking to them, or Joan of Arc heard her voices. The gods, Jaynes concludes, were 'organizations of the central nervous system...The god is part of the man...The gods are what we now call hallucinations.'[3]

According to Jaynes, the *Odyssey* followed the *Iliad* by as much as a century, and what a difference there is between the two epics. At centre stage now is wily Odysseus, not the gods. In the *Odyssey*, we are in a world of plotting and subterfuge. The gods have receded, and men take the initiative. This change, Jaynes argues, resulted from the breakdown of what he calls the bicameral mind. The human mind was no longer in two parts, one supplying the voices of the gods to the other. Now people could be in control of their thoughts and actions.

Yet it seems to me that Upper Palaeolithic people could attend to inner voices without, as Jaynes contends, being semi-automatons, unable to think for themselves. I therefore prefer to think in terms of primary and higher-order consciousness, the development of the second having taken place much earlier than the *Iliad* – at the emergence of *Homo sapiens* in Africa. Thereafter, it was culturally specific definitions of altered consciousness that determined whether people heeded their inner voices or not.

Emancipation of the mind from the imperative of voices and visions has in fact been a slow, stop-go-retreat process, one that is still incomplete. When and how did it become possible for people to stand back and contemplate their own thought processes, recognize that the voices they heard and the visions they saw came from within and not from external sources?

The controversial Yale literary critic Harold Bloom argues that it was Shakespeare who 'invented' the modern, Western, rational, independent human being. 'The dominant Shakespearean characters – Falstaff, Hamlet, Rosalind, Iago, Lear, Macbeth, Cleopatra among them – are extraordinary instances...of how new modes of consciousness come into being.'[4] Controversial he may be, but Bloom is surely right when he comments, 'I find nothing in the plays or poems to suggest a consistent supernaturalism in their author, and more perhaps to intimate a pragmatic nihilism.' Bloom agrees with A. D. Nuttall that Shakespeare 'implicitly contested the transcendentalist conception of reality'.[5] Shakespeare shows people changing, not as a result of being spoken to by gods, but by their interactions with other mortals and simply by 'taking thought', by an exercise of the individual human will. Hamlet argues with himself, not with gods or voices, as did the characters of the *Iliad* or, for that matter, Hildegaard of Bingen or Joan of Arc.

Many will feel that Bloom overstates his case when he claims that Shakespeare invented what we today accept as 'human', but he puts his finger on a key issue, on the independence of the human mind. After Shakespeare, it was the eighteenth-century Enlightenment that offered freedom from bondage, even though all Enlightenment thinkers did not take it. Today the Enlightenment receives an almost universally bad press. After two world wars and other horrors, bruised humanity feels it needs passion and commitment, not just reason. Reason, we are led to believe, is closely allied to positivism, intolerance and fascism. Yet there is no getting away from the conclusion that the Enlightenment opened up the possibility of knowing that the 'voices' came from within the human mind, not from powerful beings external to it. Optimistically, the German philosopher Immanuel Kant claimed: 'Enlightenment is man's emergence from his nonage.' Enlightenment philosophers supplied a foundation for the emancipation that Shakespeare scented. Goya summed up that new philosophy in his engraving, 'The sleep of reason brings forth monsters' (Fig. 66). Behind the man slumped on the table rise terrifying, unsettlingly anthropomorphic bats, owls, cats and dark monsters.[6]

Yet, today, even after Darwin's evolution-revolution and a string of breathtaking scientific advances, reason continues to doze, if not to sleep. New Age

66 Goya's engraving 'The sleep of reason brings forth monsters'. Goya realized that his corrupt and violent society was ignoring the spirit of the Enlightenment. In his work he explored and proclaimed the dark extremities of the human mind.

sentimentality exalts the 'spiritual' and retreats from reason. Bizarre sects control their adherents, even to mass suicide. Reports of out-of-body experiences, some in UFOs, are not uncommon. 'Urban shamanism' tries to resurrect a supposed primordial spirituality. Why should this be?

Eugene d'Aquili, until his recent death Associate Professor of Psychiatry at the University of Pennsylvania, was one of a growing band of neurologists who are tackling these questions. 'Neurotheology' takes the mental features of shamanism that we have examined and tries to find out more about them and, further, the neurology of all religions. As a starting point, d'Aquili put a twist on Lévi-Strauss's ideas and argued that myths are structured in terms of a major binary opposition, one polarity being humankind, the other some supernatural force.[7] It is the supernatural force that gives human beings the power to appear to resolve other, more specific, polarities posed by each particular myth, which may be life:death, good:evil, health:sickness, or some other imponderable. In doing so, myths appear to explain the workings of the cosmos and catastrophic events.

Allied to the resolution of such irresolvable oppositions is mystical experience, transcendence, or 'Absolute Unitary Being', the sense of being overwhelmed by ineffability and thereby achieving insights into the 'mystery' of life but without, necessarily, contact with spirit beings. As Wordsworth memorably expressed it, the 'affections gently lead us on,

> Until, the breath of this corporeal frame
> And even the motion of our human blood
> Almost suspended, we are laid asleep
> In body, and become a living soul:
> While with an eye made quiet by the power
> Of harmony, and the deep power of joy,
> We see into the life of things.

An explanation for this sense of Absolute Unitary Being – and for the other mystical experiences that we have tracked through the Upper Palaeolithic and that are still reported today – seems to lie in the human nervous system.[8] Neurobiologists are exploring what happens in the brain when people are overcome by ineffable feelings that they ascribe to divine visitation or an aesthetic oneness with the universe – what are, in effect, altered states of consciousness.[9]

The explanatory and emotional components of religion led these researchers to focus on two neurobiological processes. The first of these is what they call the 'causal operator', that is, 'the anterior convexity of the frontal lobe, the inferior parietal lobe, and their reciprocal interconnections'. I need not now explain these neurological terms save to say that they are parts of the brain and that the researchers argue that they and their interconnections automatically generate concepts of gods, powers and spirits; these 'supernatural' entities are implicated in attempts to control the environment. This 'pragmatic' component of religion is intimately linked to the second component – emotional states and altered states of consciousness that, for participants, verify the existence of spiritual entities that cause things to happen. The sense of Absolute Unitary Being – transcendence, ecstasy – is generated by 'spillover' between neural circuits in the brain, which is, in turn, caused by factors we have considered in this book – visual, auditory or tactile rhythmic driving, meditation, olfactory stimulation, fasting, and so forth. The essential elements of religion are thus wired into the brain. Cultural contexts may advance or diminish their effect, but they are always there. This, in d'Aquili and Andrew Newberg's provocative phrase, is why God won't go away.

If these neurobiologists are correct, and they have a persuasive case, the fundamental dichotomy in human behaviour and experience that I noted in the Preface – rational and non-rational beliefs and actions – will not go away in the foreseeable future. A prisoner who escapes from Socrates's cave encounters disbelief on his return. We are still a species in transition. But the neurology of mystical experiences and their persistence from the Upper Palaeolithic to the present, like the demise of Upper Palaeolithic art itself, are topics that lie beyond the scope of this book.

And yet...Who would wish to deny the wonder of Upper Palaeolithic art, Wordsworth's seeing 'into the life of things', the great music that religious devotion (and a good deal of cerebral activity as well) inspired in Bach, John Donne's wrestling with the ineffable, or a *Miserere* in the soaring acoustic of King's College chapel? If we dismiss such things as merely the functioning of the brain, are we in danger of losing something supremely valuable? Perhaps we should distinguish between, on the one hand, Wordsworth's pantheism and Donne's intellectual devotion and, on the other, the terrible belief that God is speaking directly to us and telling us not only how to order our own lives but also to impose that order on others' lives. What is in our heads is in our heads, not located beyond us. That is the crux of the matter, and it does not diminish Bach, Shakespeare, Donne and Wordsworth.

But the exaltation that those great creators excite in us does not justify mystical atavism. Shamanism and visions of a bizarre spirit realm may have worked in hunter-gatherer communities and even have produced great art; it does not follow that they will work in the present-day world or that we should today believe in personal spirit animal guides and subterranean worlds. We can catch our breath when we walk into the Hall of the Bulls without wishing to recapture and submit to the religious beliefs and regimen that produced them.

Notes

1 DISCOVERING HUMAN ANTIQUITY (PAGES 18–40)
1 Chauvet *et al.* (1996, 41–42).
2 Bégouën and Clottes (1981, 1987); for more on important finds in these caves, see Bégouën and Clottes (1991).
3 Moorhead (1969, 181).
4 Sulloway (1982).
5 George (1982, 7).
6 Darwin (1968 [1859], 453).
7 Darwin (1968 [1859], 435).
8 Daniel & Renfrew (1988, 143).
9 Darwin (1968 [1859], 458).
10 Greene (1999).
11 Childe (1942).
12 Darwin himself used the word; Darwin (1968 [1859], 455).
13 George (1982, 143).
14 Darwin (1859).
15 Darwin (1859).
16 George (1982, 140).
17 For a recent and informed overview of Upper Palaeolithic art see Clottes (2001). See also Clottes and Lewis-Williams (1998). On the distinction between deep cave art and images in better lighted areas see Clottes (1997). For recent debates see Clottes and Lewis-Williams (1996).
18 Varagnac and Chollot (1964); Clottes (1990); Sieveking (1991).
19 Kurtén (1972).
20 Pfeiffer (1982, 260).
21 Clottes *et al.* (1994).
22 See, for example, Kühn (1955); Ucko & Rosenfeld (1967); Sieveking (1979); Bahn (1997, 17–22).
23 For discussions of Altamira see Freeman (1987) and de Quirós (1991).
24 Beltran (1999, 8).
25 Kühn (1955, 48).
26 Corruchaga (1999, 22).
27 Kühn (1955, 45).
28 Kühn (1955, 48).
29 Corruchaga (1999, 24).
30 Breuil (1952, 15).
31 Breuil (1952, 154).
32 Kühn (1955, 78).
33 Beltran (1999).
34 Breuil (1952, 66).

2 SEEKING ANSWERS (PAGES 41–68)
1 Tomásková (1997).
2 See Conkey (1987, 1991); Soffer & Conkey (1997).
3 Ucko & Rosenfeld (1967, 118–19).
4 Conkey (1995, fig. 2; 1997).

5 Halverson (1987, 1992).
6 Leach (1961).
7 Lewis-Williams (1982, 429).
8 As we shall see in a later chapter the paired bison in Lascaux are an exception, and even there symmetry seems not to have been the aim of the image-maker.
9 Laming (1962, 66).
10 Cf. Layton (1987); Lewis-Williams (1991).
11 Lévi-Strauss (1969).
12 Delport (1990, 192–94).
13 Leroi-Gourhan (1968, 34).
14 Brannigan (1981); Gilbert & Mulkay (1984); Mulkay (1979).
15 Kuhn (1962).
16 E.g., Latour & Woolgar (1979); see Conkey (1997) on the intellectual history of Upper Palaeolithic art research.
17 Ingold (1992); Hacking (2000). On social construction and relativism in archaeology see Watson (1990).
18 E.g., Chalmers (1990); Hacking (1983, 2000).
19 Conkey (1980), (2001); for critique see Conkey (1990).
20 Conkey (1988).
21 Chesney (1994).
22 Conkey (1992).
23 Raphael (1945).
24 Chesney (1991, 14).
25 Chesney (1991, 14).
26 Raphael (1945, 38).
27 Raphael (1945, 2).
28 Raphael (1945, 2–3).
29 Chesney (1991, 19).
30 Chesney (1991, 3).
31 See, for example, Bloch (1983); McGuire (1992); Baert (1998).
32 Raphael (1945, 6).
33 Raphael (1945, 38).
34 Raphael (1945, 4).
35 Raphael (1945, 4, 48).
36 Raphael (1945, 51).
37 Chesney (1991, 17).
38 Chesney (1991, 11).
39 Cf. Conkey (1997, 354).
40 Laming (1959, 200).
41 Laming (1959, 180).
42 Laming (1959, 184).
43 Laming (1959, 186).
44 Laming-Emperaire (1962).
45 Laming-Emperaire (1962, 118); Chesney (1991, 19).
46 Laming-Emperaire (1962, 118, 119); translation by J. Clottes.

47 Laming-Emperaire (1962).
48 Laming-Emperaire (1972).
49 Laming (1959, 170).
50 Laming (1959, 172).
51 Barnard (2000, 125).
52 Gibbs (1998).
53 Leach (1974, 11).
54 Barnard (2000, 125).
55 Badcock (1975, 67–77).
56 Leach (1974, 16).
57 Lévi-Strauss (1967a).
58 See chapters in Leach (1967a).
59 Lévi-Strauss (1963, 229).
60 Lévi-Strauss (1963, 229).
61 Leroi-Gourhan (1968).
62 Leroi-Gourhan (1968, 19).
63 Leroi-Gourhan (1968, 118).
64 Leroi-Gourhan (1968, 20, 110).
65 Lévi-Strauss (1966); first published in French in 1962.
66 Leroi-Gourhan (1968, 19).
67 Leroi-Gourhan (1982).
68 Leroi-Gourhan (1976).
69 Leroi-Gourhan (1968, 174).
70 Leroi-Gourhan (1968, 174).
71 Lévi-Strauss (1963, 229).
72 Stevens (1975); Ucko & Rosenfeld (1967); Parkington (1969).
73 Johnson (1999).
74 Lévi-Strauss (1967b, 8).
75 Gibbs (1998, 40).
76 Conkey (2000); see also Clottes (1992) and Coudart (1999).
77 E.g., (1988); Sauvet & Wlodarczyk (1995).
78 Vialou (1986, 1987, 1991).
79 De Quirós (1999).
80 De Quirós (1999, 34).
81 Cf. Pfeiffer (1982).
82 De Quirós (1999, 56).
83 Laming-Emperaire (1962).
84 Pfeiffer (1982); Mithen (1988); Barton et al. (1994).
85 Gamble (1980, 1982, 1999); see also Jochim (1983).
86 Barton et al. (1994, 199).
87 Gilman (1984).
88 See, for example, Meillassoux (1972); Hindess & Hirst (1975); Seddon (1978).
89 Gombrich (1982). Taking a contrary view, Terrence Deacon, Professor of Biological Anthropology at Boston University, writes that Upper Palaeolithic cave paintings are 'the first concrete evidence of the storage of such symbolic information outside of a human brain' (Deacon 1997, 374; see also Donald 1991). Deacon and others who follow him confuse pictures with written records that do indeed store information and permit it to be accessed by minds in which it does not already exist.

90 Dissanayake (1995).
91 Wylie (1989).
92 Philosophers, e.g., Copi (1982), see analogy as a form of induction.
93 For an early and perceptive account of the social behaviourist position, see Mead (1934, 1964).

3 A CREATIVE ILLUSION (PAGES 69–100)
1 Tattersall (1999: 74–76); Palmer (2000: 13–18).
2 Tattersall (1999, 76).
3 Palmer (2000, 14).
4 Palmer (2000, 15).
5 For overviews, see Gamble (1991, 1999); Mellars (1989, 1990, 1994, 1996, 2000); Mellars & Stringer (1989); Knecht et al. (1993); Stringer & Gamble (1993); Byers (1994); Shreeve (1995); Tattersall (1999); Bar-Yosef (2000); Hublin (2000).
6 For a more generous view of Neanderthal aesthetics and accomplishments, see Hayden (1993).
7 See Guthrie (1990).
8 Wynn (1996).
9 Knecht et al. (1993).
10 White (1989b, 385).
11 White (1986).
12 Taborin (1993).
13 Bahn (1977).
14 White (1989, 227).
15 See, especially, Wiessner (1982, 1986) on the southern African San.
16 Binford (1981); but see Chase (1986).
17 Conkey (1980).
18 Sept (1992).
19 Farizy (1990a, 1990b).
20 White (1993).
21 White (1993, 288).
22 White (1993, 294).
23 Gargett (1989; 1999, 375–80); see Riel-Salvatore and Clark (2001) for a reply to Gargett and a lively response from him and other researchers.
24 Gargett (1999, 83–84).
25 Breuil (1952).
26 Leroi-Gourhan (1968).
27 But see Clottes (1990).
28 Chauvet et al. (1996); Clottes (1996).
29 Hahn (1970, 1971, 1993); Bosinski (1982).
30 Marshack (1991, fig. 129).
31 Wolpoff (1989).
32 Hublin et al. (1996).
33 Stringer & Gamble (1993, 132–36); Krings et al. (1997, 1999). For a review of the evidence from Portugal in favour of interbreeding if not of production of fertile offspring, see Wong (2000).
34 D'Errico et al. (1998); for a recent response see Mellars (2000).
35 Harrold (1989).
36 Gamble (1999, 377).
37 Bocquet-Appel & Demars (2000); for discussion, see Pettitt & Pike (2001) with response by Bocquet-Appel & Demars.

38 See Mellars (1996).
39 Gamble (1999, 377).
40 But see Straus (1993).
41 Mellars (1996, 415–16); for more recent discussions see Kuhn and Bietti (2000) and Kozolowski (2000).
42 White (1993a, 1993b); Gamble (1999, 380).
43 For a discussion of acculturation, see Herskovitz (1958).
44 Life in Europe at the beginning of the Upper Palaeolithic has been the topic of numerous imaginative novels, for example, William Golding's *The Inheritors*; Elizabeth Marshall Thomas's *Reindeer Moon*; Björn Kurtén's *Dance of the Tiger*; and Jean Auel's novels *The Clan of the Cave Bear*, *The Valley of the Horses*, and *The Mammoth Hunters*.
45 Stringer & Gamble (1993, 193).
46 Gamble (1999, 378).
47 Gamble (1999, 381–87).
48 Gamble (1999, 382).
49 Gamble (1999, 383).
50 Zubrow (1989).
51 Zubrow (1989, 230); see also Bocquet-Appel & Demars (2000).
52 Davidson & Noble (1989); Chase & Dibble (1987); Dibble (1989); Lieberman (1989).
53 Pinker (1994); Bickerton (1990).
54 Stringer & Gamble (1993, 88–91, 216–17); Mellars (1996, 387–91).
55 Davidson (1997).
56 Hublin *et al.* (1996).
57 Turner quoted by White (1989a, 214).
58 White (1989a, 218).
59 The evidence from the burial at Saint Césaire is inconclusive; Gamble (1999, 380–81).
60 Binford (1968).
61 It seems that some chimpanzees can be trained to perform some of these functions, perhaps up to the level of a three-year-old human child. Somewhat controversial experiments showed that these abilities in chimpanzees may give us some insight into the limitations of Neanderthals. See Savage-Rumbaugh (1986); Deacon (1997, 84ff).
62 Hahn (1993).
63 If we use 'acculturation' to denote Neanderthal/*Homo sapiens* interaction, we must take care that we do not imply inappropriate connotations, such as complete and comfortable assimilation of sets of interlocking traits. Indeed, I doubt if it is appropriate to speak of acculturation at the Transition. We must rather focus on the evidence and not become embroiled in a sterile logomachy (Demars 1998).
64 Pfeiffer (1982).
65 Mellars & Stringer (1989).
66 Davidson (1997).
67 McBrearty & Brooks (2000, 534).
68 McBrearty & Brooks (2000, 492).
69 McBrearty & Brooks (2000, 534).
70 For an accessible review see Deacon & Deacon (1999).
71 E.g., Howell (1999).
72 McBrearty & Brooks (2000, fig 13).
73 McBrearty & Brooks (2000); Deacon & Deacon (1999); Klein (2001); Henshilwood and Sealy (1997); Henshilwood *et al.* (2002).
74 McBreaty & Brooks (2000, 529).
75 McBreaty & Brooks (2000, 530).
76 See Hayden (1995) on the creation of social inequality.

4 THE MATTER OF THE MIND (PAGES 101–35)

1 Wylie (1989).
2 Glynn (1999).
3 For recent overviews of evolutionary psychology see Cummins & Allen (1998) and Kohn (2000).
4 Mithen (1996a); see also (1994, 1996b, 1998).
5 Fodor (1983); Gardner (1983); Barkow, Cosmides & Tooby (1992); Hirschfeld & Gelman (1994).
6 Chomsky (1972).
7 Chomsky (1986).
8 Bickerton (1981, 1990).
9 Mithen (1994, 36).
10 See, for example, Rose & Rose (2000).
11 Mithen (1996, fig. 33, 210–13).
12 Damasio (1999).
13 For a discussion of a possible relationship between the vividness of mental imagery and creativity see Campos & Gonzalez (1995).
14 Humphrey (1992).
15 Lutz (1992).
16 Lutz (1992, 73).
17 Lutz (1992, 76).
18 On the dangers of taking 'social construction' too far see Hacking (1999).
19 James (1982, 388). William James's brother, the writer Henry James, was also much interested in psychology, as his novels show.
20 Martindale (1981, viii).
21 Ardener (1971, xx, xxxiv).
22 Martindale (1981, 311–14).
23 McDonald (1971).
24 Dentan (1988).
25 Laughlin *et al.* (1992).
26 Laughlin *et al.* (1992, 132).
27 Cf. Laughlin *et al.* (1992, 138).
28 Martindale (1981, 255).
29 Gackenbach (1986); Price-Williams (1987).
30 Al-Issa (1977).
31 See also Siegel (1985).
32 E.g., Klüver (1926, 1942, 172–77, 1966); Knoll & Kugler (1959); Horowitz (1964); (1975); Oster (1970); Richards (1971); Eichmeier & Höfer (1974); Siegel & Jarvik (1975); Siegel (1977); Asaad & Shapiro (1986).
33 Lewis-Williams & Dowson (1988); Haviland & Haviland (1995); Haviland & Power (1995).

34 Klüver (1926, 504); Siegel (1977, 132).
35 Klüver (1926, 503); Siegel (1977, 134).
36 Knoll *et al.* (1963, 221).
37 Siegel (1977, 134).
38 Walker (1981).
39 Knoll *et al.* (1963); Siegel (1977).
40 Bressloff *et al.* (2000).
41 Horowitz (1964, 514; 1975, 164, 177, 178, 181).
42 Heinze (1986).
43 Horowitz (1975, 177).
44 Siegel (1977, 132).
45 Horowitz (1975, 178). Willis (1994); see Wilbert (1997) on Warao hallucinations.
46 Siegel & Jarvik (1975, 127, 143); Siegel (1977, 136).
47 Horowitz (1964); Grof & Grof (1980); Siegel (1980); Drab (1981).
48 Siegel (1977, 134, 1975, 139).
49 Siegel & Jarvik (1975, 113).
50 Rasmussen (1929, 124); Harner (1982, 31).
51 Boas (1900, 37).
52 Vastokas & Vastokas (1973, 53).
53 Harner (1982, 32).
54 Siegel & Jarvik (1975, 128).
55 Grof (1975, 38–39) illustrates how a clock tower changes into an owl.
56 Siegel & Jarvik (1975, 128).
57 Siegel (1977, 134).
58 Reichel-Dolmatoff (1978a, 147).
59 Klüver (1942, 181, 182).
60 E.g., Siegel & Jarvik (1975, 105).
61 Wedenoja (1990).
62 Murdock (1967).
63 Bourguignon (1973, 11); Shaara (1992).
64 Bourguignon (1973, 12); emphasis in original.
65 Reichel-Dolmatoff (1972, 1978a, 12–13, 1981).
66 Reichel-Dolmatoff (1978b, 291–92).
67 Gebhart-Sayer (1985).
68 Shirokogoroff (1935).
69 See, for example, Ränk (1967); Nordland (1967); Eliade (1972); Bourguignon (1973); Hultkranz (1973); Siikala (1982); Winkelman (1990); Atkinson (1992); Riches (1994); Vitebsky (1995a, 1995b); Thomas & Humphrey (1996); Jakobsen (1999); Narby & Huxley (2001). See also debate between Hultkranz (1998) and Hamayon (1998).
70 See Cardeña (1996) on the universalism of shamanism and a comparison between shamanism and hypnotic phenomena and the distinction between soul-loss and spirit possession.
71 Siikala (1982); Ludwig (1968).
72 Noll (1985, 445–46).
73 Siikala (1992, 105–06); see also Stephen (1989).
74 Furst (1976, 4–5); see also (1972, viii–ix).
75 McClenon (1997, 349).
76 La Barre (1980, 82–83); see also Winkelman (1992).

5 CASE STUDY 1: SOUTHERN AFRICAN SAN ROCK ART (PAGES 136–62)

1 For accounts of the Bleek family and their work see chapters in Deacon & Dowson (1996) and Lewis-Williams (2000); also Hewitt (1986) and Guenther (1989).
2 For published texts, see, for example, Bleek & Lloyd (1911); Bleek (1924); Lewis-Williams (2000).
3 There are at least two other rock art traditions in southern Africa, that made by Khoekhoen pastoralists and the distinctive, white, largely geometric images that Bantu-speaking farmers made.
4 Stow & Bleek (1930); see also Orpen (1875) for rock paintings and comments by Bleek's informants.
5 Bleek (1875, 20).
6 For introductions to San rock art see Vinnicombe (1976); Lewis-Williams (1981, 1990); Lewis-Williams & Dowson (1999).
7 Bleek (1875, 20).
8 For tales about /Kaggen see Bleek (1924); Bleek & Lloyd (1911); Lewis-Williams (2000).
9 For a full discussion of *!gi:xa* and associated words and their translation into English see Lewis-Williams (1992). For /Xam texts about *!gi:ten* see Bleek (1933a, 1933b, 1935, 1936); Lewis-Williams (2000, 255–65).
10 Marshall (1976, 1999).
11 Marshall Thomas (1959).
12 Ruby (1993).
13 For other accounts of Kalahari Desert San groups see Lee (1979); Silberbauer (1981); Guenther (1986); Wilmsen (1989); Valiente-Noailles (1993). On the San in history, see Gordon (1992, 1997).
14 On the San trance dance see Marshall (1962, 1969, 1999, 63–90); Lee (1968); Katz (1982); Katz *et al.* (1997); Keeney (1999).
15 Biesele (1993).
16 Guenther (1975, 1999).
17 Dowson (1988, 2000).
18 Blundell (in prep.).
19 Barnard (1992).
20 Biesele (1993, 70).
21 Biesele (1993, 81).
22 Biesele (1993, 81).
23 See analyses of two /Xam myths in Lewis-Williams (1996, 1997b).
24 Bleek (1875, 13).
25 Vinnicombe (1976); Lewis-Williams (1981).
26 Orpen (1874).
27 Lewis-Williams (1980, 1981).
28 Siegel (1977).
29 For compendia of accounts see Eliade (1972); Halifax (1980); Vitebsky (1995b); Musi (1997) and Bean (1992).
30 The poem is printed together with Coleridge's explanation in Dixon & Grierson (1909).
31 Biesele (1993, 70–72).
32 Biesele (1993, 72).

33 See Eliade (1972); Halifax (1980); Vitebsky (1995b); Musi (1997) and Bean (1992).
34 Biesele (1993, 72).
35 See also Lewis-Williams (1981, 1983); Lewis-Williams & Dowson (1999).
36 Lewis-Williams (1995a).
37 Lewis-Williams et al. (2000).
38 Lewis-Williams & Dowson (1990).
39 Lewis-Williams (1981, 103–16); Lewis-Williams & Dowson (1999, 92–99).
40 Bleek (1933, 309).
41 Dowson (1992).
42 Lewis-Williams (1995a).
43 Siegel (1977).
44 Sacks (1970).
45 Pager (1971, 151, 347–52).
46 E.g., Bootzin (1980, 343).
47 Lamb (1980, 144).
48 Halifax (1980, 32); Lame Deer & Erdoes (1980, 74); Neihardt (1980, 97); Munn (1973, 1(19); Christie-Murray (1978).
49 E. Wilmsen, pers. comm.
50 Orpen (1874, 8).
51 Lewis-Williams (1995b).
52 Leroi-Gourhan (1943, 1945); Dobres & Hoffman (1994); Dobres (2000).
53 Biesele (1993).
54 Lewis-Williams (1987).
55 How (1962).
56 Lewis-Williams (1986); Jolly (1986); see also Prins (1990, 1994).
57 Cf. Riddington (1988); Ingold (1993).
58 Yates & Manhire (1991).
59 Lewis-Williams & Dowson (1999, 108); Lewis-Williams & Blundell (1997).
60 Deacon (1988); Dowson (1994, 2000).
61 Stow (1905).
62 Lewis-Williams (1981).
63 See Victor Turner's work on symbolism in an African community (Turner 1967).

6 Case Study 2: North American Rock Art (pages 163–79)

1 Kroeber (1939).
2 See, for example, Steward (1929); Driver (1937); Newcomb & Kirkland (1967); Grant (1968); Ritter & Ritter (1972); Vastokas & Vastokas (1973); Wellmann (1978); Schaafsma (1980, 1992); Hedges (1982, 1992); Furst (1986); Conway & Conway (1990); Conway, T. (1993); York et al. (1993); McCreery & Malotki (1994); Ritter (1994); Turpin (1994); Haviland (1995); Boyd (1996), (1998); Stoffle et al. (2000). For an account of shamanism and altered states of consciousness in the Pacific Northwest see Jilek (1982).
3 Heizer & Baumhoff (1959, 1962); Grant (1968).
4 For a discussion of supposed North American hunting magic, see Conway (1993, 106–08) and Whitley (2000).
5 Whitley (2000, 103).
6 Whitley (2000, 103).
7 Lévi-Strauss (1977, 7).
8 Blackburn (1975, xiv).
9 Blackburn (1975, xiv).
10 Blackburn (1975, 23); see also Librado (1981).
11 Blackburn (1975, 30).
12 See also Kroeber (1925); Grant (1965); Applegate (1975).
13 Blackburn (1976, 1977).
14 Wellmann (1978, 1979a, 1979b).
15 Wilbert (1981).
16 Hedges (1976, 1982, 1992, 1994).
17 See, for example, Whitley (1992, 1994, 1998a, 1998b, 1998c, 2000); Keyser & Whitley (2000).
18 Whitley (2000).
19 For a short summary of North American religion and vision questing see Zimmerman (1996).
20 Hultkranz (1987).
21 Whitley pers. comm. See Whitley et al. (1999).
22 Hultkranz (1987, 53).
23 Whitley (2000, 77).
24 Hultkranz (1987, 53).
25 Gayton (1948).
26 Whitley (2000, 79–80).
27 Whitley (2000, 75).
28 Driver (1937).
29 Whitley (2000, 76).
30 Zigmond (1986, 406–07).
31 Cited by Keyser & Whitley (2000, 20).
32 Cited by Keyser & Whitley (2000, 20).
33 Cited by Keyser & Whitley (2000, 20).
34 Whitley (2000, 81).
35 Whitley (2000, 90).
36 Whitley (2000, 83).
37 Whitley (2000, 83); parentheses in Gayton.
38 Conway (1993, 109–10).
39 Conway (1993, 109–10).
40 Steward (1929, 225).
41 Whitley (2000, 86); see also Steward (1929, 227).
42 Whitley (2000, 86); see also Steward (1929, 227).
43 Whitley pers. comm.
44 For example, Taçon (1983).
45 Biesele pers. comm.
46 Whitley (2000, 107).
47 Whitley (2000, 105–23).
48 Lewis-Williams & Dowson (1988, 215).
49 Whitley (2000, 108).
50 Whitley (2000, 108).
51 Whitley (2000, 110).
52 Whitley (2000, 111).
53 Whitley (2000, 111).
54 Whitley (2000, 115).
55 Whitley (2000, 115).
56 Lewis-Williams et al. (1993).
57 Whitley et al. (1999, 235).
58 B. Johnson, cited by Whitley et al. (1999).

59 Whitley (1994).
60 Hultkranz (1987, 52).
61 Whitley (2000, 82).
62 Whitley (2000, 78).
63 Whitley (2000, 20).
64 Whitley (2000, 83).
65 Gayton (1930).

7 An Origin of Image-Making (pages 180–203)
1 On environmental and social change during the Upper Palaeolithic see Jochim (1983) and Gamble (1999). On altered states and social change, see Bourguignon (1973).
2 Raphael (1945, 3).
3 Breuil (1952, 23).
4 Delluc & Delluc (1986).
5 Breuil (1952, 21).
6 Forge (1970, 281).
7 See also Segall et al. (1966).
8 Forge (1970, 287).
9 Davis (1986, 1987).
10 Davis (1986, 201).
11 Davis (1986, 201).
12 Faris (1986, 203).
13 See Edelman (1987, 1989, 1992); Edelman & Tononi (2000).
14 Edelman (1994, 113).
15 Edelman (1994, 112–24).
16 Edelman (1994, 112–32).
17 Edelman (1994, 124).
18 Greenfield (1997, 2001).
19 EEG is the acronym for 'electroencephalography', a technique that measures electrical activity in various parts of the brain by means of electrodes fixed to the scalp.
20 Klüver (1926, 505, 506); see also Knoll et al. (1963, 208).
21 Siegel & Jarvik (1975, 109).
22 Siegel (1977, 134).
23 Klüver (1942, 179).
24 Reichel-Dolmatoff (1978a, 8).
25 See Clottes (1996) on thematic changes in Upper Palaeolithic art.
26 Halverson (1987, 66–67).
27 Hahn (1986, 1993).
28 Hahn (1993, 232).
29 Hahn (1993, 238).
30 Hahn (1993, 236).
31 Hahn (1986).
32 Hahn (1993, 238).
33 Clottes & Packer (2001, 177–80); Clottes (1996).
34 Hahn (1993, 231).
35 See Turner (1967) on the multiple meanings of symbols.
36 Hahn (1993, 240).
37 Hahn (1986, 1993).
38 Hahn (1993, 234).
39 Hahn (1993, 240).
40 Dowson & Porr (2001).

8 The Cave in the Mind (pages 204–27)
1 Plato (1935, 207).
2 There is debate about the applicability of 'shamanism' to Aboriginal Australian religions. Some writers believe that altered states of consciousness play no role Aboriginal religion, but I suspect that their judgment is based on a misunderstanding of what constitutes an altered state.
3 Leroi-Gourhan & Allain (1979).
4 Bégouën & Breuil (1958).
5 Leroi-Gourhan (1968); Marshack (1972).
6 Lewis-Williams & Dowson (1988).
7 Clottes & Courtin (1996); Clottes pers. comm.
8 See, for example, Graziosi (1960); Ucko & Rosenfeld (1967); Bahn & Vertut (1988); Gonnella (1999).
9 Leroi-Gourhan (1968, fig. 13).
10 Bahn & Vertut (1988, fig. 52).
11 See Clottes & Lewis-Williams (1988, fig. 83) for a photograph.
12 For photographs see Clottes (1995, figs 142, 164).
13 Freeman et al. (1987, 223–24); Beltran (1999, 34, 43, 47, 48, 152, 153, 154, 162).
14 Breuil (1952, fig. 271).
15 Eliade (1972, 50–51); Halifax (1980, 6).
16 Upper Palaeolithic vision questing has been suggested by other writers, such as Hayden (1993) and Pfeiffer (1982).
17 On sensory deprivation and visions see La Barre (1975, 14), Walker (1981, 146), Pfeiffer (1982, 211) and Siegel & Jarvik (1975).
18 Myerhoff (1974, 42).
19 Clottes & Courtin (1996, 61).
20 Clottes et al. (1992, 586–87); Clottes & Courtin (1996).
21 Lorblanchet (1992, 451).
22 Duday & Garcia (1983).
23 Lorblanchet (1992, 488–89).
24 Ucko (1992, pl. 9).
25 Ucko (1992, 188, pls 10 and 11).
26 Clottes & Courtin (1996, 60).
27 Ucko (1992, 158).
28 Clottes & Courtin (1996, 63).
29 Baffier & Feruglio (1998, 2001).
30 Lorblanchet (1991, 29).
31 Lorblanchet (1991, 30); see also Smith (1992) on the importance of breath.
32 Freeman et al. (1987, 105).
33 De Beaune (1987); de Beaune et al. (1988); de Beaune & White (1993).
34 De Beaune & White (1993, 78–79).
35 See, for example, Lakoff & Johnson (1980).
36 Jakobsen (1999, 59).
37 Kensinger (1973, 9).
38 See Levinson (1966) on auditory hallucinations in hysteria.
39 Tuzin (1984).
40 Delluc & Delluc (1990, 62–63).
41 Bahn & Vertut (1988, 69, fig. 34).

42 Needham (1967).
43 Oppitz (1992); Potapov (1996); on Lapp drums, see Manker (1996).
44 Potapov (1996, 120).
45 Vajnštejn (1996, 131).
46 Vitebsky (1995b, 79, 82).
47 Siikala (1998, 90).
48 Harner (1982, 65).
49 Neher (1961, 1962).
50 Reznikoff & Dauvois (1988); Scarre (1989); Waller 1993.
51 Waller (1993).
52 Cohen (1964, 160, 170).
53 Myerhoff (1974, 41).
54 The Greek words are variously translated.

9 CAVE AND COMMUNITY (PAGES 228–67)

1 Ingold (1992, 53). For discussions of these ideas in the context of Neolithic chambered tombs see Thomas (1990, 1991) and Lewis-Williams & Dowson (1993).
2 Cf. Vialou (1982, 1986).
3 Breuil (1952, 310–11); Gaussen (1964); Leroi-Gourhan (1968, 317).
4 Leroi-Gourhan (1968, 317); Gaussen et al. in L'art des cavernes (1984, 225–31).
5 Breuil (1952, 310).
6 Breuil (1952, 311).
7 Leroi-Gourhan (1968, 317).
8 Leroi-Gourhan (1968, 317).
9 Gaussen (1964, pl. 22).
10 Lorblanchet & Sieveking (1997).
11 For photographs see Clottes & Lewis-Williams (1996, fig. 96) and Leroi-Gourhan (1968, pl. 58).
12 Laming (1959).
13 Aujoulat (1987). Lascaux is the most extensively published Upper Palaeolithic cave. Early books include Brodrick (1949); Windels (1949); Breuil (1952, 107–51); Bataille (1955); Laming (1959). More recent guides to the cave include Delluc & Delluc (1984, 1990). The most comprehensive accounts are Ar. Leroi-Gourhan & Allain (1979); Ar. Leroi-Gourhan (1982); Leroi-Gourhan (1984); Ruspoli (1987).
14 Leroi-Gourhan (1984, fig. 2).
15 Delluc & Delluc (1990, 3).
16 Laming (1959, 67).
17 Ruspoli (1987, 109).
18 See Tuzin (1984) on miraculous voices.
19 Breuil (1952, 125).
20 Laming (1959, 78).
21 Laming (1959, 77).
22 E.g., Kehoe (1989).
23 Bégouën et al. (1993).
24 Furst (1977, 16–17).
25 Clottes, pers. comm.
26 Furst (1977, 16–21).
27 As Conkey (1980) argued for Altamira.
28 Leroi-Gourhan (1979, fig. 40).
29 Laming (1959, 80).
30 Ar. Leroi-Gourhan & Allain (1979).
31 Vialou (1979, 244, 280).
32 Breuil (1952, 147).
33 For a penetrating discussion of perspective see Kubovy (1986).
34 See, for example, Clottes & Lewis-Williams (1998, fig. 73).
35 Kubovy (1986).
36 Guthrie (1990, 93).
37 See Smith (1992).
38 Davenport & Jochim (1988).
39 Brodrick (1949, 82).
40 Eliade (1972).

10 CAVE AND CONFLICT (PAGES 268–86)

1 See Clottes (1996) on the persistence of and differential emphasis on themes found in early Aurignacian art through to the Magdalenian. More recently, he has written: 'Chauvet has also made us realise that the contents of the art did not change considerably over time' (Clottes 1998, 126). One of the most interesting changes in emphasis concerns felines and 'dangerous' animals; at the present stage of research, there appear to be more in the early rather than late Upper Palaeolithic sites.
2 Bourdieu (1977); Giddens (1984).
3 But see Bender (1989); Hayden (1990); Lewis-Williams & Dowson (1993) for related studies.
4 Foucault (1965).
5 For a review of work on the construction of personae and a specific study of personhood in the British Neolithic see Fowler (2001).
6 Sherratt (1991, 52).
7 I take 'somatic' to include haptic, or tactile, and cenesthetic hallucinations.
8 Siegel (1977); Brindley (1973, 593).
9 Pfeifer (1970, 57).
10 Pfeifer (1970, 58).
11 Winters (1975, 54).
12 Asaad (1980).
13 La Barre (1975, 12–13).
14 Klüver (1942, 199); McKellar (1972, 48–50); Fischer (1975, 222); La Barre (1975, 10); Emboden (1979, 44); Cytowic (1994).
15 Siegel (1978, 313).
16 Sedman (1966); Hare (1973); Taylor (1981).
17 Harner (1973a, 156).
18 Siegel (1992, 29).
19 Siegel (1978, 313).
20 Siegel (1978, 309–10).
21 Siegel (1978, 309).
22 Asaad (1980).
23 Goodman (1972, 58).
24 Ezekiel 34: 26.
25 Sarbin (1967, 371).
26 Halifax (1980, 189).
27 Harner (1973a, 17); see also Harner (1973b).
28 Harner (1973a, 21–22).

29 Harner (1973a, 24).
30 Bates (1992, 101–02).
31 Eliade (1972).
32 Eliade (1972, 43).
33 Eliade (1972, 43).
34 Eliade (1972, 44).
35 Eliade (1972, 44).
36 Biesele (1980, 57).
37 Katz (1982, 94).
38 Lewis-Williams (1997a, figs 2, 3 and 4).
39 Katz (1982, 46).
40 Katz (1982, 120).
41 Katz (1982, 214).
42 For further examples of 'impaled' figures in southern African rock art see Garlake (1987a, fig. 67); (1987b, fig. 6); (1995, fig. 185); Bond (1948).
43 Halifax (1982).
44 Halifax (1982, 5).
45 Leroi-Gourhan (1982, 54, chart xxviii).
46 Clottes & Courtin (1996, figs 157, 158).
47 Clottes & Courtin (1996, figs 166, 167, 168); Bahn & Vertut (1988, 152).
48 Leroi-Gourhan (1968, figs 501, 502, 514).
49 Méroc & Mazet (1977, 35–37, 70).
50 Leroi-Gourhan (1968, fig. 383).
51 Leroi-Gourhan (1968, fig. 384).
52 Méroc & Mazet (1977).
53 Lorblanchet (1984a, fig. 8).
54 Leroi-Gourhan (1982, 53).
55 Katz (1982, 46).
56 Marshall (1969, 363–64).
57 See, for example, Lewis-Williams (1981, figs 19, 20, 23, 28, 32); Lewis-Williams & Dowson (1999, figs 15, 16c, 17, 20, 28, 32a).
58 See, for example, Marshack (1972, figs 181, 182); Leroi-Gourhan (1968, fig. 57).

59 Lewis-Williams (1991).
60 Clottes & Courtin (1996, 161); Leroi-Gourhan (1982, 54).
61 Graziosi (1960, 182); Leroi-Gourhan (1968, 130); (1982, 54); Méroc & Mazet (1977, 36); Breuil (1979, 272); Clottes & Courtin (1996, 160–61).
62 Smith (1992, 84–85, 109, 114).
63 Halifax (1982).
64 Eliade (1972, 46).
65 Eliade (1972, 51).
66 Eliade (1972, 101).
67 See also Pfeiffer (1982); Hayden (1990).
68 Clottes & Courtin (1996, 159).
69 For a range of ideas on this point see Carrithers et al. (1985).
70 Hollis (1985, 222); see Rappaport (1999) on the importance of altered states in ritual.
71 Lévi-Strauss (1963, 229).
72 For a discussion of late Magdalenian cave art see Clottes (1990)

ENVOI (PAGES 287–91)
1 Jaynes (1982).
2 Iliad (19, 86–90).
3 Jaynes (1982, 74).
4 Bloom (1998, xx).
5 Bloom (1998, 3, 518–19).
6 Goya tempered his title with the following caption, 'Imagination abandoned by reason produces impossible monsters, united with her, she is the mother of the arts and the source of their wonders'.
7 D'Aquili (1978, 1986).
8 Twemlow et al. (1982).
9 Lex (1979); d'Aquili & Newberg (1993a, 1993b, 1998, 1999); Trevarthen (1986).

Bibliography and Guide to Further Reading

Al-Issa, I. 1977. Social and cultural aspects of hallucinations. *Psychological Bulletin* 84, 570–87.

Applegate, R. B. 1975. The datura cult among the Chumash. *Journal of California Anthropology* 2, 7–17.

Ardener, E. 1971. Introductory essay: social anthropology and language. In Ardener, E. (ed.) *Social Anthropology and Language*, pp. ix–cii. London: Tavistock.

Asaad, G. 1980. *Hallucinations in Clinical Psychiatry: A Guide for Mental Health Professionals*. New York: Brunner, Mazel.

Asaad, G. & Shapiro, B. 1986. Hallucinations: theoretical and clinical overview. *American Journal of Psychiatry* 143, 1088–97.

Atkinson, J. M. 1992. Shamanisms today. *Annual Review of Anthropology* 21, 307–30.

Aujoulat, N. 1987. *Le relevé des œuvres pariétales paléoliques: enregistrement et traitement des données*. Paris: Maison des Sciences de l'Homme, Documents d'Archélogie Française No. 9.

Badcock, C. R. 1975. *Lévi-Strauss: Structuralism and Sociological Theory*. London: Hutchinson.

Baert, P. 1998. *Social Theory in the Twentieth century*. Cambridge: Polity Press.

Baffier, D. & Feruglio, V. 1998. First observations on two panels of dots in the Chauvet Cave (Vallon-Pont-D'Arc, Ardèche, France). *International Newsletter on Rock Art* 21, 1–4.

Baffier, D. & Feruglio, V. 2001. Les points et les mains. In Clottes, J. (ed.) *La Grotte Chauvet: l'art des origines*, pp. 164–65. Paris: Le Seuil.

Bahn, P. 1977. Seasonal migration in south-west France during the late glacial period. *Journal of Archaeological Science* 4, 245–57.

Bahn, P. G. 1997. *Journey through the Ice Age*. London: Weidenfeld & Nicolson.

Bahn, P. G. & Vertut, J. 1988. *Images of the Ice Age*. London: Windward.

Bar-Yosef, O. 2000. The Middle and Early Upper Palaeolithic in southwest Asia and neighbouring regions. In Bar-Yosef, O. & Pilbeam, D. R. (eds) *The Geography of Neanderthals and Modern Humans in Europe and the Greater Mediterranean*, pp.107–56. Cambridge, Mass.: Peabody Museum of Archaeology and Ethnology.

Barkow, J. H., Cosmides, L. & Tooby, J. (eds) 1992. *The Adapted Mind: Evolutionary Psychology and the Generation of Culture*. Oxford: Oxford University Press.

Barnard, A. 1992. *Hunters and Herders of Southern Africa: a Comparative Ethnography of the Khoisan Peoples*. Cambridge: Cambridge University Press.

Barnard, A. 2000. *History and Theory in Anthropology*. Cambridge: Cambridge University Press.

Barton, C. M., Clark, G. A. & Cohen, A. E. 1994. Art as information: explaining Upper Palaeolithic art in western Europe. *World Archaeology* 26, 185–207.

Bataille, G. 1955. *Prehistoric Painting: Lascaux or the Birth of Art*. London: Macmillan.

Bates, C. D. 1992. Sierra Miwok shamans, 1900–1990. In Bean, L. J. (ed.) *California Indian shamanism*, pp. 97–115. Menlo Park, CA: Ballena Press.

Bean, L. J. (ed.) 1992. *California Indian Shamanism*. Menlo Park: Ballena Press.

Bégouën, H. & Breuil, H. 1958. *Les Cavernes du Volp: Trois Frères – Tuc D'Audoubert*. Paris: Flammarion. (Republished by American Rock Art Research Association, Occasional Paper 4, 1999.)

Bégouën, R. & Clottes, J. 1981. Apports mobiliers dans les cavernes du Volp (Enlène, Les Trois-Frères, Le Tuc d'Audoubert). *Altamira Symposium* pp. 157–87.

Bégouën, R. & Clottes, J. 1987. Les Trois-Frères after Breuil. *Antiquity* 61, 180–87.

Bégouën, R. & Clottes, J. 1991. Portable and wall art in the Volp caves, Montesquieu-Avantès (Ariège). *Proceedings of the Prehistoric Society* 57, 65–79.

Bégouën, R., Clottes, J., Giraud, J.-P. & Rouzaud, F. 1993. Os plantés et peintures rupestres dans la caverne d'Enlène. *Congrès National des Sociétés Historiques et Scientifiques* 118, 283–306.

Beltran, A. (ed.) 1999. *The Cave of Altamira*. New York: Harry Abrams.

Bender, B. 1989. The roots of inequality. In Miller, D., *et al.* (eds) *Domination and Resistance*, pp. 83–93. London: Unwin and Hyman.

Bernaldo de Quirós, F. 1999. The cave of Altamira: its art, its artists & its times. In Beltran, A. (ed.) *The Cave of Altamira*, pp. 25–57. New York: Harry Abrams.

Bickerton, D. 1981. *Roots of Language*. Ann Arbor: Karoma.

Bickerton, D. 1990. *Language and Species*. Chicago: Chicago University Press.

Biesele, M. 1980. Old K"au. In Halifax, J. (ed.) *Shamanic Voices: A Survey of Visionary Narratives*, pp. 54–62. Harmondsworth: Penguin.

Biesele, M. 1993. *Women Like Meat: The Folklore and Foraging Ideology of the Kalahari Ju/'hoan*. Johannesburg: Witwatersrand University Press.

Binford, L. R. 1981. *Bones: Ancient Men and Modern Myths*. New York: Academic Press.

Binford, S. R. 1968. A structural comparison of disposal of the dead in the Mousterian and Upper Palaeolithic. *Southwestern Journal of Anthropology* 24, 139–54.

Blackburn, T. C. 1975. *December's Child: A Book of Chumash oral Narratives*. Los Angeles: University of California Press.

Blackburn, T. C. 1976. A query regarding the possible hallucinogenic effects of ant ingestion in south-central California. *Journal of California Anthropology* 3, 78–81.

Blackburn, T. C. 1977. Biopsychological aspects of Chumash rock art. *Journal of California Anthropology* 4, 88–94.

Bleek, D. F. 1924. *The Mantis and his Friends*. Cape Town: Maskew Miller.

Bleek, D. F. 1933a. Beliefs and customs of the /Xam Bushmen. Part V: The Rain. *Bantu Studies* 7, 297–312.

Bleek, D. F. 1933b. Beliefs and customs of the /Xam Bushmen. Part VI: Rain-making. *Bantu Studies* 7, 375–92.

Bleek, D. F. 1935. Beliefs and customs of the /Xam Bushmen. Part VII: Sorcerers. *Bantu Studies* 9, 1–47.

Bleek, D. F. 1936. Beliefs and customs and the /Xam Bushmen. Part VIII: More about sorcerers and charms. *Bantu Studies* 10, 131–62.

Bleek, W. H. I. 1875. *Brief Account of Bushman Folklore and Other Texts*. Second Report Concerning Bushman Researches, presented to both Houses of Parliament of the Cape of Good Hope, by command of His Excellency the Governor. Cape Town: Government Printer.

Bleek, W. H. I. & Lloyd, L. C. 1911. *Specimens of Bushman Folklore*. London: George Allen. Reprint: 1968. Cape Town: Struik.

Bloch, M. 1983. *Marxism and Anthropology*. Oxford: Clarendon Press.

Boas, F. V. 1900. The mythology of the Bella Coola Indians. New York: *Memoirs of the American Museum of Natural History*, 2, 25–127.

Bocquet-Appel, J.-P. & Demars, P. Y. 2000. Neanderthal contraction and modern human colonization of Europe. *Antiquity* 74, 544–52.

Bond, G. 1948. (Cover illustration) *South African Archaeological Bulletin* 3 (11).

Bootzin, R. R. 1980. *Abnormal psychology*. Toronto: Random House.

Bosinski, G. 1982. *Die Kunst der Eiszeit in Deutschland und in der Schweiz*. Bonn: Rudolf Habelt GMBH.

Bosinski, G. 1991. The representation of female figures in the Rhineland Magdalenian. *Proceedings of the Prehistoric Society* 57, 51–64.

Bourdieu, P. 1977. *Outline of a Theory of Practice*. Cambridge: Cambridge University Press.

Bourguignon, E. (ed.) 1973. *Religion, Altered States of Consciousness and Social Change*. Columbus: Ohio State University Press.

Bourguignon, E. 1973. Introduction: a framework for the comparative study of altered states of consciousness. In Bourguignon, E. (ed.) *Religion, Altered States of Consciousness and Social Change*, pp. 3–35. Columbus: Ohio State University Press.

Boyd, C. E. 1996. Shamanistic journeys into the otherworld of the archaic Chichimec. *Latin American Antiquity* 7, 152–64.

Boyd, C. E. 1998. Pictographic evidence of peyotism in the Lower Pecos, Texas Archaic. In Chippindale, C., and Taçon, P. S. C. (eds) *The Archaeology of Rock-Art*, pp. 229–46. Cambridge: Cambridge University Press.

Brannigan, A. 1981. *The Social Basis of Scientific Discoveries*. Cambridge: Cambridge University Press.

Bressloff, P. C., Cowan, J. D., Golubitsky, M., Thomas, P. J. & Wiener, M. C. 2000. Geometric visual hallucinations, Euclidean symmetry and the functional architecture of the striate cortex. *Philosophical Transactions of the Royal Society, London*, Series B, 356, 299–330.

Breuil, H. 1952. *Four Hundred Centuries of Cave Art*. Montignac: Centre d'Etudes et de Documentation Préhistoriques.

Brindley, G. S. 1973. Sensory effects of electrical stimulation of the visual and paravisual cortex in man. In Jung, R. (ed.) *Handbook of Sensory Physiology* Vol. VII/3B, pp. 583–94. New York: Springer Verlag.

Brodrick, A. H. 1949. *Lascaux: A Commentary*. London: Lindsay Drummond.

Brodrick, A. H. 1960. *Man and his Ancestry*. London: Hutchinson.

Byers, A. M. 1994. Symboling and the Middle-Upper Palaeolithic Transition. *Current Anthropology* 35, 369–99.

Campos, A. & Gonzalez, M. A. 1995. Effects of mental imagery on creative perception. *Journal of Mental Imagery* 19, 67–76.

Cardeña, E. 1996. 'Just floating in the sky'. A comparison of hypnotic and shamanistic phenomena. *Yearbook of Cross-Cultural Medicine and psychotherapy* 1994, 85–98.

Carrithers, M., Collins, S. & Lukes, S. (eds) 1985. *The Category of the Person: Anthropology, Philosophy, History*. Cambridge: Cambridge University Press.

Chalmers, 1990. *Science and its Fabrication*. Minneapolis: University of Minnesota Press.

Chase, P. G. 1986. *The Hunters of Combe Grenal: Approaches to Middle Paleolithic Subsistence in Europe*. Oxford: British Archaeological Reports International Series 286.

Chase, P. G. & Dibble, H. L. 1987. Middle Paleolithic symbolism: a review of current evidence and interpretations. *Journal of Anthropological Archaeology* 6, 263–96.

Chauvet, J-M., Deschamps, E. B. & Hillaire, C. 1996. *Chauvet Cave: The Discovery of the World's Oldest Paintings*. London: Thames & Hudson.

Chesney, S. 1991. Max Raphael's contributions to the study of prehistoric symbol systems. In Bahn, P. and Rosenfeld, A. (eds) *Rock Art and Prehistory*. Oxford: Oxbow Books.

Chesney, S. 1994. Max Raphael (1889–1952): a pioneer of the semiotic approach to palaeolithic art. *Semiotica* 2/4, 119–24.

Childe, 1942. *What Happened in History*. Harmondsworth: Penguin Books.

Chomsky, N. 1972. *Language and the Mind*. New York: Harcourt Brace, Jovanovich.

Chomsky, N. 1986. *Knowledge of Language: Its Nature, Origin & Use*. New York: Praeger.

Christie-Murray, D. 1978. *Voices from the Gods*. London: Routledge and Kegan Paul.

Clottes, J. (ed.) 1990. *L'Art des Objets au Paléolithique, Tomes 1 et 2*. Paris: Ministère de la Culture.

Clottes, J. 1990. The parietal art of the late Magdalenian. *Antiquity* 64, 527–48.

Clottes, J. 1992. Phénomènes de mode dans l'archéologie Française. In Shay, T., and Clottes J. (eds) *The Limitations of Archaeological Knowledge*, pp. 225–45. Liège: Etudes et recherches archéologuques de 'Université de Liège, No. 49.

Clottes, J. 1995. *Les Cavernes de Niaux: art préhistorique en Ariège*. Paris: Éditions du Seuil.

Clottes, J. 1996. Thematic changes in Upper Palaeolithic art: a view from the Grotte Chauvet. *Antiquity* 70, 276–88.

Clottes, J. 1997. Art of the light and art of the depths. In Conkey, M. W., Soffer, O., Stratmann, D., and Jablonski, N. G. (eds) *Beyond Art: Pleistocene Image and Symbol*, pp. 203–16. San Francisco: California Academy of Sciences, Memoir 23.

Clottes, J. 1998. The 'Three C's': fresh avenues towards European Palaeolithic art. In Chippindale, C., and Taçon, P. S. C. (eds) *The Archaeology of Rock-Art*, pp. 112–29. Cambridge: Cambridge University Press.

Clottes, J. 2001. Paleolithic Europe. In Whitley, D. S. (ed.) *Handbook of Rock Art Research*, pp. 459–81. Walnut Creek, California: AltaMira Press.

Clottes, J. & Courtin, J. 1996. *The Cave Beneath the Sea: Paleolithic Images at Cosquer*. New York: Harry Abrams.

Clottes, J. & Packer, C. 2001. Les felines. In Clottes, J. (ed.) *La Grotte Chauvet: l'art des origines*, pp. 177–80. Paris: Le Seuil.

Clottes, J., Beltran, A., Courtin, J. & Cosquer, H. 1992. The Cosquer cave on Cape Morgiou, Marseilles. *Antiquity* 66, 583–98.

Clottes, J., Garner, M. & Maury, G. 1994. Magdalenian bison in the caves of the Ariège. *Rock Art Research* 11, 58–70.

Clottes, J., and Lewis-Williams, J. D. 1996. *Les chamanes de la préhistoire: texte intégral, polémique et réponses*. Paris: Le Seuil.

Clottes, J., and Lewis-Williams, J. D. 1998. *The Shamans of Prehistory: Trance and Magic in the Painted Caves*. New York: Harry Abrams.

Cohen, S. 1964. *The Beyond Within: The LSD Story*. New York: Atheneum.

Conkey, M. W. 1980. The identification of prehistoric hunter-gatherer aggregation sites: the case of Altamira. *Current Anthropology* 21, 609–30.

Conkey, M. W. 1987. New approaches in the search for meaning? A review of research in 'Paleolithic art'. *Journal of Field Archaeology* 14, 413–30.

Conkey, M. W. 1988. The structural analysis of Paleolithic art. In Lamberg-Karlovsky, C. C. (ed.) *Archaeological Thought in America*, pp. 135–58. Cambridge: Cambridge University Press.

Conkey, M. W. 1990. L'art mobilier et l'establisse-ment de Géoraphies sociales. In *L'art des objets au Paléolithique*, Vol. 2, *Les voies de la recherche*, pp. 163–72. Paris: Ministère de la Culture.

Conkey, M. W. 1991. Contexts of action, contexts of power: material culture and gender in the Magdalenian. In Gero, J. M. & Conkey, M. W. (eds) *Engendering Archaeology: Women and Prehistory*, 57–92. Oxford: Basil Blackwell.

Conkey, M. W. 1992. L'approache structurelle de l'art paléolithique et l'héritage d'André Leroi-Gourhan. *Les Nouvelle d'Archéologie* 48–49, 41–45.

Conkey, M. W. 1995. Making things meaningful: approaches to the interpretation of the Ice Age imagery of Europe. In Lavin, I. (ed.) *Meaning in the Visual Arts: Views from the Outside*, pp. 49–64. Princeton: Institute for Advanced Study.

Conkey, M. W. 1997. Beyond art and between the caves: thinking about context in the interpretive process. In Conkey, M. W., Soffer, O., Stratmann, D. & Jablonski, N. G. (eds) *Beyond Art: Pleistocene Image and Symbol*, pp. 343–67. San Francisco: Memoirs of the California Academy of Sciences, No. 23.

Conkey, M. W. 2000. A Spanish resistance? Social archaeology and the study of Paleolithic art in Spain. *Journal of Anthropological Research* 56, 77–93.

Conkey, M. W. 2001. Structural and semiotic approaches. In Whitley, D. S. (ed.) *Handbook of Rock Art Research*, pp. 273–310. Lanham, MD: Altamira Press.

Conway, T. 1993. *Painted Dreams: Native American Rock Art*. Minocqua, Wisconsin: North Word Press.

Conway, T. & Conway, J. 1990. *Spirits on Stone: The Agawa Pictographs*. San Luis Obispo: Heritage Discoveries.

Copi, I. M. 1982. *Introduction to Logic*. London & New York: Macmillan.

Corruchaga, J. A. L. 1999. The cave and its surroundings. In Beltran, A. (ed.) *The Cave of Altamira*, pp. 17–24. New York: Harry Abrams.

Coudart, A. 1999. Is post-processualism bound to happen everywhere? The French case. *Antiquity* 73, 161–67.

Cummins, D. D. & Allen, C. (eds) 1998. *The Evolution of Mind*. Oxford & New York: Oxford University Press.

Cytowic, R. E. 1994. *The Man who Tasted Shapes*. London: Abacus.

D'Aquili, E. G. 1978. The neurobiological bases of myth and concepts of deity. *Zygon* 13, 257–75.

D'Aquili, E. G. 1986. Myth, ritual, and the archetypal hypothesis. *Zygon* 21, 141–60.

D'Aquili, E. G. & Newberg, A. B. 1993a. Religious and mystical states: a neuropsychological model. *Zygon* 28, 177–200.

D'Aquili, E. G. & Newberg, A. B. 1993b. Liminality, trance and unitary states in ritual and meditation. *Studia Liturgica* 23, 2–34.

D'Aquili, E. G. & Newberg, A. B. 1998. The neuropsychological basis of religions, or why God won't go away. *Zygon* 33, 187–201.

D'Aquili, E. G. & Newberg, A. B. 1999. *The Mystical Mind: Probing the Biology of Religious Experience*. Minneapolis: Fortress Press.

D'Errico, F., Zilhão, J., Julien, M., Baffier, D. & Pelegrin, J. 1998. Neanderthal acculturation in western Europe? A critical review of the evidence and its interpretation. *Current Anthropology* 39, S1–S44.

Damasio, A. 1999. *The Feeling of what Happens: Body, Emotion and the Making of Consciousness.* New York: Harcourt Brace.

Daniel, G. & Renfrew, C. 1988. *The Idea of Prehistory.* Edinburgh: University of Edinburgh Press.

Darwin, C. 1968 [1859]. *On the Origin of Species by Means of Natural Selection.* Harmondsworth: Penguin Books.

Darwin, C. 1998 [1869]. *The Variation of Animals and Plants under Domestication.* Baltimore & London: John Hopkins University Press.

Davenport, D. & Jochim, M. A. 1988. The scene in the Shaft at Lascaux. *Antiquity* 62, 558–62.

Davidson, I. 1997. The power of pictures. In Conkey, M. W., Soffer, O., Stratmann, D., Jablonski, G. G. (eds) *Beyond Art: Pleistocene Image and Symbol*, pp. 125–60. San Francisco: Memoirs of the California Academy of Sciences, No. 23.

Davis, W. 1986. The origins of image making. *Current Anthropology* 27, 193–215.

Davis, W. 1987. Replication and depiction in Paleolithic art. *Representations* 19, 111–47.

De Beaune, S. 1987. Palaeolithic lamps and their specialization: a hypothesis. *Current Anthropology* 28, 569–77.

De Beaune, S. & White, R. 1993. Ice Age lamps. *Scientific American* March, 74–79.

De Beaune, S., Roussot, A. & White, R. 1988. Une lampe paléolithique retrouvée dans les collections du Field Museum of natural History, Chicago. *Bulletin de la Société Préhistorique Ariège-Pyrénées* 43, 149–60.

De Quirós, F. B. 1991. Reflections on the art of the cave of Altamira. *Proceedings of the Prehistoric Society* 57, 81–90.

Deacon, H. J. & Deacon, J. 1999. *Human Beginnings in South Africa: Uncovering the Secrets of the Stone Age.* Cape Town: David Philip.

Deacon, J. 1998. The power of a place in under-standing southern San rock engravings. *World Archaeology* 20, 129–40.

Deacon, J. & Dowson, T. A. (eds) 1996. *Voices from the Past.* Johannesburg: Witwatersrand University Press.

Deacon, T. 1997. *The Symbolic Species: the Co-Evolution of Language and the Human Brain.* Harmondsworth: Penguin.

Delluc, B. & Delluc, G. 1984. *Lascaux: art et archéologie.* Paris: Les Éditions du Périgord Noir.

Delluc, B. & Delluc, G. 1986. On the origins of image making. *Current Anthropology* 27, 371.

Delluc, B. & Delluc, G. 1990a. *Discovering Lascaux.* Bordeaux: Éditions Sud-Ouest.

Delluc, B. & Delluc, G. 1990b. Le décor des objets utilitaires du Paléolithique Supérieur. In Clottes, J. (ed.) *L'art des objets au Paléolithique* Vol. 2, Pp. 39–72. Paris: Ministère de la Culture.

Delport, H. 1990. *L'image des animaux dans l'art préhistorique.* Paris: Picard.

Demars, P.-Y. 1998. Comment on d'Errico *et al.* 1998. *Current Anthropology* 39, S24.

Dentan, R. K. 1988. Butterflies and bug hunters: reality and dreams, dreams and reality. *Psychiatric Journal of the University of Ottawa* 13(2), 51–59.

Dibble, H. L. 1989. The implications of stone tool types for the presence of language during the Lower and Middle Palaeolithic. In Mellars, P. & Stringer, C. (eds) *The Human Revolution: Behavioural and Biological Perspectives on the Origins of Modern Humans*, pp. 415–32. Edinburgh: Edinburgh University Press.

Dissanayake, E. 1995. Chimera, spandrel, or adaptation: conceptualizing art in human adaptation. *Human Nature* 6, 99–117.

Dixon, W. W. & Grierson, H. J. C. 1909. *The English Parnassus.* Oxford: Clarendon Press.

Dobres, M.-A. 2000. *Technology and Social Agency.* Oxford: Blackwell.

Dobres, M.-A. & Hoffman, C. R. 1994. Social agency and the dynamics of prehistoric technology. *Journal of Archaeological Method and Theory* 1(3), 211–58.

Donald, M. 1991. *Origins of the Modern Mind: Three Stages in the Evolution of Culture and Cognition.* Cambridge, Mass.: Harvard University Press.

Dowson, T. A. 1988. Revelations of religious reality: the individual in San rock art. *World Archaeology* 20, 116–28.

Dowson, T. A. 1992. *Rock Engravings of Southern Africa.* Johannesburg: Witwatersrand University Press.

Dowson, T. A. 1994. Reading art, writing history: rock art and social change in southern Africa. *World Archaeology* 25, 332–44.

Dowson, T. A. 2000. Painting as politics: exposing historical processes in hunter-gatherer rock art. In Schweitzer, P. P., Biesele, M. & Hitchcock, R. K. (eds) *Hunters and Gatherers in the Modern World: Conflict, Resistance & Self-Determination*, pp. 413–26. Oxford: Berghahn.

Dowson, T. A. & Porr, M. 2001. Special objects – special creatures shamanistic imagery and the Aurignacian art of south-west Germany. In Price, N. (ed.) *The Archaeology of Shamanism*, pp. 165–77. London: Routledge.

Drab, K. J. 1981. The tunnel experience: reality or hallucination? *Anabiosis* 1, 126–52.

Driver, H. E. 1937. Cultural element distributions: VI, Southern Sierra Nevada. *University of California Anthropological Records* 1(2), 53–154.

Duday, E. & Garcia, M. 1983. Les empreintes de l'homme préhistorique: la grotte de Pech Merle à Cabrerets (Lot): une relecture significative des traces de pieds humains. *Bulletin de la Société Préhistorique Française* 80, 208–15.

Edelman, G. M. 1987. *Neural Darwinism: The Theory of Neuronal Group Selection*. New York: Basic Books.

Edelman, G. M. 1989. *The Remembered Present: A Biological Theory of Consciousness*. New York: Basic Books.

Edelman, G. M. 1994. *Bright Air, Brilliant Fire: On the Matter of the Mind*. Harmondsworth: Penguin.

Edelman, G. M. & Tononi, G. 2000. *Consciousness: How Matter becomes Imagination*. Harmondsworth: Penguin.

Eichmeier, J. & Höfer, O. 1974. *Endogene Bildmuster*. Munich: Urban and Schwarzenburg.

Eliade, M. 1972. *Shamanism: Archaic Techniques of Ecstasy*. New York: Routledge and Kegan Paul.

Emboden, W. 1979. *Narcotic Plants*. New York: Macmillan.

Faris, J. 1986. Comment of Davis (1986). *Current Anthropology* 27, 203–04.

Farizy, C. 1990a. The Transition from Middle to Upper Palaeolithic at Arcy-sur-Cure (Yonne, France): technological, economic and social aspects. In Mellars, P. (ed.) *The Emergence of Modern Humans: An Archaeological Perspective*, pp. 303–26. Edinburgh: Edinburgh University Press.

Farizy, C. 1990b. Du Moustérien au Châtelperronien à Arcy-sur-Cure: un état de la question. In Farizy, C. (ed.) *Paléolithique Moyen récent et Paléolithique Supérieur ancien en Europe*. Nemours: Mémoires du Musée de Préhistorique d'Ile de France No. 3, pp. 281–90.

Fischer, R. 1975. Cartography of inner space. In Siegel, R. K. & West L. J. (eds) *Hallucinations: Behaviour, Experience & Theory*, pp. 197–239. New York: John Wiley.

Fodor, J. A. 1983. *The Modularity of Mind*. Cambridge, Mass.: MIT Press.

Forge, A. 1970. Learning to see in New Guinea. In Mayer, P. (ed.) *Socialization: The Approach From Social Anthropology*, pp. 269–90. London: Tavistock.

Fowler, C. 2001. Personhood and social relations in the British Neolithic, with a study from the Isle of Man. *Journal of Material Culture* 6, 137–63.

Freeman, D., Echegerey, J. G., de Quirós, F. B. & Ogden, J. 1987. *Altamira Revisited and Other Essays on Early Art*. Chicago: Institute for Prehistoric Investigations.

Furst, P. T. 1972. *Flesh of the Gods: The Ritual Use of Hallucinogens*. London: Allen and Unwin.

Furst, P. T. 1976. *Hallucinogens and Culture*. Novato, California: Chandler and Sharp.

Furst, P. T. 1977. The roots and continuities of shamanism. In Brodzky, A T., Daneswich, R. & Johnson, N. (eds) *Stones, Bones and Skin: Ritual and Shamanistic art*, pp. 1–28. Toronto: The Society for Art Publications.

Furst, P. T. 1986. Shamanism, the ecstatic experience & Lower Pecos art. In Shafer, H. J. (ed.) *Ancient Texans: Rock Art and Lifeways along the Lower Pecos*, pp. 210–25. Houston: Gulf Publishing Company.

Gackenbach, J. (ed.) 1986. *Sleep and Dreams: A Sourcebook*. New York: Garland.

Gamble, C. 1980. Information exchange in the Palaeolithic. *Nature* 283, 522–23.

Gamble, C. 1982. Interaction and alliance in Palaeolithic society. *Man* (N.S.) 17, 92–107.

Gamble, C. 1983. Culture and society in the Upper Palaeolithic of Europe. In Bailey, G. (ed.) *Hunter-Gatherer Economy and Prehistory: A European Perspective*, pp. 201–41. Cambridge: Cambridge University Press.

Gamble, C. 1991. The social context for European Palaeolithic art. *Proceedings of the Prehistoric Society* 57, 3–15.

Gamble, C. 1999. *The Palaeolithic Societies of Europe*. Cambridge & New York: Cambridge University Press.

Gardner, H. 1983. *Frames of Mind: The Theory of Multiple Intelligences*. New York: Basic Books.

Gargett, R. H. 1989 Grave shortcomings: the evidence for Neanderthal burial. *Current Anthropology* 30, 157–90.

Gargett, R. H. 1999. Middle Palaeolithic burial is not a dead issue: the view from Qafzeh, Saint-Césaire, Kebara, Amud & Dederiyeh. *Journal of Human Evolution* 37, 27–90.

Garlake, P. 1987a. *The Painted Caves: An Introduction to the Prehistoric Art of Zimbabwe*. Harare: Modus.

Garlake, P. 1987b. Themes in the prehistoric art of Zimbabwe. *World Archaeology* 19, 178–93.

Garlake, P. 1995. *The Hunter's Vision: The Prehistoric Art of Zimbabwe*. London: British Museum Press.

Gaussen, J. 1964. *La Grotte ornée de Gabillou*. Bordeaux: Memoire 4, Institut de Préhistoire de l'Université de Bordeaux.

Gayton, A. H. 1930. Yokuts-Mono chiefs and shamans. *University of California Publications in American Archaeology and Ethnology* 24, 361–420.

Gayton, A. H. 1948. Yokuts and Western Mono Ethnography. *University of California Anthropological Records* 5, 1–110.

Gebhart-Sayer, A. 1985. The geometric designs of the Shipibo-Conibo in ritual context. *Journal of Latin American Lore* 11, 143–75.

George, W. 1982. *Darwin*. London: Fontana.

Gibbs, W. W. 1998. From naked men to a new-world order. *Scientific American* January: 38–40.

Giddens, A. 1984. *The Constitution of Society: Outline of the Theory of Structuration*. Berkeley: University of California Press.

Gilbert, G. N. and Mulkay, M. 1984. *Opening Pandora's Box: A Sociological Analysis of Scientists'*

Discourse. Cambridge: Cambridge University Press.

Glynn, I. 1999. *An Anatomy of Thought*. London: Weidenfeld and Nicolson.

Gombrich, E. H. 1950. *The Story of Art*. London: Phaidon.

Gombrich, E. H. 1982. *The Image and the Eye*. Oxford: Phaidon.

Gonnella, S. 1999. Phenomenological remarks on the so-called 'eidetic imagery' of Paleolithic depictive representations. *Anthropology and Philosophy* 3, 27–37.

Goodman, F. 1972. *Speaking in Tongues: A Cross-Cultural Study of Glossolalia*. Chicago: University of Chicago Press.

Gordon, R. J. 1992. *The Bushman myth: the making of a Namibian underclass*. Boulder: Westview Press.

Gordon, R. J. 1997. *Picturing Bushmen: the Denver African Expedition of 1925*. Athens, Ohio: Ohio University Press.

Grant, C. 1965. *The Rock Paintings of the Chumash*. Berkeley: University of California Press.

Grant, C. 1968. *Rock Drawings of the Coso Range*. China Lake, CA: Maturango Museum.

Graziosi, P. 1960. *Palaeolithic Art*. London: Faber and Faber.

Greene, K. V. 1999. Gordon Childe and the vocabulary of revolutionary change. *Antiquity* 73, 97–109.

Greenfield, S. 1997. *The Human Brain: A Guided Tour*. London: Phœnix.

Greenfield, S. 2001. *The Private Life of the Brain*. Harmondsworth: Penguin.

Grof, S. 1975. *Realms of the Human Unconscious: Observations from LSD Research*. New York: Viking Press.

Grof, S. & Grof, C. 1980. *Beyond Death: The Gates of Consciousness*. London & New York: Thames & Hudson.

Guenther, M. 1986. *The Nharo Bushmen of Botswana: Tradition and Change*. Hamburg: Helmut Buske.

Guenther, M. G. 1975. The trance dancer as an agent of social change among the farm Bushmen of the Ghanzi District. *Botswana Notes and Records* 7, 161–66.

Guenther, M. G. 1989. *Bushman Folktales: Oral Traditions of the Nharo of Botswana and the /Xam of the Cape*. Stuttgart: Franz Steiner.

Guenther, M. G. 1999. *Tricksters and Trancers: Bushman Religion and Society*. Bloomington: Indiana University Press.

Guthrie, R. D. 1990. *Frozen Fauna of the Mammoth Steppe: The Story of Blue Babe*. Chicago: Chicago University Press.

Hacking, I. 1999. *The Social Construction of What?* Cambridge, Mass. & London: Harvard University Press.

Hacking, I. 1983. *Representing and Intervening:*

Introductory Topics in the Philosophy of Natural Science. Cambridge: Cambridge University Press.

Hahn, J. 1970. Die Stellung der männlichen Statuette aus dem Hohlenstein-Stadel in der jungpaläolithischen Kunst. *Germania* 48, 1–12.

Hahn, J. 1971. La statuette masculine de la grotte du Hohlenstein-Stadel (Wurttemberg). *L'Anthropologie* 75, 233–43.

Hahn, J. 1986. *Kraft und Aggression: Die Botschaft der Eiszeitkunst in Aurignacien?* Tübingen: Archaeologica Venatoria.

Hahn, J. 1993. Aurignacian art in Central Europe. In Knecht, H., Pike-Tay, A. & White, R. (eds) *Before Lascaux: The Complex Record of the Early Upper Palaeolithic*, pp. 229–57. Boca Raton: CRC Press.

Halifax, J. 1980. *Shamanic Voices: A Survey of Visionary Narratives*. Harmondsworth: Penguin.

Halifax, J. 1982. *Shaman: The Wounded Healer*. London & New York: Thames & Hudson.

Halverson, J. 1987. Art for art's sake in the Paleolithic. *Current Anthropology* 28, 63–89.

Halverson, J. 1992. The first pictures: perceptual foundations of Paleolithic art. *Perception* 21, 389–404.

Hamayon, R. N. 1998. 'Ecstasy' or the West-dreamt Siberian Shaman. In Wautischer, H. (ed.) *Tribal epistemologies*: essays in the philosphy of anthropology, 163–74, 188–90. Aldershot: Ashgate.

Hare, E. H. 1973. A short note on pseudo-hallucinations. *British Journal of Psychiatry* 122, 469–76.

Harlé, E. 1882. La Grotte d'Altamira près de Santander (Espagne). *Matériaux pur l'histoire de l'homme* 17, 275–83.

Harner, M. J. 1973a. Common themes in South American Indian *yagé* experiences. In Harner, M. J. (ed.) *Hallucinogens and Shamanism*, pp. 155–75. New York: Oxford University Press.

Harner, M. J. 1973b. *The Jívaro: People of the Sacred Waterfalls*. Berkeley: University of California Press.

Harner, M. J. 1982. *The Way of the Shaman*. Toronto: Bantam Books.

Harrold, F. B. 1989. Mousterian, Châtelperronian and early Aurignacian in western Europe: continuity or discontinuity? In Mellars, P. and Stringer, C. (eds) *The Human Revolution: Behavioural and Biological Perspectives on the Origins of Modern Humans*, pp. 677–713. Edinburgh: Edinburgh University Press.

Haviland, W. A. 1995. Visions in stone: a new look at the Bellows Falls petroglyphs. *Northeast Anthropology* 50, 91–107.

Haviland, W. A. & Haviland, A. de L. 1995. Glimpses of the supernatural: altered states of consciousness and the graffiti of Tikal, Guatemala. *Latin American Antiquity* 6, 295–309.

Haviland, W. A. & Power, M. W. 1995. Visions in stone: a new look at the Bellows Falls petroglyphs. *Northeast Anthropology* 50, 91–107.

Hayden, B. 1990. The cultural capacities of Neanderthals: a review and re-evaluation. *Journal of Human Evolution* 24, 113–46.

Hayden, B. 1993. The cultural capacities of Neanderthal: a review and re-evaluation. *Journal of Human Evolution* 24, 113–46.

Hayden, B. 1995. Pathways to power: principles for creating socioeconomic inequalities. In Price, T. D. & Feinman, G. M. (eds) *Foundations of Social Inequality*, pp. 15–86. New York: Plenum Press.

Hedges, K. E. 1976. Southern California rock art as shamanistic art. *American Indian Rock Art* 2, 126–38.

Hedges, K. E. 1982. Phosphenes in the context of Native American rock art. In Bock, F. (ed.) *American Indian Rock Art*, Vols 7–8, pp. 1–10. El Toro (CA): American Rock Art Research Association.

Hedges, K. E. 1992. Shamanistic aspects of California art. In Bean, L. J. (ed.) *California Indian Shamanism*, pp. 67–88. Menlo Park (CA): Ballena Press.

Hedges, K. E. 1994. Pipette dreams and the primordial snake-canoe: analysis of a hallucinatory form constant. In Turpin, S. (ed.) *Shamanism and Rock Art in North America*, pp. 103–24. San Antonio: Rock Art Foundation.

Heizer, R. F. & Baumhof, M. 1959. Great Basin petroglyphs and game trails. *Science* 129, 904–05.

Heizer, R. F. & Baumhof, M. 1962. *Prehistoric Rock Art of Nevada and Eastern California*. Berkeley: University of California Press.

Henshilwood, C. S., & Sealy, J. C. 1997. Bone artefacts from the Middle Stone Age at Blombos Cave, southern Cape, South Africa. *Current Anthropology* 38, 890–95.

Henshilwood, C. S., Sealy, J. C., Yates, R. J., Cruz-Uribe, K., Goldberg, P., Grine, F. E., Klein, R. G., Poggenpoel, C., Van Niekerk, K. L., and Watts, I. 2001a. Blombos Cave, southern Cape, South Africa: preliminary report on the 1992–1999 excavations of the Middle Stone Age levels. *Journal of Antheropological Science* 28, 421–48.

Henshilwood, C. S., d'Errico, F., Marean, C. W., Milo, R. G., and Yates, R. 2001b. An early bone tool industry from the Middle Stone Age at Blombos Cave, South Africa: implications for the origins of modern behaviour, symbolism and language. Journal of Human Evolution 41, 631–78.

Henshilwood, C. S., d'Errico, F., Yates, R., Jacobs, Z., Tribolo, C., Duller, G. A. T., Mercier, N., Sealy, J. C., Valladas, H., Watts, I., and Wintle, A. G., 2002. Emergence of Modern Human Behavior: Middle Stone Age Engravings from South Africa. *Science* 295, 1278–80. Published online: http://www.sciencemag.org.

Herskovitz, M. J. 1958. *Acculturation: The Study of Culture Contact.* Gloucester: Peter Smith.

Hewitt, R. L. 1986. *Structure, Meaning and Ritual in the Narratives of the Southern San.* Hamburg: Helmut Buske.

Hindess, B. and Hirst, P. Q. 1975. *Pre-Capitalist Modes of Production.* London: Routledge and Kegan Paul.

Hirschfeld, L. A. & Gelman, S. A. 1994. *Mapping the Mind: Domain Specificity in Cognition and Culture.* Cambridge: Cambridge University Press.

Hollis, M. 1985. Of masks and man. In Carrithers, M., Collins, S. & Lukes, S. (eds) *The Category of the Person: Anthropology, Philosophy, History.* Cambridge: Cambridge University Press.

Horowitz, M. J. 1964. The imagery of visual hallucinations. *Journal of Nervous and Mental Disease* 138, 513–23.

Horowitz, M. J. 1975. Hallucinations: an information processing approach. In Siegel, R. K. & West, L. J. (eds) *Hallucinations: Behaviour, Experience & Theory*, pp. 163–95. New York Wiley.

How, M. W. 1962. *The Mountain Bushmen of Basotoland.* Pretoria: Van Schaik.

Howard, J. 1982. *Darwin.* Oxford: Oxford University Press.

Howell, F. C. 1999. Paleo-demes, species, clades & extinctions in the Pleistocene hominid record. *Journal of Anthropological Research* 55, 191–243.

Hublin, J. J. 2000. Modern-nonmodern hominid interactions: a Mediterranean perspective. In Bar-Yosef, O., & Pilbeam, D. R. (eds) *The Geography of Neanderthals and Modern Humans in Europe and the Greater Mediterranean*, pp. 157–82. Cambridge, Mass.: Peabody Museum of Archaeology and Ethnology.

Hublin, J. J., Spoor, F., Braun, M., Zonneveld, F. & Condemi, S. 1996. A late Neanderthal associated with Upper Palaeolithic artefacts. *Nature* 381, 224–26.

Hultkranz, Å. 1973. A definition of shamanism. *Tenenos* 9, 25–37.

Hultkranz, Å. 1987. *Native Religions of North America.* San Fransisco: Harper Row.

Hultkranz, Å. 1998. The meaning of ecstasy in shamanism, & Rejoinder. In Wautischer, H. (ed.) Tribal epistemologies: essays in the philosophy of anthropology, 163–74, 188–90. Aldershot: Ashgate.

Humphrey, N. 1992. *A History of the Mind.* London: Chatto and Windus.

Ingold, T. 1992. Culture and the perception of the environment. In Croll, E. & Parkin, D. (eds) *Bush Base: Forest Farm. Culture, Environment and Development*, pp. 39–56. London: Routledge.

Ingold, T. 1993. Technology, language and intelligence: a consideration of basic concepts. In Gibson, K. & Ingold, T. (eds) *Tools, Language and Cognition in Human Evolution, pp. 449–72.* Cambridge: Cambridge University Press.

Jakobsen, M. D. 1999. *Shamanism: Traditional and Contemporary Approaches to the Mastery of Spirits and Healing*. New York: Berghahn Books.

James, W. 1982 (1902). *Varieties of Religious Experience*. London: Penguin.

Jilek, W. G. 1982. *Indian Healing: Shamanistic Ceremonialism in the Pacific Northwest Today*. Surrey, British Columbia: Hancock House Publishers.

Jochim, M. A. 1983. Palaeolithic cave art in ecological perspective. In Bailey, G. (ed.) *Hunter-Gatherer Economy and Prehistory: A European Perspective*, pp. 212–19. Cambridge: Cambridge University Press.

Johnson, M. 1999. *Archaeological Theory: An Introduction*. Oxford: Blackwell.

Jolly, P. 1986. A first generation descendant of the Transkei San. *South African Archaeological Bulletin* 41, 6–9.

Katz, K. 1982. *Boiling Energy: Community Healing among the Kalahari !Kung*. Cambridge, Mass.: Harvard University Press.

Katz, R., Biesele, M. & St. Denis, V. 1997. *Healing makes our Hearts Happy: Spirituality and Cultural Transformation among the Kalahari Ju/'hoansi*. Rochester, Vermont: Inner Traditions.

Keeney, B. (ed.) 1999. *Kalahari Bushmen Healers*. Philadelphia: Ringing Rocks Press.

Kehoe, T. F. 1989. Corralling: evidence from Upper Palaeolithic cave art. In Davis, L. B. & Reeves, B. O. K. (eds) *Hunters of the Recent Past*. One World Archaeology Vol. 7, pp. 34–45. London: Unwin Hyman.

Kensinger, K. M. 1973. *Banisteriopsis* usage among the Peruvian Cashinahua. In Harner, M. (ed.) *Hallucinogens and Shamanism*, pp. 9–14. New York: Oxford University Press.

Keyser, J. D. & Whitley, D. S. 2000. A new ethnographic reference for Columbia Plateau rock art: documenting a century of vision quest practices. *International Newsletter on Rock Art* 25, 14–20.

Klein, R. G. 2001. Southern Africa and modern human origins. *Journal of Anthropological Research* 57, 1–16.

Klüver, H. 1926. Mescal visions and eidetic vision. *American Journal of Psychology* 37, 502–15.

Klüver, H. 1942. Mechanisms of hallucinations. In McNemar, Q. & Merrill, M. A. (eds) *Studies in Personality*, pp. 175–207. New York: McGraw-Hill.

Klüver, H. 1966. *Mescal and the Mechanisms of Hallucinations*. Chicago: University of Chicago Press.

Knecht, H., Pike-Tay, A. & White, R. (eds) 1993. *Before Lascaux: The Complete Record of the Early Upper Palaeolithic*. Boca Raton: CRC Press.

Knoll, M. & Kugler, J. 1959. Subjective light pattern spectroscopy in the encephalographic frequency range. *Nature* 184, 1823.

Knoll, M., Kugler, J., Höfer, O. & Lawder, S. D. 1963.

Effects of chemical stimulation of electrically induced phosphenes on their bandwidth, shape, number & intensity. *Confinia Neurologica* 23, 201–26.

Kohn, M. 2000. *As We Know It: Coming to Terms with an Evolved Mind*. London: Granta Books.

Kozlowski, J. K. 2000. The problem of cultural continuity between the Middle and Upper Paleolithic in Central and Eastern Europe. In Bar-Yosef, O., and Pilbeam, D. (eds) *The Geography of Neandertals and Modern Humans in Europe and the Greater Mediterranean*, pp. 77–105. Cambridge, Mass.: Peabody Museum of Archaeology and Ethnology, Bulletin 8.

Krings, M., Geisert, H., Schmitz, R. W., Krainitzki, H. & Pääbo, S. 1999. DNA sequences of mito-chondrial hypervariable region II from the Neanderthal type specimen. *Proceeding of the National Academy of Science* 96, 5581–85.

Krings, M., Stone, A., Schmitz, R. W. Krainitzki, H., Stoneking, M. & Pääbo, S. 1997. Neanderthal DNA sequences and the origin of modern humans. *Cell* 90, 19–28.

Kroeber, A. L. 1925. Handbook of the Indians of California. *Bureau of American Ethnology Bulletin* 78. Washington, D.C.: Smithsonian Institution.

Kroeber, A. L. 1939. Cultural and natural areas of Native America. *University of California Publications in American Archaeology and Ethnology* 38.

Kubovy, M. 1986. *The Psychology and Perspective of Renaissance Art*. Cambridge: Cambridge University Press.

Kühn, H. 1955. *On the Track of Prehistoric Man*. London: Hutchinson.

Kuhn, L., and Bietti, A. 2000. The Late Middle and Early Upper Paleolithic in Italy. In Bar-Yosef, O., and Pilbeam, D. (eds) *The Geography of Neandertals and Modern Humans in Europe and the Greater Mediterranean*, pp. 49–76. Cambridge, Mass.: Peabody Museum of Archaeology and Ethnology, Bulletin 8.

Kuhn, T. S. 1970. *The Structure of Scientific Revolutions*. Chicago: University of Chicago Press.

Kurtén, B. 1972. The cave bear. *Scientific American* 226, 60–71.

La Barre, W. 1975 Anthropological perspectives on hallucinations and hallucinogens. In Siegel, R. K. & West, L. J. (eds) *Hallucinations: Behaviour, Experience & Theory*, pp. 9–52. New York: John Wiley.

La Barre, W. 1980. *Culture in Context*. Durham, North Carolina: Duke University Press.

Lakoff, G. & Johnson, M. 1980. *Metaphors We Live By*. Chicago: University of Chicago Press.

Lamb, F. B. 1980. Manual Córdova-Rios. In Halifax, J. (ed.) *Shamanic Voices: A Survey of Visionary Narratives*, pp. 140–48. Harmondsworth: Penguin.

Lame Deer and Erdoes, R. 1980. Lame Deer. In Halifax, J. (ed.) *Shamanic Voices: A Survey of Visionary Narratives*, pp. 70–75. Harmondsworth: Penguin.

Laming, A. 1959. *Lascaux: Paintings and Engravings*. Harmondsworth: Penguin.

Laming-Emperaire, A. 1959. *Lascaux: Paintings and Engravings*. Harmondsworth: Pelican.

Laming-Emperaire, A. 1962. *La signification de l'art rupestre Paléolithique*. Paris: Picard.

Latour, B. and Woolgar, S. 1979. *Laboratory Life: The Social Construction of Scientific Facts*. London: Sage.

Laughlin, C. D., McManus & d'Aquili, E. G. 1992. *Brain, Symbol and Experience: Toward a Neurophenomenology of Human Consciousness*. New York: Columbia University Press.

Layton, R. 1987. The use of ethnographic parallels in interpreting Upper Palaeolithic art. In Holy, L. (ed.) *Comparative Archaeology*, pp. 210–39. Oxford: Blackwell.

Leach, E. R. (ed.) 1967. *The Structural Study of Myth and Totemism*. London: Tavistock.

Leach, E. R. 1961. Golden bough or gilded twig? *Daedalus* 90, 371–87.

Leach, E. R. 1974. *Lévi-Strauss*. London: Fontana.

Lee, R. B. 1968. The sociology of !Kung Bushman trance performance. In Prince, R. (ed.) *Trance and Possession States*, pp. 35–54. Montreal: R. M. Bucke Memorial Society.

Lee, R. B. 1979. *The !Kung San: Men, Women & Work in a Foraging Society*. Cambridge: Cambridge University Press.

Leroi-Gourhan, A. 1964. *Les religions de la préhistoire*. Paris: Presses Universitaires de France.

Leroi-Gourhan, A. 1968. *The Art of Prehistoric Man in Western Europe*. London & New York: Thames & Hudson.

Leroi-Gourhan, A. 1976. Interprétation esthétique et religieuse des figures et symboles dans la préhistoire. *Archives de Sciences Sociales des Religions* 42, 5–15.

Leroi-Gourhan, A. 1982. *The Dawn of European Art: An Introduction to Palaeolithic Cave Painting*. Cambridge: Cambridge University Press.

Leroi-Gourhan, A. 1984. Grotte de Lascaux. In *L'art des cavernes: atlas des grottes ornées paléolithiques françaises*, pp. 180–200. Paris: Ministère de la Culture.

Leroi-Gourhan, Arlette & Allain, J. (eds) 1979. *Lascaux inconnu*. Paris: Éditions CNRS.

Leroi-Gourhan, Arlette. 1982. The archaeology of Lascaux Cave. *Scientific American* 246(6), 80–88.

Levinson, H. 1966. Auditory hallucinations in a case of hysteria. *British Journal of Psychiatry* 112, 19–26.

Lévi-Strauss, C. 1963. *Structural Anthropology*. Harmondsworth: Penguin.

Lévi-Strauss, C. 1966. *The Savage Mind*. London: Weidenfeld and Nicolson; Chicago: University of Chicago Press.

Lévi-Strauss, C. 1967a. The story of Asdiwal. In Leach, E. (ed.) *The Structural Study of Myth and Totemism*, pp. 49–70. London: Tavistock.

Lévi-Strauss, C. 1967b. *The Scope of Anthropology*. London: Jonathan Cape.

Lévi-Strauss, C. 1969. *Totemism*. Harmondsworth: Pelican Books.

Lévi-Strauss, C. 1977. *Structural Anthropology*, Vol. 2. London: Allen Lane.

Lewis-Williams, J. D. 1981. *Believing and Seeing: Symbolic Meanings in Southern San Rock Paintings*. London: Academic Press.

Lewis-Williams, J. D. 1983. *The Rock Art of Southern Africa*. Cambridge: Cambridge University press.

Lewis-Williams, J. D. 1986. The last testament of the southern San. *South African Archaeological Bulletin* 41, 10–11.

Lewis-Williams, J. D. 1987. A dream of eland: a unexplored component of San shamanism. *World Archaeology* 19, 165–77.

Lewis-Williams, J. D. 1990. *Discovering Southern African Rock Art*. Cape Town: David Philip.

Lewis-Williams, J. D. 1991. Wrestling with analogy: a methodological dilemma in Upper Palaeolithic art research. *Proceedings of the Prehistoric Society* 57, 149–62.

Lewis-Williams, J. D. 1992. Ethnographic evidence relating to 'trancing' and 'shamans' among southern and northern San groups. *South African Archaeological Bulletin* 47, 56–60.

Lewis-Williams, J. D. 1995a. Seeing and construing: the making and 'meaning' of a southern African rock art motif. *Cambridge Archaeological Journal* 5, 3–23.

Lewis-Williams, J. D. 1995b. Modelling the production and consumption of rock art. *South African Archaeological Bulletin* 50, 143–54.

Lewis-Williams, J. D. 1996. 'A visit to the Lion's house': structure, metaphors and sociopolitical significance in a nineteenth-century Bushman myth. In Deacon, J. & Dowson, T. A. (eds) *Voices from the Past: /Xam Bushmen and the Bleek and Lloyd Collection*, pp. 122–41. Johannesburg: Witwatersrand University Press.

Lewis-Williams, J. D. 1997a. Agency, art and altered consciousness: a motif in French (Quercy) Upper Palaeolithic parietal art. *Antiquity* 71, 810–30.

Lewis-Williams, J. D. 1997b. The Mantis, the Eland and the Meerkats: conflict and mediation in a nineteenth-century San myth. In McAllister, P. (ed.) *Culture and the Commonplace: Anthropological Essays in Honour of David Hammond-Tooke*, pp. 195–216. Special Issue of *African Studies* 56 (2). Johannesburg: Witwatersrand University Press.

Lewis-Williams, J. D. 2000. *Stories that Float from Afar: Ancestral Folklore of the /Xam San*. Cape Town: David Philip.

Lewis-Williams, J. D. & Blundell, G. 1997. New light

on finger-dots in southern African rock art: synesthesia, transformation and technique. *South African Journal of Science* 93, 51–54.

Lewis-Williams, J. D. & Dowson, T. A. 1990. Through the veil: San rock paintings and the rock face. *South African Archaeological Bulletin* 45, 5–16.

Lewis-Williams, J. D. & Dowson, T. A. 1993. On vision and power in the Neolithic: evidence from the decorated monuments. *Current Anthropology* 34, 55–65.

Lewis-Williams, J. D. & Dowson, T. A. 1999. *Images of Power: Understanding Southern African Rock Art.* (Second edition) Cape Town: Struik.

Lewis-Williams, J. D., Blundell, G., Challis, W. & Hampson, J. 2000. Threads of light: re-examining a motif in southern African San rock art. *South African Archaeological Bulletin*, 55, 123–36.

Lewis-Williams, J. D., Dowson, T. A. & Deacon, J. 1992. Rock art and changing perceptions of southern Africa's past: Ezeljagdspoort reviewed. *Antiquity* 67, 273–91.

Lex, B. 1979. The neurobiology of ritual trance. In d'Aquili, E. G., Laughlin, C. D. & McManus, J. (eds) *The Spectrum of Ritual: A Biogenetic Structural Analysis*, pp. 117–51. New York: Columbia University Press.

Librado, F. 1981. *The Eye of the Flute: Chumash Traditional History and Ritual as told by Fernando Librado Kitsepawit to John P. Harrington.* Santa Barbara: Santa Barbara Museum of Natural History.

Lieberman, P. 1989. The origins of some aspects of human language and cognition. In Mellars, P. & Stringer, C. (eds) *The Human Revolution: Behavioural and Biological Perspectives on the Origins of Modern Humans*, pp. 391–414. Edinburgh: Edinburgh University Press.

Lorblanchet, M. 1984a. Grotte de Cougnac. In *L'art des cavernes: atlas des grottes ornées Paléolithiques Françaises*: 467–74. Paris: Ministère de la Culture.

Lorblanchet, M. 1984b. Grotte de Pech-Merle. In *L'art des cavernes: atlas des grottes ornées Paléolithique Françaises*: 467–74. Paris: Ministère de la Culture.

Lorblanchet, M. 1991. Spitting images: replicating the spotted horses of Pech Merle. *Archaeology* 44(6), 25–31.

Lorblanchet, M. 1992. Finger markings in Pech Merle and their place in prehistoric art. In Lorblanchet, M. (ed.) *Rock Art in the Old World*, pp. 451–90. New Delhi: Indira Gandhi National Centre for the Arts.

Lorblanchet, M. & Sieveking, A. 1997. The monsters of Pergouset. *Cambridge Archaeological Journal* 7, 37–56.

Ludwig, A. M. 1968. Altered states of consciousness.

In Prince, R. (ed.) *Trance and Possession States*, pp. 69–95. Montreal: R. M. Bucke Memorial Society.

Lutz, C. 1992. Culture and consciousness: a problem in the anthropology of knowledge. In Kessel, F., Cole, P. & Johnson, D. (eds) *Self and Consciousness: Multiple Perspectives*, pp. 64–87. Hillsdale, NJ: Lawrence Erlman.

Manker, E. 1996. *Seite* cult and drum magic of the Lapps. In Diószegi, V. (ed.) *Folk Beliefs and Shamanistic Traditions in Siberia*, pp. 1–14. Budapest: Akadémiai Kiadó.

Marshack, A. 1972. *The Roots of Civilization.* London: Weidenfeld and Nicolson.

Marshack, A. 1991. *The Roots of Civilization: The Cognitive Beginnings of Man's First Art, Symbol and Notation.* Mount Kisco, New York: Moyer Bell.

Marshall, L. 1962. !Kung Bushman beliefs. *Africa* 32, 221–51.

Marshall, L. 1969. The medicine dance of the !Kung Bushmen. *Africa* 39, 347–81.

Marshall, L. 1976. *The !Kung of Nyae Nyae.* Cambridge, Mass.: Harvard University Press.

Marshall, L. 1999. *Nyae Nyae !Kung: Beliefs and Rites.* Cambridge, Mass.: Peabody Museum, Harvard University.

Martindale, C. 1981. *Cognition and Consciousness.* Homewood, Illinois: Dorsey Press.

McBrearty, S., & Brooks, A. S. 2000. The revolution that wasn't: a new interpretation of the origin of modern human behaviour. *Journal of Human Evolution* 39:453–63.

McClenon, J. 1997. Shamanistic healing, human evolution & the origin of religion. *Journal for the Scientific Study of Religion* 36, 345–54.

McCreery, P. & Malotki, E. 1994. *Tapamveni: The Rock Art Galleries of Petrified Forest and Beyond.* Petrified Forest, AZ: Petrified Forest Museum Association.

McDonald, C. 1971. A clinical study of hypnagogic hallucinations. *British Journal of Psychiatry* 118, 543–47.

McGuire, R. H. 1992. *A Marxist Archaeology.* New York: Academic Press.

McKellar, P. 1972. Imagery from the standpoint of introspection. In Sheehan, P. W. (ed.) *The Function and Nature of Imagery.* New York: Academic Press.

Mead, G. H. 1934. *Mind, Self and Society.* Chicago: Chicago University Press.

Mead, G. H. 1964. (ed. Reck, A. J.) *Selected Writings.* Chicago: Chicago University Press.

Meillassoux, P. A. 1972. From production to repro-duction. *Economy and Society* 1, 93–105.

Mellars, P. 1989. Major issues in the emergence of modern humans. *Current Anthropology* 30, 349–85.

Mellars, P. (ed.) 1990. *The Emergence of Modern*

Humans: An Archaeological Perspective.
Edinburgh: Edinburgh University Press.

Mellars, P. 1994. The Upper Palaeolithic Revolution. In Cunliffe, B. (ed.) *The Oxford Illustrated Prehistory of Europe.* Oxford & New York: Oxford University Press.

Mellars, P. 1996. *The Neanderthal Legacy: An Archaeological Perspective from Western Europe.* Princeton: Princeton University Press.

Mellars, P. A. 2000. The archaeological records of the Neanderthal-modern human transition in France. In Bar-Yosef, O., & Pilbeam, D. R. (eds) *The Geography of Neanderthals and Modern Humans in Europe and the Greater Mediterranean,* pp. 35–47. Cambridge, Mass.: Peabody Museum of Archaeology and Ethnology.

Mellars, P. and Stringer, C. (eds) 1989. *The Human Revolution: Behavioural and Biological Perspectives on the Origin of Modern Humans.* Edinburgh: Edinburgh University Press.

Méroc, L. & Mazet, J. 1977. *Cougnac.* Gourdon: Éditions des Grottes de Cougnac.

Mithen, S. 1988. Looking and learning: Upper Palaeolithic art and information gathering. *World Archaeology* 19, 297–327.

Mithen, S. 1994. From domain specific to generalized intelligence: a cognitive interpretation of the Middle/Upper Palaeolithic transition. In Renfrew, C. & Zubrow, E. B. W. (eds) *The Ancient Mind: Elements of Cognitive Archaeology,* pp. 29–39. Cambridge: Cambridge University Press.

Mithen, S. 1996a. *The Prehistory of the Mind: A Search for the Origins of Art, Religion and Science.* London & New York: Thames & Hudson.

Mithen, S. 1996b. Domain-specific intelligence and the Neanderthal mind. In Mellars, P. & Gibson, K. (eds) *Modelling the Early Human Mind,* pp. 217–29. Cambridge: McDonald Institute Monographs.

Mithen, S. 1998. A creative explosion? Theory of mind, language and the disembodied mind of the Upper Palaeolithic. In Mithen, S. (ed.) *Creativity in Human Evolution and Prehistory,* pp. 165–91. London & New York: Routledge.

Moorhead, A. 1969. *Darwin and the Beagle.* London: Hamish Hamilton.

Mulkay, M. 1979. *Science and the Sociology of Knowledge.* London: Allen and Unwin.

Munn, H. 1973. The mushrooms of language. In Harner, M. J. (ed.) *Hallucinations and Shamanism,* pp. 86–122. New York: Oxford University Press.

Musi, C. C. 1997. *Shamanism from East to West.* Budapest: Akadémiai Kiadó.

Myerhoff, B. G. 1974. *Peyote hunt: the sacred journey of the Huichol Indians.* Ithaca: Cornell University Press.

Narby, J., & Huxley, F. 2001. Shamans through time:

500 years on the path to knowledge. London: Thames & Hudson.

Needham, R. 1967. Percussion and transition. *Man* 2, 606–14.

Neher, A. 1961. Auditory driving observed with scalp electrodes in normal subjects. *Electroenceephalography and Clinical Neurophysiology* 13, 449–51.

Neher, A. 1962. A physiological explanation of unusual behaviour in ceremonies involving drums. *Human Biology* 34, 151–60.

Neihardt, J. G. 1980. Black Elk. In Halifax, J. (ed.), *Shamanic Voices: A Survey of Visionary Narratives,* pp. 95–102.

Newcomb, W. W. & Kirkland, F. 1967. *The Rock Art of Texas Indians.* Austin: University of Texas Press.

Noll, R. 1985. Mental imagery cultivation as a cultural phenomenon: the role of visions in shamanism. *Current Anthropology* 26, 443–61.

Norland, O. 1967. Shamanism as experiencing the 'Unreal'. In Edsman, C.-M. (ed.) *Studies in Shamanism,* pp. 166–85. Stockholm: Almqvist and Wiksell.

Oppitz, M. 1992. Drawings on shamanic drums. *RES: Anthropology and Aesthetics* 22:62–81.

Orpen, J. M. 1874. A glimpse into the mythology of the Maluti Bushmen. *Cape Monthly Magazine* (n.s.) 9(49), 1–13.

Oster, 1970. Phosphenes. *Scientific American* 222, 83–87.

Pager, H. 1971. *Ndedema.* Graz: Akademische Druck.

Palmer, D. 2000. *Neanderthal.* London: Channel 4 Books.

Parkington, J. 1969. Symbolism in cave art. *South African Archaeological Bulletin* 24, 3–11.

Pettitt, P. B. & Pike, A. W. G. 2001. Blind in a cloud of data: problems with the chronology of Neanderthal extinction and anatomically modern human expansion. With a response by J. P. Bocquet and P. Y. Demars. *Antiquity* 75, 415–20.

Pfeifer, L. 1970. A subjective report on tactile hallucinations in schizophrenia. *Journal of Clinical Psychology* 26, 57–60.

Pfeiffer, J. E. 1982. *The Creative Explosion: An Inquiry into the Origins of Art and Religion.* New York: Harper and Row.

Pinker, S. 1994. *The Language Instinct.* New York: HarperCollins.

Plato. 1935. *The Republic,* ed. A. D. Lindsay. London: Dent.

Potapov, L. P. 1996. Shamans' drums of Altaic ethnic groups. In Diószegi, V. (ed.) *Folk Beliefs and Shamanistic Traditions in Siberia,* pp. 97–126. Budapest: Akadémiai Kiadó.

Price-Williams, D. 1987. The waking dream in ethnographic perspective. In Tedlock, B. (ed.)

Dreaming: Anthropological and Psychological Interpretations, pp. 246–62.

Prins, F. E. 1990. Southern Bushman descendants in the Transkei: rock art and rain-making. *South African Journal of Ethnology* 13, 110–16.

Prins, F. E. 1994. Living in two worlds: the manipulation of power relations, identity and ideology by the last San rock artists of the Transkei, South Africa. *Natal Museum Journal of the Humanities* 6, 179–93.

Ränk, G. 1967. Shamanism as a research subject. In Edsman, C.-M. (ed.) *Studies in shamanism*, pp. 15–22. Stockholm: Almqvist and Wiksell.

Raphael, M. 1945. *Prehistoric Cave Paintings*. New York: Pantheon Books, The Bollingen Series IV.

Rappaport, R. A. 1999. *Ritual and Religion in the Making of Humanity*. Cambridge: Cambridge University Press.

Rasmussen, K. 1929. Intellectual culture of the Iglulik Eskimos. Report of the Fifth Thule Expedition 1921–24, 7(1). Copenhagen: Glydendalske Boghandel, Nordisk Forlag.

Reichel-Dolmatoff, G. 1972. The cultural context of an aboriginal hallucinogen. In Furst, P. T. (ed.) *Flesh of the Gods: The Ritual Use of Hallucinogens*, pp. 84–113. London: Allen and Unwin.

Reichel-Dolmatoff, G. 1978a. *Beyond the Milky Way: Hallucinatory Imagery of the Tukano Indians*. Los Angeles: UCLA Latin America Centre.

Reichel-Dolmatoff, G. 1978b. Drug-induced optical sensations and their relationship applied to art among some Colombian Indians. In Greenhalgh, M. & Megaw, V. (eds) *Art in Society*, pp. 289–304. London: Duckworth.

Reichel-Dolmatoff, G. 1981. Brain and mind in Desana shamanism. *Journal of Latin American Lore* 7, 73–98.

Reznikoff, I. & Dauvois, M. 1988. La dimension sonore des grottes ornées. *Bulletin de las Société Préhistorique Française* 85, 238–46.

Richards, W. 1971. The fortification illusion of migraines. *Scientific American* 224, 89–94.

Riches, D. 1994. Shamanism: the key to religion. *Man* (N.S.) 29, 381–405.

Riddington, R. 1988. Knowledge, power and the individual in subarctic hunting societies. *American Anthropologist* 90, 98–110.

Riel-Salvatore, J., and Clark, G. A. 2001. Middle and early Upper Paleolithic burials and the use of chronotypology in contemporary Paleolithic research. *Curent Anthropology* 42, 449–79.

Ritter, D. W. & Ritter, E. W. 1972. Medicine men and spirit animals in rock art of western North America. *Acts of the International Symposium on Rock Art* 97–125.

Ritter, E. W. 1994. Scratched art complexes in the desert West: symbols for socio-religious communication. In Whitley, D. S. & Loendorf, L. L. (eds) *New Light on Old Art: Recent Advances in*

Hunter-Gatherer Studies, pp. 51–66. Los Angeles: Institute of Archaeology, Monograph 36.

Rose, H. & Rose, S. (eds). 2000. *Alas, Poor Darwin: Arguments against Evolutionary Psychology*. London: Cape.

Ruby, J. (ed.) 1993. *The Cinema of John Marshall*. Reading: Harwood Academic Publishers.

Ruspoli, M. 1987. *The Cave of Lascaux: the Final Photographic Record*. London: Thames and Hudson.

Sacks, O. 1970. *Migraine: The Evolution of a Common Disorder*. London: Faber.

Sarbin, T. R. 1967. The concepts of hallucination. *Journal of Personality* 35, 359–80.

Sauvet, G. 1988. La communication graphique paléolithique. *L'Anthropologie* 92, 3–16.

Sauvet, G. and Wlodarczyk, A. 1995. Eléments d'une grammaire formelle de l'art pariétal paléolithique. *L'Anthropologie* 99, 193–211.

Savage-Rumbaugh, E. S. 1986. *Ape Language: From Conditioned Response to Symbol*. New York: Columbia University Press.

Scarre, C. 1989. Painting by resonance. *Nature* 338, 382.

Schaafsma, P. 1980. *Indian Rock Art of the Southwest*. Santa Fe: School of American Research.

Schaafsma, P. 1992. *Rock Art in New Mexico*. Sante Fe: Museum of New Mexico Press.

Seddon, D. 1978. *Relations of Production: Marxist Approaches to Economic Anthropology*. London: Frank Cass.

Sedman, G. 1966. A comparative study of pseudo-hallucinations, imagery and true hallucinations. *British Journal of Psychiatry* 112, 9–17.

Segall, M. H., Campbell, D. T. & Herskovits, M. J. 1966. *The Influence of Culture on Visual Perception*. New York: Bobbs-Merrill.

Sept, J. M. 1992. Was there no place like home? A new perspective on early hominid archaeological sites from the mapping of chimpanzee nests. *Current Anthropology* 33, 187–207.

Shaara, L. 1992. A preliminary analysis of the relationship between altered states of consciousness, healing and social structure. *American Anthropologist* 94, 145–60.

Sherratt, A. 1991. Sacred and profane substances: the ritual use of narcotics in later Neolithic Europe. In Garwood, P., Jennings, D., Skeates, R. & Toms, J. (eds) *Sacred and Profane*, pp. 50–64. Oxford: Oxford Committee for Archaeology.

Shreeve, J. 1996. *The Neanderthal Enigma*. New York: William Morrow & Co.

Siegel, R. K. 1977. Hallucinations. *Scientific American* 237, 132–40.

Siegel, R. K. 1978. Cocaine hallucinations. *American Journal of Psychiatry* 135, 309–14.

Siegel, R. K. 1980. The psychology of life after death. *American Psychologist* 35, 911–31.

Siegel, R. K. 1985. LSD hallucinations: from ergot to

electric kool-aid. *Journal of Psychoactive Drugs* 17, 247–56.

Siegel, R. K. 1992. *Fire in the Brain: Clinical Tales of Hallucinations*. New York: Dutton.

Siegel, R. K. & Jarvik, M. E. 1975. Drug-induced hallucinations in animals and man. In Siegel, R. K. & West, L. J. (eds) *Hallucinations: Behaviour, Experience & Theory, pp. 81–161*. New York: Wiley.

Sieveking, A. 1979. *The Cave Artists*. London: Thames & Hudson.

Sieveking, A. 1991. Palaeolithic art and archaeology: the mobiliary evidence. *Proceeding of the Prehistoric Society* 57, 33

Siikala, A.-L. 1982. The Siberian shaman's technique of ecstasy. In Holm, N. G. (ed.) *Religious Ecstasy*, pp. 103–121. Stockholm: Almqvist and Wiksell.

Siikala, A.-L. 1992. Shamanistic knowledge and mythical images. In Siikala, A.-L. & Hoppal, M. *Studies on Shamanism* pp. 87–113. Budapest: Akadémiai Kiadó.

Siikala, A-L. 1998. *Studies on Shamanism*, Part 1. Helsinki: Finnish Anthropological Society.

Silberbauer, G. B. 1981. *Hunter and Habitat in the Central Kalahari Desert*. Cambridge: Cambridge University Press.

Smith, N. W. 1992. *An Analysis of Ice Age art: Its Psychology and Belief System*. New York: Peter Lang.

Soffer, O. & Conkey, M. W. 1997. Studying ancient visual cultures. In Conkey, M. W., Soffer, O., Stratmann, D. & Jablonski, N. G. (eds) *Beyond Art: Pleistocene Image and Symbol*, pp. 1–16. San Francisco: Memoirs of the California Academy of Sciences, No. 23.

Stephen, M. 1989. Constructing sacred world and autonomous imagining in New Guinea. In Herdt, G. & Stephen, M. (eds) *The Religious Imagination in New Guinea*, pp. 211–36.

Stevens, A. 1975. Animals in Palaeolithic cave art: Leroi-Gourhan's hypothesis. *Antiquity* 49, 54–57.

Steward, J. 1929. Petroglyphs of California and adjoining states. *University of California Publications in American Archaeology and Ethnology* 33, 423–38.

Stoffle, R. W., Loendorf, L., Austin, D. E., Halmo, D. B., Bulletts, A. 2000. Ghost dancing in the Grand canyon: southern Paiute rock art, ceremony & cultural landscapes. *Current Anthropology* 41, 11–38.

Stow, G. W. 1905. *The Native Races of South Africa*. London: Swan Sonnenschein.

Stow, G. W. & Bleek, D. F. 1930. *Rock Paintings in South Africa: From Parts of the Eastern Province and Orange Free State; Copied by George William Stow; With an Introduction and descriptive notes by D. F. Bleek*. London: Methuen.

Straus, L. 1993. Preface. In Lévêque, F., Backer, A. M.

& Guilbaud, M. (eds) *Context of a Late Neanderthal: Implications of Multidisciplinary Research for the Transition to Upper Palaeolithic Adaptations at Saint-Césaire, Charente-Maritime, France*, pp. xi–xii. Madison, Wisconsin: Prehistory Press, Monographs in World Archaeology 16.

Stringer, C. & Gamble, C. 1993. *In Search of the Neanderthals*. London & New York: Thames & Hudson.

Sulloway, F. J. 1982. Darwin's conversion: the *Beagle* voyage and its aftermath. *Journal of the History of Biology* 15, 325–96.

Taborin, Y. 1993. Shells of the French Aurignacian and Périgordian. In Knecht, H., Pike-Tay, A. & White, R. (eds) *Before Lascaux: The Complete Record of the Early Upper Palaeolithic*, pp. 211–28. Boca Raton: CRC Press.

Taçon, P. S. C. 1983. An analysis of Dorset art in relation to prehistoric culture stress. *Inuit Studies* 7, 41–65

Tattersall, I. 1999. *The Last Neanderthal: The Rise, Success and Mysterious Extinction of our Closest Human Relatives*. New York: Westview Press.

Taylor, F. K. 1981. On pseudo-hallucinations. *Psychological Medicine* 11, 265–71.

Thomas, E. M. 1959. *The Harmless People*. New York: Knopf.

Thomas, J. 1990. Monuments from the inside: the case of the Irish megalithic tombs. *World Archaeology* 22, 168–89.

Thomas, J. 1991. *Rethinking the Neolithic*. Cambridge: Cambridge University Press.

Thomas, N. & Humphrey, C. 1996. *Shamanism, History and the State*. Ann Arbor: University of Michigan Press.

Tomásková, S. 1997. Places of art: art and archaeology in context. In Conkey, M. W., Soffer, O., Stratmann, D. & Jablonski (eds) *Beyond Art: Pleistocene Image and Symbol*, pp. 265–88. San Francisco: Memoirs of the California Academy of Sciences, No. 23.

Trevarthen, C. 1986. Brain science and the human spirit. *Zygon* 21, 161–82.

Turner, V. 1967. *The Forest of Symbols: Aspects of Ndembu Ritual*. Ithaca: Cornell University Press.

Turpin, S. 1994. On a wing and a prayer: flight metaphors in Pecos River art. In Turpin, S. (ed.) *Shamanism and Rock Art in North America*, pp. 73–102. San Antonio: Rock Art Foundation.

Tuzin, D. 1984. Miraculous voices: the auditory experience of numinous objects. *Current Anthropology* 25, 579–96.

Twemlow, S. W., Gabbard, G. O. & Jones, F. C. 1982. The out-of-body experience: a phenomenological typology based on questionaire responses. *American Journal of Psychiatry* 134, 450–55.

Ucko, P. J. & Rosenfeld, A. 1967. *Palaeolithic Cave*

Art. London: Weidenfeld & Nicolson; New York: McGraw Hill.

Ucko, P. J. 1992. Subjectivity and recording of Palaeolithic cave art. In Shay, T. and Clottes, J. (eds) *The Limitations of Archaeological Knowledge*, pp. 141–80. Liège: Etudes et Recherches Archéologiques de l'Université de Liège, No. 49.

Vajnštejn, S. I. 1996. The Tuvan (Soyot) shaman's drum and the ceremony of its 'enlivening'. In Diószegi, V. (ed.) *Folk Beliefs and Shamanistic Traditions in Siberia*, pp. 127–34. Budapest: Akadémiai Kiadó.

Valiente-Noailles, C. 1993. *The Kua: Life and Soul of the Central Kalahari Bushmen*. Rotterdam: Balkema.

Varagnac, A. & Chollot, M. 1964. *Musée des Antiquités Nationales: Collection Piette Art Mobilier Préhistorique*. Paris: Éditions des Musées Nationaux, Ministère d'État Affaires Culturelles.

Vastokas, J. M. & Vastokas, R. K. 1973. *Sacred Art of the Algonkians: A Study of the Peterborough Petroglyphs*. Peterborough: Mansard Press.

Vialou, D. 1982. Niaux, une construction symbolique magdalénienne exemplaire. *Ars Praehistorica* 1, 19–45.

Vialou, D. 1986. *L'art des grottes en Ariège Magdalénienne*. XXIIe Supplément à Gallia Préhistorique. Paris: CNRS.

Vialou, D. 1987. *L'art des cavernes: les sanctuaires de la préhistoire*. Paris: Le Rocher.

Vialou, D. 1991. *La préhistoire*. Paris: Gallimard.

Vinnicombe, P. V. *People of the Eland: Rock Paintings of the Drakensberg Bushmen as a Reflection of their Life and Thought*. Pietermaritzburg: University of Natal Press.

Vitebsky, P. 1995a. From cosmology to environmentalism: shamanism as local knowledge in a global setting. In Fardon, R. (ed.) *Counterworks*, pp. 182–203. London & New York: Routledge.

Vitebsky, P. 1995b. *The Shaman: Voyages of the Soul, Ecstasy and Healing from Siberia to the Amazon*. London: Macmillan.

Walker, J. 1981. The amateur scientist: about phosphenes. *Scientific American* 255, 142–52.

Waller, S. J. 1993. Scientific correspondence: Sound and rock art. *Nature* 363, 501.

Watson, R. A. 1990. Ozymandias, King of Kings: postprocessual radical archaeology as critique. *American Antiquity* 55, 673–89.

Wedenoja, W. 1990. Ritual trance and catharsis: a psychobiological and evolutionary perspective. In Jordan, D. K. & Schwartz, M. J. (eds) *Personality and the Cultural Construction of Society: Papers in Honour of Melford E. Spiro*, pp. 275–307.

Wellmann, K. F. 1978. North American Indian rock art and hallucinogenic drugs. *Journal of the American Medical Association* 239, 1524–27.

Wellmann, K. F. 1979a. *A Survey of North American Indian Rock Art*. Graz: Akademische Druck.

Wellmann, K. F. 1979b. North American Indian rock art: medical connotations. *New York State Journal of Medicine* 79, 1094–1105

White, R. 1986. Rediscovering French Ice Age art. *Nature* 320, 683–84.

White, R. 1989a. Toward a contextual understanding of the earliest body ornaments. In Trinkaus, E. (ed.) *The Emergence of Modern Humans: Biocultural Adaptations in the Later Pleistocene*, pp. 211–31. Cambridge: Cambridge University Press.

White, R. 1989b. Production complexity and standardization in early Aurignacian bead and pendant manufacture: evolutionary implications. In Mellars, P. & Stringer, C. (eds) *The Human Revolution: Behavioural and Biological Perspectives on the Origins of Modern Humans*, pp. 366–90. Edinburgh: Edinburgh University Press.

White, R. 1993a. Technological and social dimensions of 'Aurignacian-age' body ornaments across Europe. In Knecht, H., Pike-Tay, A. and White, R. (eds) *Before Lascaux: The Complex Record of the Early Upper Paleolithic*, pp. 277–99. Boca-Raton: CRC Press.

White, R. 1993b. A social and technological view of the Aurignacian and Castelperronian personal ornaments in SW Europe. In Cabrera-Valdés (ed.) *El origen del hombre moderno en el suroeste de Europa*, pp. 327–57. Madrid: Universidad de Educación a Distancia.

Whitley, D. S. 1992. Shamanism and rock art in far western North America. *Cambridge Archaeological Journal* 2, 89–113.

Whitley, D. S. 1994. By the hunter, for the gatherer: art, social relations and subsistence in the prehistoric Great Basin. *World Archaeology* 25, 356–77.

Whitley, D. S. 1998a. Cognitive neuroscience, shamanism and the rock art of native California. *Anthropology of Consciousness* 9, 22–37.

Whitley, D. S. 1998b. Meaning and metaphor in the Coso petroglyphs: understanding Great Basin rock art. In Younkin, E. (ed.) *Coso Rock Art: New Perspectives*, pp. 109–76. Ridgecrest (CA): Maturango Museum.

Whitley, D. S. 1998c. To find rain in the desert: landscape, gender and rock art of far western North America. In Chippindale, C. & Taçon, P. S. C. (eds) *The Archaeology of Rock Art*, pp. 11–29. Cambridge: Cambridge University Press.

Whitley, D. S. 2000. *The Art of the Shaman: Rock Art of California*. Salt Lake City: University of Utah Press.

Whitley, D. S., Dorn, R. I., Simon, J. M., Rechtman, R. & Whitley, T. K. 1999. Sally's rock shelter and the archaeology of the vision quest. *Cambridge Archaeological Journal* 9, 221–47.

Wiessner, P. 1982. Risk, reciprocity and social influences on !Kung San economics. In Lee, R. & Leacock, E. (eds) *Politics and History in Band Societies*, pp. 61–84. Cambridge: Cambridge University Press.

Wiessner, P. 1986. !Kung San networks in a generational perspective. In Biesele, M., Gordon, R. & Lee, R. (eds) *The Past and Future of !Kung Ethnography: Critical Reflections and Symbolic Perspectives: Essays in Honour of Lorna Marshall*, pp. 103–36. Hamburg: Helmut Buske Verlag.

Wilbert, J. 1997. Illuminative serpents: tobacco hallucinations of the Warao. *Journal of Latin American Lore* 20, 317–32.

Wilbert, W. 1981. Two rock art sites in Calaveras County. In Meighan, C. W. (ed.) *Messages from the Past: Studies in California Rock Art*, pp. 107–22. Los Angeles: Institute of Archaeology, UCLA.

Willis, R. 1994. New shamanism. *Anthropology Today* 10(6), 16–18.

Windels, F. 1949. *The Lascaux Cave Paintings*. London: Faber and Faber.

Winkelman, M. J. 1990. Shamans and other 'magico-religious healers': a cross-cultural study of their nature & social transformations. *Ethos* 18, 308–52.

Winkelman, M. 1992. *Shamans, Priests and Witches: A Cross-Cultural Study of Magico-Religious Practioners*. Tempe, Arizona: Arizona State University Anthropological Research Papers, No. 44.

Winters, W. D. 1975. The continuum of CNS excitatory states and hallucinations. In Siegel, R. K. & West, L. J. (eds) *Hallucinations: Behaviour, Experience & Theory*, pp. 53–70. New York: John Wiley.

Wolpoff, M. H. 1989. Multiregional evolution: the fossil alternative to Eden. In Mellars, P. and Stringer, C. (eds) *The Human Revolution: Behavioural and Biological Perspectives on the Origins of Modern Humans*, pp. 62–108. Edinburgh: Edinburgh University Press.

Wong, K. 2000. Trends in paleoanthropology. *Scientific American* April, 79–87.

Wylie, A. 1989. Archaeological cables and tacking: the implications of practice for Bernstein's 'Options beyond objectivism and relativism'. *Philosophy of Science* 19, 1–18.

Wynn, T. 1996. The evolution of tools and symbolic behaviour. In Lock, A., & Peters, C. R. (eds) Handbook of symbolic evolution, pp. 263–87. Oxford: Clarendon Press.

Yates, R. & Manhire, A. 1991. Shamanism and rock paintings: aspects of the use of rock art in the south-west Cape, South Africa. *South African Archaeological Bulletin* 46, 3–11.

York, A., Daly, R. & Arnett, C. 1993. *They Write their Dreams on the Rock Forever: Rock Writings in the Stein River Valley of British Columbia*. Vancouver: Talonbooks.

Zigmond, M. 1986. Kawaiisu. In D'Azevedo, W. L. (ed.) *Handbook of North American Indians, Vol. 11: Great Basin*, pp. 398–411. Washington, D. C.: Smithsonian Institution.

Zimmerman, L. J. 1996. *Native North America: Belief and Ritual, Visionaries, Holy People and Tricksters, Spirits of Earth and Sky*. London: Duncan Baird.

Zubrow, E. 1989. The demographic modelling of Neanderthal extinction. In Mellars, P. & Stringer, C. (eds) *The Human Revolution: Behavioural and Biological Perspectives on the Origin of Modern Humans*, pp. 212–31. Edinburgh: Edinburgh University Press.

Acknowledgments

Many people have generously assisted me over the years in many ways. I am grateful to them all. Colleagues and friends who read drafts of chapters include Patty Bass, Geoff Blundell, William Challis, Paul den Hoed, David Hammond-Tooke, Jamie Hampson, Jeremy Hollmann, Marthina Mössmer, Ghilraen Laue, Siyakha Mguni, Bill Sheehan, Benjamin Smith and David Whitley. I am also grateful to Meg Conkey with whom I have enjoyed many illuminating conversations. William Challis, David Pearce, Rory McLean and Wendy Voorveldt prepared the diagrams. I am grateful to Norbert Aujoulat, Jean Clottes, Robert Bégouën, David Whitley, and the Maison René Ginouvès (Archéologie et Ethnologie), CNRS for so kindly supplying illustrations. Marthina Mössmer mercifully collated the references and performed other computer-generated miracles with the text.

For work on the southern African San, I am deeply indebted to Lorna Marshall, Megan Biesele, Mathias Guenther and Ed Wilmsen. In North America, David Whitley, Larry Loendorf, Megan Biesele, Polly Schaafsma, Ekkehart Malotki, Carolyn Boyd, Janet Lever and John Miller took me to many rock art sites on numerous field trips. David Whitley has provided me with a great deal of information.

I am especially grateful to numerous people who made it possible for me to study Upper Palaeolithic caves in France in 1972, 1989, 1990, 1995 and 1999 and with whom I had valuable discussions. Jean Clottes, especially, has always been a fund of knowledge and a source of assistance in many ways. I am grateful to him for inviting me to serve on the International Advisory Committee for work in the Chauvet Cave. Others who have provided indispensable assistance in France include Norbert Aujoulat, Paul Bahn, Robert and Eric Bégouën, Brigitte Delluc, Jean Gaussen, Yanik Le Guillou, André Leroi-Gourhan, Michel Lorblanchet, Jaques Omnès, Aleth Plenier, Jean-Philippe Rigaud, Yoan Runeau, Dominique Sacchi, Georges Simonnet, Denis Vialou and Luc Wahl.

The work of the Rock Art Research Institute at the University of the Witwatersrand, Johannesburg, is funded by the university itself, the National Research Foundation, the Department of Tourism, Anglo American, De Beers, and the Ringing Rocks Foundation.

Finally, I thank the editorial staff of Thames & Hudson who provided encouragement when needed and always-needed advice and suggestions.

Sources of Illustrations

Unless otherwise indicated, diagrams have been supplied by the Rock Art Research Institute, University of Witwatersrand.

TEXT FIGURES
4 The Royal College of Surgeons of England.
10 Rock Art Research Institute Archives.
11 Courtesy R. Bégouën.
13 Maison René Ginouves (Archéologie et Ethnologie) CNRS.
15 After Leroi-Gourhan 1968, Chart XV.
19 After Mellars 1996, Fig. 13.6.
20 After Mellars 1996, Fig. 13.13.
22 After McBrearty & Brooks 2000, Fig. 13.
24 After Mithen 1996, 67.
27 Courtesy Jagger Library, University of Cape Town.
41–43 D. Whitley.
44 After Breuil in Bégouën & Breuil 1958.
56 After Ruspoli 1987, 200, and Leroi-Gourhan 1979.

57 After Leroi-Gourhan 1979.
58 After Leroi-Gourhan 1979.
59 After Leroi-Gourhan 1979.
60 After Leroi-Gourhan 1979.
64 After Halifax 1982, frontispiece.
66 Goya, 'The sleep of reason brings forth monsters', c. 1798.

PLATES
1 Courtesy N. Aujoulat.
2–3 Photo Rosselló.
4–5 Courtesy J. Clottes.
6 Courtesy C. Henshilwood.
7–9 Photo Rock Art Research Institute, University of the Witwatersrand.
10–11 Courtesy D. Whitley.
12–19 Courtesy J. Clottes.
20–23 Courtesy N. Aujoulat.
24–25 Courtesy R. Bégouën.
26–28 Courtesy N. Aujoulat.

Index

The Mind in the Cave